POWERPOINT® PRESENTATIONS *by DESIGN*

POWERPOINT® PRESENTATIONS *by DESIGN*

For Microsoft® Windows™ and the Apple® Macintosh®

Roger C. Parker

PUBLISHED BY
Microsoft Press
A Division of Microsoft Corporation
One Microsoft Way
Redmond, Washington 98052-6399

Copyright © 1991 by Roger C. Parker

All rights reserved. No part of the contents of this book
may be reproduced or transmitted in any form or by any means
without the written permission of the publisher.

Library of Congress Cataloging-in-Publication Data

Parker, Roger C., 1943–
    PowerPoint presentations by design / Roger C. Parker
        p.   cm.
    Includes index.
    ISBN 1-55615-266-3
    1. Macintosh (Computer)--Programming   2. Microsoft PowerPoint
(Computer program)   I. Title.
QA76.8.M3P36   1991
006.6'869--dc20   90-28247
                                                        CIP

Printed and bound in the United States of America.

2 3 4 5 6 7 8 9 ML ML 6 5 4 3 2

Distributed to the book trade in Canada by Macmillan of Canada, a division of
Canada Publishing Corporation.

Distributed to the book trade outside the United States and Canada by Penguin Books Ltd.

Penguin Books Ltd., Harmondsworth, Middlesex, England
Penguin Books Australia Ltd., Ringwood, Victoria, Australia
Penguin Books N.Z. Ltd., 182-190 Wairau Road, Auckland 10, New Zealand

British Cataloging-in-Publication Data available.

Apple® and Macintosh® are registered trademarks of Apple Computer, Incorporated. Genigraphics®
is a registered trademark of Genigraphics, Incorporated. Microsoft® and PowerPoint® are registered
trademarks and Windows™ is a trademark of Microsoft Corporation.

Acquisitions Editor: Marjorie Schlaikjer
Project Editor: Jack Litewka
Technical Editor: Mark Dodge

This book is dedicated to Robert Gaskins, director and general manager of Microsoft's Graphics Business Unit, whose vision and pioneering efforts have helped hundreds of thousands of presenters around the world do a better job of communicating in front of a group.

Contents

Acknowledgments **ix**
Preface **xi**

SECTION I: INTRODUCTION TO DESKTOP PRESENTATIONS

Chapter 1 Introduction to PowerPoint Presentations **3**
Chapter 2 Working with PowerPoint **25**

SECTION II: BASIC SKILLS

Chapter 3 Designing Your Presentation with the Storyboard Feature **59**
Chapter 4 Creating a Slide Master and Choosing a Color Scheme **79**
Chapter 5 Adding Impact to Words **103**
Chapter 6 Placing and Enhancing Files Created with Other Software Applications **147**
Chapter 7 Translating Numbers into Charts and Graphs **167**
Chapter 8 PowerPoint Tips and Techniques **201**

SECTION III: HANDS-ON POWERPOINT

Chapter 9 Preparing Handouts, Notes, and Visuals **239**
Chapter 10 Working with the "Steps to Success" Template **265**
Chapter 11 Using a Chart to Add Interest to Text Presentations **287**
Chapter 12 Using Genigraphics Backgrounds with Black-and-White Overheads **299**
Chapter 13 Working with the "Left-to-Right" Template **309**
Chapter 14 Emphasizing Sequence with the "Index Cards" Template **317**

SECTION IV: MAKEOVERS

Chapter 15 25 Ways to Improve Ordinary Slides and Overheads **329**

Index **361**

Acknowledgments

The author gratefully acknowledges the assistance of Don Miller and Cathy Harris of Microsoft's Graphics Business Unit and of PowerPoint developers Dennis Austin and Patrick Ford.

The author is also grateful for the input and perspective provided by Genigraphics' Rosemary Aboud, as well as for the insights of countless others at Genigraphics, including Kathy Lau and Bill Wassmer. For their assistance in providing slides for the color signature, "PowerPoint at Work," thanks to Peggy Piesek and Kate Dresen of Microsoft's Presentations Group, and Cathy Harris of Microsoft's Graphics Business Unit.

Most of all, the author thanks Marjorie Schlaikjer, acquisitions editor, for the enthusiasm and focus that she provided; and Jack Litewka, project editor, for his patience, politeness, and tact. Thanks also to Mark Dodge, technical editor, for his careful attention to screen dumps and instructions; and to Peggy Herman, for her attractive book design.

Preface

POWERPOINT PRESENTATIONS BY DESIGN is for people who want to look and feel their best in front of a group. The book describes how to create and deliver high-impact presentations using both the Apple Macintosh and Windows 3 versions of Microsoft PowerPoint.

POWERPOINT PRESENTATIONS BY DESIGN helps you prepare black-and-white and color overheads, 35-millimeter slides, and computer-based on-screen presentations. The book is a useful guide for newcomers to personal computing and will also help refine the skills of experienced computer users.

Whether you produce one presentation a month or daily presentations, POWERPOINT PRESENTATIONS BY DESIGN teaches you how to work more efficiently and how to create better-looking and more readable visuals, speaker notes, and audience handouts.

WHAT'S INSIDE

Section I, "Introduction to Desktop Presentations," provides an overview of PowerPoint's tools and features. By the time you reach the end of Chapter 2, you'll feel comfortable with PowerPoint's screen and be able to quickly locate desired tools.

In Section II, "Basic Skills," you'll begin to create your first PowerPoint presentation. Chapter 3 describes how to use PowerPoint's Storyboard feature to plan your presentations. Storyboards make it easy to quickly organize your ideas.

Chapter 4 describes how to create a distinctive look for your presentation by using PowerPoint's Slide Master and Color Scheme features.

Chapters 5 through 7 discuss PowerPoint's three major activities: working with words, importing artwork created with other applications, and creating charts and graphs. Chapter 8 describes advanced PowerPoint techniques. By the time you reach the end of Section II, you'll have mastered both basic and advanced PowerPoint tools and techniques.

Section III, "Hands-On PowerPoint," focuses on increasing productivity and improving the quality of your presentation visuals. Chapter 9 discusses output alternatives. Chapters 10 through 14 describe how to create and use templates to speed your work.

Section IV, "Makeovers," contains a single—but very important—chapter. Chapter 15 teaches you to identify and overcome 25 common pitfalls—so that you can add impact to ordinary slides and overheads. This chapter helps you take a fresh look at your work.

Inspiration for moving forward on your own is provided by the "PowerPoint at Work" color portfolio that contains a selection of PowerPoint color slides created by professional graphics designers.

HOW TO USE THIS BOOK

If you're new to desktop presentations and PowerPoint, you'll probably want to begin at the beginning, following the basic-to-advanced sequence.

If you're an experienced presenter, however, you might want to begin by reviewing the commands in Section II, paying particular attention to the advanced techniques described in Chapter 8. Then you'll be ready to move on to Section III.

Section III's templates and Section IV's how-to-improve suggestions are for *everyone*.

WHAT TO LOOK FORWARD TO

A successful presentation involves communicating the right information at the right time in the right way. With PowerPoint and with guidance from this book, you'll soon know how to combine the basics of effective presentation design with the PowerPoint commands and tools used to implement them.

With help from POWERPOINT PRESENTATIONS BY DESIGN, you'll soon become a master of presentations.

I
INTRODUCTION TO DESKTOP PRESENTATIONS

Introduction to PowerPoint Presentations

You're sitting in a room with other people. At the front of the room, a man stands behind a lectern, his face bent over some papers. He's reading words. No eye contact. Your eyes start to wander around the room. So does your mind. Get his point? Not likely.

Now imagine that you're sitting in another room with other people. The room lights subdued. At the front of the room, a woman stands to the side of a screen that displays a colorful, well-designed slide. She is looking at you and the others, fielding questions as she goes, conducting a conversation with you. Get her point? Very likely.

A presentation combines visual materials—such as slides or overheads—with talk that informs, motivates, or persuades. In the past, presenters relied on speeches to convey information to a group. In the modern business and professional climate, communication has become more visually oriented because people who present information find that visual communication combined with oral communication is more effective than speechmaking alone. In this chapter, you learn about the power that presentations have to deliver your ideas and information. You learn how to plan, schedule, and create an effective presentation. Then you're introduced to the ways that Microsoft PowerPoint can help you prepare your best possible presentation.

This chapter's progress resembles the process you would follow to prepare a PowerPoint presentation. On several pages you'll see visual material that is similar to a slide you might create with PowerPoint. Below the slide, you'll find explanations of the material in the slide that are similar to the oral portion of a presentation. (All you need to do is read the text aloud!)

THE POWER OF PRESENTATIONS

Presentations derive their power to communicate and to persuade by combining visual and audio elements. People retain information five times better from seeing and hearing it simultaneously than from only hearing it. Adding a visual element to your communication doubles your chances of persuading listeners and increases the chance of group consensus by about one-third. By implication, adding visual elements increases a presenter's credibility. Listeners perceive a presenter who includes visual materials as better prepared, more authoritative, and more interesting. In part, this is the result of better organization and refinement of ideas during preparation of the presentation. Presenting information visually and orally is not only more effective but also more efficient. One measure of this efficiency is the tendency for meetings in which information is presented visually to last about three-fourths as long as meetings in which only oral information is presented.

The use of visual materials as part of a presentation frees you to perform the more important functions of elaboration and clarification. Rather than read the captions to the visuals, which the audience can do much faster than you can do, you show each visual and discuss it.

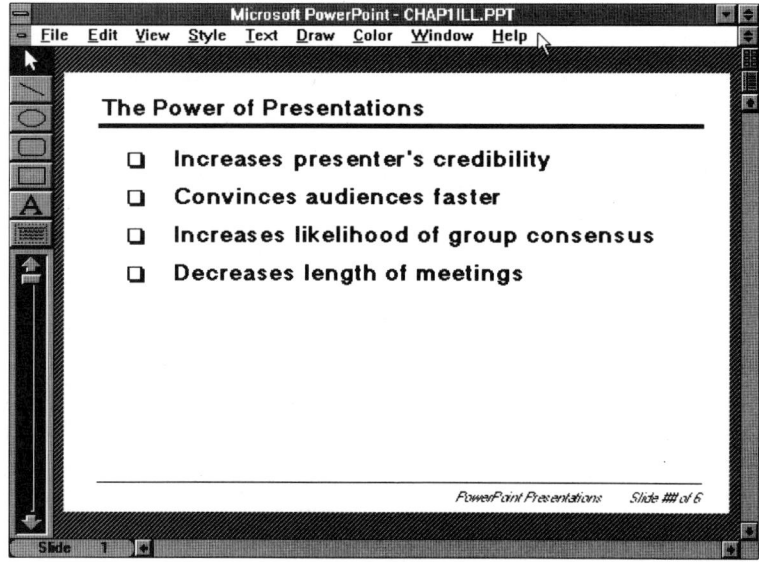

EXPLAINING THE VISUAL

Working visually gives you immediate feedback as you build your presentation. You can "see" when ideas don't fit together or when points are not well developed. You have a built-in tool for evaluating the progress and the quality of your presentation. When presenting the visual items to your audience, you can speak about the content, significance, sequence, and the sources of the evidence underlying your conclusions.

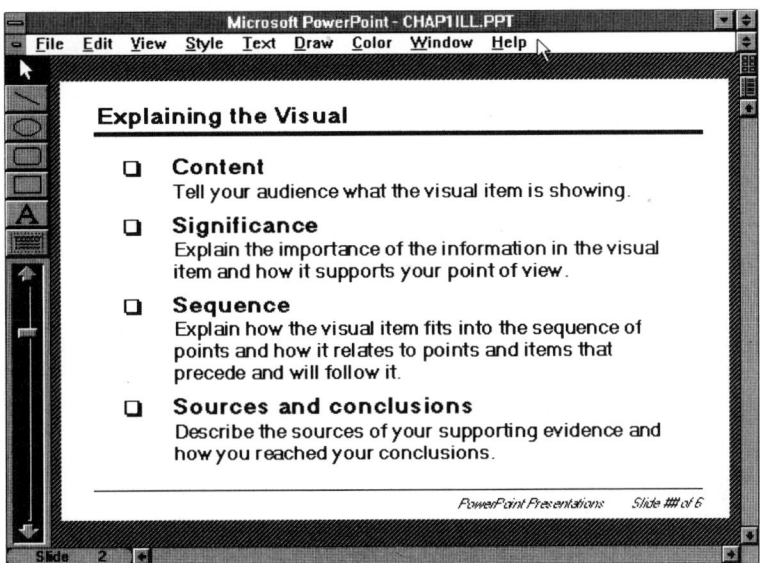

CHARACTERISTICS OF EFFECTIVE PRESENTATIONS

Effective presentations contain characteristics that improve communication. First and foremost, an effective presentation is chiefly visual. Because the presentation engages the eyes of the audience, several other communication techniques and characteristics become more readily available and more powerful. Within the boundaries of a visual item, the amount of space you can fully utilize is limited. Limited space forces you to focus on the important points and ideas, keeping the visual simple. A simple visual is more easily presented and more easily grasped, and it lends itself to visual enhancements that impress the eye.

SECTION I: INTRODUCTION TO DESKTOP PRESENTATIONS

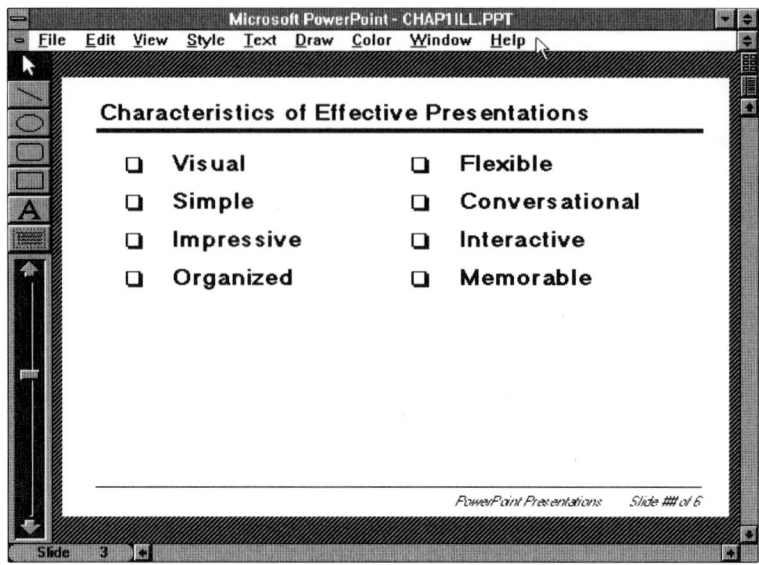

A visual item should have a consistent, well-designed appearance that conveys professionalism. A color visual attracts almost twice as much attention as a black-and-white visual, increases persuasion by almost three-fourths, and increases retention by about one-half.

Visual materials provide other benefits. Because each visual item tells its own chunk of your story, each retains a certain amount of autonomy. You can spend about the same amount of time presenting each visual, or you can spend as much or as little time on each visual as fits the audience and the circumstances. The autonomy of each visual also means that you can organize and reorganize your presentation until you find the best sequence for presentation. During the presentation, you can return easily to a previous point or jump ahead momentarily to a later one. You can insert or remove visual items at the last minute. And in future presentations, you can reuse them—with or without modifications in the oral portion of your presentation. You can also modify or remove existing visuals or add new ones. Because the visual presents the points vividly for you, leaving you to concentrate on explaining and elaborating what's shown, the accompanying oral presentation can be much more conversational—and flexible. You can make it up as you go, simply conveying your knowledge to your "friends" in the audience. With the visual elements under control, you'll find it much easier to maintain eye contact and to interact with your audience throughout the presentation, rather than taking questions only at the end of your presentation. With the visuals to guide you,

you won't lose your place or train of thought. Or if you do lose your way momentarily, the visuals get you back on track instantly.

PLANNING AN EFFECTIVE PRESENTATION—OVERVIEW

Effective presentations don't just happen: They require careful preparation and planning. The visual nature of a presentation makes much of the preparation easier, but you need to do some homework before you begin preparing the visual items, including consideration of audience, site, budget, scheduling of work, and the appropriate visual medium. (The Presentation Planning Worksheet, the Presentation Scheduling Worksheet, and the presentation-medium table, shown on the following pages, can help you with these tasks.)

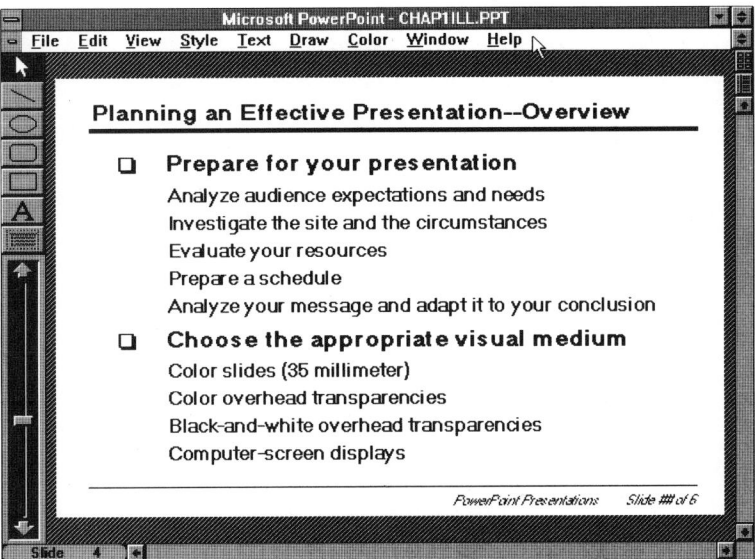

PRESENTATION PLANNING

Now you're ready to begin working on the details, as outlined in the Presentation Planning Worksheet shown on the following page. You can make a photocopy of this worksheet and use it to help define your needs; or you can create a similar worksheet and print a copy, being sure that you store a "master" in memory for future use. (Take advantage of these options with the other worksheets in this chapter.)

PRESENTATION PLANNING WORKSHEET

Audience

What are the characteristics of your audience?

How many people will be attending your presentation?

How receptive is your audience likely to be to your ideas?

How much audience interaction do you desire?

Circumstances

Where will you be delivering your presentation?

How long will your presentation last?

Schedule

How much time do you have to prepare your presentation?

Resources

How much money is available to prepare visual materials?

What support staff, if any, can help with preparations?

What equipment will be available for displaying your visual materials?

Audience

Who is your audience? Are you presenting a proposal to the board of directors or to your company's highest-level managers? Are you presenting the latest company policy decision to line supervisors or to your staff? Are you presenting the results of your research to peers and colleagues? Or are you conducting a workshop or seminar? In each of these circumstances, you might choose a specific approach and style of presentation as well as tailor the types of visual materials you'll prepare.

How large is the audience? Are you presenting to a group of 12 or to a conference plenary session of 2000? For the small group, your visual materials might be low-key so as to invite the type of commentary common to a working session. You might provide handouts on which they can write notes and comments. For the plenary session, your visuals must be (so to speak) "writ large." You might not be able to afford to make copies of your visuals for everyone, or it might be awkward to distribute so many handouts, so you might prefer to use dramatic and powerful visuals.

How much audience participation do you want? At one extreme, you might be conducting a working session in which ideas and plans are being generated in a fluid interaction between presenter and audience. For such interactive situations, you want your visual materials to suggest openness, and you want the participants to feel free to write on and alter the visual materials as the group's thinking progresses. At the other extreme, you might be conducting a formal, information-dispersal session. For such a situation, you would simply present your message and only answer questions to clarify the message for everyone. You want to minimize audience interaction, so you can use visual materials that suggest closure.

What is the audience's initial attitude toward your message? Hostility? Indifference? Involvement? Agreement? The expected response of the audience to your message can influence the style and content of your presentation—not only the type, quality, and design of your visuals but also your entire approach to the subject. For example, your approach in presenting your company's new dress code to your staff might be very different from your approach in presenting a fabulous new product to a meeting full of enthusiastic sales representatives.

Circumstances

Where will you give your presentation? In a drafty conference hall? Or in a plush corporate board room? Or crammed into a cozy little meeting room?

Does the meeting place have any special significance? (There have been Alcoholics Anonymous meetings in a cocktail lounge—that is, in a *closed* cocktail lounge.) The site might be conducive to your presentation, or the site might be a setup for distractions and disruptions. Imagine, for example, preparing beautiful 35-millimeter slides for a noon meeting in a room with uncurtained windows having a southern exposure. Or imagine trying to present your visual materials in a room with no electrical outlet near the location where you need to set up your projection equipment.

In addition to the joys and woes of the site, you need to adapt the style, content, and medium of your presentation to the circumstances. A long or complex presentation in a dark room might put people to sleep, even if the subject is important or the message exciting. For such a presentation, try using several visual media, which require you to turn the lights up and down after short intervals. Provide for audience participation and interaction. Keep your visual materials very lively yet simple. Find as many ways to add impact to your presentation as you can. And remember that people perform more productively when they believe they're being noticed.

Resources and Schedule

For every presentation, you'll need three resources in addition to your ideas and your talent for presenting them in visual form. You need time, money, and equipment. The availability of these resources determines, to some extent, the style and quality of your visual materials.

PRESENTATION SCHEDULING

Every presentation takes time to create—figuring out the materials you need, designing and preparing them, and producing (or reproducing) them. If you reuse materials from a previous presentation, you nevertheless need to analyze your audience and check out the site, as well as modify reusable visual items. Printing, duplicating, special processing for slides or overheads—each of these takes time. Even if you're printing your visual materials in your office, you need to allow enough time to print the entire set of visual materials. Visual materials, especially those that contain charts or graphics, take longer to print on a laser printer than a page that contains only text. Color printers print even more slowly than black-and-white printers. If you know how much lead time you have to prepare your presentation and how long it takes to print a visual, you can adjust the number and type of visual materials you use so that you can complete your preparations on time.

PRESENTATION SCHEDULING WORKSHEET

Date of Presentation:

Visual Materials

Deadline for receiving completed visual material (allow time for sorting, placing in holders or trays, and rehearsal):

Shipping time from service bureau to you:

Time required to prepare visual materials in final form:

Date materials arrive at service bureau, or date you begin printing:

Shipping time to the service bureau:

Deadline for shipping files to service bureau:

Time required to produce PowerPoint file for visual materials:

Time required to plan your presentation:

Notes and Audience Handouts

Time required to print, duplicate, collate, and bind handouts:

Deadline for preparing notes and handouts:

To establish a realistic schedule for your preparations, work backwards from the date of the presentation. Starting with the last step of your preparations, estimate the time (in days or fractions of a day) you need to complete each step. After you estimate the time for each step, you'll see when you should have started (yesterday at the latest!), and you can try to find ways to shorten each step (if necessary). The Presentation Scheduling Worksheet shown on the previous page can help you estimate your schedule.

All the time in the world to prepare? Or no time left at all? In either of these situations, you have to count your money. What's the budget for your presentation? If the budget is small, you need to prepare inexpensive (and possibly fewer) visual items. If the budget is generous, you can prepare elaborate visual items. If the time is short and the budget is large, you might be able to employ additional people and equipment to shorten preparation time.

After time and money are known quantities, you need to check on the equipment available to display your visual materials at the presentation site. If the site is your own building, you can check this out readily—just remember to reserve the equipment. If the site is remote, you might need to take equipment with you: Do you have money to ship the equipment? Or can you carry it with you? If you plan to display your visual materials by using a computer, you should consider having a backup computer available as well as backup disks that contain all your materials. For last-minute adjustments, you might even consider shipping a printer with you if one is not available at (or near) the site of your presentation. For peace of mind, you need to create a list of the equipment you'll use and to finalize arrangements for your presentation.

ANALYZING YOUR MESSAGE

Successful presentations are focused—short and to the point. They take only as much time as is necessary to communicate essential information. Focus and simplicity derive from clarity of purpose, important ideas, supporting evidence, and the organization of your message. Use the questions in the Analyzing Your Message Worksheet shown on the facing page as a checklist to help you critique your message.

It's important to be very clear about what you want to accomplish. In most presentations, you'll want to compare, inform, motivate, persuade, reinforce, and train, or at least you'll want to accomplish some of these goals. But choose one or two of these goals as most important, and use any of the others (as appropriate) to support your main purpose. Next, align your purposes with the central idea you want to communicate. Everything you say and everything

ANALYZING YOUR MESSAGE WORKSHEET

Purpose

What are you trying to accomplish?

Is your goal to compare, inform, motivate, persuade, reinforce, or train?

Central Idea

What is the single most important idea you want to communicate?

Can you organize your presentation around this idea?

Can this idea be reinforced in every visual item?

Supporting Evidence

What evidence is available to support your central idea?

Does this evidence consist of charts, diagrams, lists, maps, numbers, words, or quotations?

Organization

What information should you present first? Last? In the middle?

What sequence of ideas, issues, themes, points should you follow?

How can you arrange your visual items so that they build on one another?

you show should reveal, support, and reinforce your central idea. With your presentation focused on its purpose and main idea, you can marshal supporting evidence in a variety of forms. As you consider various visual formats, think ahead to the presentation medium you intend to use. Can that medium present all your visual items well? If not, you might consider using alternative evidence or additional media to support your message.

With purpose, main idea, and evidence analyzed, you organize the message so that it communicates most effectively. You might want to proceed from general ideas to specific examples, or you might want to proceed from specific ideas to general ideas. You can present problems and then solutions, or sometimes you can present your message as a chronology. Whichever ordering scheme you choose, your presentation should have a definite beginning, middle, and ending. Along the way, sequence your visual items so that they build on previous items and support your main idea.

CHOOSING THE RIGHT PRESENTATION MEDIUM

You can choose color slides, color transparencies, black-and-white transparencies, and the computer screen as your presentation medium. Consideration of image quality, cost, lead time, and so forth will dictate your choice.

Color Slides (35 millimeter)

For the greatest visual impact and the most professional image, 35-millimeter (35mm) color slides provide "boardroom-quality" visual images. The colors are bright, the shadings are smooth, and the details are sharp. If your presentation is in a formal setting or for a group of 100 or more people, slides are your likely choice because they're easy to transport and because a slide projector is usually available at any site. By creating a sequence of slides, you can "build" a visual item; the first slide shows one point, the next slide shows the first point and a second one (perhaps highlighted), and so on. Or you can add pieces to a graphical image.

On the other hand, slides are expensive, and you must send your files to a service bureau for processing, which requires time. Most service bureaus offer overnight, 1-day, and 2-day processing. The shorter the processing time, the more expensive the processing.

Slide shows, however, also have potential liabilities. Slides sit in a fixed order. You've seen presentations during which some slides are "skipped" by advancing quickly, forward or backward, past them; some people are irritated by such skipping, and they lose their concentration. Because the room lights must be dimmed, the audience can't take notes, and you can't maintain eye contact or gauge audience reaction. Many people dislike sitting for a long time in a darkened room; some might nod off. Slides are best used for short presentations.

Choosing the Right Presentation Medium

Media Type	Cost	Group	Time	Flexibility
Color Slides (35mm)	High	Over 100; formal; passive	Service bureau (overnight, 1 day, or 2 days); short presentations	Fixed order
Color Transparencies	Medium to high	Under 50; formal; interactive	Printing (hours); longer presentations	Rearrange or omit during presentation
Black-and-White Transparencies	Low	Under 50; informal; training; staff meetings	Printing (minutes); longer presentations and working sessions	Add, remove, rearrange, and modify during presentation
Computer Screen	Low	Small	Preparation only	Interactive; update and display immediately

Color Transparencies

For formal and professional presentations to groups of up to 50 people, color transparencies offer the impact of color slides, with much more flexibility during your presentation and at a much lower cost. When you use transparencies, you can leave the room lights turned up. The audience can take notes, and you can maintain eye contact and optimal interaction. You can rearrange or omit transparencies during the presentation, depending on time constraints or audience feedback. If you have a color printer in your office, you can print the overheads shortly before you have to leave for the presentation.

Be aware, however, that color printing is not a speedy process, taking several minutes per page; 5 or 6 minutes per page can be typical. For a presentation of two dozen overheads, printing can take 2 or 3 hours. You can also send the materials to a service bureau for color printing, which will often result in higher-quality images. If you decide to use a service bureau, then you must build into your schedule the time needed for shipping, processing, and return of the overheads.

Black-and-White Transparencies

You can write on black-and-white transparencies. Based on audience comments and questions, you can add, remove, rearrange, and modify transparencies during your presentation. Modifying a transparency encourages audience participation, which makes black-and-white transparencies very useful for training and for informal and staff-meeting presentations. These transparencies cost less than color slides or color transparencies.

The image quality of black-and-white transparencies is best suited to outlines and patterns, although limited use of gray backgrounds is possible. You need to be careful using these because grays and patterns can obscure text and distort graphical images.

Computer Screen

For small groups, you can display your visual materials on a computer screen. If the site is equipped with special large-screen monitors, you can display your visuals through the computer to large groups. Projector pads that sit on top of overhead projectors permit you to display computer-based visuals to a medium-size group.

The image quality of visuals displayed through a computer screen depends on the quality of the computer monitor or projector pad. The quality can vary widely. If you use a VGA monitor or one of better quality, the image quality will be excellent. Using a computer to display your visual materials has significant advantages. First, preparation time is limited to the preparation of the content and format of the visuals; no extra printing or service-bureau time is required. Second, a computer-based presentation allows for a high level of interaction; you can advance or return to any display instantly, and you can create new visuals based on audience feedback and display them immediately. Third, computer-based visuals are less expensive than slides and transparencies. Note: If you choose to present your material using a computer, you should have a backup computer and monitor available in case of breakdown.

POWERPOINT'S CONTRIBUTION

PowerPoint contributes to the effectiveness of your presentation in a variety of ways.

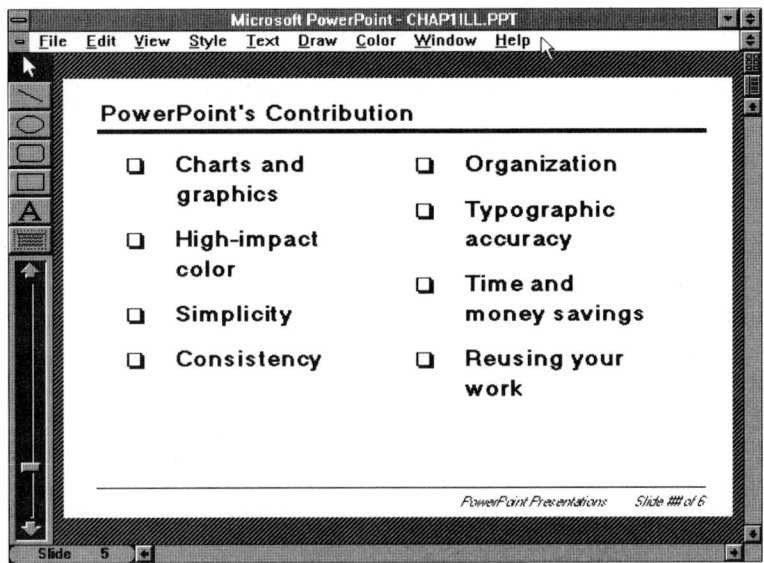

Charts and Graphics

Windows PowerPoint allows you to create over 45 types of charts. In PowerPoint for the Macintosh, you can easily import charts created with Microsoft Excel for the Macintosh. In both versions, you can create graphic effects and incorporate them into your visuals. You can add smoothly shaded backgrounds, or you can insert any of the hundreds of professionally drawn illustrations included in PowerPoint. With PowerPoint's extensive drawing tools, you can also develop your own illustrations.

High-Impact Color

Microsoft Corporation worked with Genigraphics, Incorporated, the country's most experienced slide-production service, to develop the PowerPoint Color Scheme system. The Color Scheme helps you select background, foreground, and accent colors that work well together rather than fight each other. PowerPoint contains 5000 color groupings (called "palettes") selected by design professionals as well as color recommendations for 35mm slides, overhead color transparencies, and computer-screen presentations. And if you include any of PowerPoint's illustrations in a visual item, you can easily recolor the illustrations to match the chosen color scheme of your presentation.

Simplicity

Most of the time, you'll work directly on the visual item. Doing so provides instant and constant feedback because you're always working with the "view" that you'll display. You see immediately how the text and graphics appear on the visual. Seeing your work as you build it encourages you to edit as you work and thereby refine your thoughts. For a quick start in preparing a visual, you can also import an outline from a word processor or from an outline-generating program.

Consistency

As the graphics in this chapter illustrate, your slides can have a consistent appearance. Notice that each slide has a title with a thick underline. At the bottom of the slide is the presentation identification and the slide number plus the total number of slides. Within each slide, the points appear with a consistent format.

PowerPoint makes it easy to set up a consistent appearance. First you create a master slide. The master slide contains all the elements that are the same in every slide—color scheme, format of the title line, the presentation identification (date, logo, firm, presenter), and graphic elements such as borders, lines, boxes, bullets, shading, and so on. Then, for each slide, you fill in the other text and graphics you want to display. PowerPoint's Styles feature makes it easy to choose identical typeface, type size, type style, and text color for all your visuals. Figure 1-1 shows a master slide and a slide created from it. In later chapters you'll see the consistency of appearance given by the style and placement of common elements based on a master slide.

Organization

Effective presentations are built on the progressive disclosure of ideas. The visual items form a sequence that builds toward an understanding and acceptance of the presented ideas and that makes the audience more amenable to your suggestions. To help you organize your presentation, PowerPoint provides a Title Sorter view and a Slide Sorter view, shown in Figure 1-2 on page 20.

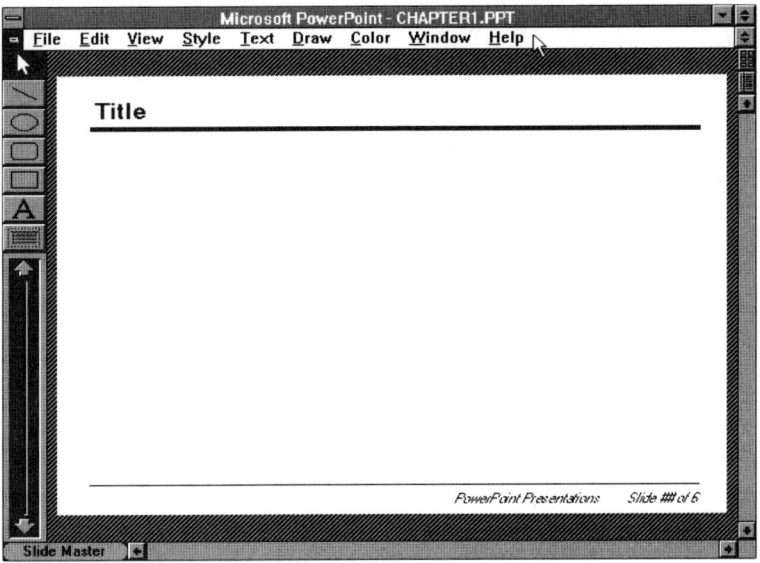

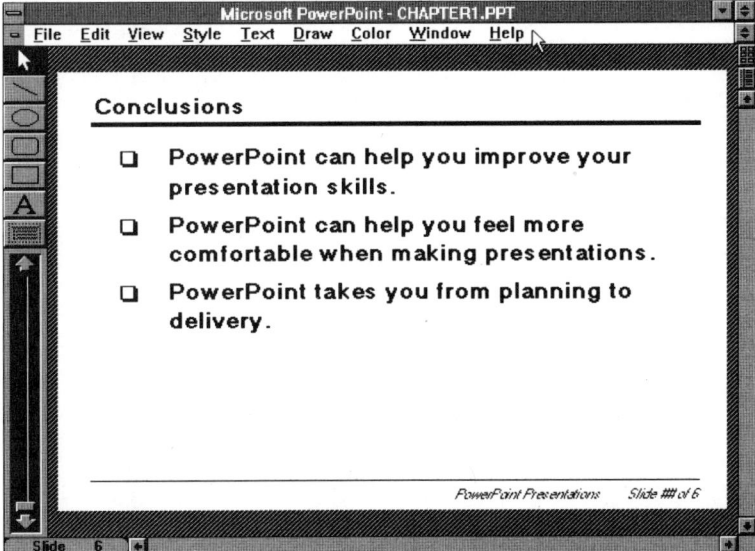

Figure 1-1. Master slide (top) and a filled-in slide (bottom) created from the master slide.

SECTION I: INTRODUCTION TO DESKTOP PRESENTATIONS

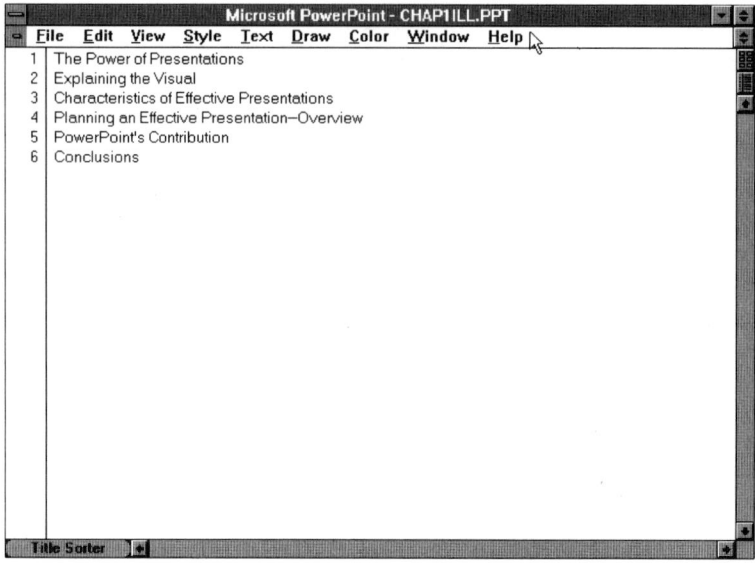

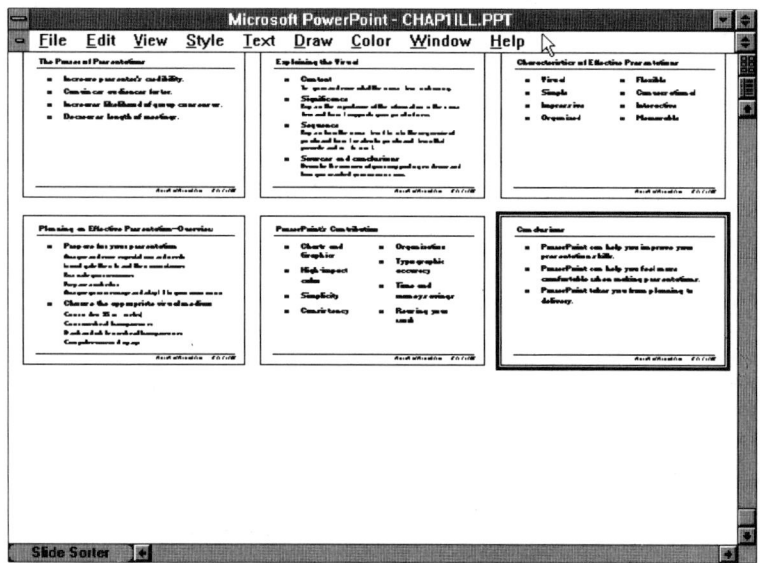

Figure 1-2. *The Title Sorter view (top) and the Slide Sorter view (bottom) make it easy to organize your presentation.*

Typographic Accuracy

Spelling and typographical errors on visual materials detract from your message. Someone in the audience is sure to spot the errors and point them out, thus challenging your credibility. PowerPoint contains a spelling checker, so you can easily and quickly check the spelling of the text in your visual materials, notes, and handouts.

Time and Money Savings

PowerPoint helps you prepare additional items that enhance your presentation. After you prepare the visual items, you can use PowerPoint to convert them to notes for your presentation and to handouts for your audience—instead of spending additional time and money creating your notes and handouts.

PowerPoint can help you create a Notes page to accompany every visual item. Each Notes page contains a reduced-size image of a visual plus space for you to insert key phrases and supporting material, which you can refer to during your presentation. Figure 1-3 shows a sample Notes page, which you can easily create for each visual item.

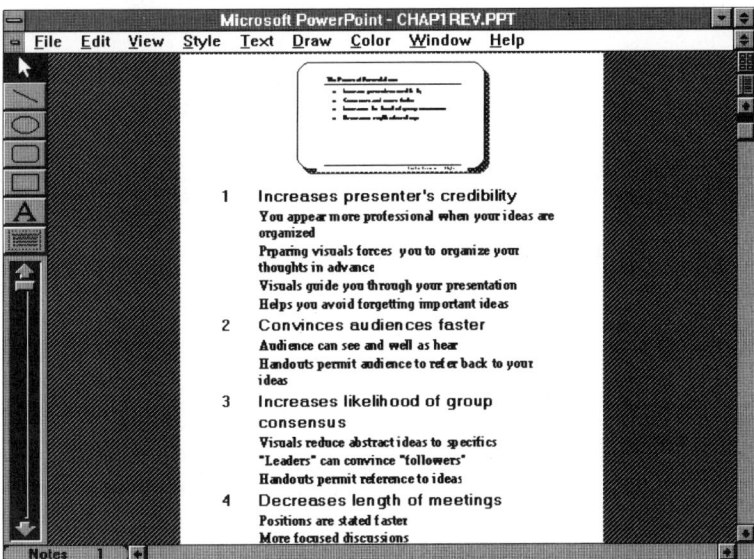

Figure 1-3. A sample Notes page.

Handouts add tangibility and follow-through to your presentation. With a handout in hand, the audience can follow your presentation more easily (especially for those who have difficulty seeing the displayed visual materials), and they can take notes on a handout. Your audience can refer to your handouts at a later date to help them recall your ideas or report what they learned. Also, your audience can share your visual materials with others who were unable to attend your presentation.

A Handout Page can contain two, three, four, or six reduced-size images of visuals. Figure 1-4 shows a sample Handout Page, which you can create easily from your visuals by using PowerPoint.

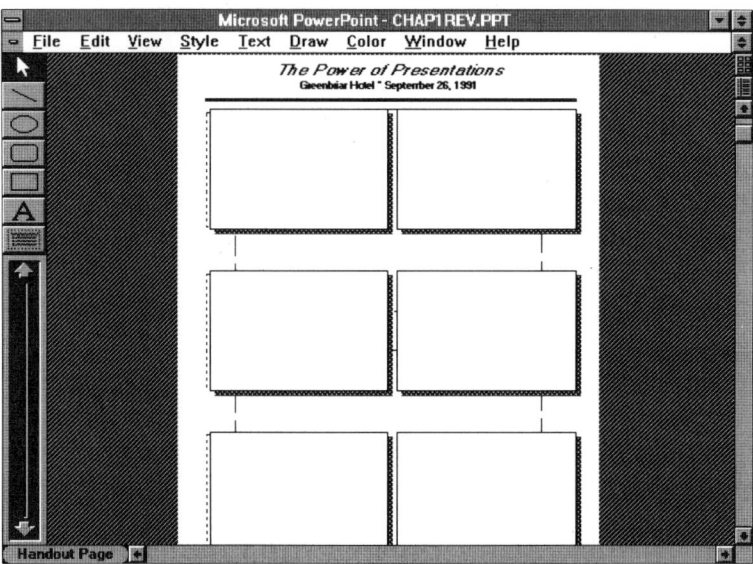

Figure 1-4. A sample Handout Page.

Reusing and Reworking Your Slides

In addition to the time and money saved by converting visual items into notes and handouts, PowerPoint lets you reuse slides from one presentation in another. You can use the slides "as is," or you can modify existing slides to fit the new presentation. This capability saves you the effort and time it would take to create the slides from scratch.

CONCLUSION

PowerPoint can revolutionize your attitudes toward talking in front of a group. As you become more comfortable working with PowerPoint, you'll find yourself producing increasingly effective and attractive visual materials. You'll feel more pride in your work and greater confidence while preparing and delivering a presentation. You might even begin to look forward to preparing presentations.

Most important of all, always keep in mind that the better those in attendance remember your points, the more likely they are to remember you.

Working with PowerPoint

Regardless of the complexity or type of presentation you're working on, and regardless of whether you're using PowerPoint for Windows (hereinafter Windows PowerPoint) or PowerPoint for the Macintosh (hereinafter Macintosh PowerPoint), you'll find PowerPoint easy to use. PowerPoint is based on a few basic commands and features that will soon become second nature to you. This chapter reviews the basics of PowerPoint. In later chapters, you'll find more detailed descriptions of the topics introduced here.

By the end of this chapter, you'll not only know how to load PowerPoint and be familiar with its tools and the commands grouped under the menus at the top of the screen, you'll also know how to target the appropriate presentation output device.

You can then begin working on your first PowerPoint presentation!

BECOMING FAMILIAR WITH THE POWERPOINT SCREEN

The first step is to start PowerPoint.

- ◆ If you're using Macintosh PowerPoint, double-click on the PowerPoint program name or icon (depending on whether you display program names or icons on the Macintosh desktop or on the startup screen).

SECTION I: INTRODUCTION TO DESKTOP PRESENTATIONS

◆ If you're using Windows PowerPoint, double-click on the Applications Group icon, and then double-click on the PowerPoint icon.

In either case, the PowerPoint screen appears. (See Figure 2-1.) You can begin working on the blank slide in front of you. One of PowerPoint's most important virtues is immediately apparent: PowerPoint offers a simple, clean screen that provides all the tools you need to create effective visuals within the working area.

The PowerPoint Screen

If you're using Macintosh PowerPoint, an Apple icon and several menu names appear across the top of the screen. If you're using Windows PowerPoint, the words *Microsoft PowerPoint* appear on the top line, and the menu bar appears on the second line. The word *Title* appears in the top center of the PowerPoint working area. The Title plays an important role in rearranging your visuals.

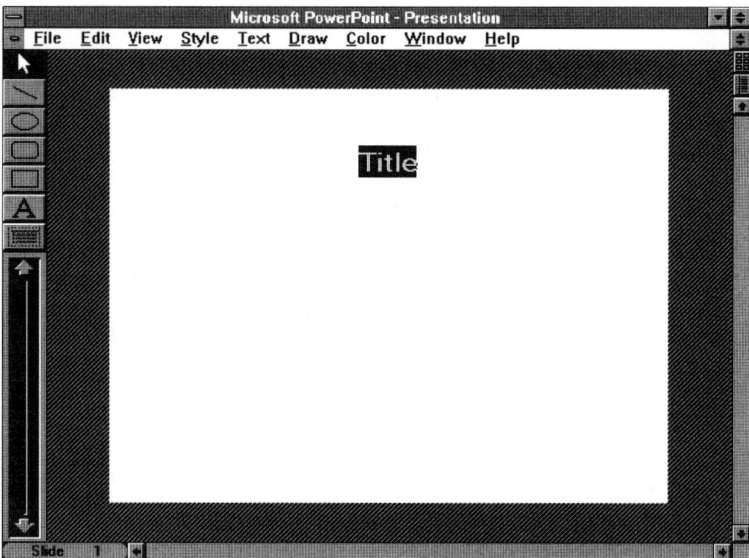

Figure 2-1. *PowerPoint's screen contains a working area and the tools you need to work efficiently. (This screen is from the Windows version of PowerPoint.)*

To access the commands in the menus located along the top of the screen, point to the desired menu and hold down the mouse button—the left mouse button if you're using Windows PowerPoint. To choose a command, drag the pointer down through the menu and release it when the desired command is highlighted—as indicated by white letters against a black background.

An arrow pointing to the right indicates that additional options are available by moving the mouse to the right. Three dots indicate that a dialog box must be filled in.

Keyboard Shortcuts

In Macintosh PowerPoint, letters to the right of certain commands indicate that you can directly access those commands by simultaneously holding down the Command key while pressing the indicated letter.

Windows PowerPoint offers even more extensive keyboard shortcuts, allowing you to directly access any command without using the mouse.

- Start by pressing the Alt key, followed by the first letter of the menu you want to open. Notice that the menu opens *and remains open*.

- To access a particular command, press the key corresponding to the underlined letter. This activates the command and closes the menu.

PowerPoint's Menus

PowerPoint's commands reside in menus located at the top of the screen. I'll discuss the menus, moving from left to right.

Apple or Windows symbol

One of the most important commands located under the Apple icon is the Chooser, which allows you to target the type of printer or output device you'll be using to produce your presentation. (See Figure 2-2 on the following page.) You also access PowerPoint's online Help by clicking on the Apple icon.

If you're using Windows PowerPoint, the commands contained under the horizontal line—which represents the Windows symbol—allow you to adjust the size of the screen area as well as to switch between applications.

SECTION I: INTRODUCTION TO DESKTOP PRESENTATIONS

Figure 2-2.
The Apple Chooser command lets you target the output device you're going to use to produce your Macintosh Power-Point presentation.

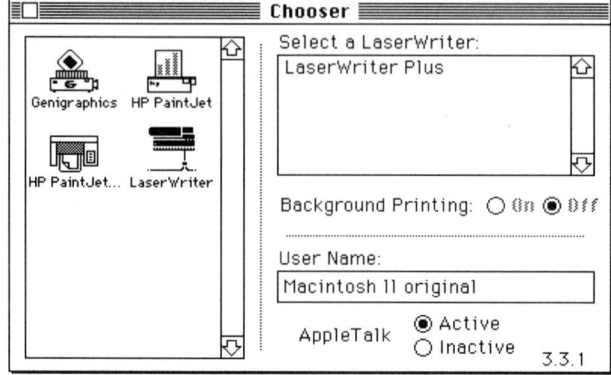

File

The File menu contains commands that allow you to open new or existing presentations, save your work, and import files created with other software programs, as well as access the Slide Show feature that is used for computer-based on-screen presentations or for previewing your visuals from the audience's perspective. (See Figure 2-3: The Macintosh version is shown at the left; the Windows version is shown at the right.)

One of the few major differences between Windows PowerPoint and Macintosh PowerPoint is that the File menu of the Windows version contains an Insert command. This allows you to create, format, and add charts, worksheets, and graphs to your presentation. (Macintosh users typically create charts, worksheets, and graphs using Microsoft Excel and then import them through the Clipboard.)

Figure 2-3.
The File menu commands let you retrieve and save your presentation or preview it by using the Slide Show feature. (Macintosh version, left; Windows version, right.)

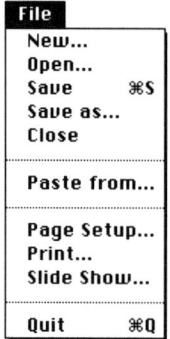
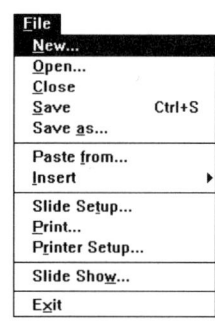

In addition, the File menu of Windows PowerPoint contains a Printer Setup command that allows you to target different printers for visuals and for preparing Notes and Handout pages.

Edit

The Edit menu contains commands that allow you to handle text and graphics on individual slides. (See Figure 2-4.) These include copying and pasting to the Clipboard, grouping items together, and sending text and graphical objects to the front or to the rear. The Edit menu also contains the New Slide command used to add new slides to your presentation.

The Edit menu of Windows PowerPoint contains two commands not found in Macintosh PowerPoint. Crop Picture allows you to eliminate unneeded information at the top, bottom, or sides of an imported graphic. Edit Graph allows you to alter or reformat a previously placed graph.

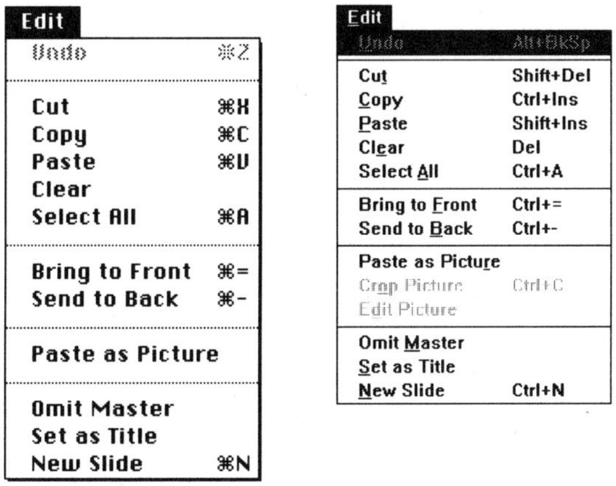

Figure 2-4.
The Edit menu commands let you add, delete, move, or group items or layer them on top of each other. (Macintosh version, left; Windows verison, right.)

Edit	
Undo	⌘Z
Cut	⌘X
Copy	⌘C
Paste	⌘V
Clear	
Select All	⌘A
Bring to Front	⌘=
Send to Back	⌘-
Paste as Picture	
Omit Master	
Set as Title	
New Slide	⌘N

Edit	
Undo	Alt+BkSp
Cut	Shift+Del
Copy	Ctrl+Ins
Paste	Shift+Ins
Clear	Del
Select All	Ctrl+A
Bring to Front	Ctrl+=
Send to Back	Ctrl+-
Paste as Picture	
Crop Picture	Ctrl+C
Edit Picture	
Omit Master	
Set as Title	
New Slide	Ctrl+N

View

The View menu contains commands that allow you to choose the degree of magnification at which you want to work. (See Figure 2-5 on the following page.) It also allows you to choose to work on slides, Notes, or Handouts. The View command also accesses the Title Sorter and Slide Sorter views, which you'll use to copy, delete, or rearrange the order of your visuals. Perhaps the most important View command is the Slide Master command, which allows you to add elements that will be automatically added to all slides.

SECTION I: INTRODUCTION TO DESKTOP PRESENTATIONS

Figure 2-5.
The View menu commands let you work on a portion of your visual with great precision or choose a smaller view in order to get an overall view. (Macintosh version, left; Windows version, right.)

PowerPoint's Notes view allows you to prepare the idea sheet that you'll use to rehearse and deliver your presentation. Each Notes sheet contains a reduced-size image of the visual plus space in which to enter the phrases or supporting data that you want to discuss while displaying the visual.

PowerPoint's Handout Master view allows you to format the pages that you'll give to your audience. You can add presentation title, date, page number, and other information to the Handout pages. Each Handout page can contain two, four, six, or eight reduced-size images of each visual.

Style

The Style menu contains commands that allow you to choose the desired typeface, type size, and type style. (See Figure 2-6.) You can also store and retrieve styles. The Styles command helps you work faster and improve the appearance of your visuals by permitting you to choose quickly and consistently the appropriate typeface, type size, type style, and color. Macintosh PowerPoint includes two additional font styles—Outline and Shadow.

Figure 2-6.
The Style menu commands let you determine the appearance of the words used in your presentation visuals. (Macintosh version, left; Windows version, right.)

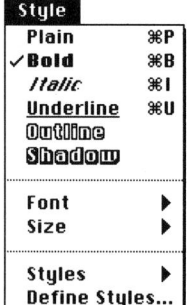
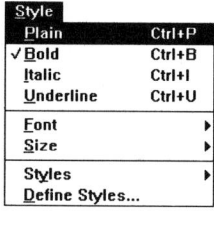

Text

The Text menu contains commands that allow you to refine the placement of words and numbers. (See Figure 2-7.) You can choose desired text alignment (flush left, flush right, centered, or justified) and fine-tune line and paragraph spacing as well as adjust the depth of tabs and indents. The Text menu also contains PowerPoint's spelling checker, which can help you avoid embarrassing typographical errors. The Find/Replace command (in Macintosh PowerPoint) or the Find/Change command (in Windows PowerPoint) allows you to easily update older presentations as well as double-check for overused words.

Figure 2-7.
The Text menu commands let you choose among flush-left, centered, and flush-right text placement, indent items in a list as well as refine line and paragraph spacing. (Macintosh version, left; Windows verison, right.)

Draw

The Draw menu contains commands that allow you to establish the appearance of objects created with PowerPoint's Line and Rectangle drawing tools. You can specify line thickness and background patterns, determine the presence or absence of shadows, and add arrowheads to lines. (See Figure 2-8 on the following page.) Other Draw commands allow you to hide or reveal alignment guides. You can also disable the background grid, allowing you to place objects next to, but not quite touching, each other. You can also choose to either hide or reveal object edges; revealing text and object edges often makes it easier to move objects.

SECTION I: INTRODUCTION TO DESKTOP PRESENTATIONS

Figure 2-8.
The Draw menu commands let you specify such characteristics as line thickness and patterns. (Macintosh version, left; Windows version, right.)

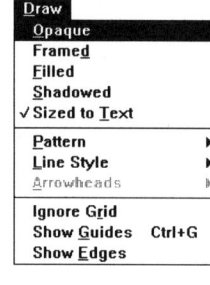

Color

The Color menu contains commands that allow you to select or alter the colors used in your visuals. (See Figure 2-9.) You can choose and manipulate a slide's background color and shading as well as choose the colors used for lines and boxes, imported graphics, shadows, and text. You can choose and modify the Color Scheme settings used throughout your presentation, and you can also add colors.

Figure 2-9.
The Color menu commands let you control color usage and shading in your visuals. (Macintosh version, left; Windows version, right.)

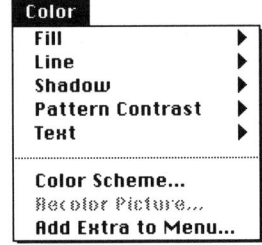 

Window

PowerPoint allows you to open more than one presentation file at a time. This makes it easy to share visuals and color schemes among presentations. The Window menu, as shown in Figure 2-10, displays the titles of each active presentation, allowing you to switch between them easily. In Windows Power-Point, the Arrange All command allows you to view all open presentations on screen simultaneously, while the Fit To Page Size command scales the active window to display only the active area, cropping out the background.

Chapter 2: Working with PowerPoint

Figure 2-10.
The Window menu commands let you open more than one presentation file at a time. (Macintosh version, left; Windows version, right.)

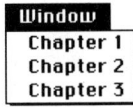
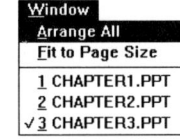

Help When You Need It

PowerPoint's Help feature is found in different locations in the Macintosh and Windows versions. To locate Help when using Macintosh PowerPoint, click on the Apple icon. Windows PowerPoint contains its own Help menu, located to the right of the other menus.

Using either version, you can quickly locate information by clicking on the index and dragging the mouse through the various commands, releasing the mouse button when you reach the desired command.

Selection and Drawing Tools

PowerPoint's selection and drawing tools are grouped along the left edge of the screen. As we describe these tools, working from top to bottom, notice how the commands in the menus along the top of the screen are used to modify the appearance of the objects and text they create.

Arrow tool

The Arrow tool, a white arrow on a dark background that points up and slightly to the left, allows you to select a text element or graphical object for deletion, movement, or modification. For example, if you're at your computer and have loaded PowerPoint, first click the Arrow tool, and then click on *Title*. Notice that a "fuzzy border" appears. (See Figure 2-11 on the following page.) Click anywhere on this border and hold down the mouse button. You can now reposition the Title box by dragging it anywhere on the slide. Release the button and the Title box will remain in the new location.

Windows PowerPoint offers an even faster way to select and move an object. Simply click anywhere on the object with the right mouse button and hold it down. You can immediately drag it to a new position.

33

SECTION I: INTRODUCTION TO DESKTOP PRESENTATIONS

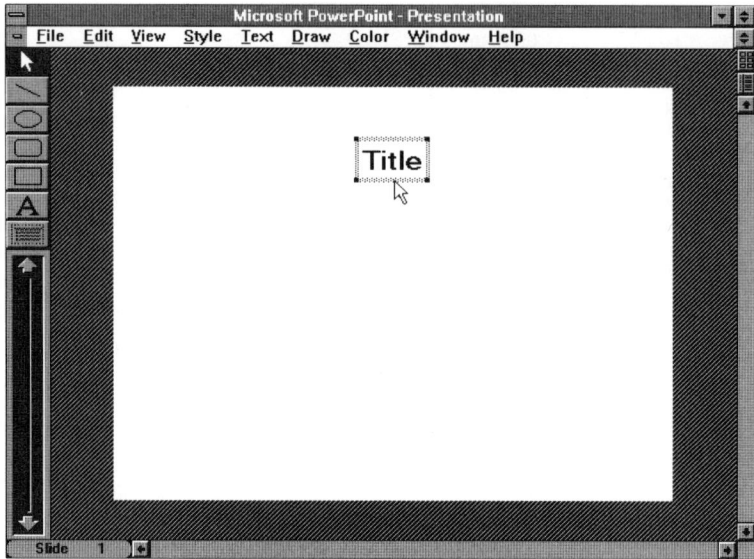

Figure 2-11. *To move a text or graphical object using the Arrow tool, click on one of its "fuzzy borders" and, while holding down the mouse button, drag the object.*

Line tool

The Line tool allows you to add rules—or lines of different weight—to your visuals. To use the Line tool, choose it by clicking on its icon. Place the cursor anywhere on the screen, hold down the mouse button as you move the mouse in the desired direction, and then release. (See Figure 2-12.) Notice how a line is drawn between the cursor's original location and where you release the mouse button.

Notice that after you release the mouse button, the line is surrounded by the fuzzy border and has a dot at each end. These indicate that the line is currently selected. While the line is selected, you can use the commands in the Draw menu to change the characteristics of the line. For example, you can open the Draw menu by clicking on it and choose the Line Style command.

To change the line's thickness to one of the alternatives presented, select the desired alternative by highlighting it, and release the mouse button. (See Figure 2-13.) While the line is still selected, open the Draw menu again and choose the Arrowheads command. Select the bottom alternative by releasing the mouse button. The line now has a completely different appearance.

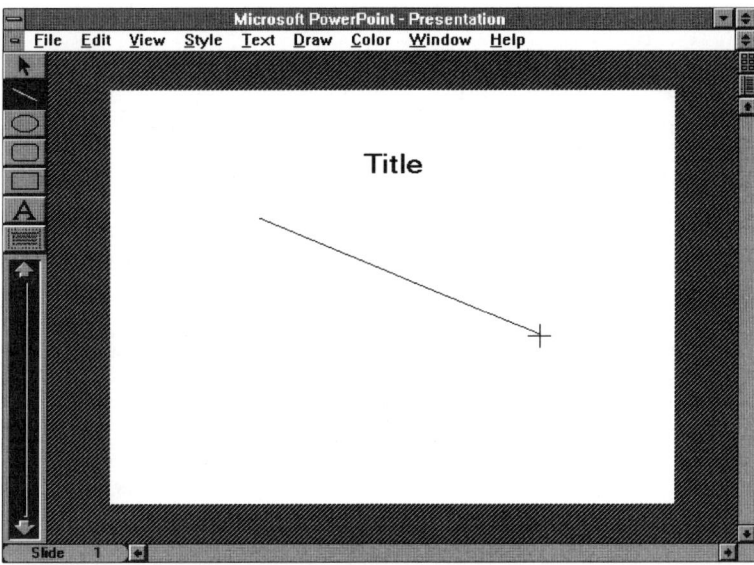

Figure 2-12. *A line before modification. (See Figure 2-13.)*

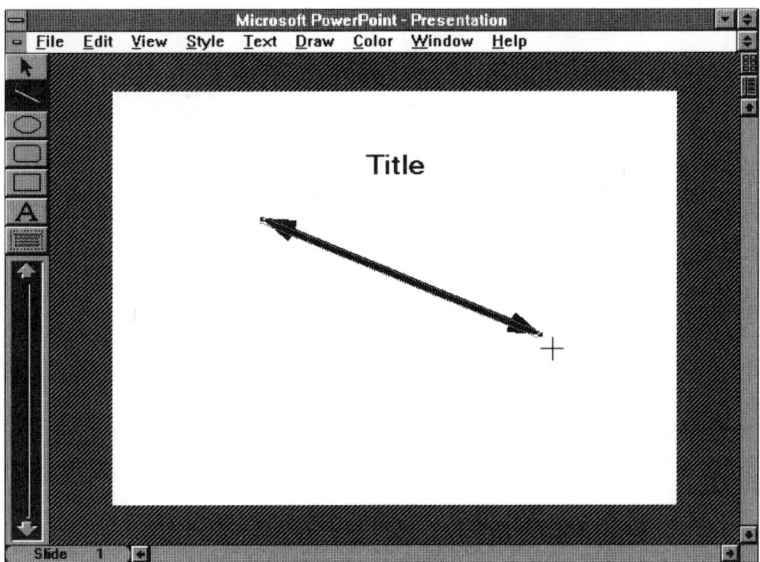

Figure 2-13. *The line after modification by means of the Draw menu commands. (See Figure 2-12.)*

Oval, Rounded Rectangle, and Rectangle drawing tools

The Oval, Rounded Rectangle, and Rectangle tools allow you to draw ovals, rectangles with round corners, and rectangles with square corners. You can also draw circles and squares by holding down the Shift key while the Oval or Rectangle tools are selected. You choose a tool by clicking on it. For example, click on the Rounded Rectangle tool. Place the cursor in the upper left corner of the screen, click and hold down the mouse button, drag the mouse toward the lower right corner of the screen, and release the button. (See Figure 2-14.) You've just drawn a rectangle with rounded corners.

After you've created the rounded rectangle, but while it is still selected, open the Draw menu and choose Filled. The rounded rectangle becomes a solid. Next, open the Draw menu again and choose Pattern. Hold down the mouse button and click on the square containing the lines pointing diagonally to the upper right. Release the mouse button, and the appearance of the box changes completely. (See Figure 2-15.)

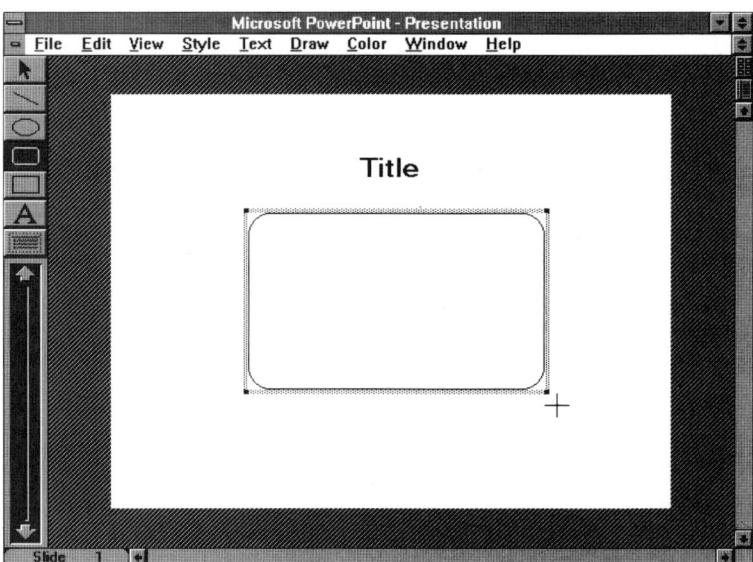

Figure 2-14. *A rounded rectangle before modification. (See Figure 2-15.)*

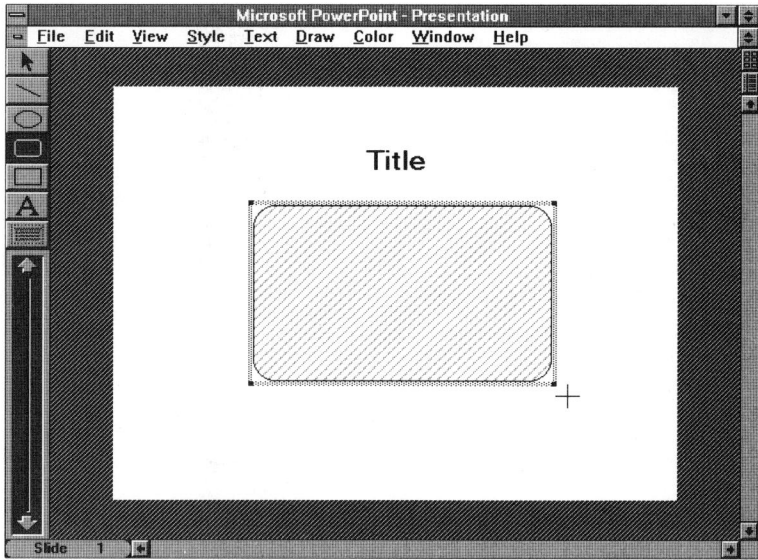

Figure 2-15. *The rounded rectangle after modification by means of the Draw menu's Pattern command. (See Figure 2-14.)*

Labeler tool

The Labeler tool—represented by the A-shaped icon—allows you to add a short phrase or a single sentence to your slide or overhead. Choose the Labeler tool by clicking on its A-shaped icon. Use the mouse to place the cursor where you want the text to appear on the screen. Click the mouse button once. Notice that the cursor has turned into a flashing (vertical) insertion point. Type *Format Text*. The words you typed appear to the left of the insertion point. (See Figure 2-16 on the following page.)

After you've typed the words *Format Text*, click on the Arrow tool and click on the words you just typed. Notice that the fuzzy border surrounds the words. Open the Style menu and choose Size. Choose *96*, the largest size that appears. Notice how PowerPoint instantly reformats the words. (See Figure 2-17 on the following page.) If you did not choose to install the large fonts when you first installed the PowerPoint program, the text on your screen might appear more jagged than the text shown in Figure 2-17.

SECTION I: INTRODUCTION TO DESKTOP PRESENTATIONS

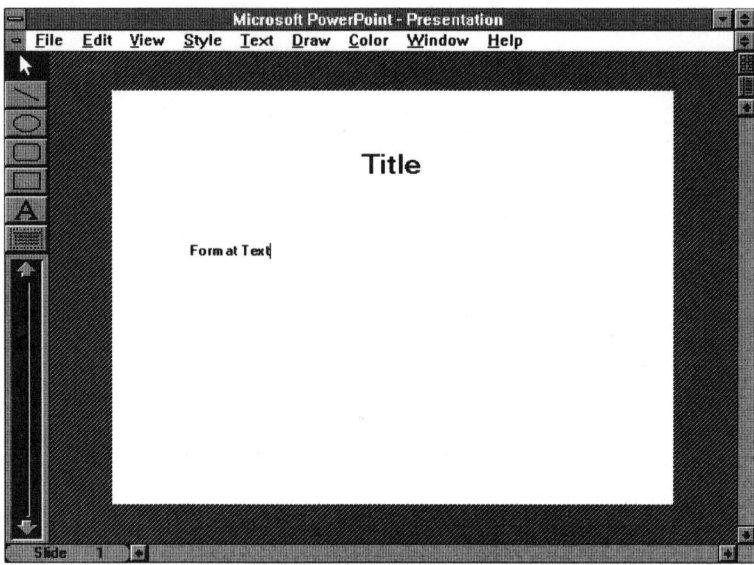

Figure 2-16. Text before modification. (See Figure 2-17.)

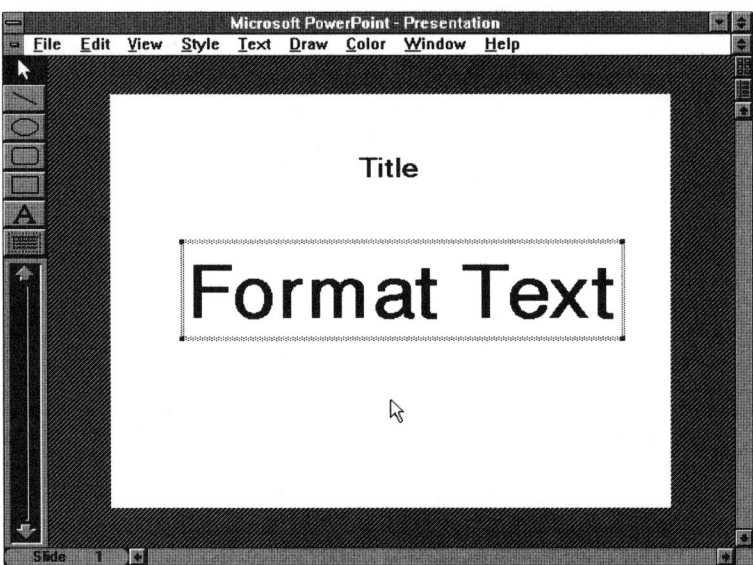

Figure 2-17. The text after modification by means of the Style menu's Size command. (See Figure 2-16.)

Word Processing tool

The Word Processing tool allows you to enter extended amounts of text—including lists formatted as indented outlines—to your presentation. Click on the Word Processing tool. To create a text area, position the cursor at the upper left corner of the area where you want text to appear. Click the mouse button and hold it down while dragging the cursor to the lower right corner of the desired text area. Release the mouse button and type the following: *PowerPoint permits you to format your words for maximum visual impact and legibility, making it easier for the audience to quickly grasp your ideas.* PowerPoint's graphical user interface instantly shows you the results of your formatting instructions. (See Figure 2-18.) Notice how the words "wrap" at the end of each line—that is, how one line ends and the next begins...automatically.

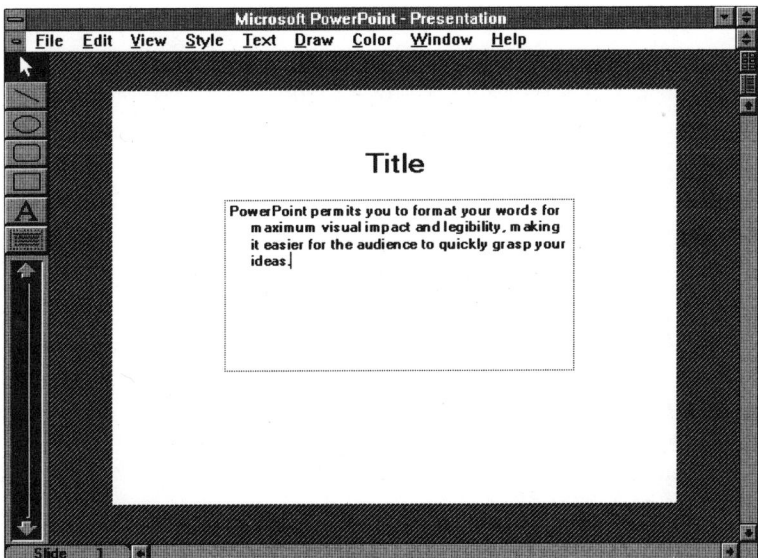

Figure 2-18. *Automatic end-of-line word wrap as well as adjustable indents and line spacing are among the capabilities of the Word Processing tool.*

Moving Between Slides

To experience how easy it is to move forward and backward through a PowerPoint presentation, choose the Open command from the File menu. Double-click on the "Columbus" presentation. (Notice that you don't need to close your first presentation. PowerPoint allows you to have more than one presentation open at a time.)

When the first slide appears, click on the Downward arrow of the Slide Changer tool at the lower left edge of the screen (beneath the Word Processing tool). Notice how you move further into the presentation, one visual at a time, each time you click on the Downward arrow.

To review previous slides, click on the Upward arrow directly below the Word Processing tool. Each time you click, you'll move toward the beginning of your presentation, one slide at a time.

Notice that the horizontal bar (the "level control" marker) located between the Upward and Downward arrows allows you to quickly advance to the approximate location of any desired visual. Simply click on the level control marker and hold down the mouse button while you drag the marker to the approximate slide location. Once there, use the Upward and Downward arrows to pinpoint the slide's exact location.

Notice that the slide number of the selected slide is always displayed in the Slide Number box at the lower left of your screen. This box also indicates whether you're in the Slide Master view and indicates the number of the Notes page on which you're working.

Selecting Image Area

While the "Columbus" presentation is on the screen, you can experiment with various levels of magnification selected from the View menu. Choose the Full Size command.

Most computer screens are unable to display an entire slide or visual when Full Size has been chosen from the View menu. (See Figure 2-19.) Many monitors are not even able to display the complete image at 66% Size. Therefore, you need a method by which to see a portion of the image.

The arrows pointing to the left and right at the bottom of the screen allow you to scroll to the left or right across the surface of a slide or overhead displayed at Full Size or 66% Size, so you see a portion of the image. This permits you to work with greater precision.

Likewise, the up and down arrows along the right edge of the PowerPoint screen allow you to scroll up or down across the surface of a slide or overhead displayed at Full Size or 66% Size. (See Figure 2-20.)

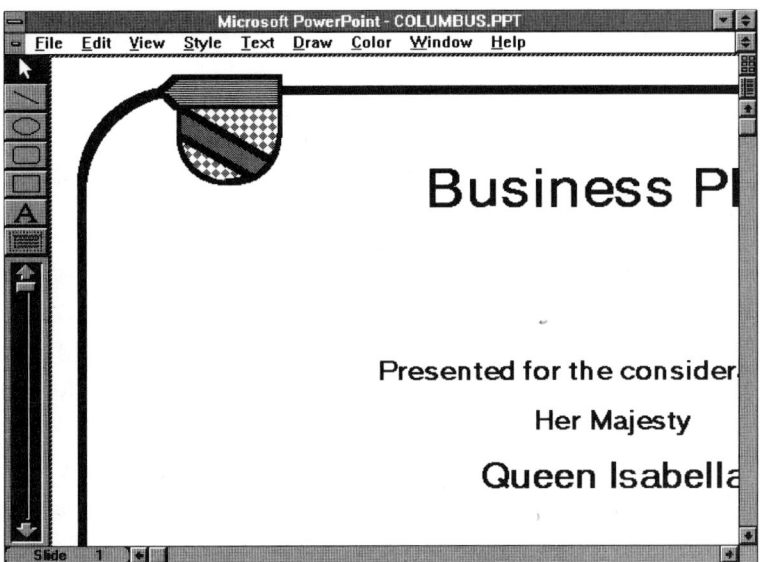

Figure 2-19. View of the "Columbus" screen with Full Size chosen from the View menu.

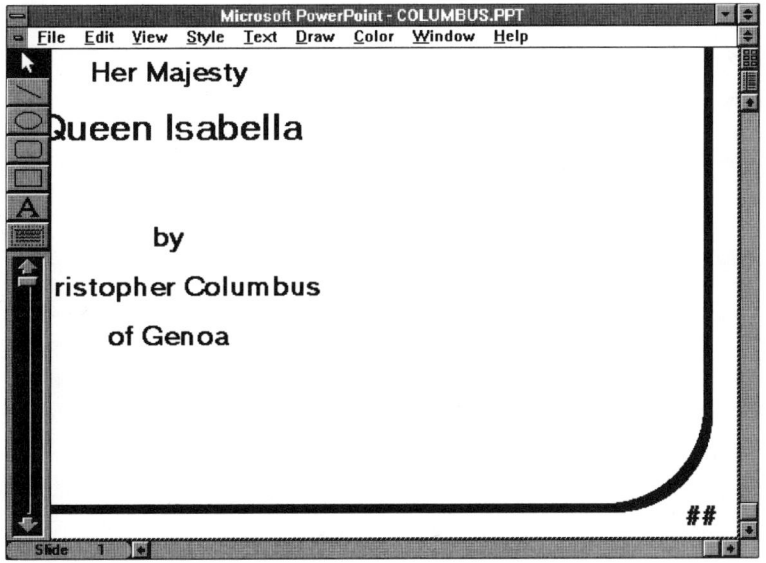

Figure 2-20. The view shown in Figure 2-19 has been moved down and to the right with the down and right arrows at the lower right of the screen, providing a new partial image of the "Columbus" screen.

Slide Sorter and Title Sorter Views—Shortcuts

The PowerPoint screen contains two important "shorthand" boxes located at the upper right. These permit you to select the Slide Sorter view or, immediately below it, the Title Sorter view. These views make it easy to rearrange your presentation visuals—along with the Notes and Handout pages that accompany them.

Slide Sorter

Click on the top box when you want to go directly to the Slide Sorter view. (You can also choose Slide Sorter from the View menu.) The Slide Sorter displays thumbnails—reduced-size versions—of each of your slides. (See Figure 2-21.) Choose the Slide Sorter view when you want to reorganize your presentation.

To move a slide to a new location, select it by clicking on it. A heavy border surrounds the slide. Hold down the mouse button and drag the slide to a new location. Release the mouse button when the cursor appears between the slides where you want to insert the selected slide.

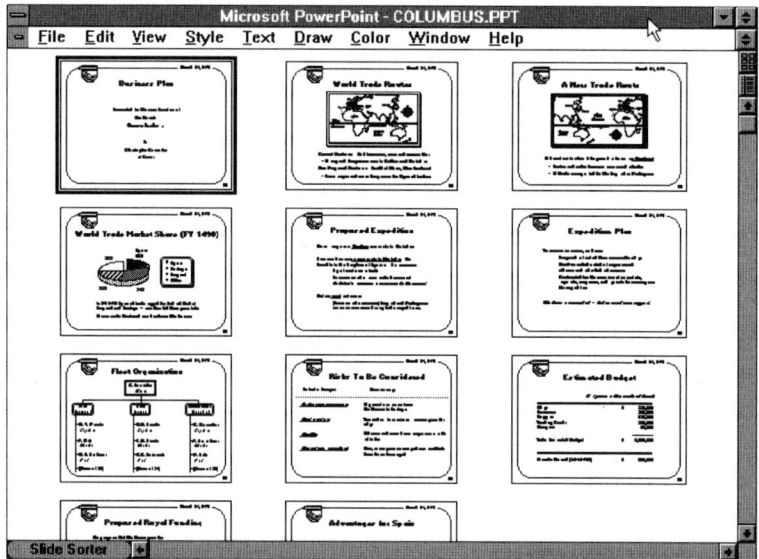

Figure 2-21. *The Slide Sorter view makes it easy to rearrange your presentation.*

Title Sorter

Click on the box below the Slide Sorter—the one with parallel horizontal lines—when you want to go directly to the Title Sorter view. (You can also choose Title Sorter from the View menu.) The Title Sorter displays a list of slide titles. (See Figure 2-22.) Reorganizing a presentation using the Title Sorter is faster than using the Slide Sorter because the computer does not have to redraw each slide on the screen.

To reorganize your presentation using the Title Sorter, select the slide you want to move by clicking on its title. The selected title will appear "reversed"—that is, white letters against a black background. Hold down the mouse button and drag the slide to a new location. Notice the horizontal bar with arrow, which indicates possible locations. Release the mouse button at the desired location.

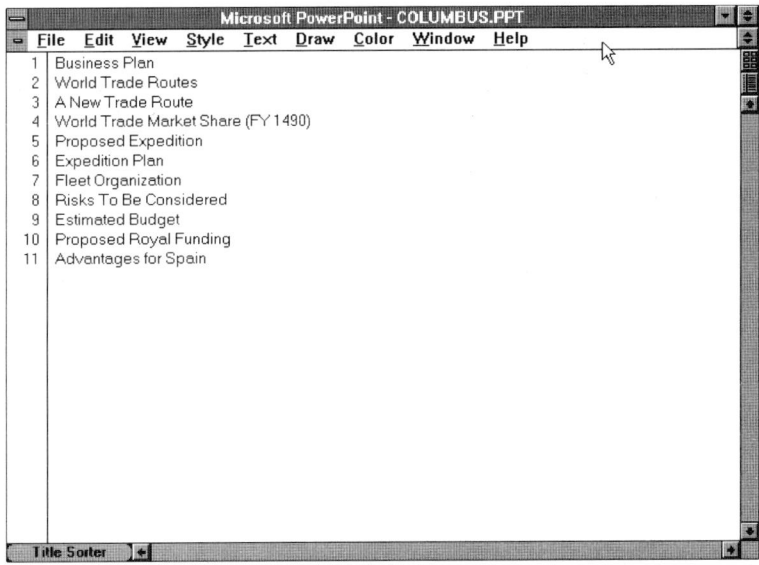

Figure 2-22. *The Title Sorter view offers a fast way to reorganize your presentation.*

Returning to Slide View

PowerPoint offers two ways that you can return to the slide you were last working on before you entered Slide Sorter or Title Sorter view.

- ◆ Open the View menu and click on Slides (#_). The number next to the pound sign is the number of the last slide on which you were working.

- Use the appropriate keyboard shortcut: Command-D (in Macintosh PowerPoint) or Ctrl-D (in Windows PowerPoint).

In addition, the Title Sorter and Slide Sorter views make it easy to go directly to a specific slide. When in Slide Sorter view, you can go to the Slide view of a specific visual simply by double-clicking on it. To go directly to a specific slide from the Title Sorter view, double-click on the title.

Closing the sample "Columbus" presentation

After you've become acquainted with these PowerPoint features, close the "Columbus" presentation by opening the File menu and choosing Close. If you have not made any changes, it will close immediately. If you *have* modified it, you'll be asked whether you want to make the changes permanent.

When the Save Changes dialog box appears, choose No. This returns you to the original "untitled" presentation.

ADDING, COPYING, AND DELETING SLIDES

You can add a new slide to your presentation in two ways.

- Choose New Slide from the Edit menu.
- Use the appropriate keyboard shortcut: Command-N (in Macintosh PowerPoint) or Ctrl-N (in Windows PowerPoint).

New slides can be added in Slide, Slide Sorter, or Title Sorter view.

Slides can be deleted in Slide Sorter or Title Sorter view. Simply click on the slide you want to delete and choose Clear from the Edit menu. Or, as a keyboard shortcut, use the Backspace or Delete key.

If you want to delete or move more than one slide at a time, hold down the Shift key as you click on the slides. This allows you to "grab" several slides and delete them or move them to a new location in the same presentation. (Note: You can also use this shortcut to copy several slides to a *different* presentation.)

You can copy slides in either the Slide Sorter or the Title Sorter view. To copy a slide, click on the slide itself (in Slide Sorter view) or on its title (in Title Sorter view), and choose the Copy command from the Edit menu. Position the cursor where you want the new slide inserted and choose Paste from the Edit menu.

PLACING, MANIPULATING, AND ALIGNING TEXT AND GRAPHICS

You can import previously created graphics files into PowerPoint presentations in several ways. Following are some commands that you'll use to import, move, resize, align, and layer text and graphical objects.

Importing Previously Created Text and Graphics Files

PowerPoint offers three ways to import text and graphics.

Paste From

You'll frequently use the Paste From command, located on the File menu, to import previously prepared text or graphics files. In addition to importing graphics created with drawing and paint programs, you can also import outlines prepared with various word processing files.

Paste

The Paste command, located in the Edit menu, is used with the Cut and Copy commands. You can use Paste in conjunction with Cut to move text or a graphic from one slide to another, and you can use Paste with Copy to add copies of a graphic to a slide or to create a background consisting of several parallel lines.

Paste As Picture

The Paste As Picture command is used with Cut to combine two (or more) text or graphic objects into a single object that can be moved or resized as a single graphic. (See Figures 2-23 and 2-24 on the following page.) Paste As Picture is also used to recolor imported graphics.

Using the following procedure, you can group individual objects (for example, the ones shown in Figure 2-23) into a single image.

1. Click on the Arrow tool, the topmost tool at the left side of the screen that is used for selection. (This arrow points up and slightly to the left and is white on a dark background.) Start by selecting all the objects: Hold down the Shift key as you click on each item. (Or you can draw a selection box around the group of objects.) You'll be able to tell when the objects have been selected because the fuzzy borders will be visible.

SECTION I: INTRODUCTION TO DESKTOP PRESENTATIONS

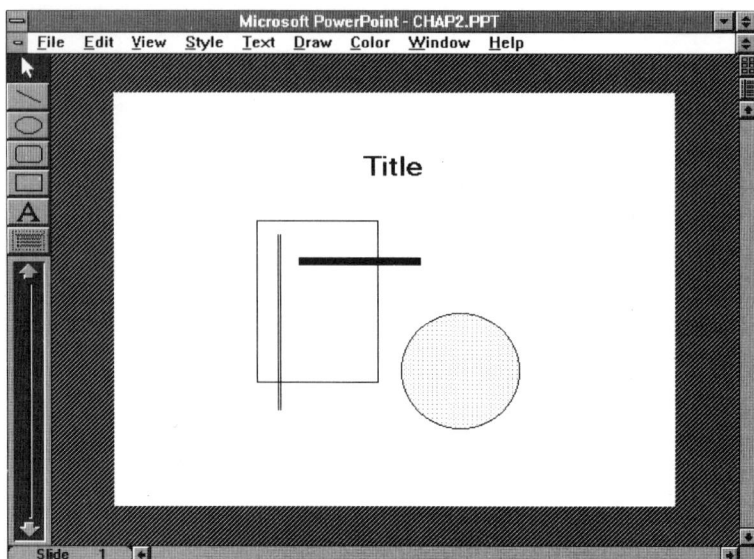

Figure 2-23. Lines, box, and circle before they are grouped together. (See Figure 2-24.)

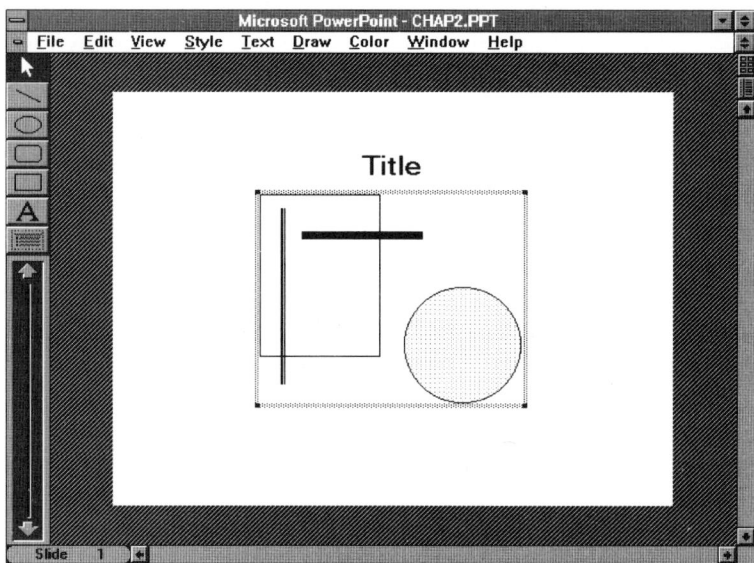

Figure 2-24. Lines, box, and circle after the Cut and Paste As Picture commands have been used to group them. The objects can now be resized and moved as a single unit. (See Figure 2-23.)

2. Cut the objects by choosing Cut from the Edit menu. Or use the Command-X keyboard shortcut for Macintosh PowerPoint or the Shift-Del keyboard shortcut for Windows PowerPoint.

3. Click on Paste As Picture from the Edit menu. The objects will appear in the center of the screen, within a box. (See Figure 2-24.)

The lines, circle, and box can now be resized and moved as a single unit.

Warning

After grouping objects with the Cut and Paste As Picture commands, you cannot separate them and manipulate the individual parts—that is, you cannot *un*group the visual.

Resizing Graphics

To resize a graphical object, click on one of the four corner buttons and drag it in the desired direction.

- To widen or narrow the image, drag the button horizontally.

- To make the image taller or shorter, drag the button vertically.

- To simultaneously increase or decrease image size both horizontally and vertically, drag one of the corner buttons in a diagonal direction.

- To maintain the original's aspect ratio—or height-to-width ratio—hold down the Shift key while dragging one of the corner buttons diagonally. The image will be proportionately increased or decreased in size.

- To maintain the original's height or width, hold down the Shift key while dragging one of the corner buttons horizontally or vertically. The image will be constrained vertically while you drag horizontally, and vice-versa.

Deleting, Moving, and Copying Text and Graphics

To delete a text element or a graphical image, first click on it. Then:

- To place it in your computer's memory for pasting later to a different position—or a different slide—choose Cut from the Edit menu.

- To leave the original in its present position for pasting elsewhere at a later time, choose Copy from the Edit menu.
- To delete the original without placing it in the computer's memory, choose Clear from the Edit menu.

Aligning Text and Graphics

PowerPoint alignment and measuring tools reside in its Show Guides command (located near the bottom of the Draw menu), and they are accessed by using a keyboard shortcut: Command-G (in Macintosh PowerPoint) or Ctrl-G (in Windows PowerPoint).

When you select Show Guides, a pair of centered vertical and horizontal lines appear on your screen. These lines are guides that function as on-screen straightedges, helping you align objects on your slide. These guides also exert a magnetic attraction on the sides or the center of text or on graphical objects that are within $\frac{1}{6}$ inch of a guide.

Aligning objects by using the horizontal guide

To see how PowerPoint's alignment tool operates, choose the Rectangle tool and press the Shift key to draw a square. While it remains selected, open the Draw menu and choose Filled. Then choose the Oval tool and press the Shift key to draw a circle. Choose a pattern from the Draw menu while the circle is selected. (See Figure 2-25.)

If the guides are not already present, choose Show Guides from the Draw menu, or use the appropriate keyboard shortcut.

- Command-G in Macintosh PowerPoint
- Ctrl-G in Windows PowerPoint

As you've seen, the horizontal and vertical guides are centered on the screen when you open a new presentation; this is also the case when you toggle between Show Guides and Hide Guides. (See Figure 2-26.)

Select the horizontal guide by clicking on it and, while holding down the mouse button, drag the horizontal guide above the two images.

Select the square by clicking on it. Grab one of the borders and, while holding down the mouse button, raise the square until its top edge touches the horizontal guide. Notice that if you try to raise the square higher, the image will hesitate until you force it by dragging with a more determined hand.

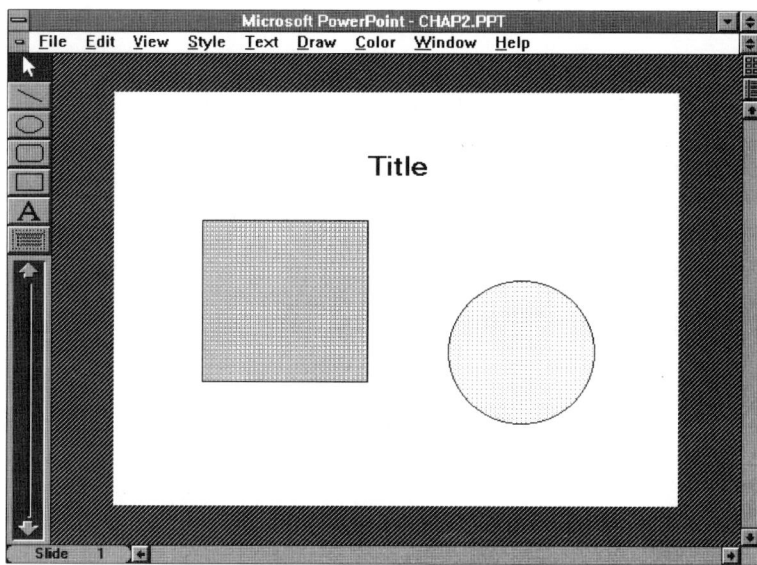

Figure 2-25. *Location of a square and a circle before repositioning. (See Figure 2-26.)*

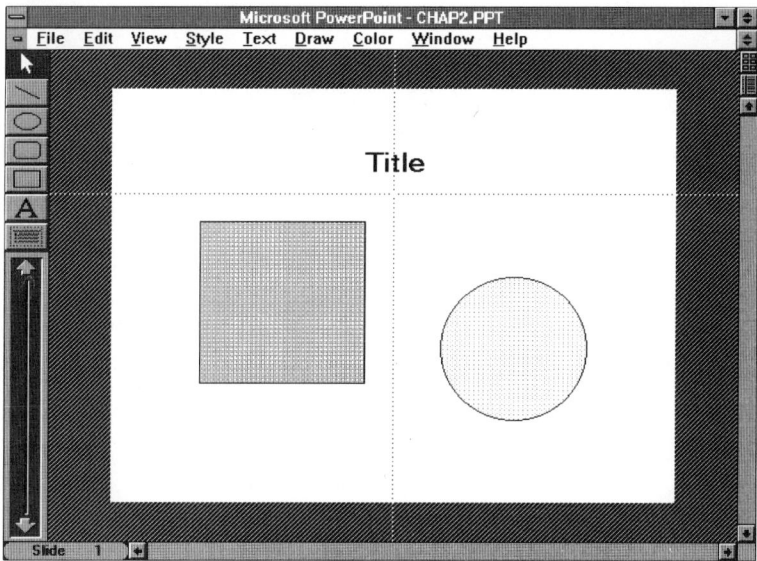

Figure 2-26. *Horizontal guide moved to desired position above the square and the circle. (See Figures 2-25 and 2-27.)*

Select the circle. Raise it until the top edge touches the horizontal guide. (See Figure 2-27.)

To align the bottoms of graphical images, grab the horizontal guide and move it down until it's located where you want to align the bottom edges of the box and the circle. Select the objects and release them when the bottom edges of their fuzzy borders approach the horizontal guide.

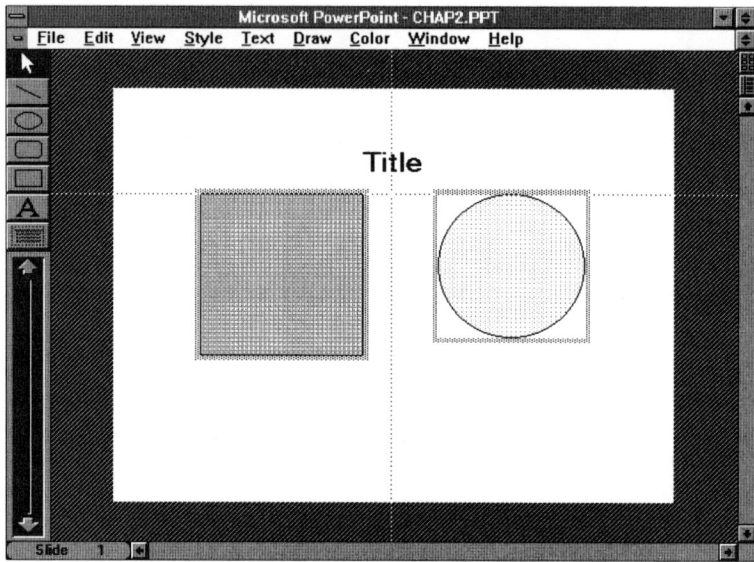

Figure 2-27. The square and the circle aligned with repositioned horizontal guide. (See Figure 2-26.)

Centering objects

You can also use the horizontal and vertical alignment guides to align the centers of graphical images.

Reposition the alignment guides in the center of the screen by toggling them on or off. You can do this in two ways:

- ◆ Alternately choose Hide Guides and Show Guides from the Draw menu.
- ◆ Use the appropriate keyboard shortcut: Command-G (in Macintosh PowerPoint) or Ctrl-G (in Windows PowerPoint).

As you raise or lower each graphical image above or below the horizontal guide, notice that it tends to stick when the image is centered over the horizontal guide.

Aligning objects by using the vertical guide

You can use the vertical guides to align either the left or the right edge of a graphic or to horizontally center the graphic.

Measuring

You can also use the alignment guides as extremely accurate measuring tools. Select the horizontal alignment guide and drag it up. Notice the arrow and the number that appear. (See Figure 2-28.) These indicate the direction and distance you have moved the guide from the center of the slide. Select the vertical alignment guide by clicking on it and dragging it to the left. Again, an arrow and a number appear that indicate the direction and distance you have moved the guide from the center of the slide.

By noting the distances from the center of your slides and overheads, you can maintain presentation consistency. For example, you can ensure that all borders, titles, and text blocks are the same distance from the center of the screen.

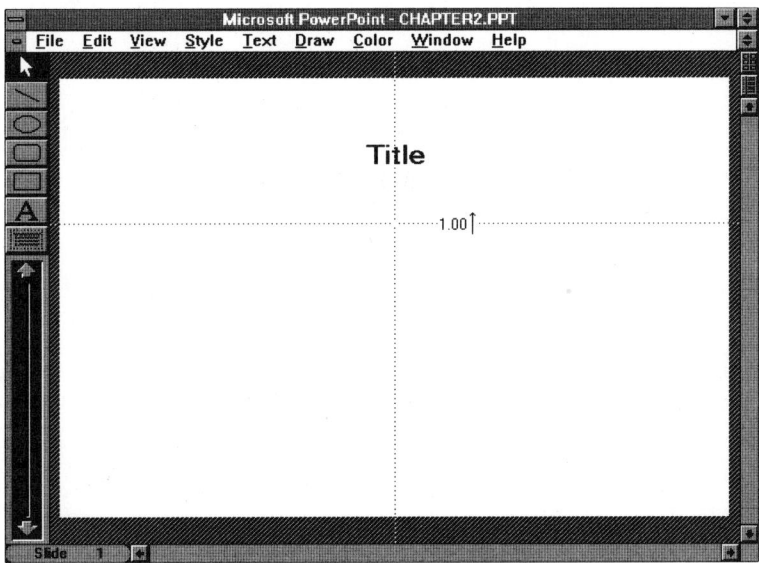

Figure 2-28. *Horizontal and vertical guides used to measure distances from the center of a slide. The arrow and the number show how far the horizontal guide has been moved upward.*

TARGETING OUTPUT DEVICES

If you're approaching PowerPoint from a word processing or desktop publishing perspective, you might be surprised at how important it is to target (or select) the output device you'll be using to produce your presentation visuals—*before* you begin work.

The output device you choose is important in several ways. It influences the dimensions of your visuals. (The various makes and models of printers, film recorders, projection pads, and monitors offer different image areas.) In addition, the output device also often limits typeface alternatives and the types of graphics file formats you can incorporate into your presentation.

Your options include

- Black-and-white laser printers (such as the Apple LaserWriter IINT or the Hewlett-Packard LaserJet)
- Color ink-jet printers (such as the Hewlett-Packard PaintJet or PaintJet XL or color thermal printers such as those made by NEC, QMS, and Tektronix)
- Film recorders (such as the Presentation Technologies MR-1)
- Genigraphics service bureaus, which are located throughout the United States
- Computer-based presentations that use projection pads or direct-view monitors

The table in Figure 2-29 summarizes the advantages and disadvantages of the available options.

You might frequently use more than one output device to prepare a presentation. For example, you might print proofs of your slides and overheads as well as speaker's Notes and audience Handouts on an office laser printer but send your color slides or overhead transparencies to Genigraphics for production of color slides or overhead transparencies.

The basis of your decision, of course, is the Presentation Planning Worksheet described in Chapter 1.

Format	Pros	Cons
On-Screen Presentations	Special effects such as builds, charts, and graphs can be updated during presentation. Good color quality and saturation. Easy to move throughout presentation, going directly to desired visual.	Limited to small groups. Inconvenient to move computer and screen from place to place. Advisable to have backup unit available. Type enhancement software such as Adobe Type Manager or Bitstream Facelift recommended.
Projector Pads	Permits interactive presentations to larger groups. Units are small and easily transported (but require presence of overhead projector and computer).	Many units limited to black-and-white or gray scales. Color models differ in image quality and can be costly. Requires computer as source. Backup units advisable. Adobe Type Manager or Bitstream Facelift can improve type quality.
Black-and-White Ink-Jet and Laser Printers	Practical: You probably already own one. PostScript printers reproduce full range of Adobe typefaces, scanned images, and drawings created with PostScript illustration programs.	Limited creative options. Chart and graph segments represented by gray shades or angled lines.
Color Ink-Jet Printers	Low cost. Ideal for last-minute color overhead transparencies. Some units capable of excellent image quality, saturated colors, sharp images, and smooth shadings.	Color models differ in image quality. Low-cost models often exhibit noticeable dot pattern and are best at reproducing primary colors. Secondary colors reproduced by dithering—placing dots of alternating color next to each other. Limited selection of typefaces, which can be overcome by Adobe Type Manager or Bitstream Facelift. Units differ in ability to reproduce PostScript images.

Figure 2-29. *A few of the advantages and disadvantages of the output devices available for imaging presentation visuals.*   *(continued)*

Figure 2-29. continued

Format	Pros	Cons
Color Thermal Printers	Improved image quality. Ideal for color proofing. Reproduces full range of Adobe typefaces, scanned images, and drawings created with PostScript illustration programs.	Handouts sometimes can't be copied due to heat buildup. Units differ in capability to create overhead transparencies. Same typeface limitations as for color ink-jet printers.
Film Recorders	Excellent color saturation and smooth shadings. Ideal for high-volume production environments.	High initial investment. Typically ties up computer during slide preparation, which can take significant amounts of time. Film must be developed and mounted in slide holders, which extends turnaround time. Units typically cannot reproduce scanned images or PostScript images.
Genigraphics	Excellent image quality, sharp images, and smooth shadings for color slides and overheads. Overnight and two-day service available. Files can be sent via modem to imaging centers throughout the country.	Expensive. Unable to reproduce scanned images and drawings created with PostScript illustration programs.

Using the Apple Chooser

If you're working with Macintosh PowerPoint, click on the Apple icon and choose the Chooser command. Click on the icon representing the printer that you want to use to output your visuals, and select its name from the list to the right, if necessary. If you're going to send your files to Genigraphics for high-resolution imaging, click on the Genigraphics icon.

Next, choose Page Setup from the File menu to fine-tune your selection. In addition to the Apple page-setup dialog box, you'll see a PowerPoint Slide Setup dialog box. (See Figure 2-30.) In Windows PowerPoint, Slide Setup is a separate command on the File menu. You'll usually choose Presentation Format (a Genigraphics Driver setup), but you can also create custom sizes.

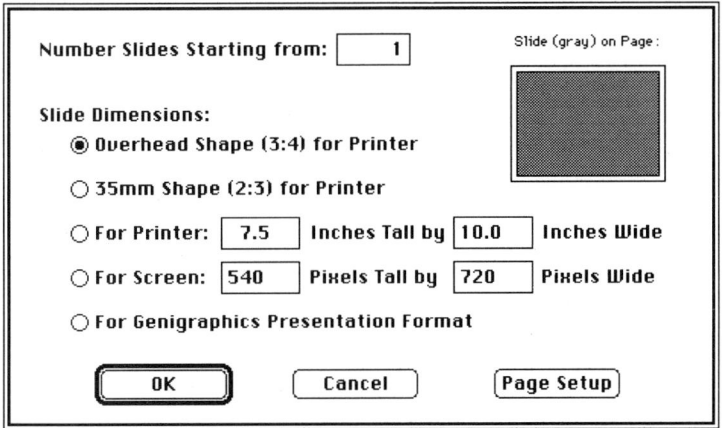

Figure 2-30. This is the Slide Setup dialog box for Macintosh PowerPoint. It appears when you choose the Page Setup command.

Later you'll need to reopen the Chooser if you want to use your LaserWriter to print proofs of your slides or print Notes or Handouts.

Targeting Printers When Using Windows PowerPoint

If you're working with Windows PowerPoint, targeting printers is a two-step procedure. First, target the output device that you'll use to produce your visuals. Then target the printer that you'll use to print proofs as well as Notes and Handouts. (See Figure 2-31.) Notice that you can specify the specific fonts, font cartridges, or downloadable fonts available with your printer.

Figure 2-31.
Printer Setup dialog box in Windows PowerPoint.

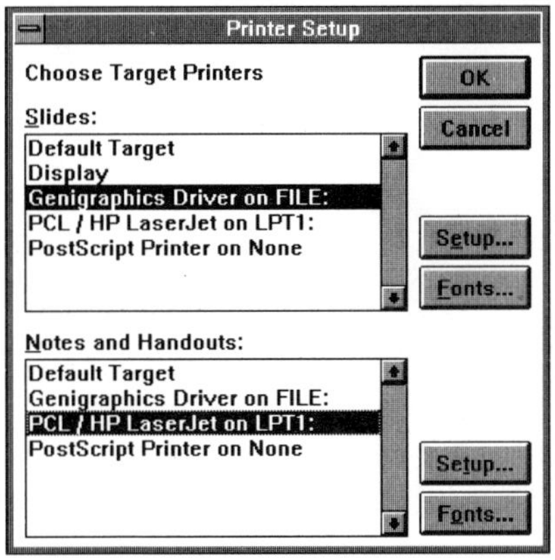

Because Windows PowerPoint allows you to target different output devices for visuals, drafts, Notes, and Handouts in advance, you don't need to open the Chooser and run Page Setup each time you print a different portion of your presentation.

II

BASIC SKILLS

Designing Your Presentation with the Storyboard Feature

A strong initial design provides the foundation for an effective presentation. Design refers to the planning of both the content and the appearance of your presentation visuals. In this chapter, you'll see how PowerPoint's Storyboard feature helps you immediately begin to generate ideas, organize their sequence, and develop a unique look for your visuals. In the next chapter, we use PowerPoint's Slide Master and Color Scheme to translate these designs into a consistent format that will unify all of your presentation visuals.

Three steps are involved in designing your PowerPoint presentation.

1. *Prepare PowerPoint Storyboards.* The Storyboard form (or page) helps you quickly develop a first, or working, draft of your presentation. The Storyboard form is a page that contains three empty rectangles (which are to contain visuals) as well as space to jot down ideas (on horizontal lines) as they occur to you. The Storyboard form encourages you to generate ideas and quickly write them down using paper and pencil.

2. *Determine presentation content and sequence.* Start by jotting down the ideas you want to include in each visual, and then refine your work by separating main ideas from supporting ideas. Determine

what you'll show and what you'll tell. Organize your presentation so that it has a distinct beginning, middle, and end. Develop a way to pace your presentation and to keep your audience informed of your progress.

3. *Develop a "look" for your presentation visuals.* Choose the size and placement of the title, choose an appropriate border, and locate graphic and text elements—such as your firm's logo or the presentation's title—that will appear on every visual.

In this chapter and in those that follow, we'll build on the planning begun in the previous chapter to create a sample PowerPoint presentation. The example we'll use will be based on the "Promoting Specialist" concept. As we prepare our presentation, we'll be able to take a more detailed look at Slide Master, Color Scheme, and typographic and drawing tools. We'll also see how easy it is to enhance your presentation with charts and tables.

PREPARE POWERPOINT STORYBOARDS

The Storyboard feature is similar to the storyboards that are used, for example, by advertising agencies when planning a television advertisement.

Storyboards help make your presentation as tangible as possible at as early a stage as possible. By encouraging you to work on your presentation using a pencil and paper, the Storyboard form encourages the rapid development of ideas. Most people find that they generate ideas more quickly when they work with paper and pencil than when they sit in front of a blank computer screen. In addition, by concentrating on content as early as possible, you gain additional time for formatting, refining, reorganizing, and rehearsing your presentation later on—and these steps are the ones that transform adequate presentations into excellent presentations.

Printing Storyboards

To print PowerPoint Storyboards, do the following.

1. Start PowerPoint (if it isn't already started).

2. Locate the Storyboard Forms folder (in Macintosh PowerPoint) or the Template\Strybrds subdirectory (in Windows PowerPoint).

3. Choose either 35mm Slide format or Overhead Transparency format depending on the type of presentation you're planning.

4. If you're using Macintosh PowerPoint, use the Chooser to target the Apple LaserWriter (or other printer). If you're using Windows PowerPoint, double-check that you've targeted the appropriate output device for drafts, Notes, and Handouts.

5. Choose Print from the File menu. (See Figure 3-1.)

6. Deselect Slides by clicking on the box next to Slides (in Macintosh PowerPoint) or by clicking another button (in Windows PowerPoint).

7. Click the box or button next to *Handouts [3 per page]*.

8. Enter the number of copies you want to print (see below).

9. Click the OK button or press the Enter key.

If you're just getting started with PowerPoint, you might want to print storyboards for both 35mm slides and overhead transparencies (also called overhead slides). Notice that overheads are slightly narrower and shorter than slides.

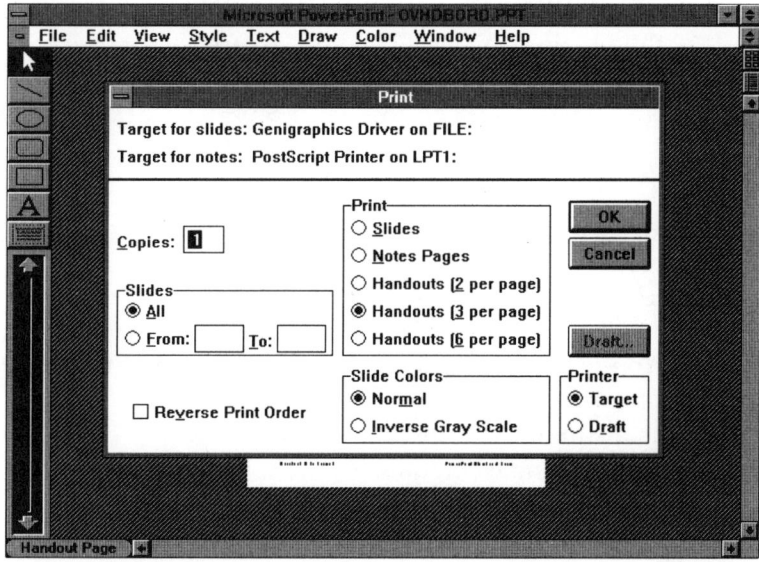

Figure 3-1. *Printing the Storyboard form by choosing the Print command from the File menu.*

Each Storyboard "visual" (that is, the empty rectangle) is accompanied by a series of horizontal lines. (See Figure 3-2.) The rectangle provides space to make rough drawings of the contents of each visual. The horizontal lines (to the right of the rectangle) provide space to write down—yes, using pencil or pen!—additional ideas or to remind yourself of points to mention during the presentation.

Work as quickly as you can comfortably. Avoid the temptation to make ultraneat Storyboards. Remember that you're the only person who will see them! You'll have time enough later to choose precisely the right words and introduce ideas in a logical order. All you want to do at this point is to get your creative juices flowing—to begin thinking about the information you want to include in your presentation and the order in which it will be introduced.

Notice that the top of each Storyboard form contains a place for you to record the presentation's title, date, and page number. This information will help you project-manage your presentation. (The page numbers are useful if you accidentally drop your Storyboards.)

Printing the correct number of Storyboard forms

As a rough rule of thumb, prepare one slide or transparency for every 2 minutes of presentation. Thus, if you're planning a 30-minute presentation, print out five pages of Storyboards. (Recall that each Storyboard page contains three slides or overheads.)

DETERMINE PRESENTATION CONTENT AND SEQUENCE

Early on you'll need to determine what information you're going to include in your presentation. You might decide to begin your presentation with a title slide, followed by a preview slide that presents the information that will follow, and to end with a summary of the information already presented. This follows the traditional ordering technique:

1. Tell the audience what you're going to tell them.
2. Then tell them.
3. Finally, conclude with a summary of what you've told them.

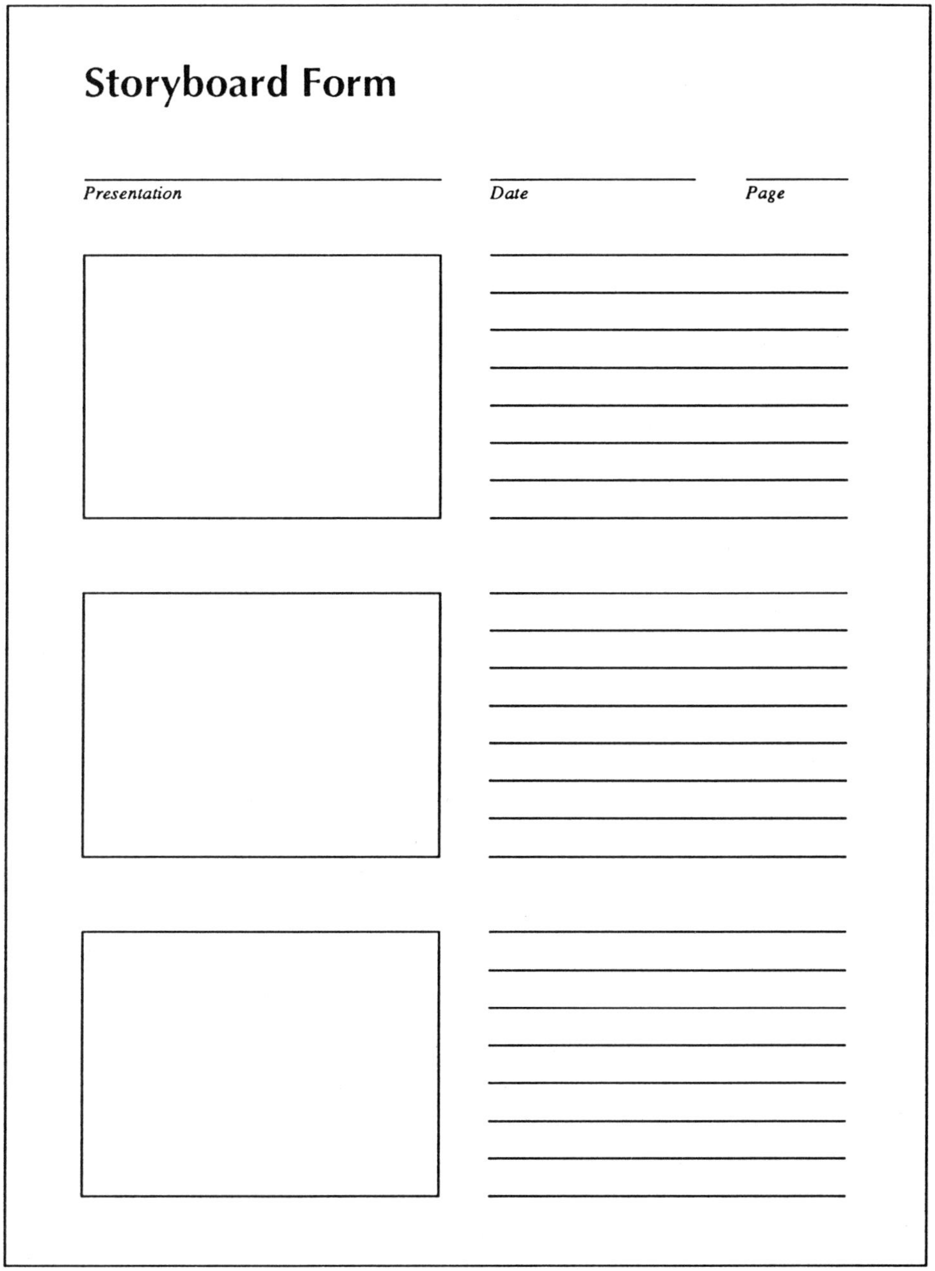
Storyboard Form

Presentation *Date* *Page*

Figure 3-2. *Using the Storyboard feature to plan the content and the appearance of your presentation.*

Possible Organizing Concepts

You might choose to organize your presentation along the following lines.

Beginning

- *Introduction.* Begin by stating the problem—in this example, that most businessmen are either "Promoters" or "Specialists."

- *Implications.* Describe the consequences of the above problem. (In this case, you can describe the advantages and disadvantages of "Promoters" and "Specialists.")

- *Offer alternatives.* Discuss possible ways of attacking the problem. (In this case, you might suggest ways of attempting to accommodate both positions—or to avoid either position.)

- *Take a stand.* Present your preferred approach—the one you are advocating—and describe its advantages. (The "Promoting Specialist" position adopts the strengths and avoids the weaknesses of "Pure Promoters" and "Pure Specialists.")

Middle

- *Describe the first step necessary to implement your program.* Include a few details to support your step. (The first step might be, for example, to analyze your own inclinations.)

- *Describe subsequent steps,* with supporting arguments or details. (Show how the mistakes of others can be avoided.)

- *Analyze* the costs involved.

- *Compare* costs and benefits of the suggested alternative with those of the rejected alternatives.

- *Summarize* the desired conclusion you're advocating.

End

- *Conclusion.* Restate your premise. (Success comes to those who adopt the strengths and avoid the weaknesses of the "Pure Promoters" and "Pure Specialists.")

Strive for Simplicity

As you work with the Storyboard feature, limit each slide or overhead to a *single idea*. These ideas will become the titles of each visual. Later you can go back and add three or four supporting points to each title.

The samples in Figure 3-3 on the following page show handwritten drafts of filled-in Storyboard forms for the "Promoting Specialist" presentation. Notice how ideas quickly begin to flow after you overcome your initial inertia and begin working. Soon, instead of worrying that you don't have enough material for your presentation, you'll be concerned that you have *too much* information to choose from!

Sources of Ideas

If you find yourself in need of inspiration, try looking for that spark in categories such as the following.

Quotations and endorsements

Can you come up with a statement by a famous individual, or someone known to your audience, that will support your cause? Can you use this statement as an attention getter?

Examples

What evidence do you have to support your ideas? Where have your ideas been successfully put to work? How well did they succeed? Examples are especially powerful when presented in anecdotal form.

Facts and figures

How can you quantify the success of your ideas? Can you point to specific sales, profit increases, reduced arrests, or improved voter turnout? The advantage of facts and figures is that numbers can be converted into very convincing charts and graphs.

Comparisons

Can you provide convincing before-and-after or either-or comparisons that will support your presentation's premise? Comparison visuals make it easy for your audience to grasp the benefits of the position you are arguing.

Don't be concerned about the superficiality of your first efforts. The idea is to begin working, to have a starting point that you can build on. Chances are that your storyboards will quickly gain in sophistication as you work on them. Ideas will build on ideas.

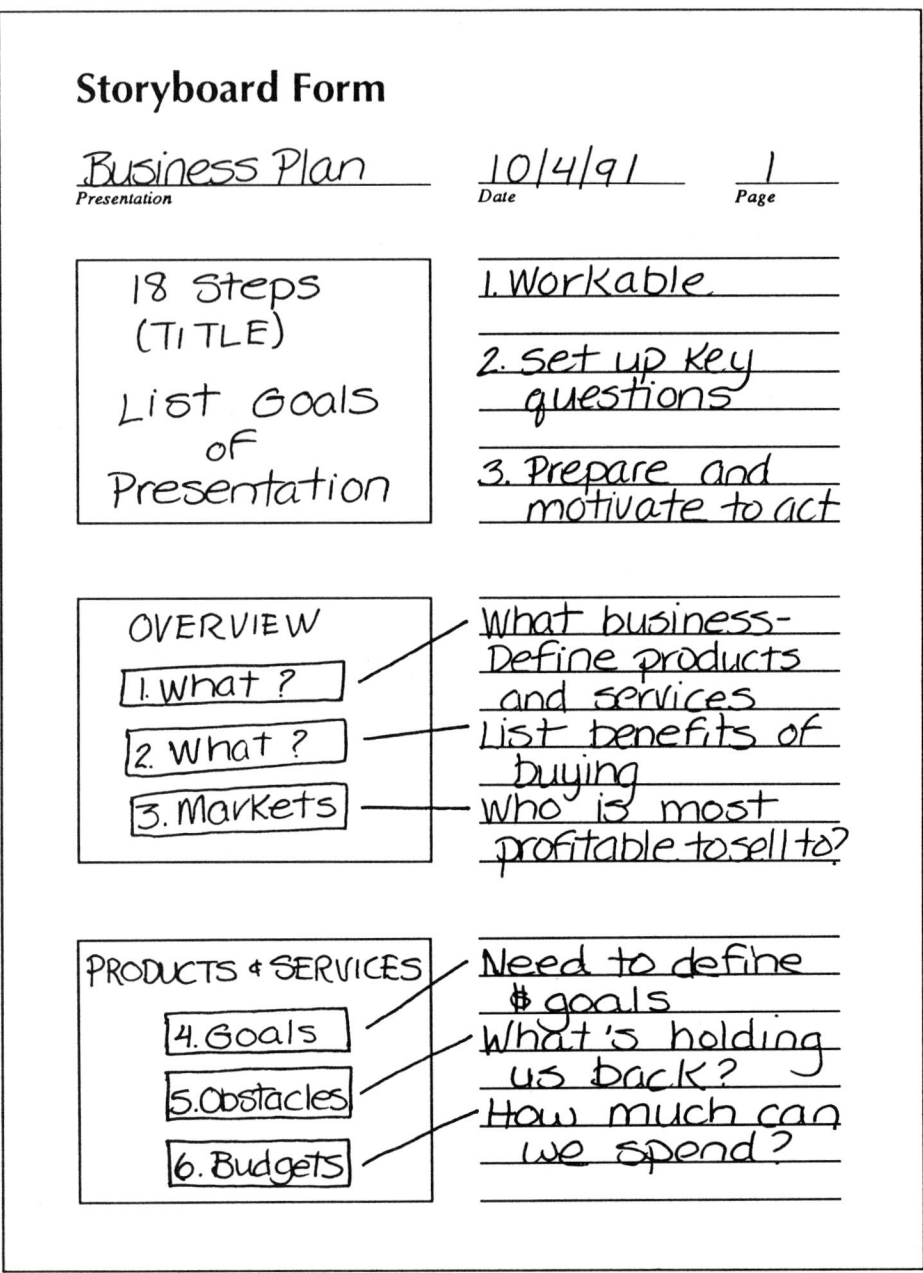

Figure 3-3. Sample storyboards for a "Promoting Specialist" presentation.

Avoid Presentation Overkill

One of the most important decisions you have to make is *deciding between what you'll show and what you'll tell*. As you come up with an idea, you need to decide whether to communicate it visually or verbally.

Avoid the temptation to include too much information in your visuals. Think of your visuals as road maps or signposts—guiding the way but not taking you the entire distance.

Avoid creating visuals so crowded with information that they replace the presenter. Including too much information in your visuals has several disadvantages.

Smaller type size

As you increase the number of words in your visuals, you're forced to use a smaller type size, making it more difficult for people in the back of the room to decipher your visuals.

Audience overload

Most people are unable to listen and read simultaneously. When a visual containing a lot of information first appears on the screen, many in your audience will tune you out while they read the visuals. The more your audience has to read, the less your audience can listen.

Loss of personal contact

The audience came because they want to hear you speak. They want to hear your interpretation of the information presented in the visuals. They'll judge your message partly by noting the expression on your face and the inflections in your voice. If your visuals contain too much information, you might end up repeating your visuals word for word—an invitation to audience boredom and a surefire way to dampen your enthusiasm—and theirs.

When you limit your visuals to a few words, however, you're forced to become more involved in your presentation as you elaborate on the ideas presented. Instead of reading aloud the same text that your audience can see and read, you can interpret and explain. This encourages you to be more conversational, enthusiastic, and relaxed.

Categories of Visuals

As you prepare your storyboards, you also need to determine which format communicates the information best. Your options include

- Lists
- Quotations
- Charts
- Illustrations or scanned images
- Tables

Self-Editing

As you work with the Storyboard feature, search for ways to replace long words with short words. As you sketch in the content of your Storyboard thumbnails, eliminate unnecessary verbs and adjectives. *Strive to reduce the number of words in your visuals to the minimum necessary to provide a guide for your verbal discussion.*

As you review your storyboards, be alert for visuals that develop more than one point. Look for places where information contained on a visual can be divided among two or more visuals. For example, the "before" overhead shown in Figure 3-4 contained three ideas, each with its own supporting information. The overhead looked "busy"—simply too much to read. When the information contained in the "before" visual was divided among three separate visuals, several things occurred.

First, legibility improved because a larger type size could be used and the layout could be redesigned. (See Figure 3-5.) Second, the audience's attention became focused on one idea at a time. This made it easier for the audience to relate the supporting information to the idea being presented.

Instead of three ideas and eight supporting pieces of evidence squeezed into a single visual, each visual now contains a single idea with its supporting information.

Chapter 3: Designing Your Presentation with the Storyboard Feature

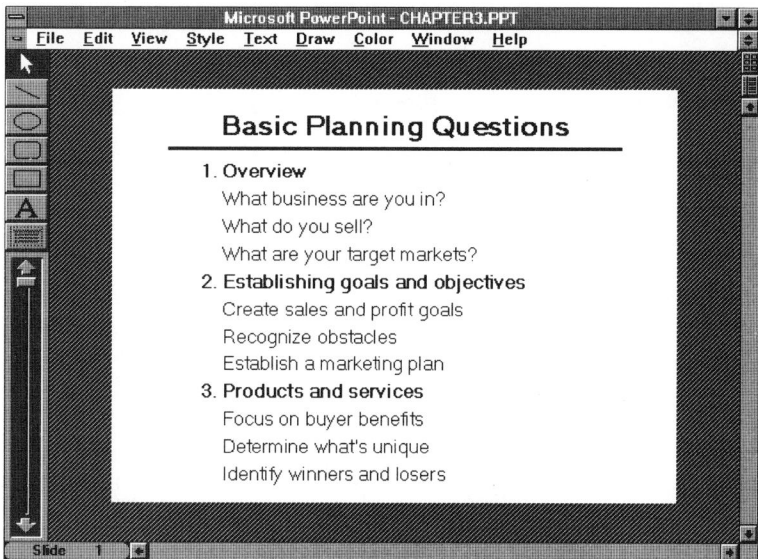

Figure 3-4. *The original ("before") overhead, containing three separate ideas, forcing the use of a small type size. (See Figure 3-5.)*

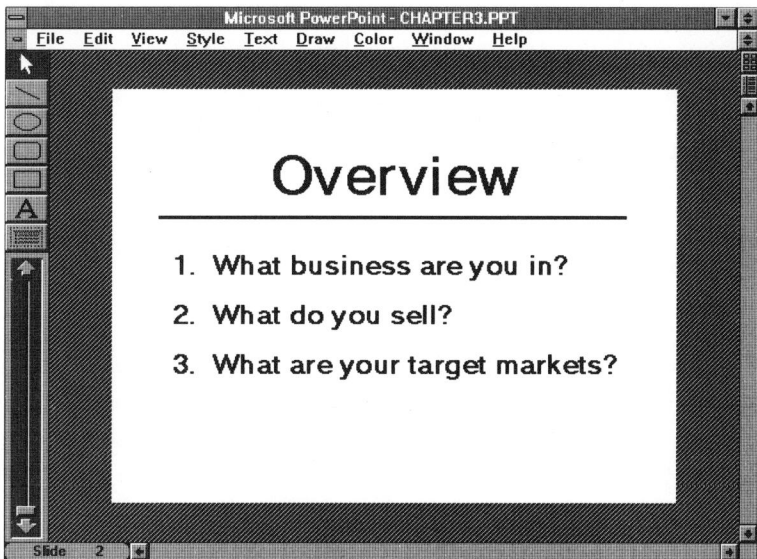

Figure 3-5. *The revised ("after") overhead, showing the increased impact achieved by focusing on fewer points set in a larger type size. (See Figure 3-4.)*

Working with Imported Outlines

Although the Storyboard feature makes it easy to begin working on presentation content, you might be more comfortable working with word processed outlines.

Several dedicated outlining programs are available. In addition, PowerPoint permits you to import outlines prepared with word processing programs such as Microsoft Word or Word for Windows. Using an existing program obviates the need to purchase and learn an additional software program. Microsoft Word and Word for Windows make it easy to work in outline format—entering ideas, changing the level of ideas, and reorganizing the order in which the ideas are presented.

After the outlines have been prepared and saved, you can import them into your PowerPoint presentation by choosing the Paste From command from the File menu, as described in Chapter 10. When you do this, the first level of each topic becomes the title of each visual. Supporting ideas appear as indented text.

Refining Your Presentation

As you work, new ideas are likely to turn up, and older ideas might get discarded. Although your final presentation is likely to differ significantly from your initial storyboards, remember that the initial storyboards are vital to getting started in the right direction as quickly as possible. Later, working with PowerPoint, you'll have ample time to refine your ideas using the Title Sorter and Slide Sorter views.

You're likely to have additional ideas as the storyboards help shape your presentation into an increasingly cohesive form.

DEVELOP A "LOOK" FOR YOUR PRESENTATION VISUALS

The Storyboard feature also offers you an opportunity to begin developing a unique look for your presentation. Working with a pencil and paper on the Storyboard form encourages you to try out various layouts for your visuals.

Design Considerations

Effective presentation visuals are based on the following four overriding concepts.

Simplicity

Your presentation visuals gain impact to the extent that they're as simple as possible. Edit ruthlessly; eliminate unnecessary words and graphic accents. Your visuals exist to reinforce your message, not to overwhelm it.

Contrast

The various text and graphic elements in your visuals gain impact to the extent they contrast with each other. Important information, for example, should be significantly larger than subordinate, or supporting, information. Presentation titles should visually contrast with the text that they introduce.

Contrast adds visual interest to your presentation and improves your audience's retention of your ideas by helping them quickly locate important information. The members of your audience should be able to immediately locate the title of each visual and smoothly move on to supporting information. Lesser information (such as qualifiers or presentation titles) should be subordinate in size and attention-getting ability.

Consistency

Your presentation visuals should each be unique, yet share a common look. The most visible consistency tools include backgrounds, borders, colors, title placement, and typography. All your titles, for example, should be set in the same typeface, type size, and color.

Completeness

Each visual should tell a whole story. In addition to containing text and graphics that support the premise listed in the title, your presentation can be unified by adding repeating elements such as your firm's logo, the presentation date and title, and (when appropriate) the audience's "name."

Try Different Layout Alternatives

The starting point for designing your presentation visuals is to use—by sketching by hand—your newly printed Storyboards to try out different locations for repeating elements such as

- Borders
- The Title, or summary statement, that introduces each visual
- Repeating information (such as a logo or the title or the date of a presentation)

After you've arrived at a satisfactory arrangement using Storyboard Forms, you can translate your ideas to the computer, creating a Slide Master and choosing a Color Scheme as described in the next chapter.

Borders

Start by experimenting with different types of borders, changing their location, shape, and thickness. (See Figure 3-6.) Experiment with square boxes, rounded corner boxes, and horizontal bars at the top and bottom of each slide, and so forth.

Next, determine border size. Options include thin rules, thick rules, single rules, and double rules.

Remember that borders don't need to be equal on all four sides. Sometimes top and bottom borders are sufficient.

Borders exist to focus your audience's attention on the content of your visuals. Avoid locating borders so far from the text, however, that there is no logical connection between border and content. Be sure to leave enough "breathing room" between your borders and the edges of your slide or overhead.

Titles

Next, try out different locations for the title—the phrase or sentence that introduces and summarizes each slide or overhead. (See Figure 3-7 on page 74.) Experiment with different alignments. Should the titles be centered or set flush left? How large should the titles be relative to the rest of the visual?

You can also experiment with ways of enhancing slide titles—perhaps using a horizontal rule under them or placing them in shadowed boxes.

Repeating information

Now decide where your firm's logo looks best. Do you want it placed upper left, centered at the top or bottom of each visual, or placed at the lower right of each slide?

Symmetrical vs. asymmetrical layouts

One of your most important decisions is whether you want your presentation visuals to have a centered, symmetrical layout or an off-center, asymmetrical layout. You can center the title, or you can offset the title to the left and indent supporting materials to the right. (See Figure 3-8 on page 75.)

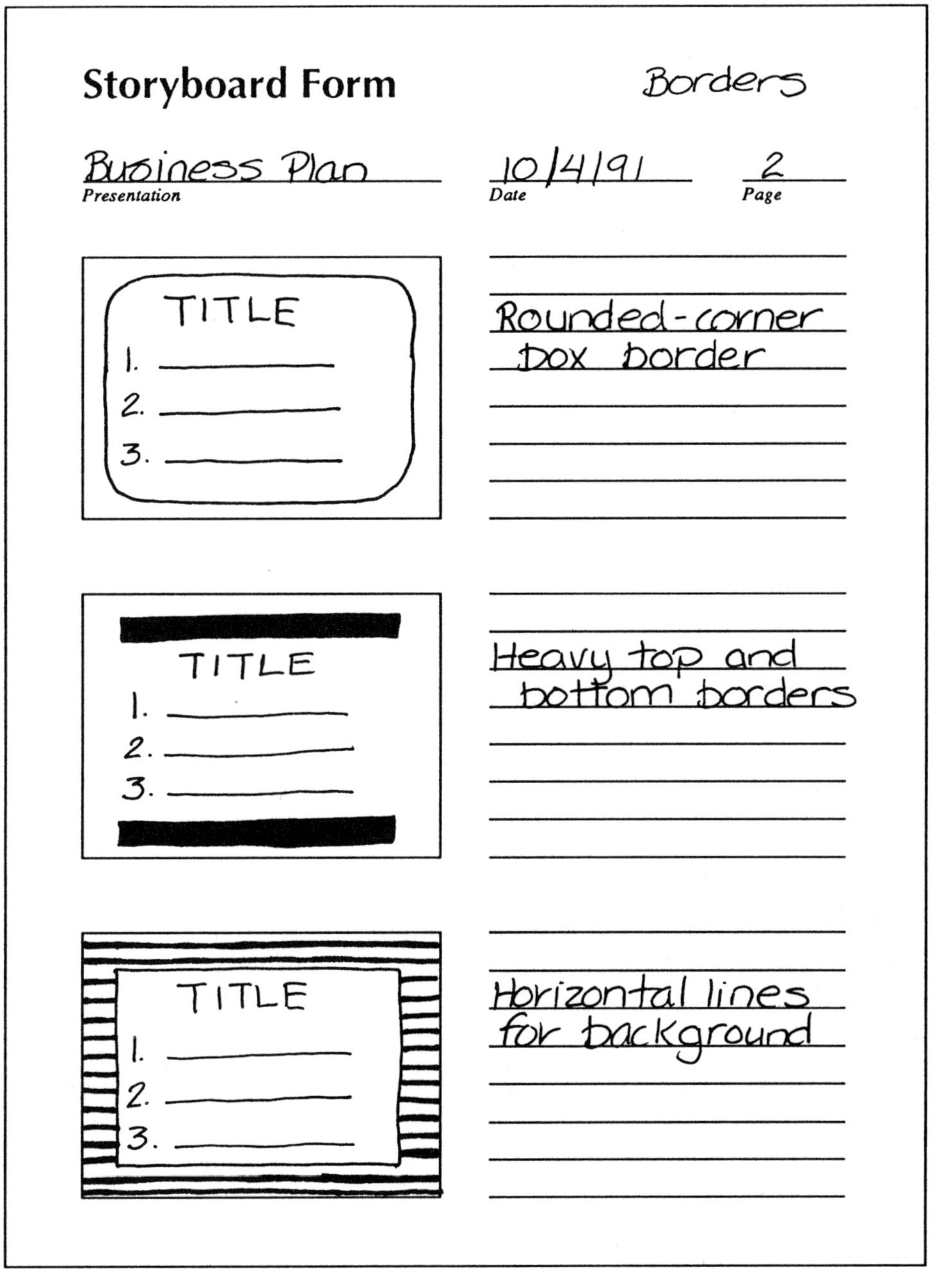

Figure 3-6. Using the Storyboard feature to try out different types of borders.

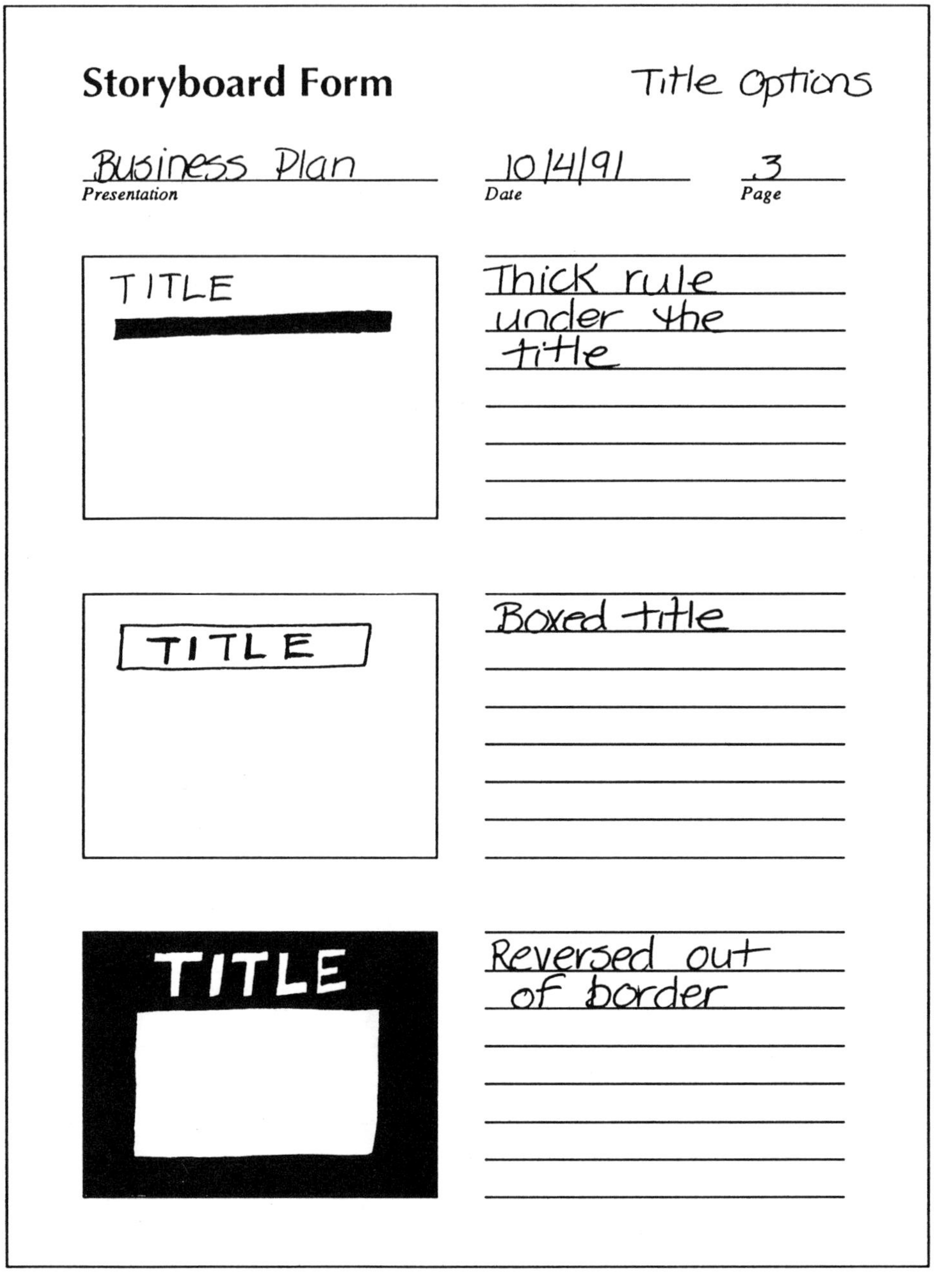

SECTION II: BASIC SKILLS

Figure 3-7. Using the Storyboard feature to try out different title placements, alignments, sizes, and backgrounds.

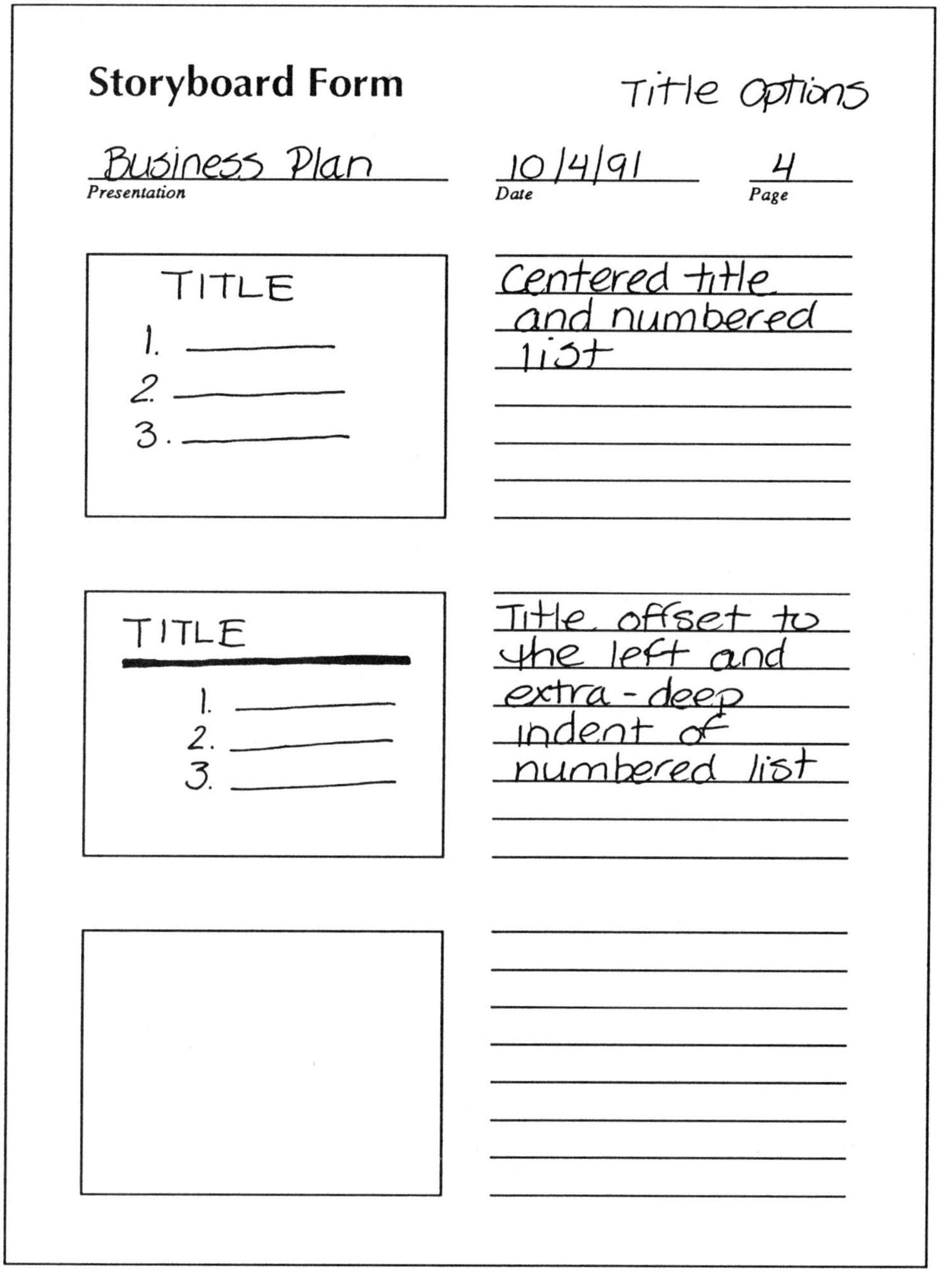

Chapter 3: Designing Your Presentation with the Storyboard Feature

Storyboard Form — Title Options

Business Plan — 10/4/91 — 4
Presentation — *Date* — *Page*

TITLE
1. ___
2. ___
3. ___

Centered title and numbered list

TITLE
1. ___
2. ___
3. ___

Title offset to the left and extra-deep indent of numbered list

Figure 3-8. *A centered ("traditional") layout and an off-center layout with the title offset to the left and text offset to the right.*

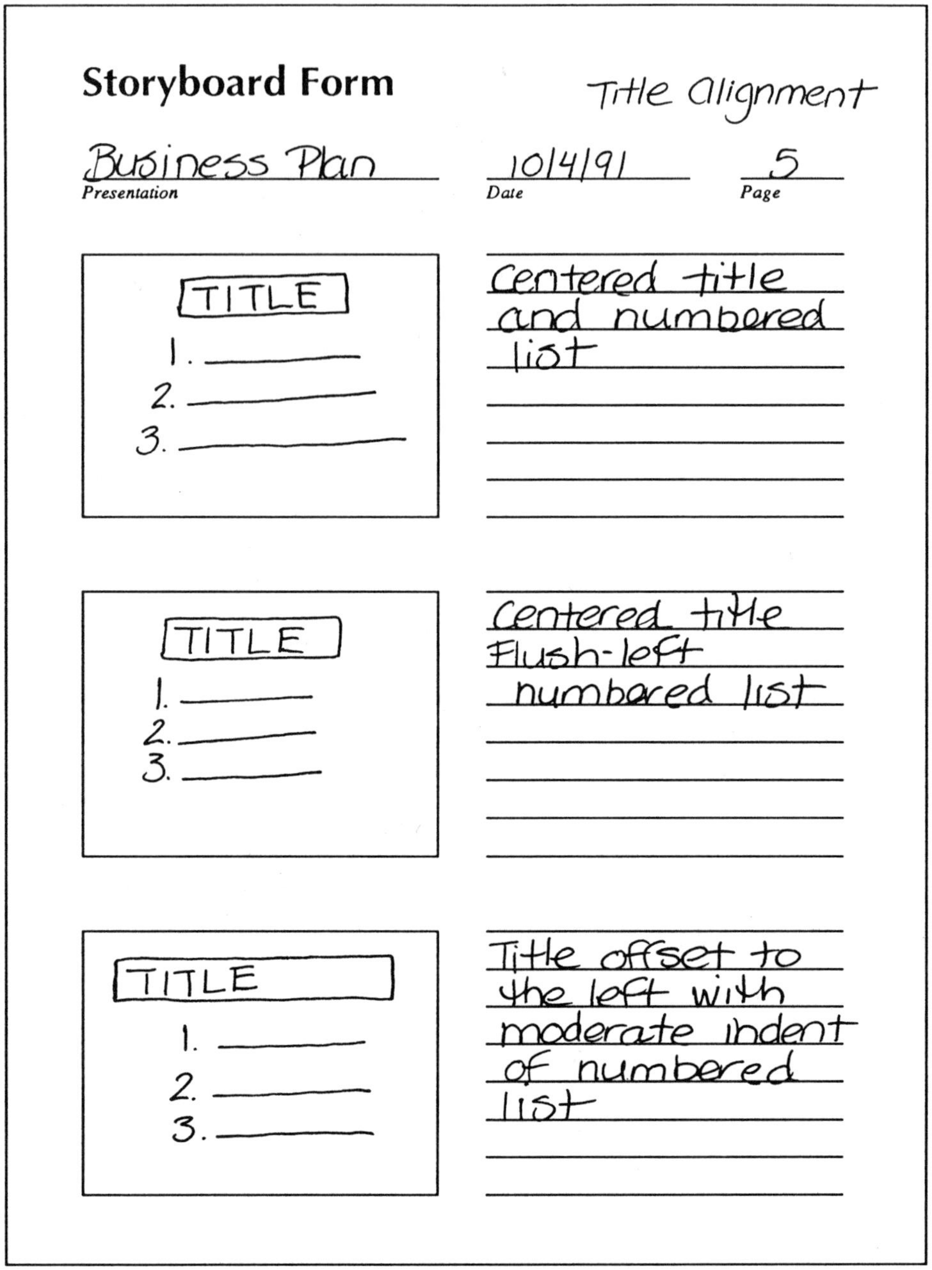

SECTION II: BASIC SKILLS

Storyboard Form — Title Alignment

Presentation: Business Plan
Date: 10/4/91
Page: 5

[TITLE]
1. ___
2. ___
3. ___

Centered title and numbered list

[TITLE]
1. ___
2. ___
3. ___

Centered title
Flush-left numbered list

[TITLE]
1. ___
2. ___
3. ___

Title offset to the left with moderate indent of numbered list

Figure 3-9. Using the Storyboard feature to try out different alignments.

Finally, experiment with both options—centered and flush-left text. (See Figure 3-9 on the facing page.) If your presentation includes a lot of text presented in outline (or list) format, you might use centered text set in a large type size for short quotations but use flush-left text in small type for lists.

You can also decide whether to use numbers or bullets in front of listed items.

EVALUATING YOUR PROGRESS

As you prepare your presentation Storyboards, ask yourself the following questions:

- ◆ Did I print the correct number of Storyboards for the time available?
- ◆ Have I limited the content of each visual to a single idea, reinforced by three or four supporting statements or examples?
- ◆ Have I indicated whether each item of supporting information is best displayed in quotations, lists, charts, or visuals?
- ◆ Are ideas introduced in a logical sequence?
- ◆ Have I replaced long words with short words and eliminated verbs and qualifiers wherever possible?
- ◆ Have I paced my presentation appropriately, creating a logical beginning, middle, and end?
- ◆ Do borders draw attention to my visuals without overwhelming their content?
- ◆ Are titles large enough to be easily located?

Creating a Slide Master and Choosing a Color Scheme

Two important steps are required to create a "look" for your presentation.

1. *Create a Slide Master.* PowerPoint's Slide Master feature is the basic building block for each of your presentation visuals. The Slide Master maintains continuity throughout all your visuals by ensuring consistent placement of borders, titles, and other elements repeated on each visual.

2. *Choose a Color Scheme.* Color is one of the most powerful tools available. Color permits you to orchestrate the emotional tone of your presentation as well as provide selective emphasis where you want it. PowerPoint's Color Scheme feature helps you choose precisely the right combination of background, foreground, and accent colors.

As you create the Slide Master described in this chapter, you'll gain a further understanding of PowerPoint's many drawing tools.

CREATE A SLIDE MASTER

The Slide Master feature provides a consistent background on which you construct individual slides and overhead transparencies. The Slide Master ensures the consistency of

- Borders and graphic accents
- Title placement and accents
- Repeating information (such as presentation identification, presenter's or client's name, presentation date, and company logo)

Slide Master View

Start PowerPoint (if it is not already started) by double-clicking on the PowerPoint Program icon.

When a screen appears containing only the word *Title*, choose Slide Master from the View menu. Notice that the words *Slide Master* appear at the lower left side of your screen.

Any text or graphics you add while in Slide Master view will be added to all your visuals.

Adding a border to the Slide Master

You can add a border to the Slide Master by using one of the drawing tools: the Line tool, the Rounded Rectangle tool, or the Rectangle tool. (You can use the Rounded Rectangle tool to draw rectangles and squares with rounded corners. You can use the Rectangle tool to draw rectangles and squares whose corners form a right angle.)

You can frame the top and bottom of your slides with horizontal rules. This technique can create an open, contemporary feeling. These rules can be as thin or thick as you want. You can place rules of equal thickness at the top and bottom of each slide, or you can weight either the top or the bottom of your slides with a heavier (thicker) rule.

You can also use either the Rounded Rectangle tool or the Rectangle tool to frame the entire slide with a box—that is, four connected lines of equal thickness.

Creating a border with the Line tool

To draw horizontal, vertical, or diagonal lines, click on the Line tool at the left side of the PowerPoint screen. Click on the screen where you want the line to begin and drag the pointer in the direction you want the line to extend. Release the mouse button when you've drawn the desired length of line.

Note: Hold down the Shift key while dragging if you want to create horizontal, vertical, or 45-degree diagonal lines.

Choosing a line thickness

You can select a line thickness at three times:

♦ Before you choose the Line tool

♦ After you draw the line, and while it's still selected—as indicated by the border and the dots, or handles, at each end

♦ Later, after you reselect the line by clicking on it

For example, while the line is still selected—as indicated by the border and buttons on each end—choose Line Style from the Draw menu. (See Figure 4-1.) A submenu box appears, showing available options.

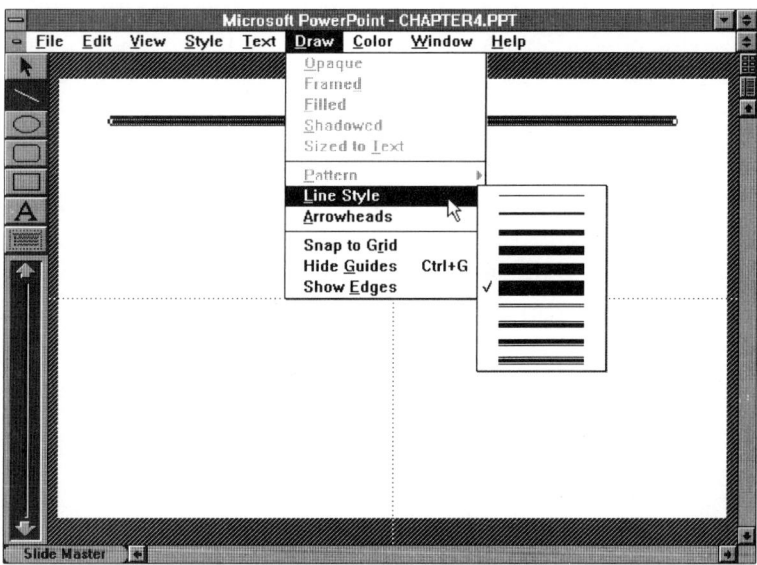

Figure 4-1. You can create borders from lines of several thicknesses by choosing Line Style from the Draw menu.

Creating a border with a box-drawing tool

To create a boxed border around your presentation, do the following.

- Choose Show Guides from the Draw menu (if the alignment guides are not already visible).
- Choose either the Rounded Rectangle tool or the Rectangle tool to create a boxed border.
- Choose a line thickness. (See Figure 4-1.)

After choosing one of the box-drawing tools (Rounded Rectangle or Rectangle), click on the screen at one corner of the box and drag the pointer diagonally toward the other corner.

If you want to center the border on the screen, click on the center of the screen where the horizontal and vertical guides intersect and hold down the Option key (in Macintosh PowerPoint) or the Ctrl key (in Windows PowerPoint) as you drag the pointer away from the center of the screen toward one of the corners.

As with the Line tool described above, you can adjust border thickness before you choose either of the box-drawing tools or after the border has been drawn but while the border is still selected. Alternatively, you can modify the thickness of previously created borders by clicking on those borders. Again, choose Line Style from the Draw menu to define the border thickness.

Placing and Emphasizing Titles

When you place the title, you can add a rule or box for emphasis. Consistent title placement and treatment create a more professional-looking presentation that makes it easier for an audience to follow the development of ideas.

Each slide or overhead should have a title. When you create your presentation, deciding on the title might help you focus the contents of each slide or overhead on a single thought. The use of titles also makes it possible to quickly reorganize a presentation using PowerPoint's Title Sorter.

Locating the title

To relocate the title in the Slide Master view, choose the Arrow tool and click on the word *Title* at the upper center of your screen. (Note: The Arrow tool is a selection tool.) When *Title* is selected (as evidenced by a fuzzy border), you can move *Title* to a different location by grabbing its fuzzy border and dragging it. If you're using Windows PowerPoint, you can also select and move the title using the right mouse button.

If you want to accentuate the title, you can choose Left alignment from the Text menu and use the Line tool to add a horizontal rule below each title. (See Figure 4-2.) In the next chapter, you'll learn how to format the title by returning to the Slide Master view and choosing a typeface, type size, type style, and color most appropriate to your presentation.

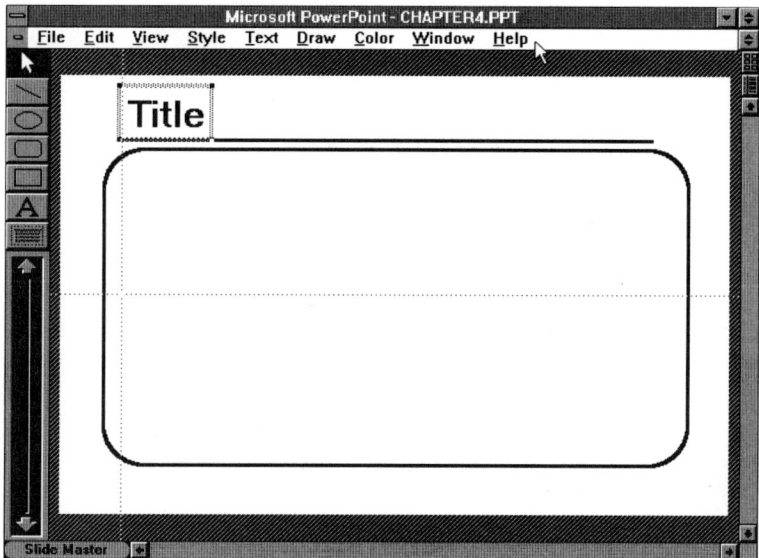

Figure 4-2. *You can create a distinct look by placing the slide title off center and adding a rule below it.*

Framing a title by adding a background

You can also add emphasis to titles by framing them. The frame will change in size to accommodate the number of words contained in the title.

To frame a title, choose Framed from the Draw menu while it is selected. (See Figure 4-3 on the following page.) You can pick out an appropriate line thickness from the options available by choosing Line Style from the Draw menu.

To add a box behind the title, choose Filled from the Draw menu while the title is selected. (See Figure 4-4 on the following page.) This box will automatically resize itself to accommodate the number of words in the title.

SECTION II: BASIC SKILLS

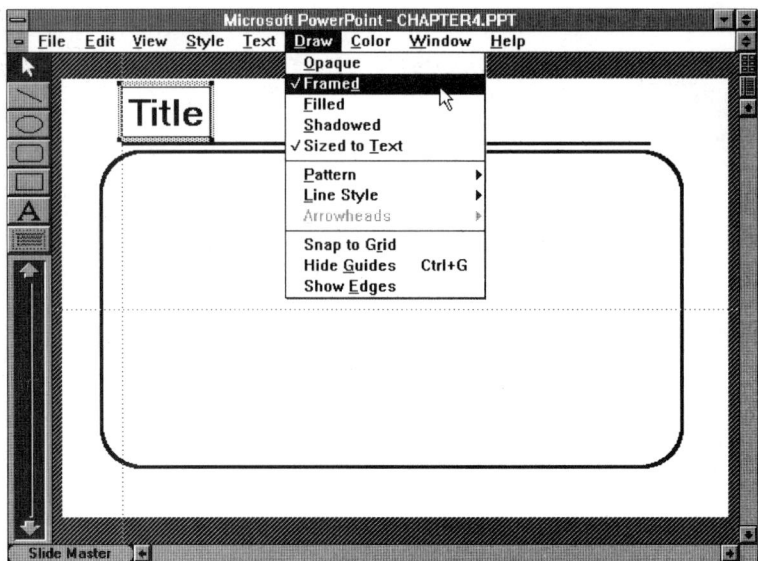

Figure 4-3. *You can add emphasis to slide titles by choosing Framed from the Draw menu.*

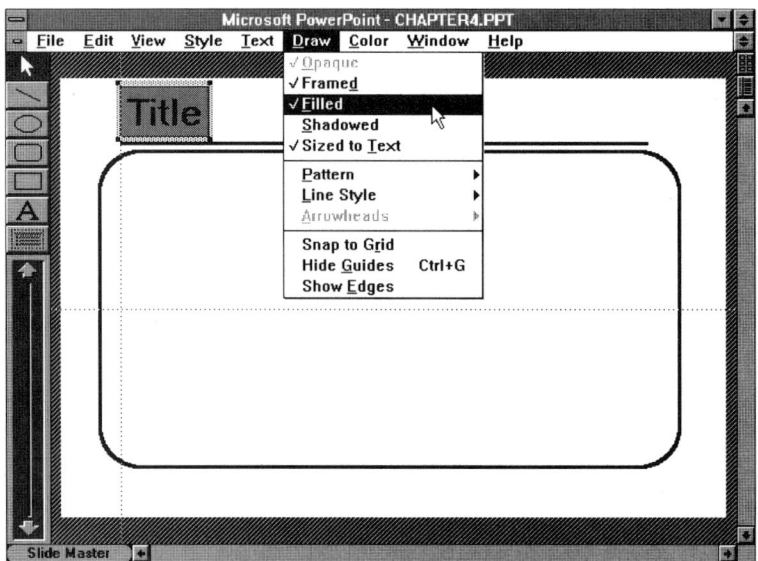

Figure 4-4. *By choosing Filled from the Draw menu, you can enhance titles with a box that expands or contracts to accommodate the number of words in each title.*

Adding Presentation Information

You can add text or visuals that you want to include on every slide or overhead transparency.

Often you'll want to include a company's or association's logo on the Slide Master. To add a logo to a Slide Master, choose Paste From from the File menu. Scroll through the folders (in Macintosh PowerPoint) or subdirectories (in Windows PowerPoint) on your computer screen until you find the file containing the logo. When it is highlighted, double-click on it, or click OK.

When the logo first appears on the slide, it's likely to be too large. You can resize an imported graphic file by clicking on one of the corner buttons and dragging the button while holding down the Shift key. This preserves the height-to-width ratio of the logo. (This process is described in greater detail in Chapter 6.)

When you import a logo, be sure that the logo has been saved in a file format compatible with the output device you'll be using to produce your presentation. (See Chapter 7 for more information about placing and resizing imported graphics.)

Fine-Tuning Your Slide Master

Attention to detail is extremely important at this stage. Precise positioning is vital to the design quality of all the slides and overheads created using the Slide Master.

- Use the vertical guide to align *Title* and the box containing the Presentation Associates logo with each other.
- Use the horizontal guide to bottom-align the Presentation Associates logo and the presentation date.
- Align the right edge of the date with the right edge of the horizontal rule. Accent *Title* by dragging the vertical guide into proper position.

Notice how the Presentation Associates logo in Figure 4-5 (on the following page) has been placed outside the lower left border of each slide. The Presentation Associates name has been spelled out and aligned flush left, balanced by the name of the seminar aligned flush right.

SECTION II: BASIC SKILLS

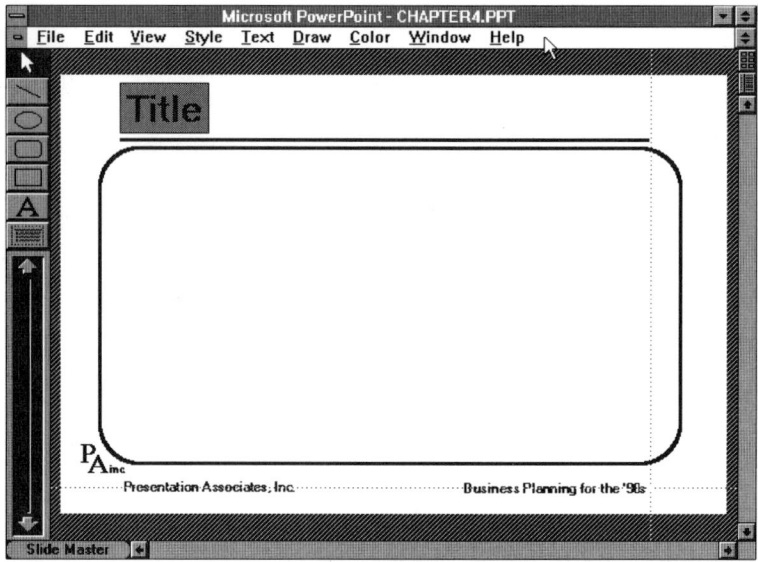

Figure 4-5. *Finished Slide Master with borders, titles, and presentation information.*

Numbering Slides and Overheads

You can easily number your slides and overheads. You'll appreciate this feature if you should accidentally drop your slides or overheads on the way to a presentation!

To number your slides and overheads, be sure the Slide Master is active, and then select the Labeler tool by clicking on the large A at the left side of the screen and enter two pound-sign symbols (##). You can include these symbols with text, as in *Slide* ##.

Slide and overhead numbers will be updated automatically whenever you add, delete, or reorganize visuals in Slide Sorter or Title Sorter view.

You can also add temporary date and time symbols to your Slide Masters. This is a convenience feature that helps you keep track of the various proof copies of your presentation that you print as you rework your presentation.

♦ The date symbol consists of two slashes (//).

♦ The time symbol consists of two colons (::).

You'll probably want to delete these symbols from the Slide Master before printing the final copy of your slides and overheads.

86

Changing Views and Hiding Grids

While creating a Slide Master, you'll probably want to switch frequently between an overall view of your slide and a magnified view of it. You can do this by alternately choosing Full Size and 66% from the View menu.

Occasionally, to accomplish precise positioning, you might find it necessary to select Hide Grid from the Draw menu. This allows you to place items *close to* (but not touching) each other. You can turn the Grid, and its magnetic attraction, back on by choosing Show Grid.

Returning to Slide View

After you've placed the various elements in position, choose Slide #1 from the View menu or use a keyboard shortcut: Command-D (in Macintosh PowerPoint) or Ctrl-D (in Windows PowerPoint).

At this stage, if you're creating black-and-white overhead transparencies, you can immediately begin working on your presentation. If you're creating 35mm color slides or color overhead transparencies, the next step is to choose a Color Scheme for your presentation.

Omitting a Slide Master

Occasionally you might run into a situation where you need a more flexible working surface—for example, you might want to work on a slide that has the same Slide Background as your other slides, but it might lack borders, accents, and other repeating elements.

When you run into this situation, choose Omit Master from the Edit menu. The title will be properly positioned and formatted and the Slide Background will be present, but all other repeating elements from the Slide Master will be eliminated.

CHOOSE A COLOR SCHEME

Color plays an important role in establishing the mood of your presentation by influencing your audience's emotional responses. In addition, color plays a major role in determining how legible your presentation is.

Different colors elicit different emotional responses. Grays and blues are often used to create a "cool," "corporate," or "impersonal" atmosphere, while reds and oranges generate excitement. Colors can reflect seasonal themes—the greens and blues of summer, the browns and oranges of autumn, or the reds and greens of Christmas.

The proper use of colors makes it easier for your audience to read and understand your message. White or yellow text against a black background, for example, is easier to read than gray text against a blue background. This is because increased contrast makes it easier for your audience's eyes to separate the text and its background.

Presentation Environments

The presentation environment should influence your choice of colors. Different color combinations work best for slides, overhead transparencies, and computer-based on-screen presentations.

- ◆ Light colors with dark text work best for color overhead transparencies that are viewed in normal room lighting.
- ◆ Dark backgrounds with light text work best for 35mm color slides that are viewed in darkened rooms.

You don't need to be an artist or a scientist to choose the right colors for your presentation. The Color Scheme feature, created in conjunction with Genigraphics, provides color combinations that have been chosen by experts because they work well together. Each Color Scheme is based on a unique combination of foreground, background, and accent colors.

Previewing Genigraphics Suggested Color Schemes

If you're working with a Macintosh II computer equipped with a color monitor, you can preview the Genigraphics Suggested Color Schemes by opening one of the sample Color Schemes. (See Figure 4-6.) If you're using an Apple Macintosh II equipped with a color graphics monitor, double-click on the Color Schemes folder and—depending on the type of presentation you're creating—choose one of the following:

- ◆ Genigraphics 35mm Scheme
- ◆ Genigraphics Overhead Scheme
- ◆ Genigraphics On-Screen Scheme

If you're using Windows PowerPoint, click on the Color Scheme subdirectory (colorsch) and load the appropriate file by clicking on its name.

Chapter 4: Creating a Slide Master and Choosing a Color Scheme

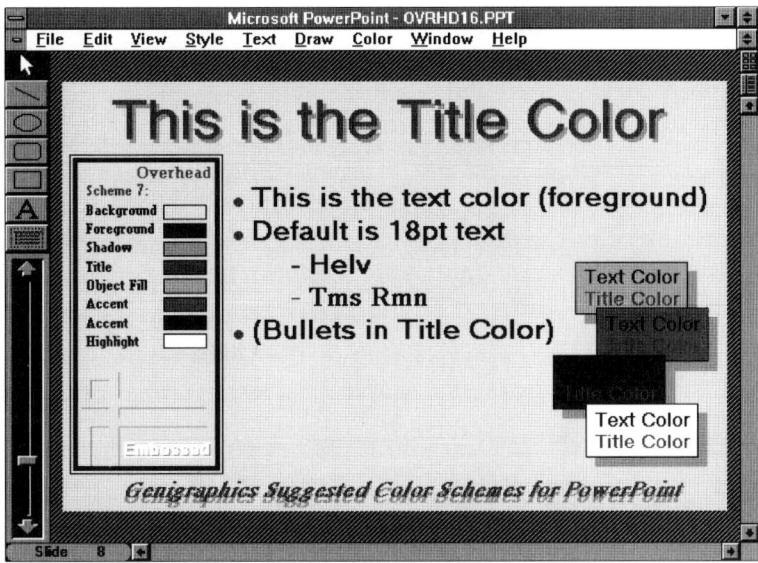

Figure 4-6. *The Genigraphics sample Color Schemes.*

By clicking on the Downward arrow at the lower left of the PowerPoint screen, you can move through the color samples provided for each type of presentation.

Over 40 combinations are included. The same Slide Master has been used for each sample so that you can see how the various background, foreground, and accent colors work together (without being distracted by differing slide content). As you preview the samples, notice how you react differently to each color scheme. You'll undoubtedly feel that some color combinations appear more "right" for your presentation than others.

Using an Existing Genigraphics Color Scheme

To use one of Genigraphics' sample 35mm slide, overhead transparency, or on-screen video Color Schemes for your presentation, do the following.

1. After you've selected the slide containing the Genigraphics Suggested Color Scheme you want to use in your presentation, choose the Color Scheme command on the Color menu.

2. With the Color Scheme dialog box still active, open the Window menu and select the title of the presentation you're working on—perhaps "Untitled" (if you haven't saved it yet).

3. When your presentation appears, open the Window menu and choose Color Scheme. The Color Scheme dialog box for the Genigraphics file (as shown in Figure 4-7) now appears.

4. Click on the Apply To All Slides option and then click on the Apply button. If you're using Macintosh PowerPoint, close the Color Scheme by clicking on the small box at the upper left. If you're using Windows PowerPoint, press Ctrl-F4. The Color Scheme used in the Genigraphics sample has now been applied to your presentation.

Finally, open the Window menu, and choose the Genigraphics Overhead Schemes file. When the Genigraphics file appears, close it without saving it.

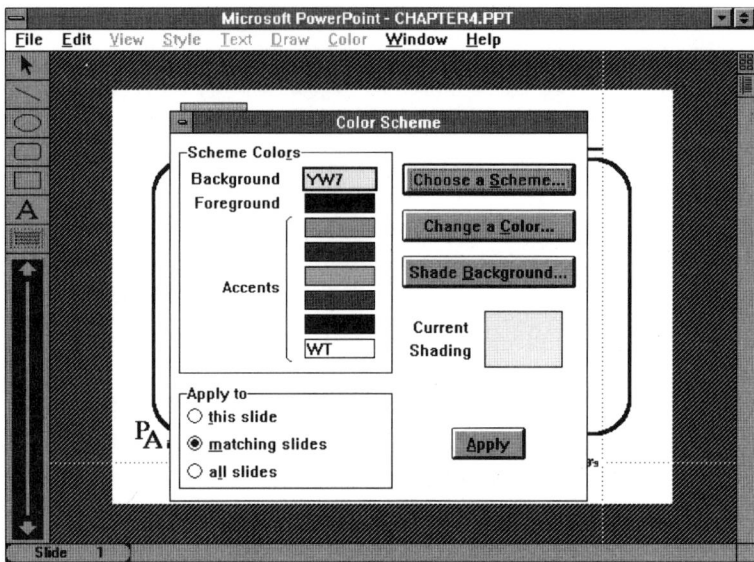

Figure 4-7. The Color Scheme dialog box lets you customize a new presentation or revise the Color Scheme of an existing presentation.

Creating Your Own Color Scheme

To create a color scheme, begin by choosing Color Scheme from the Color menu. This brings you to the Color Scheme dialog box. Now do the following.

◆ Click on Choose A Scheme. (The Choose A Scheme dialog box appears, as shown in Figure 4-8.)

Chapter 4: Creating a Slide Master and Choosing a Color Scheme

- ◆ Choose an appropriate Background color.
- ◆ Choose a compatible Foreground color.
- ◆ Choose Accents.

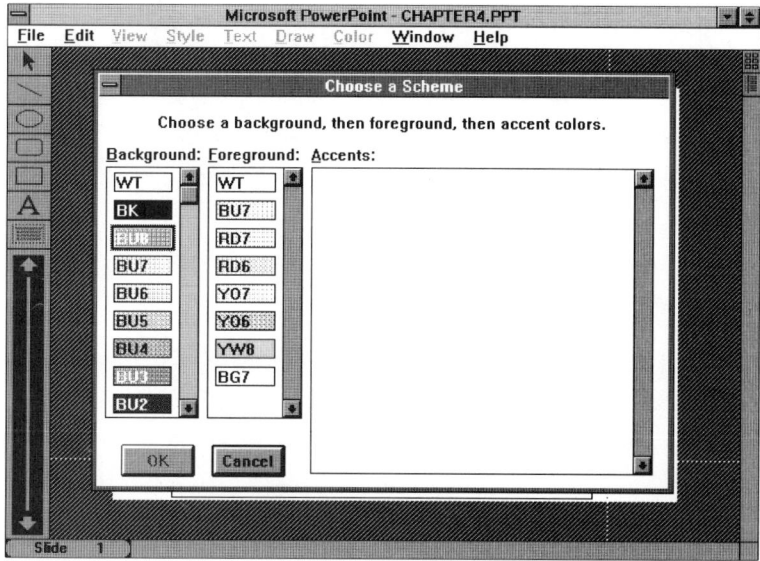

Figure 4-8. *You create a Color Scheme by choosing the colors you want—first for Background and then for Foreground.*

Choosing a background color

To preview your Background color choices, click on the up or down arrow in the Background box to move through the options. (See Figure 4-9 on the following page.) After you've become more comfortable with the Color Scheme feature, you can use the scroll box between the arrows to go directly to the area where preferred options are likely to be located.

As you preview your choices, consider the emotional responses you want to evoke from your audience. Do you want to project a cool and impersonal atmosphere, or do you want to appear warm and friendly? (Which "C" do you want to project: "Corporate" or "Creative"?)

When you come to a Background color that appeals to you, click on it. PowerPoint then prompts you to choose a foreground color.

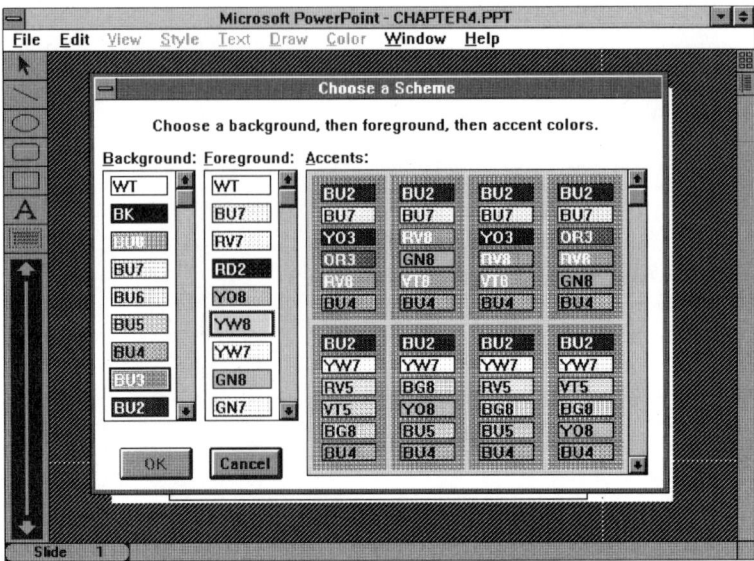

Figure 4-9. *The last step in choosing a Color Scheme is to choose a set of accent colors.*

Choosing a foreground color

The Foreground color is used for rules and text. The Foreground color options appear immediately after you choose a background. (See Figure 4-9.) Again, you can scroll through the various options PowerPoint offers by clicking on the up or down arrow or by using the scroll box.

In general, the greater the contrast between Background and Foreground colors, the easier it will be to read your slides. If Foreground and Background colors are similar to each other, the words will blend into the background. A light blue foreground against a dark blue background, for example, will rarely succeed. To help you avoid contrast problems, the Color Scheme feature limits your foreground choices to those that will provide effective contrast against the previously chosen background.

Choosing accents

The final step in choosing a Color Scheme is to choose remaining accent colors. (See Figure 4-9.) For most combinations of Background and Foreground colors, Genigraphics and PowerPoint offer you six alternative accent colors. In the Choose A Scheme dialog box, you can select one of eight sets of six accent colors to complement your choices of foreground and background colors. These sets of Accents are displayed against the background that you've chosen, separated by horizontal and vertical rules in the foreground that you've chosen. Click on the desired accent set.

When you're satisfied with your choices, click OK or press Enter. This returns you to the Color Scheme dialog box, which now displays the foreground, background, and accents that you chose.

Adding a Shaded Background

The Shade Background feature permits you to add visual impact and a professional touch to your presentation. By adding a subtle light-to-dark transition to your background, you can add visual interest without drawing so much attention to the background that it detracts from your message.

To add a shaded background to your Slide Master, choose Color Scheme from the Color menu. This time, however, click on Shade Background. (See Figure 4-10.) The Shade Background dialog box appears, offering a variety of ways to add interest—but not confusion—to your Slide Master background.

Choose None if you want a single background tone.

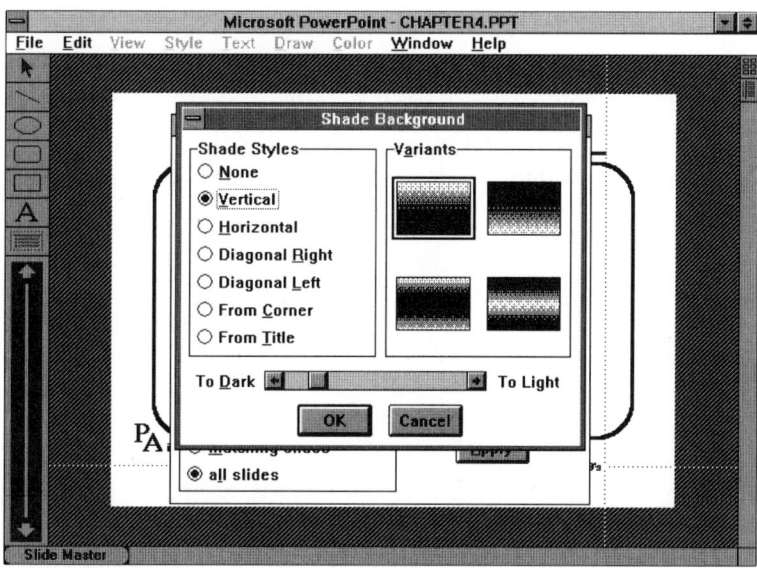

Figure 4-10. *The Shade Background dialog box lets you shade background colors horizontally, vertically, diagonally, from the corner, or from the Slide title.*

If you choose Vertical, you are presented with four choices of background shading effects. These include gradual shading transitions from

- Light at the top of the screen to dark at the bottom
- Dark at the top of the screen to light at the bottom
- Light at the top and bottom of the screen to dark in the middle
- Dark at the top and bottom of the screen to light in the middle

Click on the box that corresponds to the shading option you want.

Other options

Four styles of shading, similar to the Vertical options, are available if you choose Horizontal, Diagonal Right, or Diagonal Left. In contrast, if you choose From Corner, you choose a smooth diagonal transition from a highlight located in one of the four corners to a "spreading" dark.

Shading a title

One of the most interesting ways in which you can add interest to a Slide Background is to choose the Shade From Title command. Two options are available.

- The Slide Master highlight can be placed behind the title, with a gradual transition to dark away from the title.
- The title can be placed against the darkest part of the background with a gradual transition to light elsewhere in the slide.

Adjusting shading range

Regardless of the shading option you choose, you can control how much of a light-to-dark transition takes place in your slides. The To Dark...To Light bar allows you to adjust the precise range of the transition.

- By clicking on the To Dark arrow or by moving the scroll box in the middle, you can make the darker areas increasingly dark.
- By clicking on the To Light arrow, the darkest areas of the slide background become progressively lighter.

As you manipulate the To Light...To Dark bar, you can see the effect of your changes in the Preview boxes directly above the To Light...To Dark bar.

If you've chosen Shade From Title and are modifying the To Light…To Dark bar, remember to maintain sufficient contrast between the Title text and the background. It's possible, for example, to lighten or darken the background of a title so much that the letters become difficult, if not impossible, to read. Again, the greater the text-to-background contrast, the better.

Applying a Color Scheme

After you've chosen the particular background shading option you want, click OK or press Enter. This returns you to the Color Scheme dialog box, which presents three alternatives.

- ◆ Choose Apply To All Slides if you want to apply the chosen shading option to your Slide Master. (This will replace a previously chosen Color and Shading Scheme.)
- ◆ Choose Apply To This Slide if you want to modify only the currently active slide.
- ◆ Choose Apply To Matching Slides if you want to modify all slides that have the same color scheme as the currently active slide.

Using Macintosh PowerPoint, click the Close box at the upper left of the Color Scheme box to remove it from the screen. If you're using Windows PowerPoint, do the following.

- ◆ Open the Window menu at the upper left of the Color Scheme dialog box, and choose Close.
- ◆ Choose the Ctrl-F4 keyboard shortcut.

When choosing a new Color Scheme for a Slide Master, remember that only new slides will be affected unless you select Apply To All Slides.

REFINING COLOR SCHEMES

After you've chosen a Color Scheme for your presentation, you can fine-tune it to your specific needs. You can reformat your Slide Master by changing the order of colors, adding colors, replacing colors, and removing colors.

Changing the Order of a Color Scheme

You can make a major change in the appearance of your presentation without introducing new colors by simply changing the order of the colors in the Color Scheme. This feature permits you to customize your presentation without destroying the integrity of the original Genigraphics-developed Color Scheme or of the palette you created.

The Color Scheme is based on eight colors displayed vertically. The position of each color determines where it will be placed in each slide. Later in this chapter, we'll see how this permits you to change the appearance of your slides and overheads without adding new colors simply by changing the stacking order of the colors.

Here is the default color order of the Slide Master.

- *Background color.* This is the most important color on the slide because all others appear against it.

- *Foreground color.* The Foreground color is used for rules and boxes; it is also used for text (but not titles) entered with one of PowerPoint's three text editing tools. (Titles have their own color; see *Title color*, below.)

- *Shadow color.* The Shadow color is usually a darker version of the Background color.

- *Title color.* The Title color is often applied to bullets that are used to emphasize items placed in a list.

- *Object Fill color.* The Object Fill color is used to fill circles, squares, and rectangles; it is also used as a background for boxes created with PowerPoint's Word Processing tool.

- *Accent colors.* The next two colors are accent colors that can be used, as desired, for additional highlights. (Note: The six colors that are below Background and Foreground are referred to generically as "accents.")

- *Highlight color.* The Highlight color is the last color in the list.

To replace any color in the Color Scheme hierarchy with another color, simply grab the desired color and move it to the position of the original color. (See Figures 4-11 and 4-12.) When you return to your presentation by clicking on the desired Apply option, your presentation will be recolored according to the most recent stacking order of the colors.

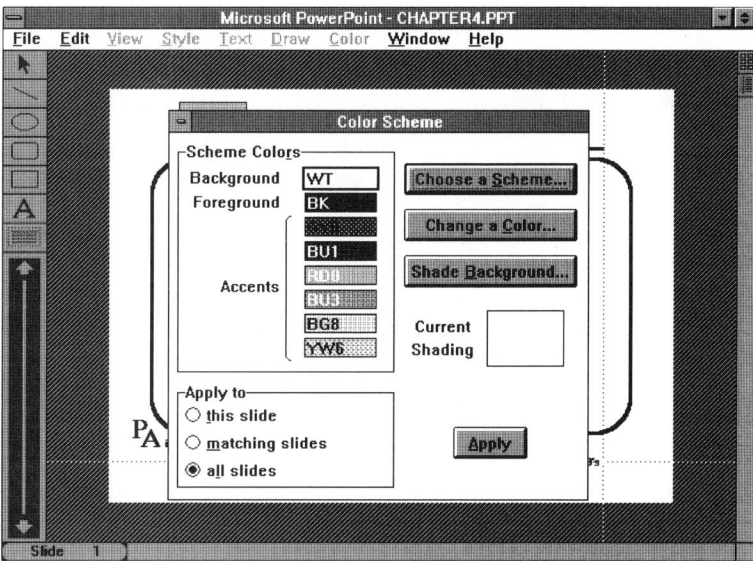

Figure 4-11. *Original Color Scheme: Notice the position of yellow and red. (See Figure 4-12.)*

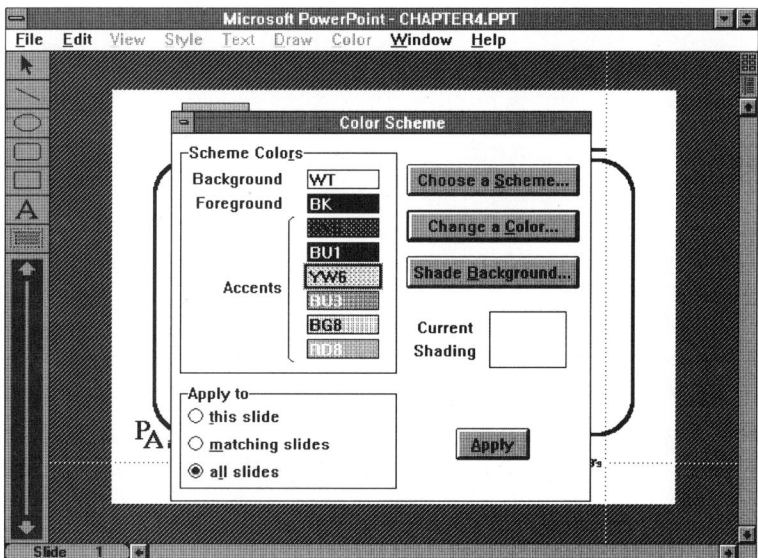

Figure 4-12. *Revised Color Scheme: Notice the new (reversed) positions of yellow and red. (See Figure 4-11.)*

Adding Colors

To add a color to the eight basic Color Scheme colors, choose the Add Extra To Menu command, located at the bottom of the Color menu. (See Figure 4-13.)

To add a new color to your Color Scheme, first click on the color and then click on Add. You can add several colors.

Black and white are probably the first colors you might consider adding, if they're not already present in your original Color Scheme. Black and white provide a strong contrast to existing light or dark colors.

If you're not satisfied with the first 90 color choices offered, click on More Colors. The Select A Color dialog box appears, offering access to the full complement of colors available on your computer.

When you're finished, click OK.

The next time you choose Fill, Line, Shadow, Pattern Contrast, or Text from the Color menu, your recently added colors will appear along with the eight basic Color Scheme options.

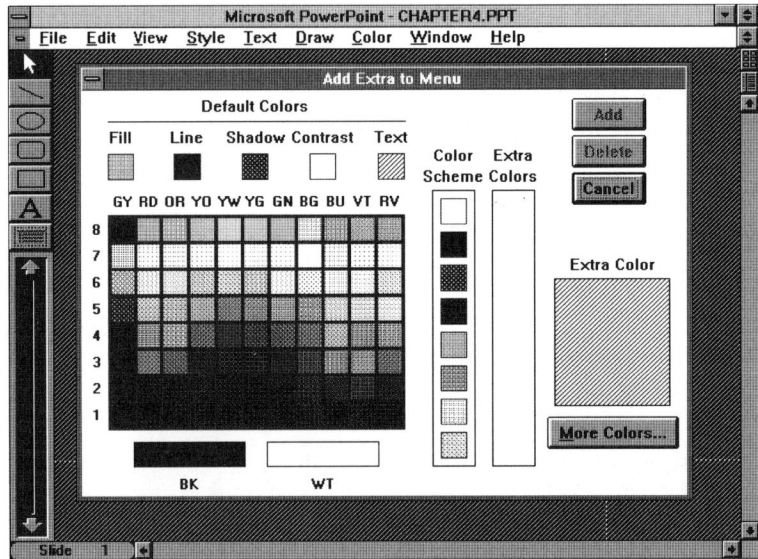

Figure 4-13. *The Add feature of the Add Extra To Menu dialog box lets you add extra colors (often black or white) to your original Color Scheme.*

Chapter 4: Creating a Slide Master and Choosing a Color Scheme

Removing Colors

You can add up to eight colors to the original eight colors of the Color Scheme. When you select an added color, the Delete button (in Macintosh PowerPoint) or the Remove button (in Windows PowerPoint) becomes activated. This gives you an opportunity to remove one of the eight added colors. (Note: Although you can change the original eight colors, you cannot remove them.)

To remove a color, choose it by clicking on it and then click on the Delete or Remove button. You can then add a different color.

Changing Colors

You can further customize your presentation by replacing one of the original eight colors with a new one. To replace a Color Scheme color with a new one, choose Color Scheme from the Color menu and click on Change A Color. This brings you to the Change A Color dialog box. (See Figure 4-14.) To replace an existing color, do the following.

◆ Choose the Color Scheme color you want to change by clicking on it. The color you're changing can be one of the original eight Color Scheme colors or one of your newly added colors.

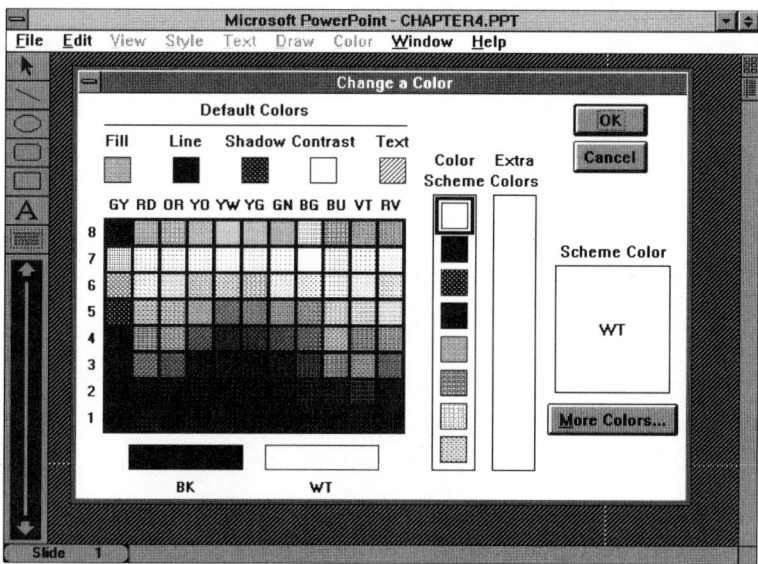

Figure 4-14. *The Change A Color dialog box lets you modify individual Color Scheme colors.*

- Next, replace it by choosing black, white, or another one of the colors shown in the Change Color menu, or click on More Colors and choose a replacement color from the Select A Color dialog box. Either way, your choice is immediately reflected in the Color Scheme preview box.

When you're satisfied with your substitution, click OK or press Enter.

Changing the Colors of an Existing Presentation

PowerPoint makes it easy to recolor an existing presentation at any time. You can do this in two ways.

- You can choose a new Color Scheme by choosing Color Scheme, choosing new Background, Foreground, and Accents colors, and choosing Apply To All Slides.

- You can change the order of the colors and then choose Apply To All Slides.

If you're unsure of how good your changes will look, you can save your original presentation with a name that suggests its color—for example, "New Business, Blue"—and then immediately choose the Save As command and save it under different names—for example, "New Business, Red."

Preparing Color Presentations on Computers with Black-and-White Screens

You can use PowerPoint to create color presentations on computers with black-and-white monitors. For example, when you choose the Color Scheme command from the Color menu with an Apple Macintosh Plus or an SE, the dialog box displays abbreviations for the eight basic colors.

- WT (white)
- BK (black)
- GY5 (gray)
- BU1 (dark blue)
- RD8 (red)
- BU3 (blue)
- BG8 (cyan)
- YW6 (yellow)

In addition, you can use a Macintosh Plus or an SE to modify presentations originally created on a Macintosh II equipped with a color monitor. The PowerPoint documentation includes Color Chart, which helps you reference the 90 Genigraphics colors that can be included in color presentations.

Hardware Considerations

With Windows PowerPoint, colors can appear grainy, and shaded backgrounds will be only roughly approximated on your screen. This is because of the limitations of the standard Video Graphics Array (VGA) card, which creates colors by dithering. Dithering approximates colors by closely positioning individual pixels of color. Dithering requires that your eye and brain combine the pixels into the desired colors and shades.

This graininess is apparent only on a color monitor. When you print your overheads on a color ink-jet or thermal printer or send 35mm slides to Genigraphics for imaging, the colors will be fully saturated and smooth.

If you're using a standard VGA color monitor, you can dramatically improve color quality by replacing your current color card with an improved color driver.

Improving monitor performance is virtually a necessity if you're preparing presentations to be displayed to small groups on your computer screen.

EVALUATING YOUR PROGRESS

After you've created a Slide Master and Color Scheme that represent the visual identity of your company or association, you can use them over and over. The following questions will help you evaluate how close you've come to achieving your intent.

- ◆ Have I chosen an appropriate border?
- ◆ Does the title appear in a logical location on my Slide Master?
- ◆ Have I added all necessary presentation information to each Slide Master?
- ◆ Are the Color Scheme and Background Shading appropriate both for anticipated lighting conditions and for the desired atmosphere?
- ◆ Do the Color Scheme and logo treatment accurately portray and reinforce the identity of my company or association?

Adding Impact to Words

Words form the basis of most presentations. Your presentations will succeed to the extent that your words emerge with clarity and visual impact.

The following six steps allow you to add words to your PowerPoint presentations.

- *Choose the right tool for entering text.* You can use the Labeler tool, the Attached Label feature, or the Word Processor tool.

- *Format the text.* It's essential that you choose the right typeface, type size, and type style. In addition, you need to choose the appropriate text alignment and fine-tune such details as line spacing, tabs, and indents.

- *Edit your words.* Editing is an essential part of successful presentation design. Your visuals will improve to the extent that you rigorously eliminate unnecessary words and replace long words with short words whenever possible. Visual fine-tuning is also necessary to eliminate widows—that is, instances of a word or two isolated on a line.

- *Add text enhancements.* You can use frames, background fills, shadows, colors, and bullets to add emphasis to your words.

- *Establish styles and defaults.* The Styles command allows you to make typeface, type size, type style, and color choices in advance.

Defaults allow you to preselect borders and backgrounds. The use of Styles and defaults helps ensure consistency and saves you time by increasing your efficiency.

- *Refine your work.* Use the Spelling command and the Find command to eliminate embarrassing typographical errors and identify overused words.

A fuller discussion of these steps follows.

CHOOSE THE RIGHT TOOL FOR ENTERING TEXT

PowerPoint provides three tools for entering text on Slide Masters, individual slides, or overheads. Each tool has advantages and limitations.

Labeler Tool

Use the Labeler tool to add individual words or short phrases to your visuals. (Remember that the "A" icon at the left of the screen is the stand-in for the Labeler tool.) Labeler tool applications include

- Customizing a presentation by adding the presenter's or client's name, presentation title, date, or slide number to the Slide Master
- Creating callouts that identify parts of a chart, graph, or drawing on individual slides
- Indicating the source of information presented in a chart or illustration
- Adding disclaimers or author and illustrator credits

Advantages of the Labeler tool

- The Labeler tool is easy to use.
- After the text is created, it can be permanently locked to surrounding objects using the Cut and Paste As Picture commands.

Limitations of the Labeler tool

- The Labeler tool lacks the wordwrap capability; lines will continue beyond the right edge of your screen or slide unless you enter a hard return where you want a line break.

- You have no control over line spacing.
- You cannot edit words after you have locked them to adjacent objects using PowerPoint's Cut command and Paste As Picture command.

Working with the Labeler Tool

Choose the "A" (Labeler tool) icon from the left side of your screen. Then click on the slide location where you want to insert text and start typing. Enter a hard return whenever you want to end one line and enter a second line of text.

Attached Label Feature

Use the Attached Label feature to add text to the center of a rectangle, square, oval, or circle you've previously created. (See Figure 5-1 on the following page.) Use the Attached Label feature to create

- Information presented in tables
- Organizational and flow charts
- Presentations similar to the "Steps to Success" template described in Section III

Advantages of the Attached Label feature

- Text is locked to the object, yet the text can be edited at any time.
- Objects can accommodate multiple typefaces, type sizes, and type styles.
- Text is automatically centered horizontally *and* vertically in the object.
- Object is automatically resized if the text is reformatted (if Sized To Text is chosen from the Draw menu, as described below).

Limitations of the Attached Label feature

- You have limited control over vertical text position.
- The Attached Label feature lacks the wordwrap capability.
- Text cannot be justified.
- You have no control over line spacing.

SECTION II: BASIC SKILLS

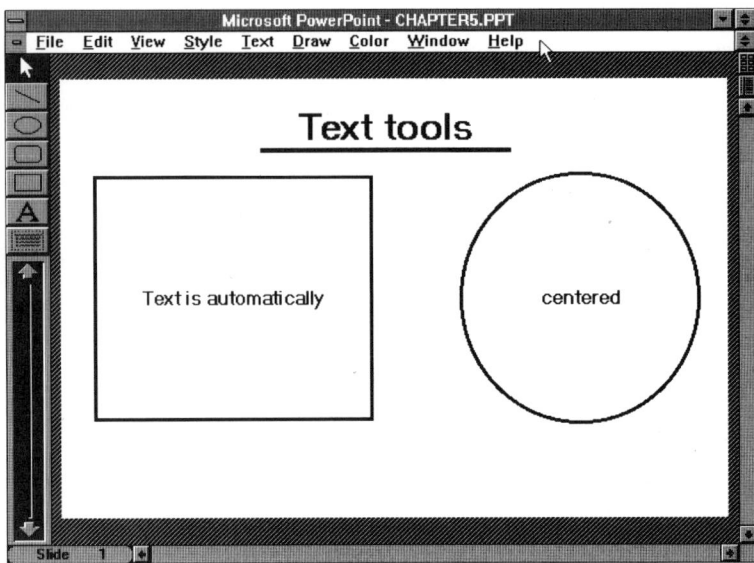

Figure 5-1. The Attached Label feature centers text in objects created with the Oval, Rounded Rectangle, or Rectangle tool.

Working with the Attached Label feature

Start by creating an object using the Oval tool, the Rounded Rectangle tool, or the Rectangle tool.

Next, with the object selected, simply start typing. The words you type appear, centered in the object.

Text added with the Attached Label feature becomes a part of the object in which you inserted the text—that is, part of the rectangle, circle, and so forth. They cannot be separated. If the object is moved, the text moves with it (unlike text entered with the Labeler tool).

Sized To Text option

The Sized To Text command located in the Draw menu allows the object to enlarge or shrink to accommodate the text. (See Figure 5-2.)

With Sized To Text chosen, if the object were narrower than the lines of text, the object would expand to accommodate the text.

You can choose Sized To Text at any time. Objects automatically resize themselves if you reformat previously entered text.

Chapter 5: Adding Impact to Words

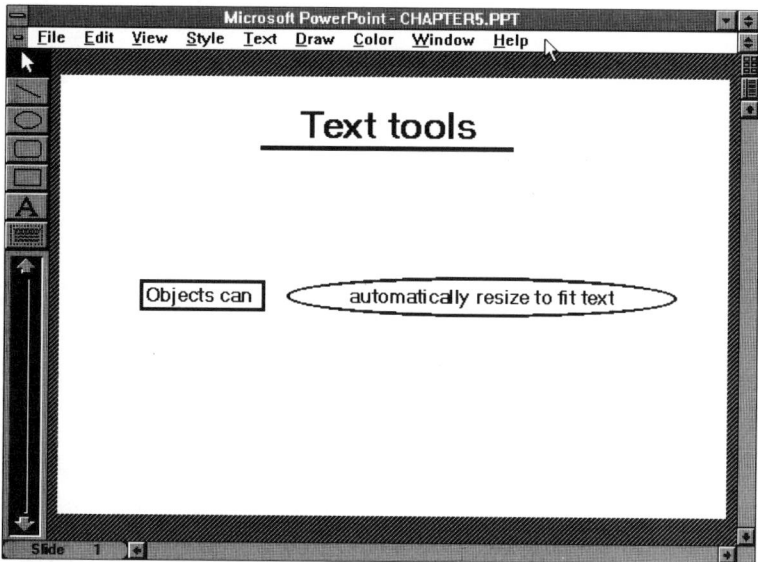

Figure 5-2. *Choose the Sized To Text command if you want to expand or contract the object to accommodate your text.*

Word Processor Tool

The Word Processor tool is PowerPoint's most powerful text tool, providing full control over the appearance of text. The Word Processor tool is your basic tool for most text entry applications. Use the Word Processor tool to add text to

- ◆ Title and summary slides
- ◆ Slides containing lengthy quotations
- ◆ Wide, single-column lists in sentence or indented-outline format
- ◆ Double-column lists of words or short phrases
- ◆ Text or numeric information presented in table form

Advantages

- ◆ The Word Processor tool offers full control over alignment, line spacing, tabs, and indents.

- You can create lists with multiple levels of indents.
- Decimal tabs allow you to create tables.
- Backgrounds, frames, and shadows can be sized automatically to fit content.
- The Copy and Paste commands allow you to create parallel Word Processor boxes for two-column lists.
- Word Processor boxes can be resized at any time, and the lines will be reformatted as needed.

Limitations

- You must create the Word Processor box before you add text.
- Word Processor boxes must be created on each slide. Placing such a box on the Slide Master does not result in its appearing automatically on each individual slide.

Working with the Word Processor Tool

First, click on the Word Processor icon, which is at the bottom of the list of tool icons that appear along the left side of your screen.

Next, click on the place where you want the upper left corner of the Word Processor box to appear. (See Figure 5-3.) Then, while holding down the mouse button, drag the cursor to the lower right corner of the desired Word Processor box. Release the mouse button when you have defined the height and width of the Word Processor box.

A flashing cursor appears at the upper left corner inside the Word Processor box. Start typing, and your words appear from that point on. When your words fill up one line, the following words appear at the beginning of the next line. (Notice that PowerPoint does not hyphenate a word to split it between two lines because hyphenation is rarely desirable in slides or overheads.)

Helpful shortcut

Macintosh PowerPoint contains a handy keyboard shortcut. After you've chosen the Word Processor tool, you can use the Enter key (not the Return key) to toggle between choosing the Word Processor box (for movement or reformatting) and the Text tool (for selecting and highlighting individual words or phrases for editing or deleting).

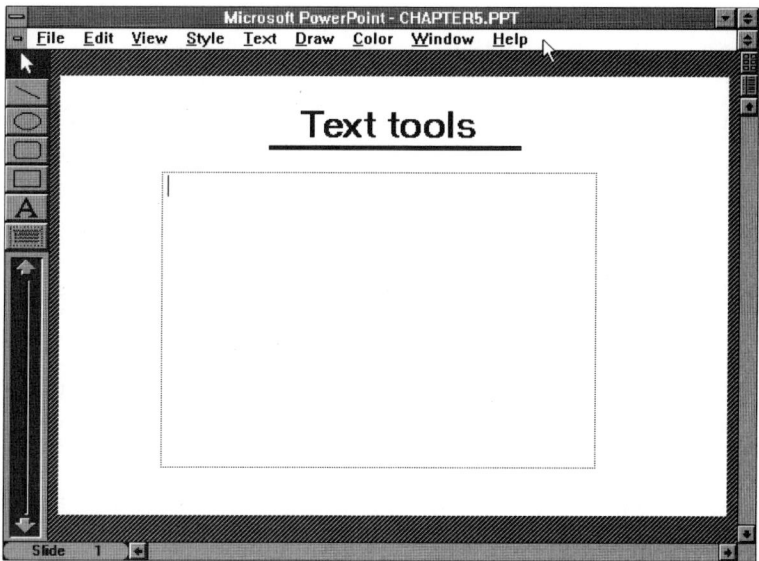

Figure 5-3. *Defining a Word Processor box.*

FORMAT THE TEXT

Text formatting involves using the typeface (Font), type size (Size), and type style (Style) commands located in the Style menu. It also involves employing the alignment and indent features found in the Text menu.

The first step in formatting your presentation is to choose the appropriate typeface. This decision involves

- ◆ Thinking about how your presentation will be produced. In particular, consider the type of printer or film recorder that you'll use to produce your slides and overheads.

- ◆ Examining the characteristics of the typefaces themselves. This involves aesthetic decisions as well as evaluation of typeface legibility under varying conditions.

Output Device Limitations

Your freedom to choose typefaces is limited by the capability of your output device to print them. Output devices are limited in the number of typefaces they can reproduce.

For example, with Macintosh PowerPoint, if you're preparing black-and-white overhead transparencies on a PostScript laser printer such as the Apple LaserWriter IINT (or equivalent), you enjoy complete freedom to use any of the fonts built into your laser printer as well as the full range of downloadable PostScript typefaces available from firms such as Adobe, Monotype, URW, and Kingsley ATF. These typefaces are sent from your computer's hard disk to the printer as needed. This gives you access to thousands of typefaces.

If you're producing color overhead transparencies on a color PostScript printer such as those made by QMS or Tektronix, you can choose any PostScript typeface.

Likewise, with Windows PowerPoint, if you're producing black-and-white overhead transparencies on a Hewlett-Packard LaserJet Series III, you can choose any of the Bitstream (or any other firms') typefaces.

If you're using the Adobe Type Manager with Macintosh PowerPoint or Windows PowerPoint, you can also use any Adobe PostScript typeface with a wide variety of black-and-white or color ink-jet or thermal printers made by Hewlett-Packard or Tektronix. The Adobe Type Manager also makes a major improvement in on-screen, computer-based presentations delivered using PowerPoint's Slide Show feature.

But, if you're producing color slides on a film recorder, or if you're sending your files to an outside service bureau such as Genigraphics, you need to be more careful in choosing your typefaces. In this case, you're limited to the specific typeface options offered by your particular output device or service bureau.

If you're using Genigraphic's nationwide chain of service bureaus to create color slides or overhead transparencies in either the Macintosh or MS-DOS environments, for example, you can choose the same 35 typefaces built into most PostScript printers such as the LaserWriter IINT. The Genigraphics typeface lineup includes three serif faces, two sans serif faces, one "decorative" face, and one typeface that resembles typewritten output, as well as a symbol collection.

Typeface Design and Legibility

After you've narrowed your typeface options down to those that your output device can handle, choosing the right typeface involves looking at five basic typeface design characteristics that help differentiate one typeface from another. These are as follows:

- Serif vs. sans serif
- Stress
- X-height
- Font metrics
- Symbols

Serif vs. sans serif

Serifs are small extensions, or decorations, at the edges of each letter that enhance the readability of words by helping guide the reader's eyes from letter to letter. (See Figure 5-4. Notice that Figures 5-4 through 5-9 show the Macintosh screen.) Serif typefaces communicate a "classic" or "conversational" tone. The most commonly available serif typefaces are

- Bookman
- New Century Schoolbook
- Palatino
- Times Roman

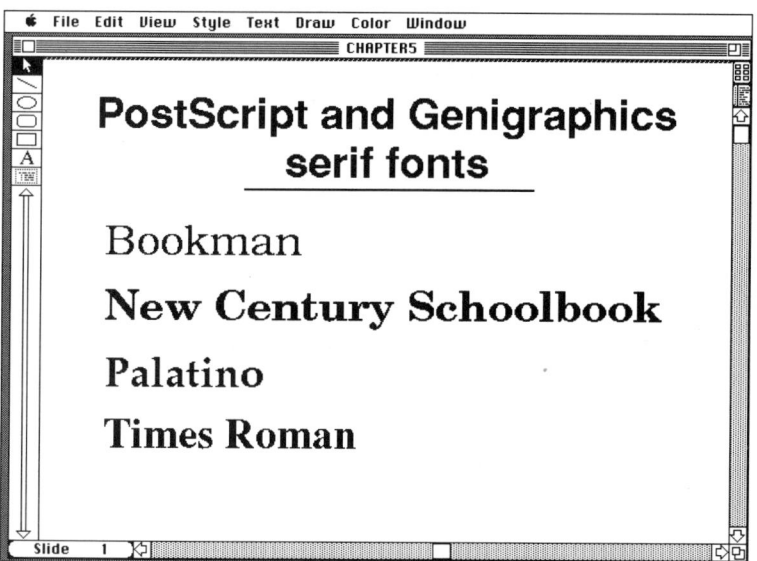

Figure 5-4. When using a PostScript printer, or when sending your files to Genigraphics, you can choose serif fonts such as Bookman, New Century Schoolbook, Palatino, and Times Roman.

These serif faces are built into PostScript printers and are also available from Bitstream (and other companies) as downloadable fonts. You can also use them in color slides and overheads produced by Genigraphics.

Compare Palatino's "classic" appearance with the more robust Bookman. Notice how Times Roman fits in more words per line.

Sans serif means "without serif." The design of these typefaces is more simple and straightforward. (See Figure 5-5.) Sans serif typefaces are often more legible from a distance.

The most commonly available sans serif typefaces are

- ◆ Avant Garde
- ◆ Helvetica
- ◆ Helvetica Narrow

These sans serif typefaces are built into PostScript printers and can also be used in color slides and overheads produced by Genigraphics.

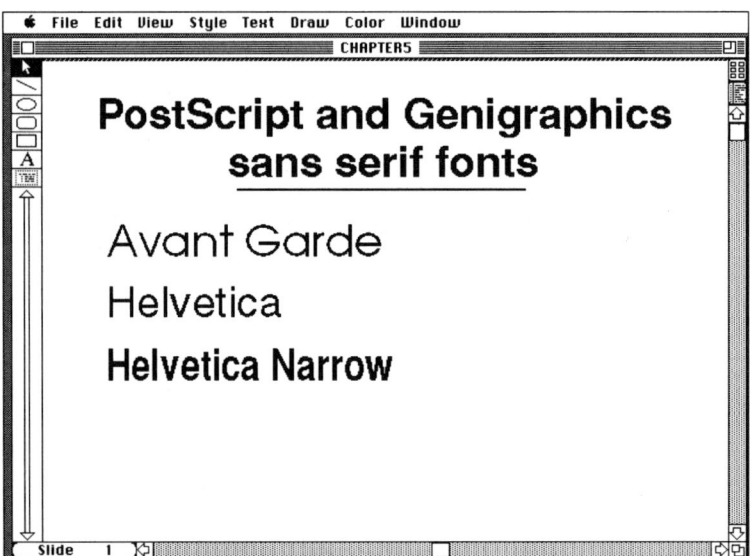

Figure 5-5. When using a PostScript printer, or when sending your files to Genigraphics, you can choose sans serif fonts such as Avant Garde, Helvetica, and Helvetica Narrow.

The presence or absence of serifs influences both the appearance and the legibility of your slides and overhead transparencies. For example, at small sizes, the serif fonts can add visual confusion or become "lost." Sans serif fonts often project a contemporary feeling.

Special typefaces

You can use two special-purpose typefaces—Courier and Zapf Chancery—when sending PowerPoint files to Genigraphics.

Courier resembles typewritten copy. (See Figure 5-6.) Zapf Chancery is an elegant script face that can be used for title slides.

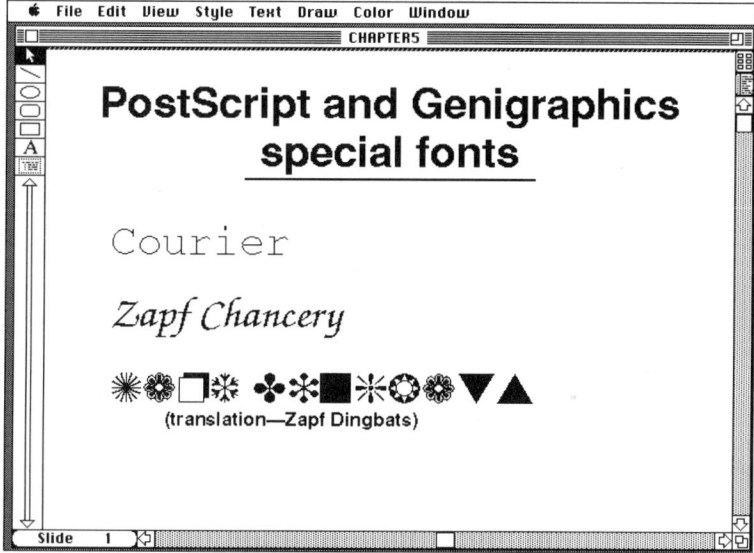

Figure 5-6. *Courier can add a look of "fast-breaking news" to your visuals. Zapf Chancery is a script typeface useful for titles. The Zapf Dingbats symbols can be used instead of bullets to introduce items in a list.*

Stress

Stress refers to changes in the thickness ("weight") of individual letters. High-stress typefaces exhibit a significant difference between the thick and thin strokes. Low-stress typefaces exhibit less difference between thick and thin strokes. In Figure 5-7 on the following page, notice that Bookman has less variance in stroke thickness than Times Roman.

SECTION II: BASIC SKILLS

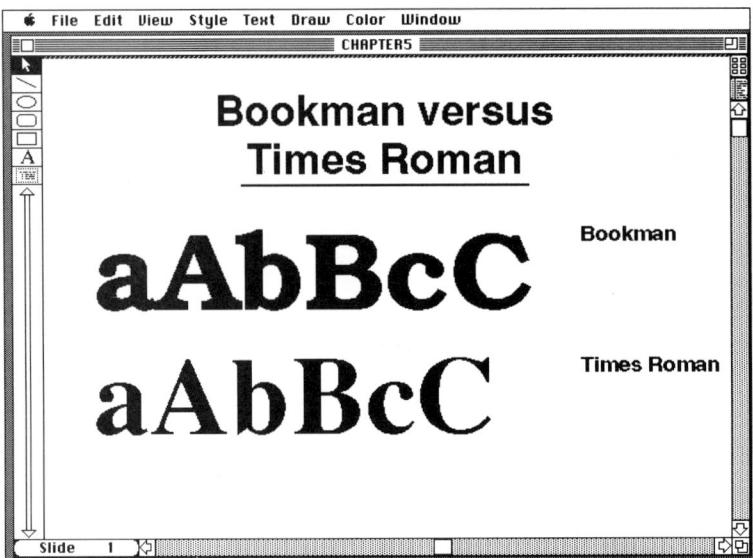

Figure 5-7. Compare Bookman's relatively even stroke weight with Times Roman's pronounced differences between thick and thin strokes.

Stress is an important consideration in choosing a presentation typeface because thin strokes can become "lost" at small sizes, especially if insufficient contrast exists between the text and its background.

X-height

The x-height of a typeface refers to the height of lowercase letters (such as c's, m's, and x's) containing neither ascenders nor descenders. Ascenders are the tall strokes of b's, d's, l's and t's. Descenders are the portions of the letters that fall below the baseline of letters, contained in such letters as p's, q's, and y's.

For presentation purposes, typefaces with a high x-height (such as Bookman) are easier to read from a distance than typefaces with a lower x-height (such as Times Roman).

Font metrics

Font metrics refers to the width and character spacing of individual letters. Some typefaces are characterized by wider letters than others, with the letters often more tightly spaced.

Letter width and spacing have a great impact on presentation legibility. For example, Helvetica is often a better choice than Avant Garde because the letters are a bit narrower. (See Figure 5-8.) The a, e, m, n, o, and p of the Avant Garde font are somewhat less distinguishable than those same letters of the Helvetica font. Such differences become more pronounced as viewing distance increases.

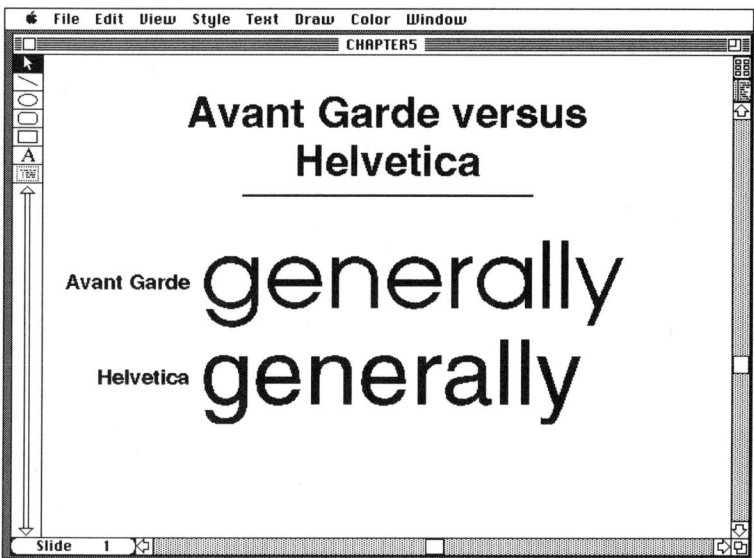

Figure 5-8. Helvetica letters are narrower and more distinct than those of Avant Garde, which increases readability when used for blocks of text. In Avant Garde, the letters e and a are relatively similar in shape; in Helvetica, e and a are visually unique.

Symbols

Zapf Dingbats is a typeface option available with PostScript printers and from Genigraphics. The Zapf Dingbats font consists of a wide variety of asterisks, boxes, bullets, check marks, open and closed ballot boxes, and pointing hands. (See Figure 5-9 on the following page.) These symbols can be used to add character and interest to visuals consisting entirely of text.

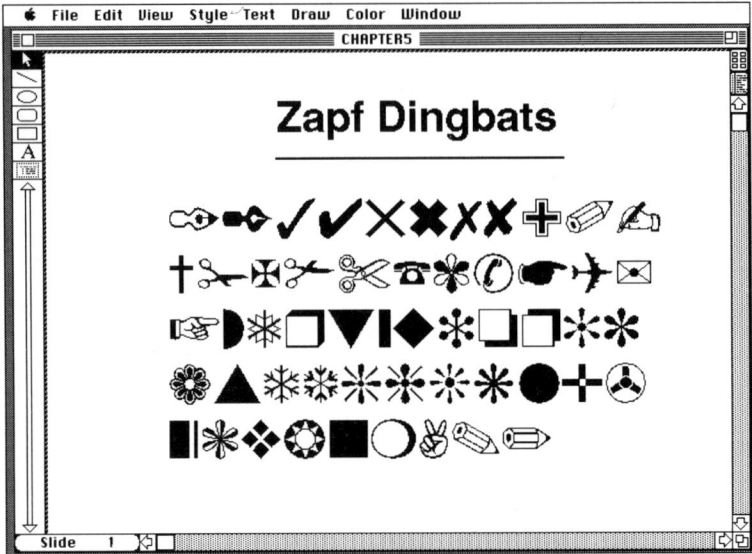

Figure 5-9. *A few of the symbols in the Zapf Dingbats font.*

Locating symbols

Using Macintosh PowerPoint, you can easily locate specific Zapf Dingbat symbols by using the Macintosh Keycaps desk accessory.

To use Keycaps, click on the Apple icon and choose Keycaps. Next, from the Keycaps menu, choose the typeface you want displayed—in this case, Zapf Dingbats. The keyboard on the screen of your computer shows the location of every symbol, accessed by pressing

- ◆ The keyboard character by itself
- ◆ The keyboard character in conjunction with either the Shift or Option key
- ◆ The character key in conjunction with both the Shift and Option keys

Windows PowerPoint also helps you locate any Zapf Dingbats symbol.

- ◆ Open the Help menu, and choose Keyboard. (See Figure 5-10.)
- ◆ Double-click on Zapf Dingbat Keyboard (1 of 6).

You'll see a three-column table that associates keyboard characters with what appears on your slide when the Zapf Dingbats font is chosen.

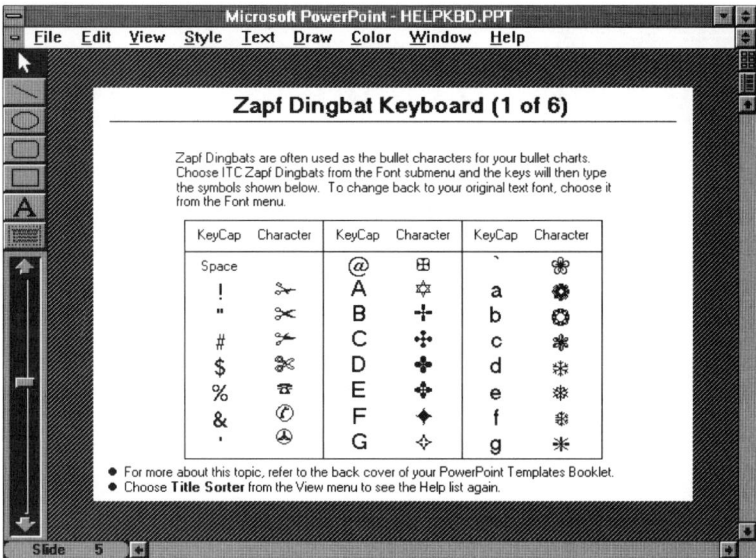

Figure 5-10. The Help menu of Windows PowerPoint makes it easy to choose any Zapf Dingbats symbol.

There are six help screens in all. Click on the Upward or Downward arrow until you find the specific Zapf Dingbats symbol you want. The last three screens contain symbols that can be accessed only by pressing the Alt key and entering the character's numeric code.

Choosing Typefaces

To choose a typeface, first select the text by clicking on it. Then open the Style menu and choose Font. A list of available fonts appears. Hold down the mouse button while you scroll through available typeface alternatives, and release it when the name of the desired typeface is highlighted.

Only those typeface options available with the output device you've selected will be listed.

Adding contrast to your slides

You can add visual interest to your slides and overheads by using different typefaces for various categories of information. (See Figure 5-11 on the following page.) You should exercise great care when mixing fonts, however.

SECTION II: BASIC SKILLS

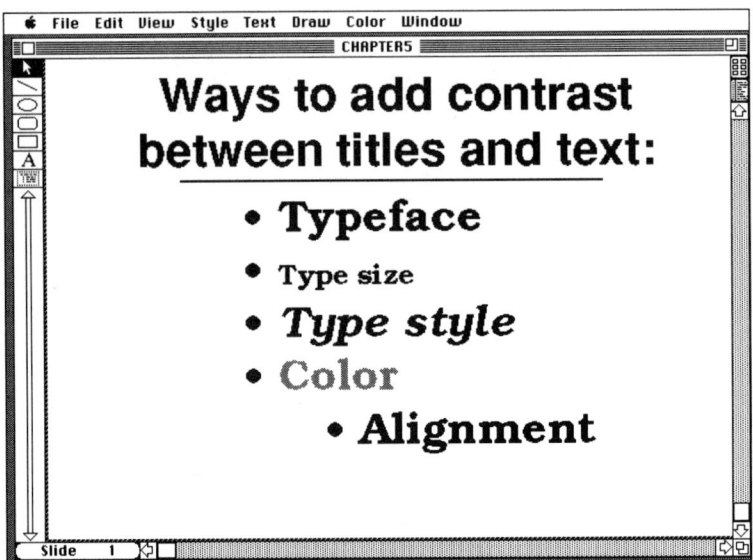

Figure 5-11. *Some of the ways you can add contrast to your visuals.*

Whenever you change a typeface, be sure that the change is a major one. For example, you're better off contrasting *significantly different* typefaces than typefaces that are only *slightly* different.

One of the safest typeface combinations is the contrasting of titles set in a sans serif typeface with lists or supporting material set in a serif typeface. For example, Helvetica titles with Bookman body copy is a classic combination.

A slide containing a title that is set in Helvetica with Avant Garde supporting material simply wouldn't look as strong as Helvetica with Bookman. (See Figure 5-12.) Helvetica and Avant Garde look enough alike to be similar, yet enough different to look "wrong" together.

Likewise, a Bookman title with Times Roman body copy (shown in Figure 5-13) has nowhere near the impact of a Helvetica/Bookman combination. As in many other cases, opposites attract.

Always exercise restraint when mixing typefaces. Each slide should contain only a few well chosen typefaces—three at most. In addition, your typeface decisions should remain consistent from slide to slide. For example, the typeface you used for titles in Slide 1 should also be used for titles throughout your presentation. Likewise, your typeface choices for supporting information and callouts should remain the same throughout your presentation.

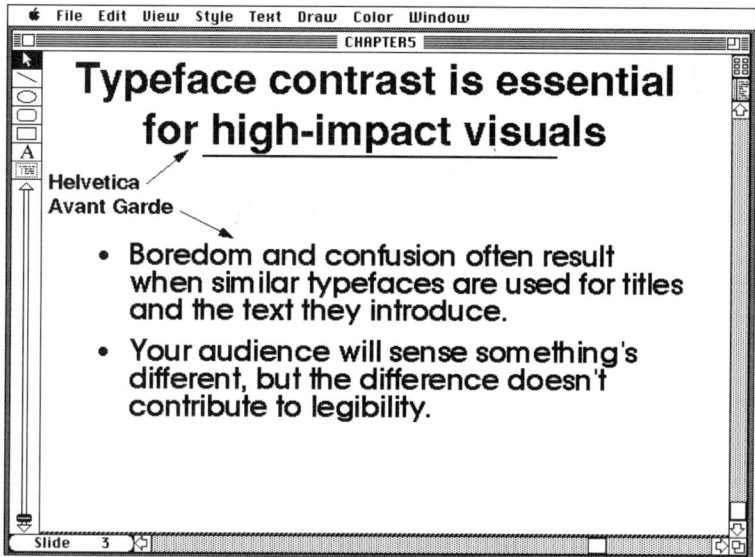

Figure 5-12. Helvetica and Avant Garde do not provide enough contrast for impact.

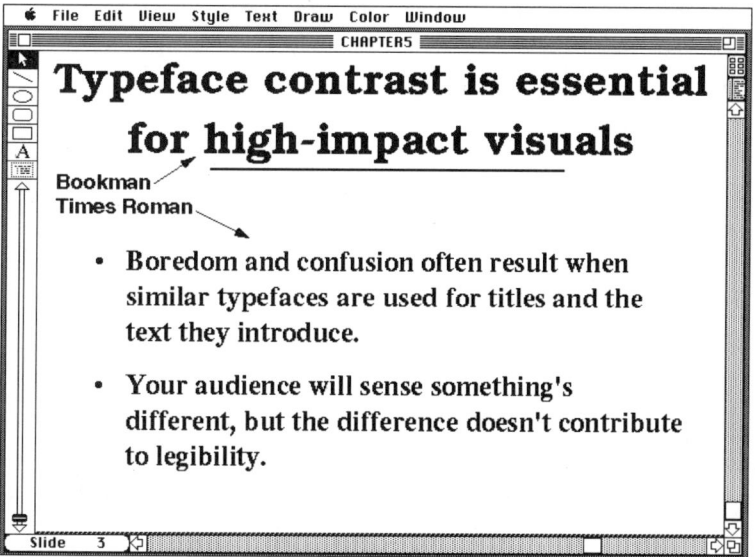

Figure 5-13. Bookman and Times Roman also lack the contrast needed for impact.

Choosing the Appropriate Type Size

Type is measured in points; 72 points equals an inch. The larger the typeface you choose, the more legible it will be—especially from the back of the room. (See Figure 5-14.) However, a larger typeface means that fewer words will fit on each line of your slides or overheads.

To choose a type size, select the text and choose the Size command from the Style menu. Scroll through the list of available options and release the mouse button when the desired type size is highlighted (appears as white type against a black background).

Like typefaces, type sizes are output device dependent. If you're using a PostScript printer to prepare black-and-white or color overhead transparencies, for example, you can safely use the "other" option that allows you to specify nonstandard type sizes.

With Windows PowerPoint, however, if you're creating black-and-white overhead transparencies with a Hewlett-Packard LaserJet printer, you're limited to the type sizes available on the font cartridge you might be using or the sizes of the Bitstream downloadable typefaces you've previously created.

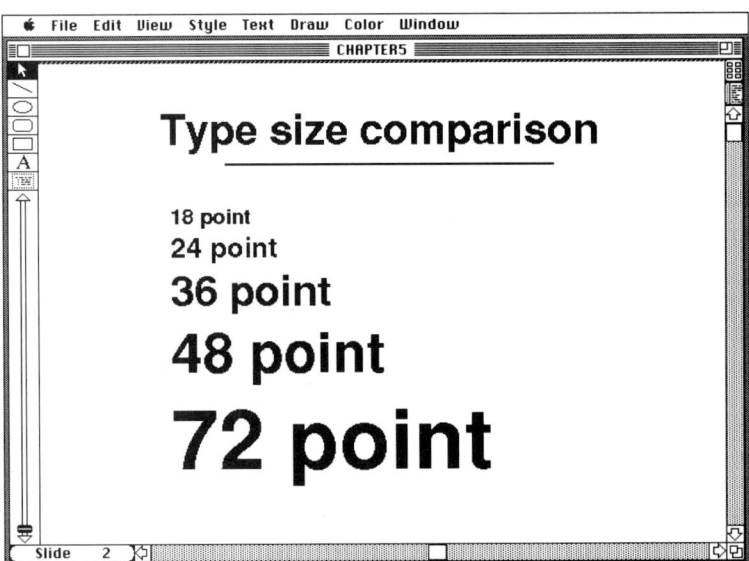

Figure 5-14. *A comparison of 18-point, 24-point, 36-point, 48-point, and 72-point type. (Not actual size.)*

Likewise, if you're preparing color slides or overheads for Genigraphics to prepare, you must limit your type size choices to the alternatives listed on the Size submenu. This ensures that line lengths will remain unchanged.

Type size considerations

A close relationship exists between type size, legibility, and the number of words you can place on a slide. (See Figure 5-15.) A close correlation should also exist between the importance of the message and the size of the type used to communicate it.

- Important information (such as titles) should be significantly larger than supporting information (such as copyright information or the date of the presentation).
- As type size increases, legibility also increases, but the number of words that can fit on a slide decreases.
- As type size decreases, legibility decreases, but you can fit more words on a slide or overhead.

Your success in designing effective presentations depends largely on your willingness to work with this fundamental relationship. Because you can't

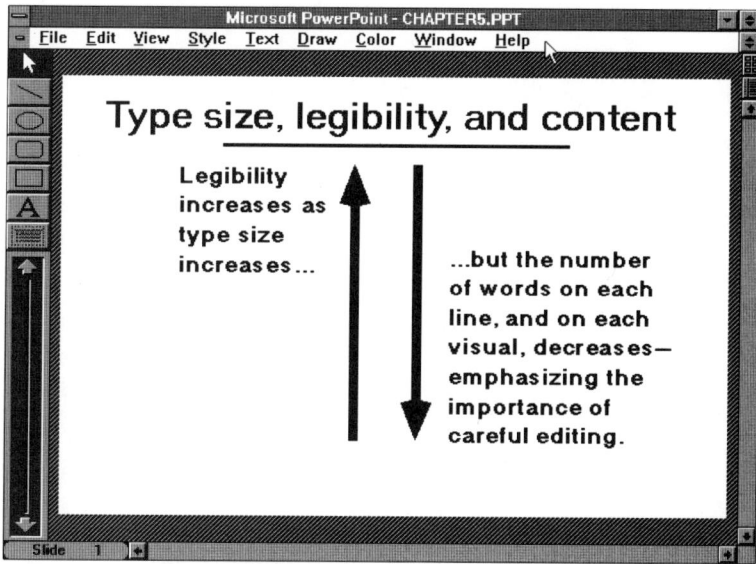

Figure 5-15. *An intimate relationship exists between type size, legibility, and the number of words you can fit in each visual.*

have both large type and a lot of words, you'll need to rigorously edit your words and reorganize your presentation so that each slide contains a bare minimum of words.

Using size for contrast

In general, your visuals will improve in appearance and communicate better to the extent that you provide appropriate type size contrast between the various text elements.

The following example lacks impact because the title, numbers, and body copy do not contrast with one another sufficiently. When all the type is roughly the same size, as in Figure 5-16, the type blends together. As a result, the visual lacks a focal point.

By setting the title and introductory numbers significantly larger than the body copy, however, you can create the contrast necessary both to add visual interest to a slide and to organize the information. (See Figure 5-17.) By setting the title larger than the body copy, the title emerges with added impact. Now an appropriate relationship exists between the size of the type and the importance of the message. In addition, by setting the numbers in a significantly larger size than the adjacent body copy, the numbers do a better job of organizing the list.

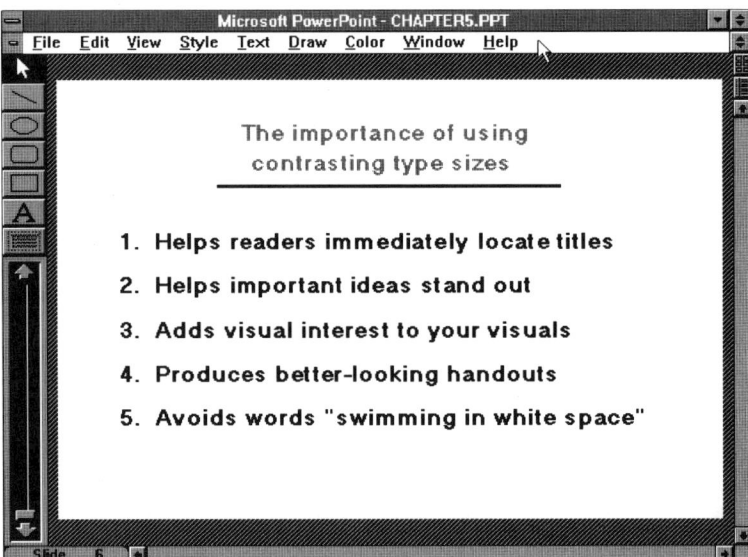

Figure 5-16. *An insufficient type size contrast between the title and the list it introduces produces a boring visual.*

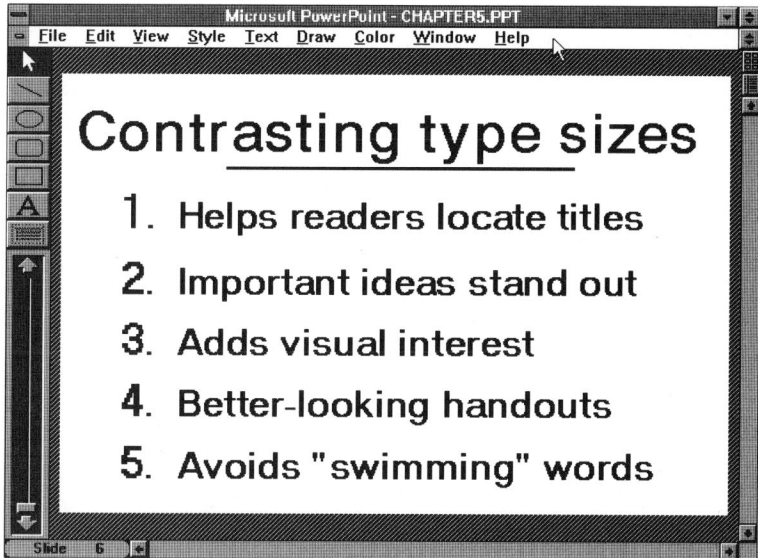

Figure 5-17. By simply increasing the type size contrast of title, numbers, and text, a visual can become more interesting and better organized.

As it is with choosing typefaces, consistency is a virtue. Type size choices made on Slide 1 should be maintained throughout the slides that follow. Each slide should contain only a few, major type size options. The use of a few well-chosen type sizes adds unity to your presentation and helps your audience quickly categorize and understand the information contained on each slide.

Choosing the Appropriate Type Style

Type style options include bold, italic, bold italic, and underline. In Macintosh PowerPoint, the outline and shadow styles are also available. There are two ways to select style options.

- ◆ Choose an option from the Style menu.
- ◆ Use the keyboard shortcuts listed next to the options in the Style menu.

Use of the keyboard shortcuts will soon become second nature to you. They speed your work by eliminating the need to remove your hand from the keyboard and reach for the mouse.

- ◆ *Plain* refers to unmodified type. At small sizes, Plain type might be too light to be read comfortably from long distances.

- *Bold* type is characterized by thicker strokes. Although bold type is often preferable, thick strokes in a small font can cause the counters—enclosed areas of white space within individual letters—to close up, thus reducing typeface legibility in a bold type of small size.
- *Italic* adds momentum, irony, or a conversational tone to your words.
- *Underlining* should be used with discretion. Often, the line interferes with typeface descenders, reducing both typeface attractiveness and legibility.

Macintosh PowerPoint includes two Style options not available with Windows PowerPoint:

- *Outline* can be used for slide titles and short phrases but should not be used for lengthy phrases.
- *Shadow* can enhance typeface legibility by helping the type contrast with its background. As with bold type, however, legibility is often reduced at small sizes because the open spaces within letters become lost.

You can toggle a style selection on or off by alternately selecting and deselecting it. More than one style formatting option may be applied at a time. For example, bold italic type is chosen by clicking on both Bold and Italic.

- *Bold italic* is an ideal way to add emphasis to quotations, subtitles, or short phrases.

Contrasting type styles can greatly enhance your presentation. Visual style can communicate a hierarchy of information. Bold titles, for example, signal (in a visual way) that their content is more important than the Plain text that provides supporting details.

Uppercase text

Whenever possible, avoid the temptation to set long titles or headings in uppercase type. Words set entirely in uppercase type are more difficult to read than words set in all lowercase type or in a combination of uppercase and lowercase type. Readers recognize words by their shapes, which are created by the alternating pattern created by descenders and ascenders. (See Figure 5-18.) Words set entirely in uppercase type are more difficult to recognize because they lack shape—they're simply rectangles.

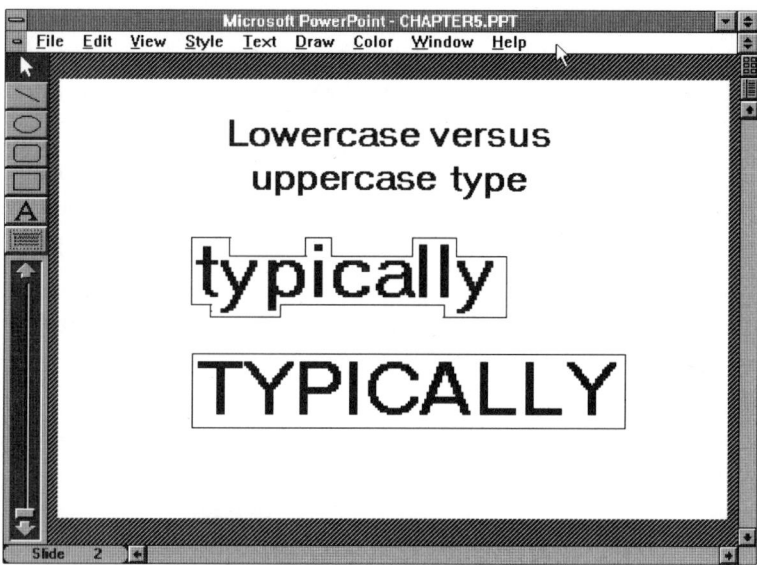

Figure 5-18. *Compare the unique shape formed by the ascenders and descenders in the word set in lowercase type with the plain rectangle formed by the word set in uppercase type.*

Choosing an Appropriate Text Alignment

If you've used desktop-publishing software, you're likely to be familiar with the various alignment options available to you from the text menu. Options include Left, Center, Right, and Justify.

Left-aligned type is easiest to read because each line, regardless of length, begins at the same starting point.

Centered text is often overused. Although appropriate for short, one-line phrases (such as titles), centered text is more difficult to read than left-aligned text. This is because readers must search for the beginning of each line, which can become tiresome in long passages.

You can improve the readability of centered text by breaking the lines at points where readers would normally pause.

Flush-right text can be used to anchor two or three lines of text to a large illustration located to the right of it. Readers are likely to find it difficult to read more than three lines of right-aligned text because they must search for the beginning of each line.

If you're using the Word Processor tool, you can justify text. Justified text is characterized by lines of equal length—that is, each line is flush left *and* flush right. Spacing between words is manipulated to fill out each line.

Justified text should also be used with discretion. Because PowerPoint doesn't automatically hyphenate and run down—or split—words over two lines, if your text consists only of a few words set in a rather large type size, you might inadvertently end up with large, visually distracting "holes" (white spaces) in your text, as shown in Figure 5-19.

The Word Processor tool offers a decimal-alignment feature. This allows you to create tables with numbers—say, dollars-and-cents figures—aligned around a decimal point.

To create decimal-aligned tables, create a Word Processor box. Then choose Show Text Ruler from the Text menu. With the Text Ruler exposed, click-and-drag the tab icon with the dot inside and insert it at the desired spot below the ruler scale. Numbers tabbed to this point in the Word Processor box will align around the decimal point.

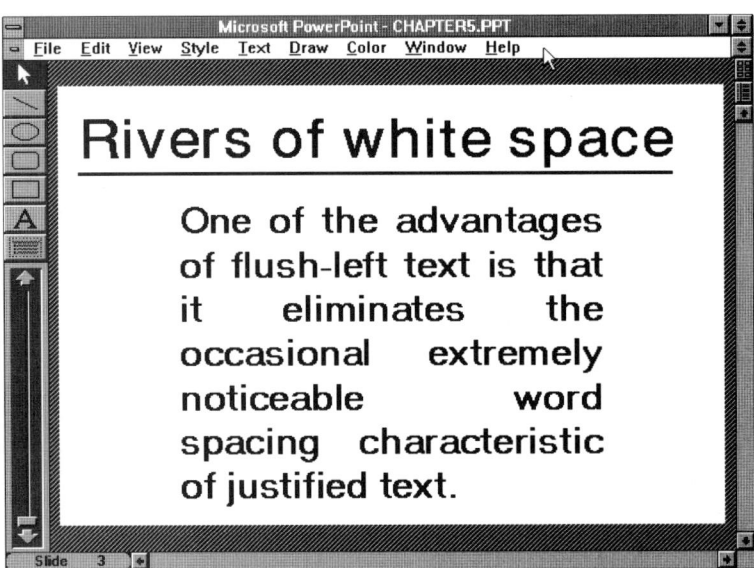

Figure 5-19. *Justified text set in a large type size often results in large gaps between words.*

All three text tools allow you to choose the appropriate alignment option before or after you've typed your words.

For example, before you click on the Word Processor or Labeler tool icon, you can choose Left, Centered, or Right alignment from the Text menu by clicking on the desired option. Or you can modify the alignment of previously entered text by clicking on the box surrounding the words and then choosing Left, Centered, or Right from the Text menu. (Note: You can justify only text entered with the Word Processor tool.)

Adjusting Tabs and Indents

You can improve the appearance of your slides and overheads by using tabs and indents.

After you've created a Word Processor box, choose Show Text Ruler from the Text menu. If you're preparing a list with items introduced by bullets, you can determine how far from the left each level of text will be indented. You can also adjust the space between text and bullets.

To deepen an indent (the space between the bulleted first line and the other lines of each paragraph), click-and-drag the lower dotted vertical line and position it to the right.

A first-line hanging indent is a design in which the first line of each paragraph begins to the left of each paragraph (allowing bullets to be surrounded by white space). To eliminate a first-line hanging indent, line up the first and second dotted lines of each indent on the text ruler and delete the tab that was used to separate the bullet from the first line of text.

Entering indented text

PowerPoint can handle lists with up to five levels of indents.

When preparing a list in outline fashion with a Word Processor box, open the Text menu and choose Indent Right to advance to the next indent. Or you can use the appropriate keyboard shortcut: Command-R (in Macintosh PowerPoint) or Ctrl-R (in Windows PowerPoint).

To return text to a higher level in the outline, open the Text menu and choose the Indent Left command, or use Command-L (in Macintosh PowerPoint) or Ctrl-L (in Windows PowerPoint).

SECTION II: BASIC SKILLS

Adjusting Line Spacing

When using the Word Processor tool, you can modify line and paragraph spacing by using the Line Spacing command in the Text menu. Line spacing refers to the vertical distance between lines. Note: You cannot modify line or paragraph spacing for text entered with PowerPoint's Labeler tool or Attached Label feature.

Reducing line spacing can help unify adjacent lines, visually isolated quotations, or listed items occupying two or more lines. (See Figures 5-20 and 5-21.)

Paragraph spacing influences the vertical distance between lines separated by a hard carriage return. Additional space between paragraphs helps isolate the paragraphs. Additional paragraph spacing also helps separate listed items from an introductory paragraph.

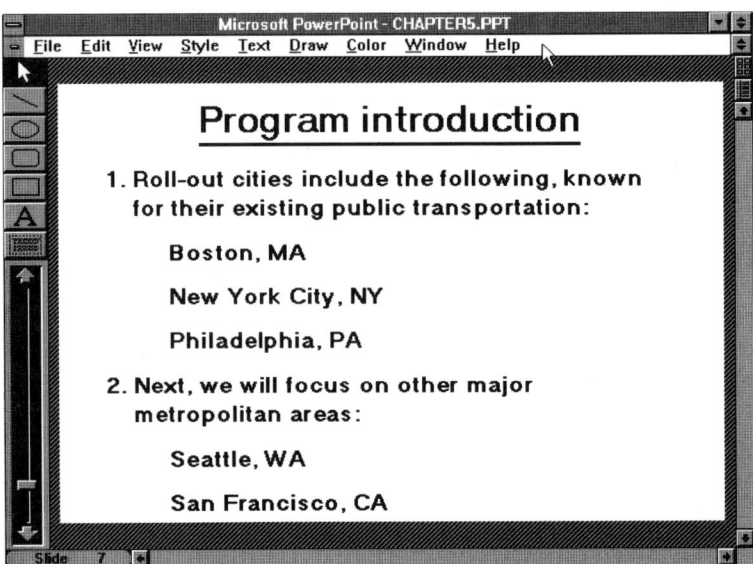

Figure 5-20. *The results of PowerPoint's line spacing and paragraph spacing defaults can be seen in this visual.*

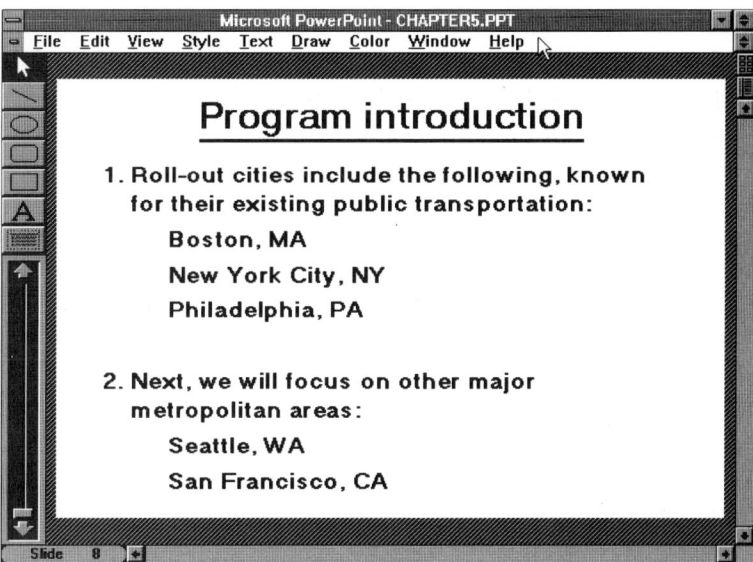

Figure 5-21. *Notice how reducing the line spacing in Figure 5-20 slightly and adding line spacing before #2 improve the appearance of the list.*

Formatting Text

Text formatting can be done at any time. Regardless of the tool you use to enter text, you can do your formatting

- ◆ Before you enter the text
- ◆ After you've entered the text

To format text before you enter it, make your typeface, type size, type style, alignment, indents, and line-spacing decisions *before* you choose the Labeler tool, Attached Label feature, or Word Processor tool.

You can reformat previously entered text in three ways.

Clicking in a text box

If all the text in a box is to be *identically formatted* (or reformatted), click *anywhere in the text box*. When the box has been selected—as indicated by the presence of its gray border and corner buttons—choose the Style or Text attributes you want to apply to *all the text* in the box.

Formatting phrases and sentences

If you want to *selectively format* individual letters, words, or sentences, first select the text box by clicking on it. When the flashing vertical I-beam appears, click on the space before the letter, word, or sentence and—while holding down the mouse button—drag the text tool through the desired words, highlighting them. Release the mouse button when you have completed highlighting the words you want to reformat. Then apply the desired Style or Text attributes.

Formatting individual words

Double-clicking is a shortcut that helps you highlight individual words quickly. You can highlight a word simply by double-clicking on it with the I-beam pointer.

EDIT YOUR WORDS

Editing is an essential part of the presentation-design process. Your presentation will improve if you constantly review your work and edit previously entered text. This involves

- Eliminating unnecessary words
- Searching for one word that will do the work of two
- Replacing long words with short words

To edit previously entered text

- Click anywhere in the text block.
- Double-click on the word you want to replace or highlight the word or phrase you want to replace by dragging the I-beam through it.

After you highlight one or more words, you can

- Permanently eliminate the word or phrase by choosing Clear or by pressing the Backspace or Delete key
- Move the word to a different location by using the Cut and Paste commands
- Directly type in a replacement word, phrase, or sentence

Although editing is often thought of in terms of content, visual editing will play a major role in the success of your presentation. Visual editing includes techniques such as the elimination of words isolated by themselves on a line. These can be very distracting.

Often you can eliminate *widows*—a word or part of a word isolated on a line—by removing or replacing a word in a previous line or by temporarily increasing the width of the box containing the text. Notice the distracting widow in Figure 5-22.

You can eliminate the widow by judicious editing—in this case, simply by replacing a long two-word phrase ("The discretionary") with one medium-long word ("Optional"), as shown in Figure 5-23 on the following page.

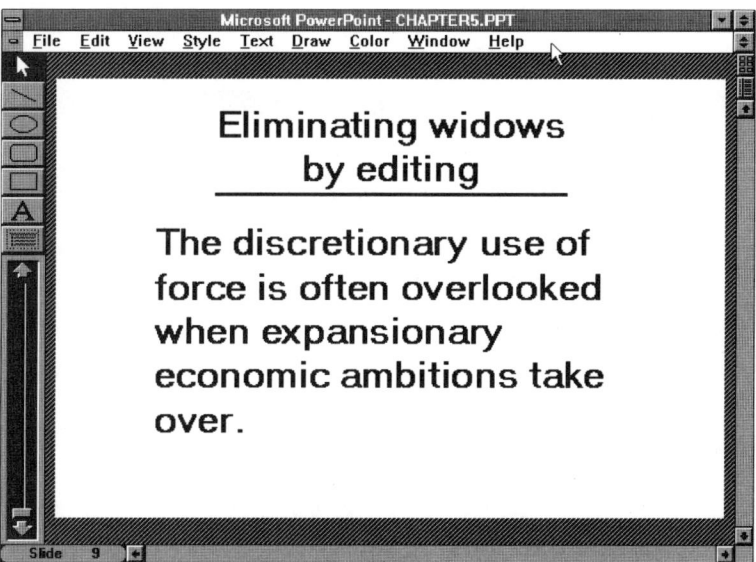

Figure 5-22. *Notice how the single word on a line by itself (a widow) distracts your eye.*

SECTION II: BASIC SKILLS

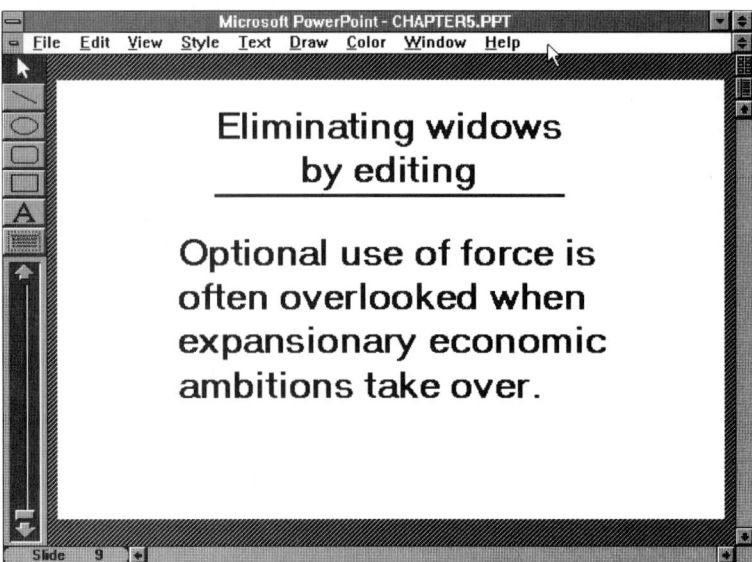

Figure 5-23. Replacing the first two words in Figure 5-22 ("The discretionary") with one word ("Optional") eliminates the widow.

ADD TEXT ENHANCEMENTS

In addition to allowing you to choose the typeface, type size, type style, alignment, indents, and line spacing most appropriate to your text, you can manipulate the backgrounds against which text will appear. You can also use color to enhance your text.

Enhancements Located in the Draw Menu

By themselves or used together, the following Draw menu commands can greatly enhance the appearance of text contained in your visuals.

Opaque

The Opaque command determines how the text will relate to objects already present on the slide—either objects present on the Slide Master or objects added to the individual slide you're working on. If you choose Opaque, the text hides objects located behind it, as shown in Figure 5-24.

If you don't choose Opaque, text appears in front of any previously placed objects. (See Figure 5-25.)

132

Chapter 5: Adding Impact to Words

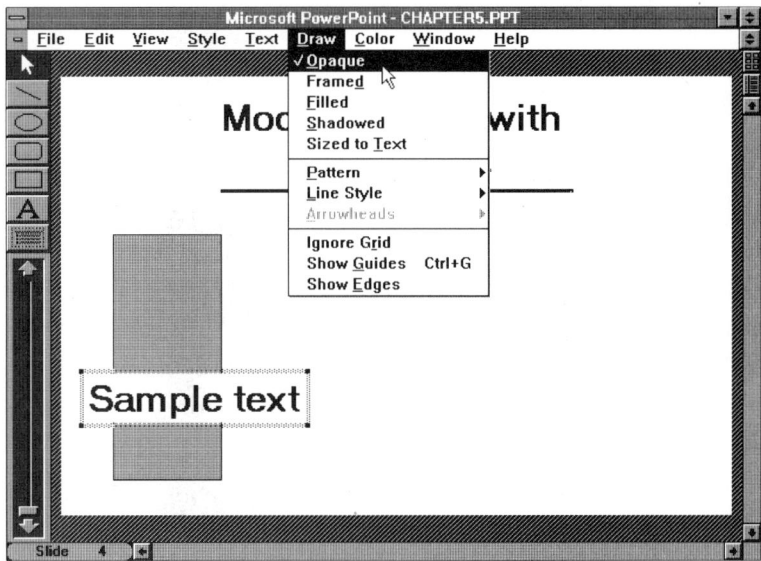

Figure 5-24. *When you open the Draw menu and choose Opaque, the text hides objects located behind it.*

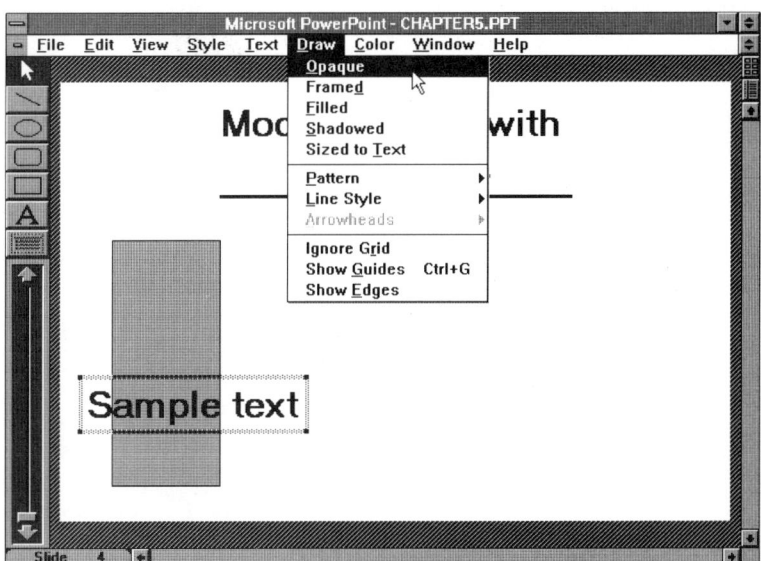

Figure 5-25. *When the Opaque command is not chosen, the text appears against whatever background objects are present.*

Framed

The Framed command allows you to create a box around text entered using the Word Processor or Labeler tools. (See Figure 5-26.) Framed can be used with Opaque either selected or deselected.

The Line Style command allows you to choose the desired thickness of the frame surrounding the text. Six line thicknesses are available, as are double or triple lines.

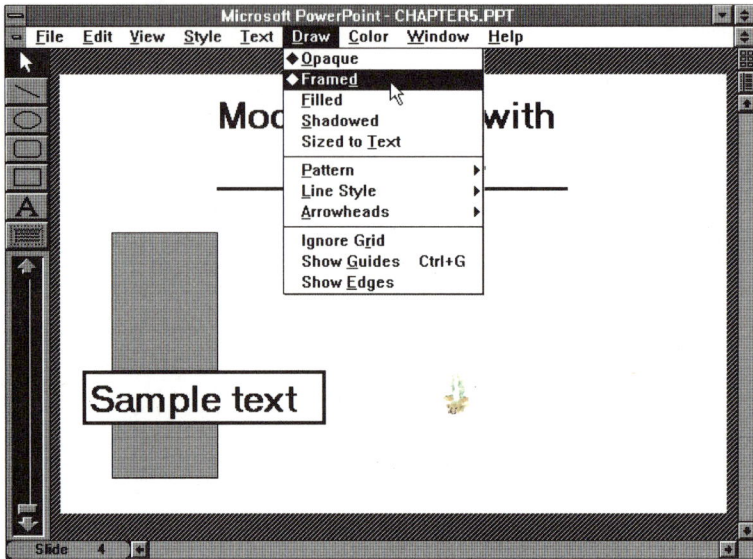

Figure 5-26. *Choose Framed from the Draw menu if you want to outline the text area.*

Filled

The Filled command allows you to emphasize your words by placing them against a background that helps them stand apart from the slide background.

To choose among various solid, shaded, and lined backgrounds, choose the Pattern command from the Draw menu and click on the desired background. (See Figure 5-27.)

Chapter 5: Adding Impact to Words

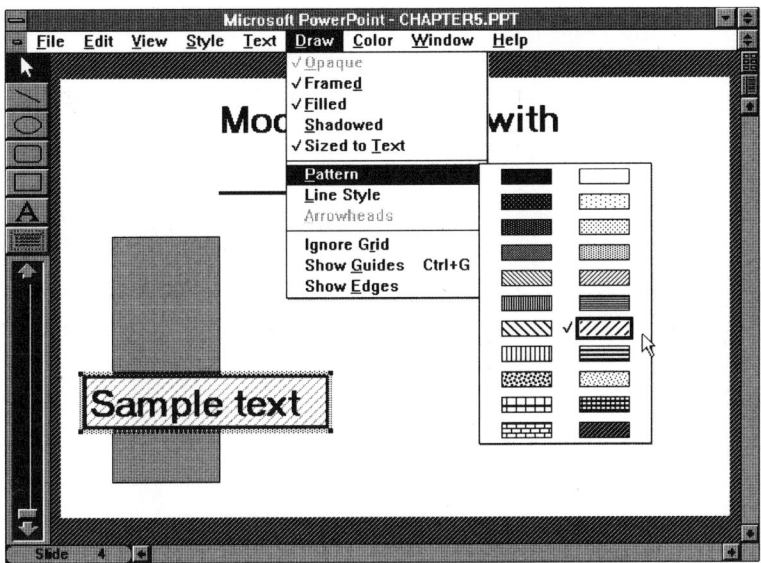

Figure 5-27. *The Pattern dialog box lets you enhance text by means of a variety of backgrounds.*

Shadowed

When you choose the Shadowed command, the text is automatically made Opaque. (See Figure 5-28 on the following page.) Notice that Shadowed *refers to the box* surrounding the text, *not* to the text itself. Don't confuse the Shadowed command in the Draw menu with the Shadow text style located in the Text menu of Macintosh PowerPoint, which refers to the way the letters themselves appear on your slide or overhead.

Sized To Text

Choose the Sized To Text command if you want the text frame or background to expand or shrink to accommodate the number of words in the type size you've chosen.

If you don't choose Sized To Text, the text frame and outline remain the same, even if you edit the text or reduce the type size. (See Figure 5-29 on the following page.)

SECTION II: BASIC SKILLS

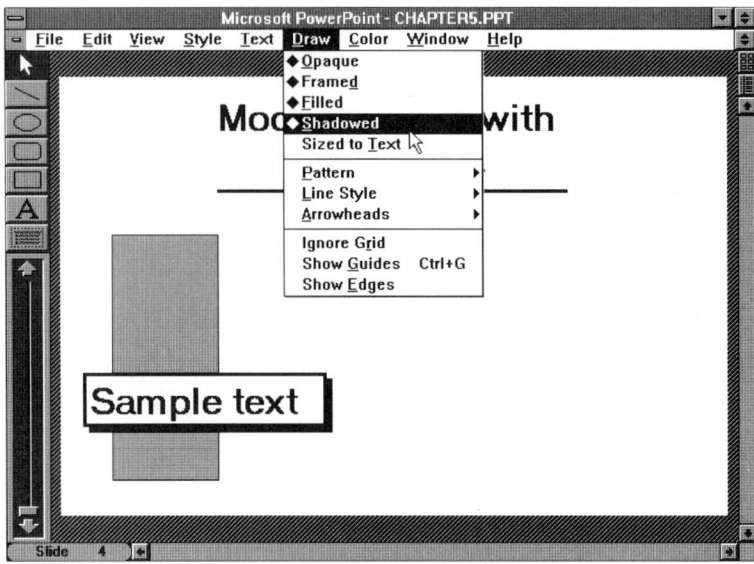

Figure 5-28. The Shadowed command makes text opaque and creates a three-dimensional effect.

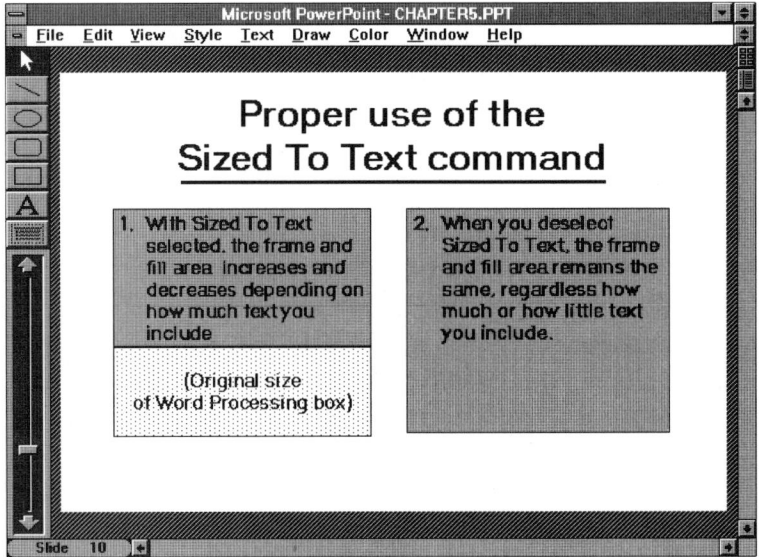

Figure 5-29. Do not choose the Sized To Text command if you want an identical text frame and background on each slide.

Working with Color

Color is one of the most important text enhancements available. You can enhance your words by means of color in four ways.

- ◆ Choose the colors you want before you choose the Labeler tool, Attached Label feature, or Word Processor tool.
- ◆ Select a text box or object by clicking on it.
- ◆ Highlight a word by double-clicking on it.
- ◆ Select a phrase or sentence by dragging the text tool through it.

In addition, you can establish styles and defaults to speed your work and ensure slide-to-slide consistency. Styles and defaults, as described later in this chapter, will also make it easier to quickly make major changes throughout your presentation.

Color menu

The Color menu contains the commands that allow you to enhance your presentation by controlling the color of words and their surroundings.

- ◆ Choose the Fill command when you want to see the background against which your words appear.
- ◆ Choose the Line command to specify the color of the frame surrounding your words.
- ◆ Choose the Shadow command to specify a color to add a three-dimensional effect to the box containing your words.
- ◆ Choose the Text command to specify the color of the words themselves.

In addition, the Pattern Contrast command allows you to place type against a two-color background that uses different colors for foreground and background accents.

In each case, the color options you're presented with are determined by the Color Scheme you adopt when planning and designing your presentation. The first options you're presented with are based on the many years of experience Genigraphics has had in choosing compatible colors.

Color considerations

Color is one of the most powerful design tools. Your presentations gain in impact and legibility to the extent that you provide sufficient contrast between text and surrounding backgrounds. This can be accomplished by using

- Dark-colored text against light backgrounds
- Light-colored text against dark backgrounds

These backgrounds can be either the background colors of the Slide Masters or the backgrounds created using the Filled and Shadowed tools created with the Draw menu and colored with the Color menu.

For example, a Word Processor box with a dark background can be placed against a Slide Master that has a light background. Or a light-colored Word Processor box can be placed against a dark-colored Slide Master. In either case, the result is the same: The audience's attention is drawn to the words.

Insufficient color contrast seriously weakens your presentation. For example, light-colored text against a light-colored background is both visually boring and hard to read. The same is true of dark text against a dark background.

The same principles of contrast apply to frames and shadows. A light-colored frame surrounding a light background lacks impact, as does a dark frame surrounding a dark background.

Using color consistently

Your presentations will gain in strength to the extent that you build unity and contrast into your color combinations. Adjacent colors should work well together and also be different enough to remain distinct. The Text, Frame and Fill colors used on Slide 1 should be repeated throughout your presentation. The only exception to this is when you use color to pace your presentation. For example, you might use different colors for the visuals located in the beginning, middle, and end of your presentation. Within these segments, however, your text color choices should remain the same.

Using color with numbers and bullets

Another way you can add visual interest to your presentation is to use contrasting colors for the bullets, numbers, or Zapf Dingbats you use to organize lists. Simply highlight the bullet, number, or symbol, and then choose Text from the Color menu. Choose a color that provides a strong contrast to the text it introduces, or choose the same color for the bullets as you're using for the title.

Using color to create text builds

You can also use color to create text "builds," which are used to introduce text on an item-by-item or line-by-line basis. This technique is described in Chapter 8, "PowerPoint Tips and Techniques."

ESTABLISH STYLES AND DEFAULTS

The Style features makes it easy to maintain consistency throughout your presentation. You can create style definitions by specifying the following major text attributes.

- Typeface
- Type size
- Type style
- Color

Defining Styles

You can define a style from scratch or you can use previously formatted text as the basis for creating a "Style by example."

Creating a new style

To create a new style, choose Define Styles from the Style menu. (See Figure 5-30 on the following page.) Click on the Font box, and a list of available typefaces appears. (In Windows PowerPoint, click on the arrow to the right of the box to activate the drop-down list.) Hold down the mouse button as you scroll through the list. Release the mouse button when you've chosen a typeface.

Next, click on the Color box and, while holding down the mouse button, scroll through the list of colors and release the mouse button when the desired color is highlighted.

In Windows PowerPoint, use the same procedure to select a font size using the Size box. In Macintosh PowerPoint, choose the leftmost Size box, and scroll through the list of available alternatives; or if you're using a PostScript laser printer, enter a specific size in the rightmost box.

Next, click on the type style alternative, or alternatives, you want: Bold, Italic, Underline, Outline, or Shadow for Macintosh PowerPoint and Bold, Italic, and Underline for Windows PowerPoint.

SECTION II: BASIC SKILLS

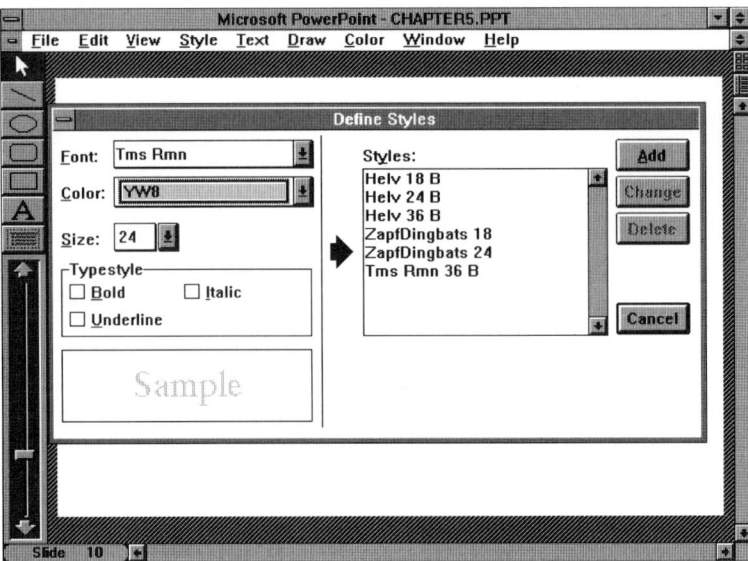

Figure 5-30. The Define Styles command makes it easy to preselect typeface, type size, type style, and color attributes.

Notice that each of your choices is reflected in actual size, in the colors chosen, in the preview window. When you're satisfied with your choices, click on the Add button.

Previewing your work

To preview your work, open the Style menu and choose Styles. If you're working with a color monitor, the various styles you've created will appear in color. This makes it easy to differentiate the style definition for 36-point Helvetica, in red, from the style definition for 36-point Helvetica, in blue.

Creating styles by example

You can also create a style by selecting and highlighting previously formatted text.

Start by selecting the text box. Then drag the I-beam through the words to highlight them. While the text is highlighted, choose Define Styles from the Style menu. Notice that the text appears in the Preview window. Click on Add; if you're satisfied with your choice, click on Done. The new style definition appears the next time you choose the Style menu.

Applying Styles

You can apply a Style to new text in two ways.

- ◆ You can choose a Style *before* you choose the Labeler tool, Attached Label feature, or Word Processor tool.

- ◆ You can choose a Style after you've chosen the text tool but before you begin entering the text.

You can also apply a Style to previously entered text either by selecting the text box or by highlighting the individual words, phrases, or sentences you want to reformat.

One option is to first open the Style menu and choose the Styles command, and—while holding down the mouse button—scroll through the list of available styles. (See Figure 5-31.) Release the mouse button when the style you want is highlighted.

Figure 5-31. *The Styles command, located on the Style menu, lets you scroll through a list of previously prepared styles.*

Notice that each style is accompanied by a numbered keyboard shortcut. Applying styles with these keyboard shortcuts will quickly become second nature to you. If you don't use a keyboard shortcut, you'll have to use the following sequence.

1. Remove your hands from the keyboard.
2. Use the mouse to open the Style menu.
3. Choose Styles.
4. Scroll through the list of previously defined styles while holding down the mouse button.
5. Release the mouse button when the Style you want is highlighted.

If you do use a keyboard shortcut, you can simply choose the style you want by doing the following.

- In Macintosh PowerPoint, hold down the Command key while entering the number associated with the Style.
- In Windows PowerPoint, hold down the Ctrl key while entering the number associated with the Style.

Rearranging styles

You can quickly rearrange the order of the styles in your Style menu. You might want to move frequently used styles closer to the top of the menu.

To move a style to a more convenient location, choose Define Styles and click on the style you want to move. Drag it to the new position while holding down the mouse button. Release the mouse button at the new location, and the Style definitions will be automatically renumbered to reflect the new order.

Removing styles

You can remove an infrequently used style definition from the Define Styles dialog box by clicking on it and clicking the Remove button in Macintosh PowerPoint, or the Delete button in Windows PowerPoint. PowerPoint will renumber the styles that remain to compensate for the missing number.

Establishing Text Defaults

In addition to defining typeface, type size, type style, and color, you can also set defaults for styles, text alignment, tabs, indents and line spacing.

Style default

To preselect your most frequently used style, choose the Arrow tool and click on an empty part of the screen. Open the Style menu and choose Styles. Click on the style you'll be using most frequently.

Text-alignment default

To specify a default text alignment, choose the Arrow tool and click on a blank part of the screen. Open the Text menu and choose Left, Right, Centered, or Justified.

Tabs, indents, and line-spacing defaults

Choose the Word Processor tool. Then choose Show Text Ruler and adjust tabs and indents. Now choose Line Spacing and set the appropriate line and paragraph spacing. After you're satisfied with your choices, choose Set As Default from the Text menu. Click on the Set It button, and the indents and line spacing will be in effect the next time you use the Word Processor tool.

The active Style and Text defaults are indicated by a small diamond. The next time you enter text, your defaults will dictate the appearance of your text.

These defaults are saved with your presentation. Unless you create a Default Presentation, as described in Chapter 8, however, you'll need to rechoose these defaults each time you open a new presentation.

REFINE YOUR WORK

The final step in adding text to your presentation involves checking for proper spelling and being sure that you haven't overused certain words.

The Spelling Command

You can avoid embarrassing typographical errors by using the spelling checker. To check your presentation, choose the Spelling command from the Text menu. (See Figure 5-32 on the following page.) The Spelling dialog box appears, and PowerPoint checks your entire presentation—including handout materials—for misspelled words.

When PowerPoint encounters an unfamiliar word, you can instruct it to

- Accept the word—for example, a client's name or a technical term
- Suggest an alternative spelling

SECTION II: BASIC SKILLS

- ◆ Check the word against PowerPoint's dictionary of exceptions
- ◆ Add the word to PowerPoint's "Added Words" dictionary

You can create as many specialized dictionaries as you need. You might create one dictionary for legal terms, another for medical terms, and so forth. To create a specialized dictionary, click the Added Words button. A dialog box opens, allowing you to add the word to the Added Words dictionary (the default), create a new dictionary, or open a previously created dictionary. A list of words contained in the selected dictionary appears in the dialog box. You can use the plus button and the minus button to add or delete words from the dictionary.

Note: PowerPoint's spelling checker can share specialized dictionaries created for Microsoft Word, eliminating the need to frequently add client names or specialized terminology.

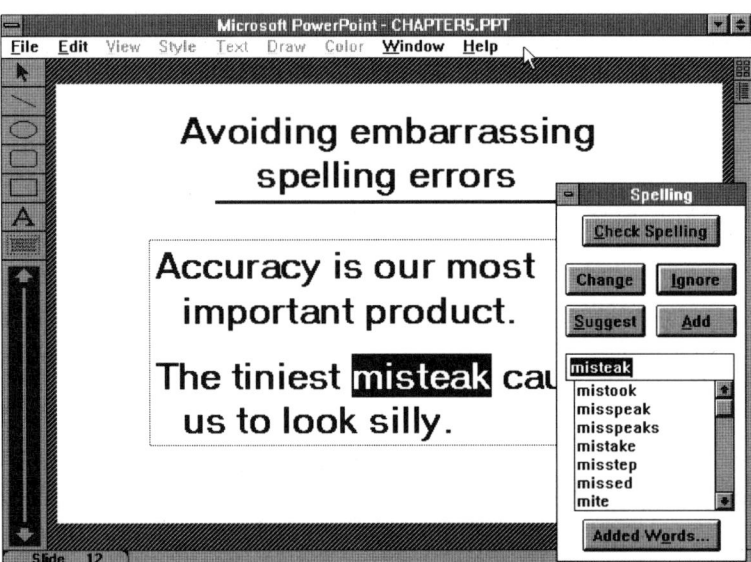

Figure 5-32. Use the Spelling command to avoid distracting and embarrassing errors.

The Find Commands

The Text menu also includes the Find/Replace command (in Macintosh PowerPoint), the Find/Change command (in Windows PowerPoint), and the Find Next command (in Macintosh and Windows versions).

You can use Find/Replace or Find/Change to customize an existing presentation for a new audience. For example, PowerPoint can search through your slides and handouts to locate every appearance of the previous audience's name and replace it with a new audience's name. (See Figure 5-33.) This feature can save you hours of work as well as improve accuracy.

The Find/Replace command can search and replace one word at a time or automatically replace all the occurrences throughout the presentation. You can also choose to match whole words regardless of case, all-uppercase words, or all-lowercase words.

The Find Next command allows you to monitor your use of words to avoid the inadvertent overuse of a word or phrase. Find Next searches your presentation for specified words or phrases, advances you to the next occurrence of the word or phrase, and highlights it. At this point, you can substitute a different word.

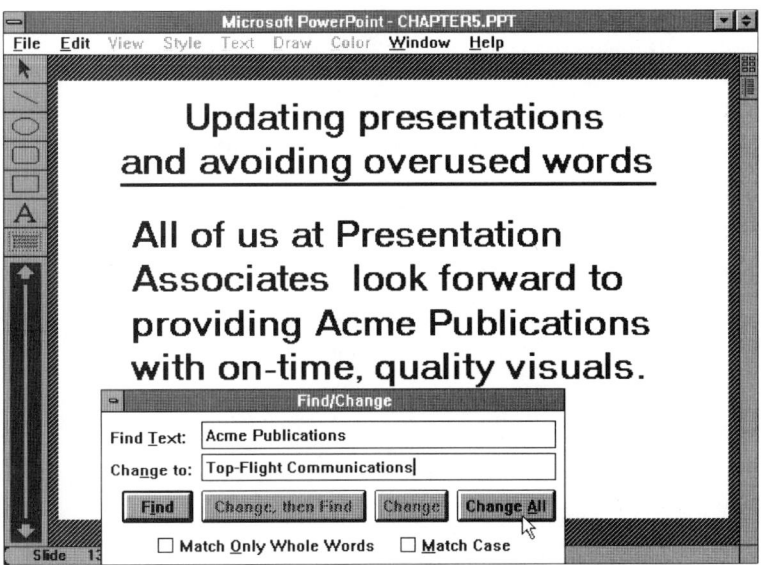

Figure 5-33. You can use the Find/Change command in Windows PowerPoint to update a presentation for a new client. (You use the Find/Replace command in Macintosh PowerPoint.)

ON-SCREEN LEGIBILITY

The legibility of words displayed during computer-based on-screen presentations can be greatly improved by using utilities such as Adobe Type Manager (available for both the Apple Macintosh and Windows 3.0 environments) and Bitstream Facelift (Windows 3.0 environment only).

These utilities improve the quality of on-screen presentations by replacing jagged letters with smooth ones. Adobe Type Manager and Bitstream FaceLift also permit you to use a wider variety of typeface alternatives with laser and ink-jet printers. Users of non-Postscript printers (such as Hewlett-Packard LaserJets and PaintJets) can access the entire Adobe typeface library.

EVALUATING YOUR PROGRESS

As you review your text formatting decisions, ask yourself the following questions.

- ◆ Did I choose the right text tool to place each category of text?
- ◆ Did I place my titles in the same relative position on each slide?
- ◆ Did I use the same typeface, type size, type style, alignment, color, and enhancements for all titles?
- ◆ Have I been consistent in the way I've placed, formatted, and enhanced text by using the Word Processor tool?
- ◆ Have I rigorously edited text, eliminating unnecessary words and avoiding long words and technical jargon?
- ◆ Have I included so much copy in my slides and overheads that my presence isn't needed at the presentation?
- ◆ Did I use the Spelling command frequently while preparing my presentation? Did I use it one last time before I printed my overheads or sent my slides to Genigraphics for production? (Typographical errors have a way of creeping in during last-minute changes.)
- ◆ Did I use the Find Next command to eliminate overused words?

Placing and Enhancing Files Created with Other Software Applications

You can enhance your visuals by adding a wide variety of graphical images created with other software programs. These can include charts, illustrations, scanned images, and images created using specialized programs—such as Microsoft Project for Windows. In addition, PowerPoint includes over 400 professionally drawn Genigraphics illustrations.

In this chapter, you'll learn how to import, resize, crop, and recolor graphical images as well as how to enhance them with frames, backgrounds, and shadows.

Three steps are involved in working with graphics files created by other software programs.

- ◆ *Choose a compatible file format.* Before importing a file, be sure that your output device is capable of reproducing it.

- ◆ *Import, resize, and crop the image.* PowerPoint's moving, resizing, and cropping commands allow you to place and modify graphics until they look their best.

- *Enhance the image.* You can further enhance your presentation by recoloring images and adding frames and backgrounds.

CHOOSE A COMPATIBLE FILE FORMAT

Many of the same principles that influence your typeface choices, described in Chapter 5, also influence your ability to work with previously prepared graphics files. Your choice of graphics file formats is limited by the output device you'll be using to produce your slides and overheads.

Although PowerPoint can import a wide variety of graphics formats, the capability to reproduce them is limited by the output device you'll be using to prepare 35mm slides, overheads, or on-screen presentations.

Black-and-White Transparencies

If you're preparing black-and-white overhead transparencies with a PostScript printer such as the Apple LaserWriter IINT, you can work with the widest variety of file formats, including graphics stored as Encapsulated PostScript Files created by programs such as Adobe Illustrator and Aldus Freehand. You can also work with scanned images saved as a Tag Image File Format (TIFF). You can choose graphics prepared with either Paint-type programs such as Claris MacPaint II and Windows Paint or draw-type programs such as Claris MacDraw II.

35mm Slides and Color Transparencies

If you're producing color overheads that will be printed on a color PostScript printer such as those available from NEC, QMS, or Tektronix, you can also include graphics saved in a wide variety of file formats.

Your choices are more limited, however, if you're preparing color transparencies with printers such as the Hewlett-Packard PaintJet or PaintJet XL or with other non-PostScript color printers. Unless your ink-jet or thermal color printer is specifically called a PostScript printer, you won't be able to satisfactorily reproduce Encapsulated PostScript (EPS) files, scanned images, or Paint-type files.

If you're using a non-PostScript film recorder, or if you're sending your PowerPoint files to Genigraphics for production of color slides or color overheads, you should also avoid graphics saved as EPS files.

If you attempt to reproduce an image saved as an EPS file on a non-PostScript output device, your presentation will contain a relatively coarse, unattractive image resembling an extremely grainy picture. This is because the printer or film recorder can reproduce only the relatively coarse image shown on the screen of your computer, not the actual stored image. Similarly, you're likely to be disappointed by the reproduction quality of graphical images created by Paint-type programs or scanned photographic images.

When working with film recorders or Genigraphics, restrict yourself to black-and-white (PICT) or color (PICT2) files. These file formats provide the best reproduction and the greatest flexibility for resizing and recoloring.

On-Screen Presentations

The same limitations that pertain to 35mm slides and color transparencies also pertain when you produce computer-based presentations using either liquid crystal display (LCD) projection panels or presentations viewed on your computer screen.

IMPORT, RESIZE, AND CROP THE IMAGE

Notice that the File and Edit menus contain three Paste commands.

- ◆ Use the Paste From command (located in the File menu) to import files prepared *and saved* with other software programs. (PowerPoint's Paste From command is similar to the Import and Place commands found in other software programs.)

- ◆ Use the Paste command (located in the Edit menu) to import files through the Apple Macintosh or Windows 3 Clipboard. If you're using Macintosh PowerPoint, you also use Paste to import images stored in the Macintosh Scrapbook. You also use Paste, in conjunction with the Copy command, to import any of the more than 400 Genigraphics illustrations included with Macintosh PowerPoint and Windows PowerPoint.

- ◆ Use the Paste As Picture command in conjunction with the Cut command when you want to group objects together permanently.

How to Use PowerPoint's Paste Commands

You'll use the three Paste commands for different functions, depending on when the graphics file was created and on the particular hardware and software you're using.

Paste From command

To import a file prepared, created, and saved with software programs such as Adobe Illustrator, Microsoft Excel, Claris MacDraw, and Corel Draw or Micrografx Designer for Windows, choose the Paste From command from the File menu.

Scroll through your computer's various folders or subdirectories until you find the desired file. When it is highlighted, double-click on it and click OK or press Return. The desired image appears in the center of your PowerPoint screen, outlined by a fuzzy box. You can then move, resize, or crop it as described below.

Paste command

Use the Paste command to import graphics through the Apple Macintosh or Windows 3 Clipboard. If your computer has sufficient memory available, you can work with PowerPoint and a drawing program at the same time. You'll be able to switch quickly back and forth between them, importing graphical images as soon as you create them.

If you create, for example, an image with a drawing program, you can copy it to the Macintosh or Windows Clipboard, return to PowerPoint, and choose Paste. The image appears on your PowerPoint slide, allowing you to move, resize, crop, or enhance it.

The Paste command is also used to import the Genigraphics illustrations included with PowerPoint. If you're using Macintosh PowerPoint, you'll use Paste to import charts created with Microsoft Excel. (See Chapter 7.)

Paste As Picture command

As described in Chapter 2, the Paste As Picture command is used in conjunction with the Cut command to group text or graphical objects.

Working with Genigraphics Illustrations

PowerPoint contains over 400 pieces of color clip art from the Genigraphics library. You can use these professionally drawn images to enhance presentations based on 35mm slides, overhead transparencies, and on-screen presentations. The Genigraphics illustrations offer exceptional quality and flexibility. You can use them on black-and-white overheads printed on PostScript laser printers or on 35mm slides and color overheads produced from files you send to Genigraphics. (Note: The Genigraphics library contains over 20,000 images that can be put into your PowerPoint, for a fee.)

The following categories of Genigraphics illustrations are included in PowerPoint.

- Animals
- Architecture (buildings, city skylines, and so forth)
- Backgrounds
- Business
- Education
- Entertainment
- Household
- International
- Maps
- People
- Presentation helpers (pointing hands, arrows, and so forth)
- Scientific
- Sports
- Technical
- Transportation

Locating a specific image

To make it easy to locate a specific Genigraphics illustration, each image is stored as an individual PowerPoint file. Each illustration is also stored as an individual slide. (See Figure 6-1 on the following page.)

To preview the Genigraphics artwork included with PowerPoint, do the following.

1. Choose Open from the File menu.
2. If you're using Macintosh PowerPoint, choose the Genigraphics clip-art folder. If you're using Windows PowerPoint, choose the Genigraphics clip-art subdirectory (clipart).
3. Scroll through the list of categories. Double-click on the title of the desired clip-art category, for example, Architecture or People. Or click on Open, or press Return.

4. When the PowerPoint file containing the selected category of Genigraphics clip-art appears, use the Upward and Downward arrows located at the left of the PowerPoint screen to scroll through each file, previewing the images stored on each slide.

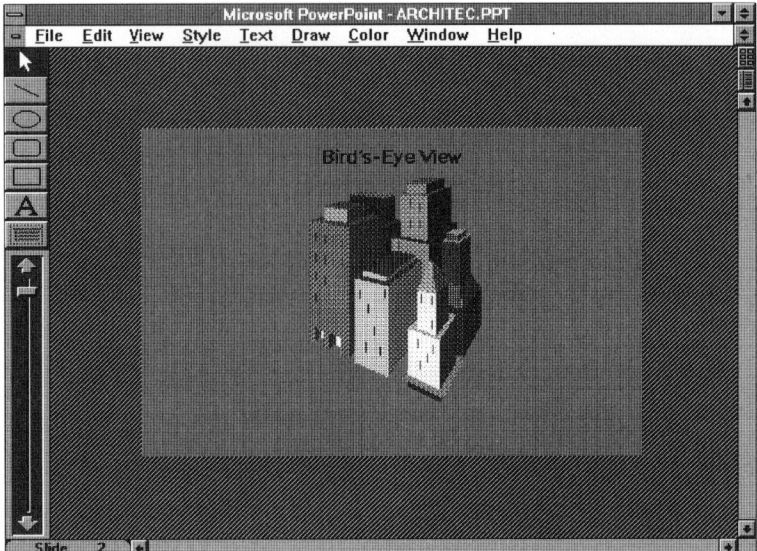

Figure 6-1. Each Genigraphics illustration is stored as an individual PowerPoint slide, making it easy to preview available images.

Importing a Genigraphics illustration

1. When you locate a desired Genigraphics image, select it by clicking on it.

2. While it is selected, choose Copy from the Edit menu. (This places the image in the Apple Macintosh or Windows 3 Clipboard.)

3. Close the Genigraphics file.

4. Paste the image onto the desired slide of your original PowerPoint presentation.

Separating and repeating Genigraphics images

Many Genigraphics images can be used in more than one way. Several of the Genigraphics clip-art items consist of individual pieces that can be used in multiple. For example:

◆ Slide 17 of the Business file contains a coin that can be copied and pasted to create a pile of coins. (See Figure 6-2.)

Chapter 6: Placing and Enhancing Files Created with Other Software Applications

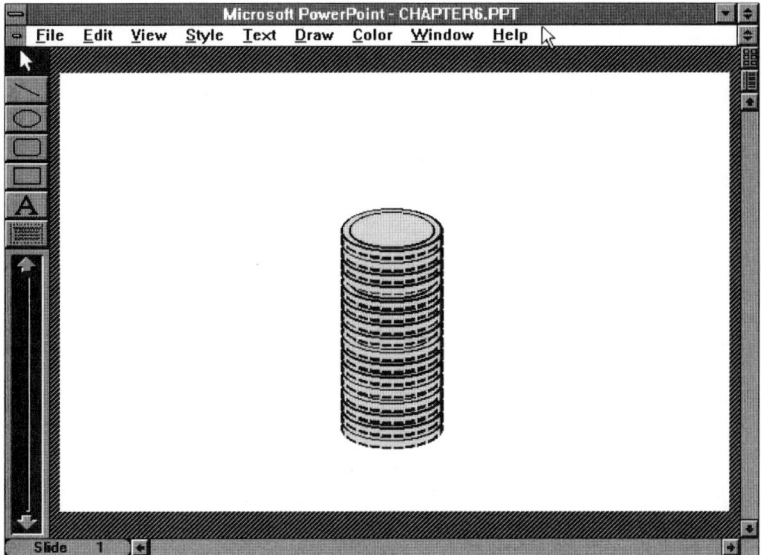

Figure 6-2. *Genigraphics illustrations take on a new look when they are used in multiple. Here, a single coin has become a pile with the "help" of the Paste command.*

- Slide 7 of the Business file contains a desk, file cabinet, calendar, and clock that can be used individually.

- Slide 12 of the People-2 file contains 10 separate people; the slide can be used over and over again—especially if the people are recolored to disguise their common origin.

In addition, many of the backgrounds found in the Genigraphics Color Special Effects sample files can be copied and used as the basis for new presentations, as described in Chapter 12. In this case, you use the Genigraphics clip art as the basis for the presentation Slide Master.

To import an element from one of the Genigraphics Color Special Effects sample files, do the following.

1. Select the appropriate Genigraphics illustration. (See the list of Genigraphics sample files, at the top of the next page.)

2. Copy the desired artwork into the Clipboard.

3. Return to your original presentation, and use Paste to place the image on the Slide Master of your new presentation.

The following is a list of Genigraphics sample files containing reusable backgrounds.

- The "perspective grid," on Slide 17 of the Background file. It can be copied and used in another location.
- The "sunken horizon," on Slide 18 of the Background file.
- The "perspective" drawing, on Slide 19 of the Background file.
- The "stars," found on Slide 22.

Using the Macintosh Scrapbook Feature

The Macintosh Scrapbook desk accessory can be used to increase your efficiency. The Scrapbook permits you to save multiple images in one location for easy retrieval. These images remain accessible even after you turn off your computer at the end of a work session. The Scrapbook allows you to

- Save several images at a time
- Easily preview available images
- Save time by storing images from different software programs

Storing images using the Macintosh Scrapbook

To use the Macintosh Scrapbook feature, do the following.

1. Select an image from one of the files in the Genigraphic clip-art folder.
2. Click on the image, and copy it by using the Copy command.
3. Open the Scrapbook, and use the Paste command to place the image in the Scrapbook.
4. Close the Scrapbook by clicking on the Close box at the upper left.
5. Select another image from the same Genigraphics clip-art file, and use Copy to place it.
6. Once again, open the Scrapbook, and use Paste to place the image in the Scrapbook. Notice that a second page of the Scrapbook is opened.

The two small numbers, separated by a slash, at the lower left of the Scrapbook window indicate the number of the current image and the total number of stored images. (See Figure 6-3.)

Chapter 6: Placing and Enhancing Files Created with Other Software Applications

Figure 6-3. The Macintosh Scrapbook feature lets you open multiple Scrapbook files.

Notice that the first images stored in the Scrapbook are pushed to the right and that the newest images have the highest number.

Placing a Scrapbook image into a PowerPoint presentation

To import an image stored in the Macintosh Scrapbook into a PowerPoint presentation, open the Scrapbook and preview your stored images by clicking on the left and right arrows, or use the elevator box in the middle to rapidly advance to the approximate location of the desired image.

1. When you reach the desired image, click on it and copy it by using the Copy command.

2. Select your target PowerPoint presentation by clicking on any part of the slide. This action sends the Scrapbook behind the presentation.

3. Paste the image onto your PowerPoint presentation.

4. To select another Scrapbook image, click on the portion of the Scrapbook window visible at the bottom of your screen and repeat the process of selecting, copying, and pasting. When finished, close the Scrapbook by clicking on the Close box at the upper left.

Remember that, unlike images in the Macintosh Clipboard, images stored in the Scrapbook remain when you turn off your computer. Thus, when you resume work on your presentation, the same images will still be available in the Scrapbook. This allows you to store frequently used images in the Scrapbook. It also allows you to devote one working session to selecting visuals and pasting them into the Scrapbook and a later session to placing them on individual PowerPoint slides.

Moving Images

Regardless of how you import a graphic, you can move it to a new location after you have placed it on the PowerPoint screen. To move a graphic in both Macintosh PowerPoint and Windows PowerPoint, do the following.

1. Select the object by clicking on it (unless it's already selected).
2. Relocate it by clicking on one of the fuzzy borders surrounding the image and holding down the mouse button while you drag the image in the direction you want to move it.
3. Release the mouse button and click elsewhere on the slide when the graphic is in the desired location.

In addition, if you're using Windows PowerPoint, you can use the right mouse button to both select an object by clicking on it and immediately move it. This is a great time-saver.

Resizing Images

Regardless of an image's origin, resizing permits you to dramatically change the appearance of a graphic.

To resize an image, do the following.

1. Select it by clicking on it (unless it is already selected).
2. Click on one of the buttons located at one of the four corners.
3. To enlarge the image, drag the button away from the image. To shrink the image, drag the button into the image. Dragging the button horizontally distorts the image sideways, and dragging the button vertically changes the height of the image.

Resizing typically distorts the graphic by changing its aspect ratio (height-to-width ratio), as shown in Figures 6-4 and 6-5.

Chapter 6: Placing and Enhancing Files Created with Other Software Applications

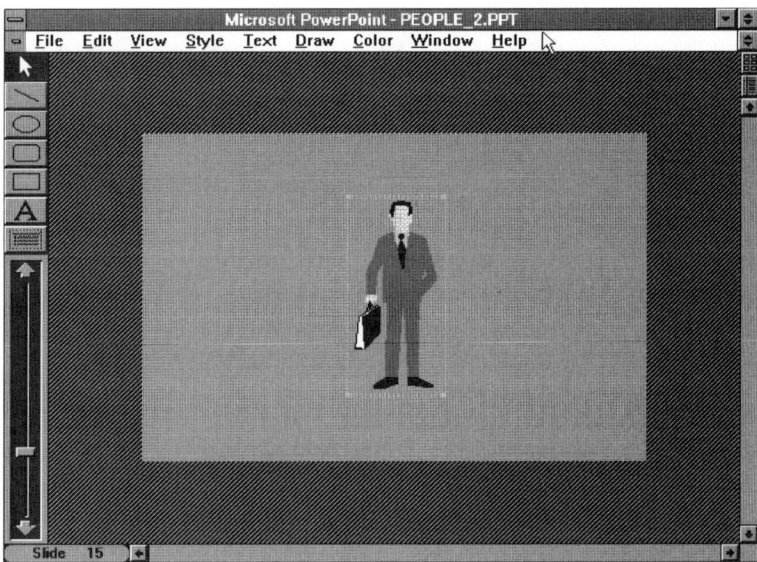

Figure 6-4. *Compare this original Genigraphics illustration with the distorted version shown in Figure 6-5.*

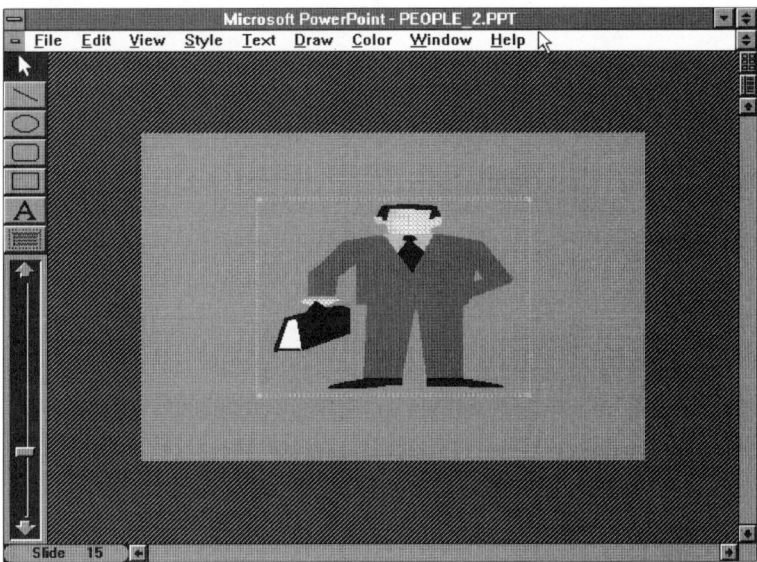

Figure 6-5. *This is the distorted version of the original Genigraphics illustration shown in Figure 6-4.*

157

Maintaining an object's original aspect ratio

To avoid unintentionally distorting the image, hold down the Shift key as you drag one of the corner buttons at approximately a 45-degree angle. (See Figure 6-6.) This resizes the graphic but maintains its original proportions.

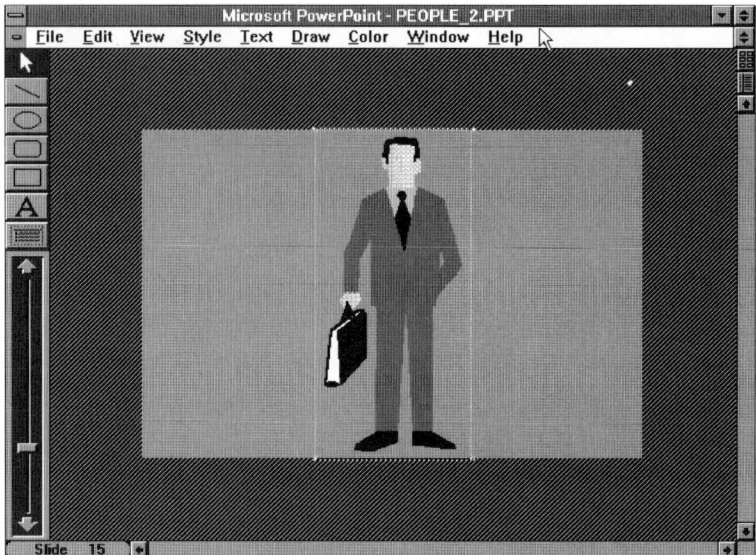

Figure 6-6. *Hold down the Shift key while resizing an image if you want to retain the original height-to-width ratio of the Genigraphics illustration shown in Figure 6-4.*

Maintaining both location and aspect ratio

You can resize an image from its center, maintaining its original location while making it larger or smaller. This saves you time because you don't need to relocate the graphic after it has been resized.

- ◆ Hold down both the Shift key and the Option key (Shift-Option) if you're using Macintosh PowerPoint.

- ◆ Hold down both the Shift key and the Ctrl key (Shift-Ctrl) if you're using Windows PowerPoint.

Cropping Images

Cropping involves trimming a portion of an imported image—from the top, bottom, or sides. Cropping eliminates extraneous detail at the edges of an image. Cropping also changes the shape of the image.

Chapter 6: Placing and Enhancing Files Created with Other Software Applications

The Crop Picture command of Windows PowerPoint is located in the Edit menu. You can also access it by using the Ctrl-C keyboard shortcut. The Crop Picture command creates a pair of "scissors" (called the cropping tool) that can be used on one of the corner buttons. (See Figure 6-7.)

To crop an object with Macintosh PowerPoint, first select the object. Then click on one of the corner buttons and drag horizontally or vertically while holding down the Command key. You can simultaneously crop from the top and one side of the object by clicking on one of the buttons at the top of the object and dragging diagonally while holding down the Command key.

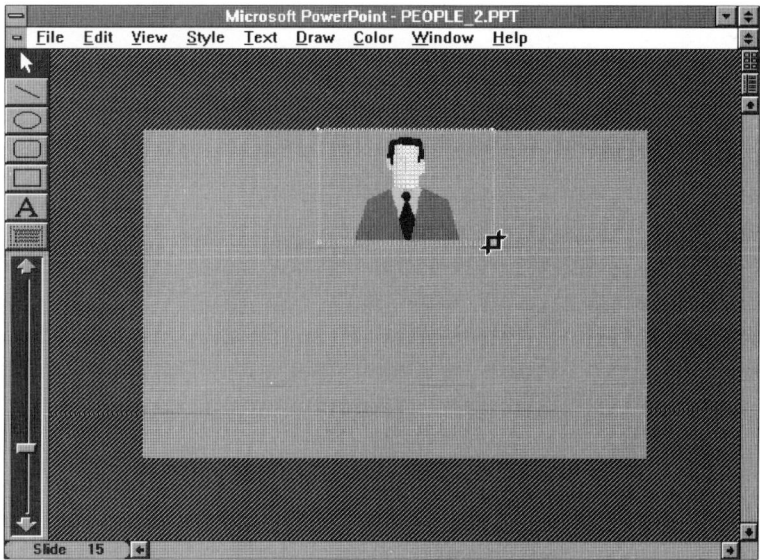

Figure 6-7. *The Crop Picture command, located on the Edit menu of Windows PowerPoint, lets you define the part of an image that you want to use.*

Returning an image to its original size

You can return a cropped image to its original size. To "uncrop" an image with Windows PowerPoint, select the image, open the Edit menu and choose the Crop Picture command (or press Ctrl-C), click on one of the corner buttons with the cropping-tool cursor, and move in the desired direction. This allows you to restore the image to its original dimensions and proportions. In Macintosh PowerPoint, you can uncrop an image by holding down the Command key while dragging the corner button.

ENHANCE THE IMAGE

In addition to moving, resizing, and cropping images, you can camouflage the origins of existing artwork by recoloring it to match your presentation's Color Scheme. You can also choose various framing and background effects.

Recoloring Imported Graphics

You can use the Recolor Picture command, located in the Color menu, to make the colors of imported graphical images match your Slide Master's Color Scheme. This integrates the graphical image into your presentation, enhancing its professionalism and preserving slide-to-slide consistency.

If you don't use the Recolor Picture command, you run the risk of creating color clashes between the imported images and those images already defined by your presentation's Color Scheme. Lack of color coordination can also make it seem as if the presentation had been thrown together hastily.

To recolor an imported image, select it by clicking anywhere on it. When the fuzzy border appears, open the Color menu and choose Recolor Picture. The Recolor Picture dialog box presents you with a reduced-size version of the graphic plus two vertical rows of boxes (Change, From, and To) along the right side. (See Figure 6-8.)

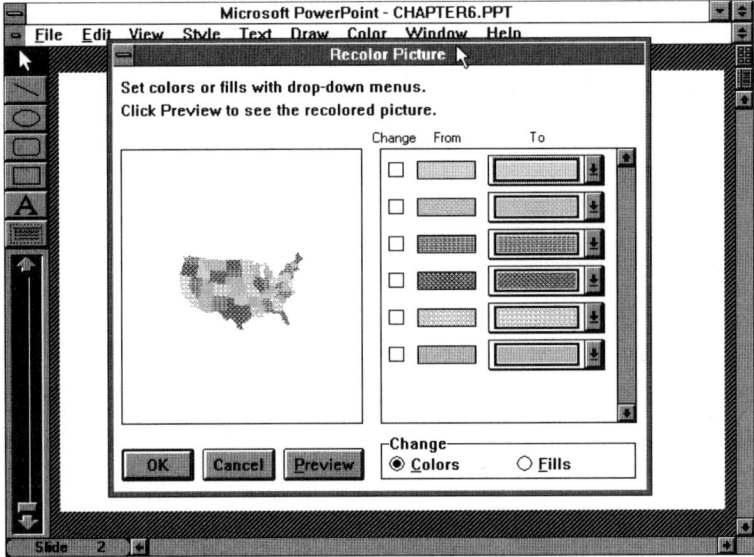

Figure 6-8. *The Recolor Picture dialog box lets you replace colors of imported graphical images with ones that are compatible with your presentation's Color Scheme.*

Chapter 6: Placing and Enhancing Files Created with Other Software Applications

Choose the Change Patterns option if you imported an image through the Macintosh Scrapbook or if you imported an Excel chart by using the Paste command. (See Figure 6-9.) These techniques replace colors with patterns. Choose the Change Colors option if you imported the image as a previously saved file using the Paste From command.

- Select an existing color from the image by clicking on the Change box associated with the corresponding color.

- When you click on the corresponding box to the right, you'll be presented with a list of colors compatible with your presentation's existing Color Scheme. Select a replacement color. Change as many colors as you want.

- When you've finished choosing replacement colors, click on Preview to see how the recolored image looks.

- If you like what you see in the Preview box, click OK or press Return.

When you return to Slide View, you'll notice that the graphic looks as if it "belongs."

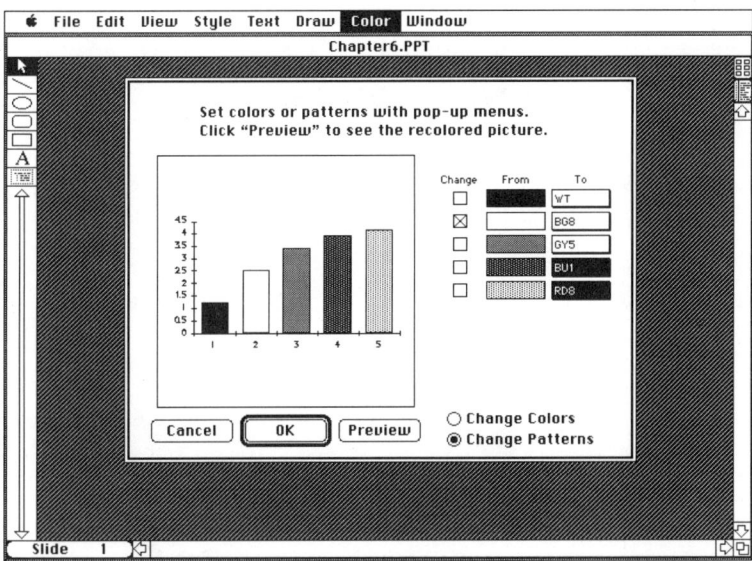

Figure 6-9. The Recolor Picture dialog box lets you replace the colors of an imported image. Here, a color used in a chart created with Microsoft Excel is being changed.

Adding Frames, Backgrounds, and Shadows

You can add frames, backgrounds, and shadows to graphics either before you import them or after they have been placed. These frames and backgrounds can either draw attention to the graphics or help integrate them into the overall look of your presentation.

Use the following Draw menu commands to enhance imported graphics.

- ◆ Opaque
- ◆ Framed
- ◆ Filled
- ◆ Shadowed

First, select the imported graphic by clicking on it. Next, open the Draw menu and choose one of the commands listed above.

Opaque

If you choose the Opaque command, the imported graphic appears with a background that is the same color as the slide background—but in front of any previously placed objects. (See Figure 6-10.)

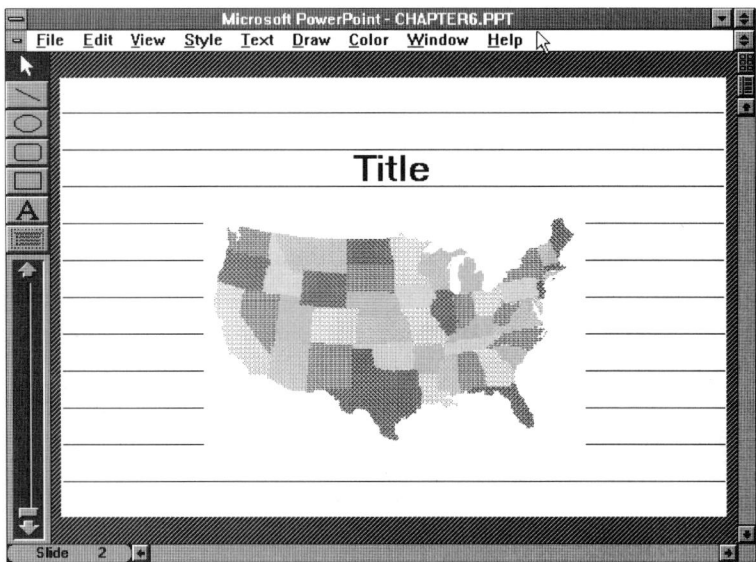

Figure 6-10. *An imported object with Opaque selected.*

Chapter 6: Placing and Enhancing Files Created with Other Software Applications

If you deselect Opaque, only the graphical image appears in front of previously placed background objects. (See Figure 6-11.)

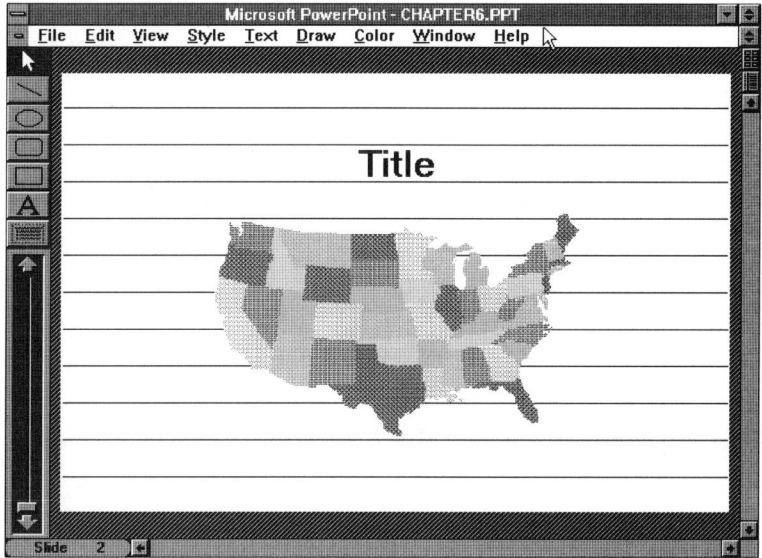

Figure 6-11. *Imported object with Opaque deselected.*

Framed

Choose the Framed command if you want to outline an object. (See Figure 6-12 on the following page.) You can pick the width of the frame by choosing the Line command located in the Draw menu. You can pick the color of the line by choosing Line from the Color menu.

Filled

If you choose the Filled command, the object appears against its own colored background. (See Figure 6-13 on the following page.) To change the color of the background, choose Fill from the Color menu. To change the pattern of the background, choose Pattern from the Draw menu. To place the object against a two-color background, choose Pattern Contrast from the Color menu.

SECTION II: BASIC SKILLS

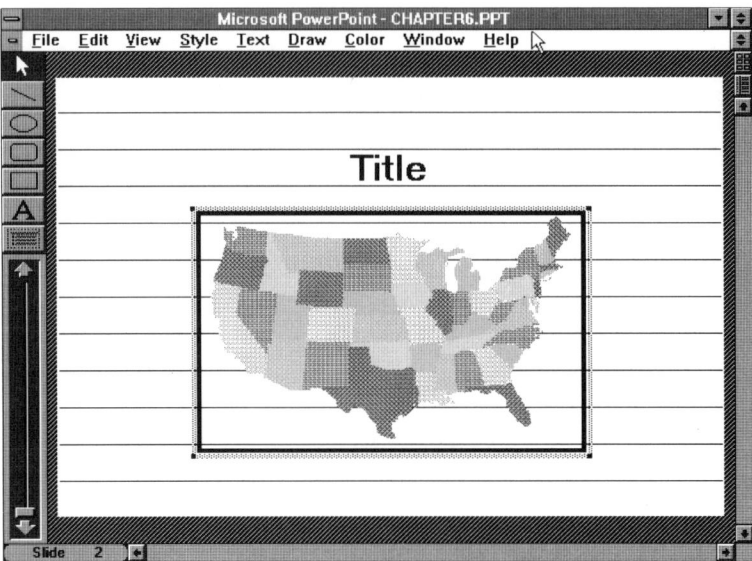

Figure 6-12. The Framed command lets you outline an imported graphic.

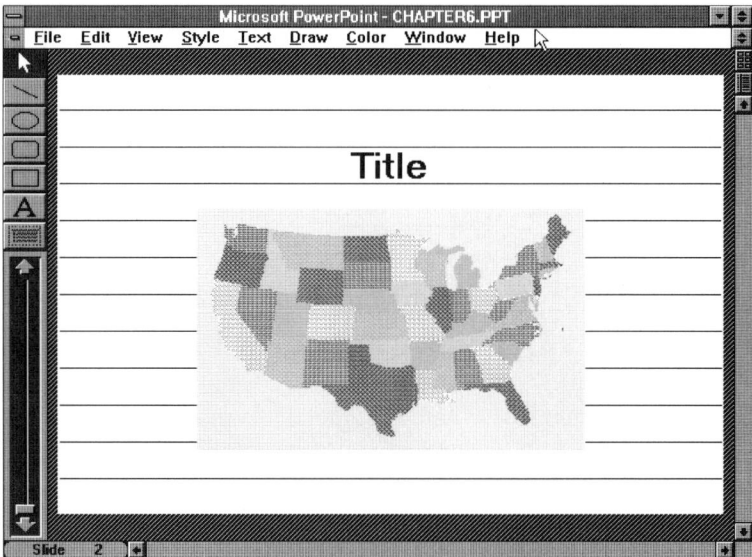

Figure 6-13. The Filled command lets you enhance an object by placing it against its own background.

Framed and Filled

If you choose both Framed and Filled, the object becomes clearly distinct from the Slide Master background. (See Figure 6-14.)

You can add further impact by choosing a patterned background. You can choose a second color for contrast by choosing the Patterned Contrast command from the Color menu, resulting in a two-color background.

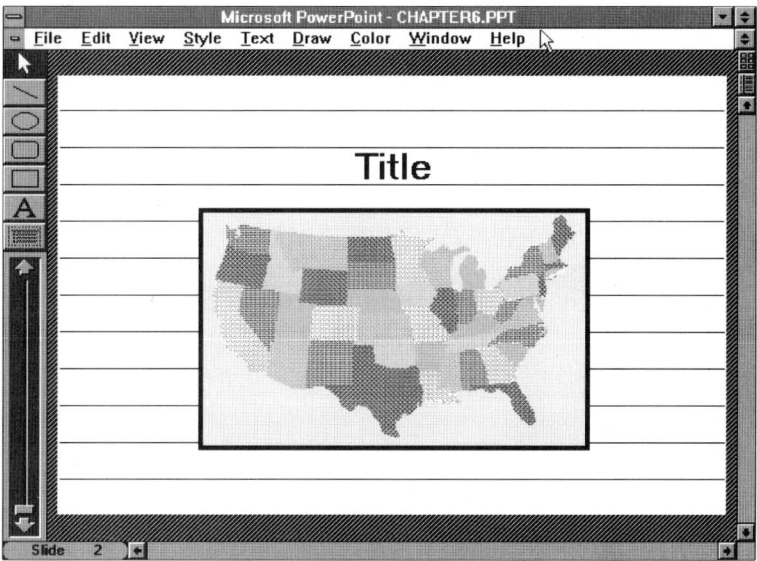

Figure 6-14. *The Framed and Filled commands, used together, let you emphasize an object by separating it from its background.*

Shadowed

You can add further emphasis to a framed and filled graphic by adding a shadow to it. Open the Color menu, and choose Shadow to choose an appropriate shadow color. (See Figure 6-15 on the following page.)

SECTION II: BASIC SKILLS

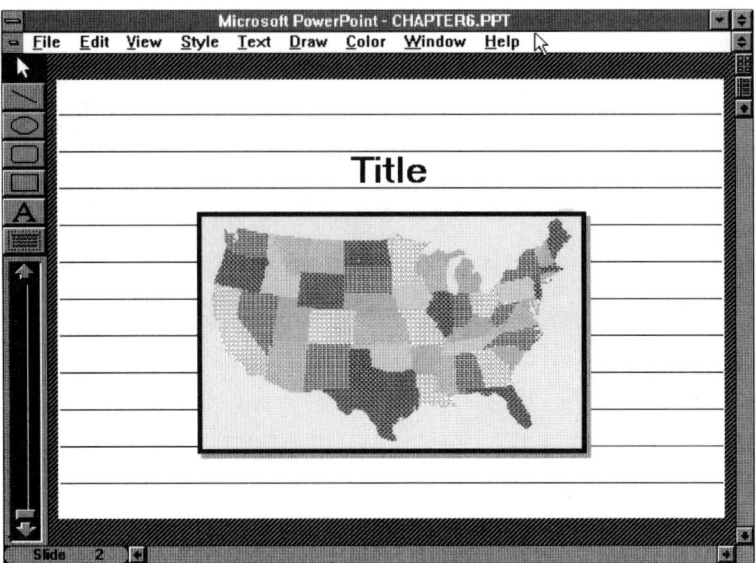

Figure 6-15. The Color menu's Shadow command, when applied to a graphic already framed and filled, results in a graphic that stands out the most.

EVALUATING YOUR PROGRESS

To evaluate your work, review each visual. As each slide appears on your computer screen, ask yourself the following questions.

- ◆ Are the graphical images appropriately sized so that they're neither so small that they're hard to see nor so large that they dominate the slide?

- ◆ Did I crop the images so that only the most important parts of the image remain?

- ◆ Do the colors of the imported graphics match the Color Scheme used in my presentation?

- ◆ How effectively did I use the Draw commands to enhance imported graphics?

- ◆ Was I careful to include only graphics file formats compatible with the output device I'll use to prepare my slides or overheads?

Translating Numbers into Charts and Graphs

People respond more immediately to visual images than to numbers alone and are more likely to remember images than numbers. Charts can express relationships and trends far more effectively than numbers. Charts allow you to transform even the most data-intensive presentation into memorable visuals your audience will react to favorably.

Windows PowerPoint contains a powerful graphing utility, PowerPoint Graph, that allows you to create a wide variety of charts. Microsoft Excel offers you the same capability whether you're using Windows PowerPoint or Macintosh PowerPoint. With Graph, you can easily create the type of chart that best illuminates the information and results in the interpretation you want to communicate. Graph also helps you format the chart so that it becomes an integral part of your presentation.

Follow these four steps when adding charts to your presentation visuals.

- *Enter the source data.* Charts derive from data organized in columns and rows. If you're using Macintosh PowerPoint, enter data in a Microsoft Excel worksheet. If you're using Windows PowerPoint, enter data in PowerPoint's built-in Datasheet. With both programs, you can also import information stored in previously created spreadsheets.

- ◆ *Create the right type of chart.* Several basic types of charts plus numerous variations are available. Choose the type of chart best suited to displaying the interpretation you want to stress. After creating the chart, you can format it to strengthen your message.

- ◆ *Format the chart.* PowerPoint allows you to format each part of the chart for maximum legibility and visual impact.

- ◆ *Place, resize, and enhance the chart.* The final step is to place the chart and integrate it into the overall design of your presentation, often recoloring it to correspond to or match your presentation's Color Scheme.

ENTER THE SOURCE DATA

You begin to create a chart by entering the information you want to display in chart form.

Windows PowerPoint

If you're using Windows PowerPoint, open the File menu and choose Insert Graph. The Datasheet and a default chart appear. (See Figure 7-1.)

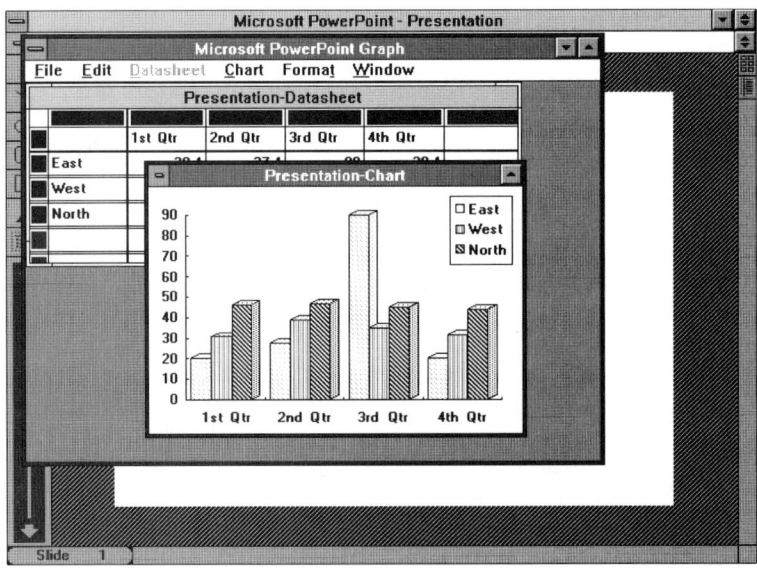

Figure 7-1. *The PowerPoint Windows Datasheet plus default chart.*

Notice that both the chart and the Datasheet are visible. To enter data, click on part of the Datasheet. To format the chart—or to choose a different type of chart—click on the chart.

The chart is updated as you enter information in the Datasheet. To observe this, replace the default *27.4* in the first row of the 2nd Qtr quarter with *500* and press Enter. Notice how the chart is instantly redrawn.

To eliminate previously entered data in the Datasheet (so you can begin working with a "clean" Datasheet), open the Edit menu and choose Select All. Next, open the Edit menu and choose Clear. If you prefer to use the Del keyboard shortcut, PowerPoint will ask you whether you want to clear data or formatting information or both. Choose Data, and then press Enter. You can now enter the numbers required for your chart.

To observe the power and flexibility of PowerPoint's Graph, take a few moments to enter the data in the table below in the Datasheet. (If you're working with Microsoft Excel, enter the same data in an Excel worksheet, as described below under "Importing Previously Entered Data.")

	1990	1991	1992	1993
East	500	550	600	640
West	900	860	750	800
North	125	250	325	450
South	780	800	650	650

Importing previously entered data

Using Windows PowerPoint, you can import data from existing spreadsheets into the Datasheet. To import data, do the following.

1. Click on the Datasheet.
2. Open the File menu.
3. Choose Import Data.

You can then change directories and scroll through previously prepared spreadsheets until you find the spreadsheet you want. When you locate that spreadsheet, double-click on its title or select the title from the list, and then click OK.

Working with Microsoft Excel in Macintosh PowerPoint

If you're using Macintosh PowerPoint, the first step in creating a chart is to start Microsoft Excel. If your Macintosh has enough memory to permit you to use MultiFinder, you'll be able to work faster because you'll be able to start both Excel and Macintosh PowerPoint and quickly switch between them.

When a blank Excel worksheet appears, enter the sample data contained in the table on the preceding page.

Working with Microsoft Excel in Windows PowerPoint

If you're using the Windows version of PowerPoint, you can create a chart using Microsoft Excel in one of two ways. You can start Microsoft Excel and enter your data as you normally would. Or you can choose the Insert command from the File menu and select the Excel Chart option. PowerPoint will automatically start Excel and open a new chart window titled "1PowerPoint." When you're finished with formatting (as explained later in this chapter), you can open a new or existing Excel chart or worksheet and copy the chart or worksheet data into the PowerPoint chart window.

CREATE THE RIGHT TYPE OF CHART

Microsoft Excel and Windows PowerPoint together can create a wide variety of charts and graphs. These include multiple versions of the six basic types of charts: area, bar, column, line, pie, and scatter.

Choosing the appropriate type of chart is a two-step process based on the data you want to display and the audience reaction you're after. To create a chart using either Windows PowerPoint or Microsoft Excel, do the following.

1. Determine the appropriate type of chart.
2. Choose the variation that best illustrates your data.

Using Windows PowerPoint

Choose the default chart by clicking on it. Next, open the Chart menu, and choose the type of chart you want from the menu options. After you choose a chart type, PowerPoint presents you with reduced-size versions of the available variations for that chart type. Double-click on the variation you want. The information you have previously entered in the PowerPoint Datasheet will instantly be translated into the type of chart you have chosen.

You might want to spend some time observing how the above data you entered in the Datasheet appears when you choose the following chart types.

Area

Area charts display comparative amounts as well as trends. Relative quantities as well as the direction of change are easily communicated. Options include versions that total 100 percent (options 2 and 7) as well as versions that drop lines (option 3) and background grids (option 4).

As the chart options in Figure 7-2 demonstrate, the alternatives located in the top row are three-dimensional versions, and those in the bottom row are flat, or two-dimensional.

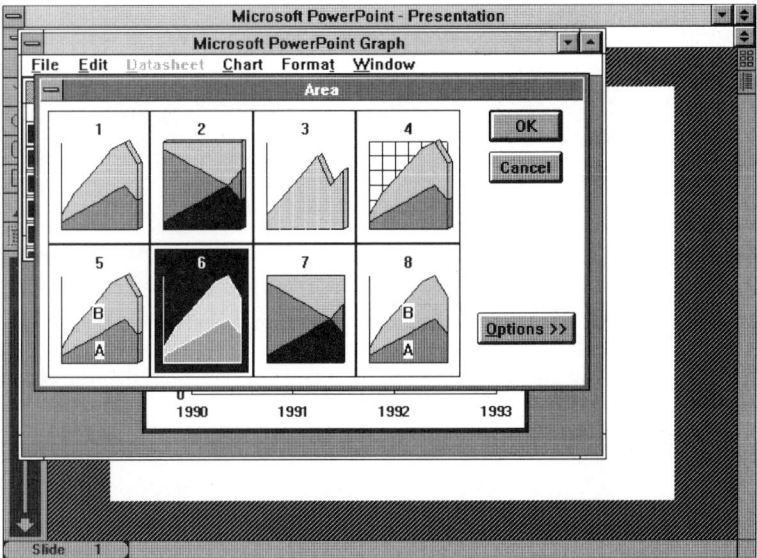

Figure 7-2. PowerPoint's area charts can be three-dimensional versions (top row) or flat versions (bottom row).

Bar

Horizontal bar charts (shown in Figure 7-3 on the following page) are used to quantify comparisons. Options include side-by-side bar placement (options 1 and 5), stacked bars (options 2 and 6), overlapped bars (option 7), and bars that extend to the left and right from a common starting point—useful for showing plus and minus figures (option 4). Options 3 and 8 total 100 percent.

SECTION II: BASIC SKILLS

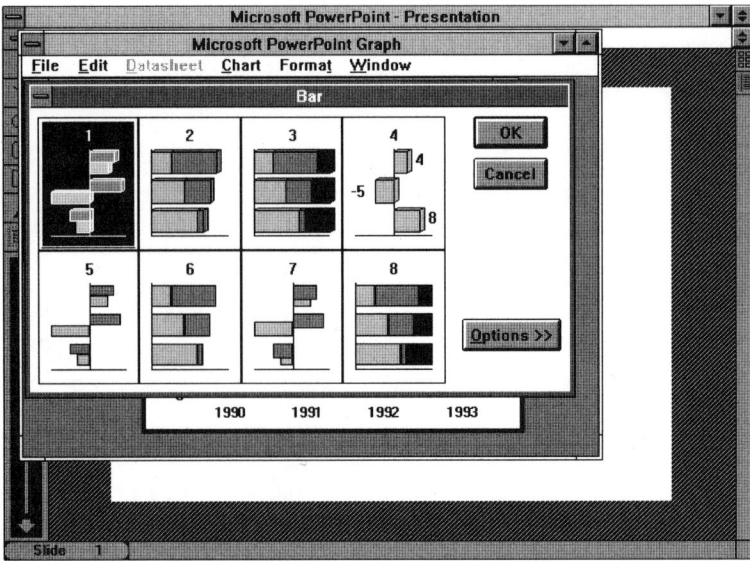

Figure 7-3. You can choose from among side-by-side, stacked, overlapping, and left–right bar charts.

Column

Column charts are similar to horizontal bar charts except that the data is displayed vertically. (See Figure 7-4.) Column charts include three-dimensional versions and flat (two-dimensional) versions.

Line

Choose a line, or "fever," chart when you want to display trends. (See Figure 7-5.) For example, you can display only lines (option 2), lines plus data points (options 1, 4, 5, and 6), or only data points (option 3). Notice that option 6 is a logarithmic chart, which is useful when the rate of change is exponential. Options 7 and 8 are high–low charts, commonly used for stock prices.

Pie

Choose pie charts when you want to emphasize part-to-whole relationships. (See Figure 7-6 on page 174.) Options include two-dimensional or three-dimensional images, exploded charts, and charts that compute the percentages for each slide (options 5 and 8).

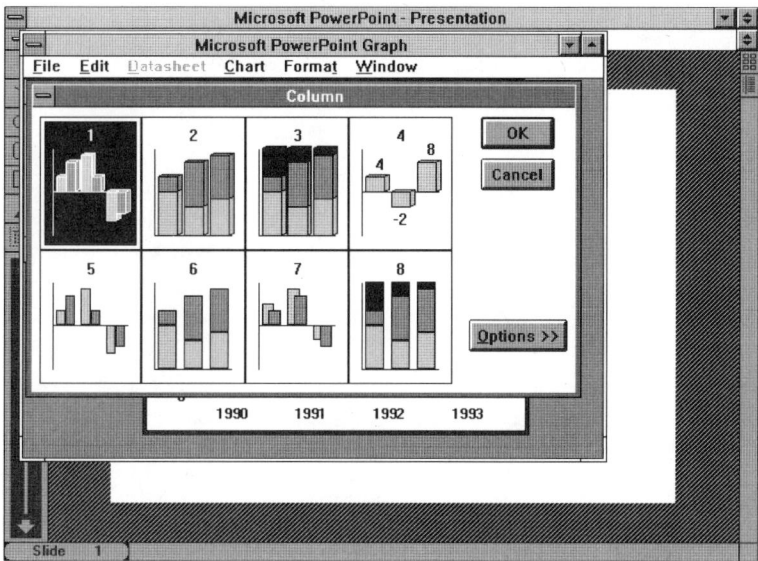

Figure 7-4. *You can choose from among various column-chart options.*

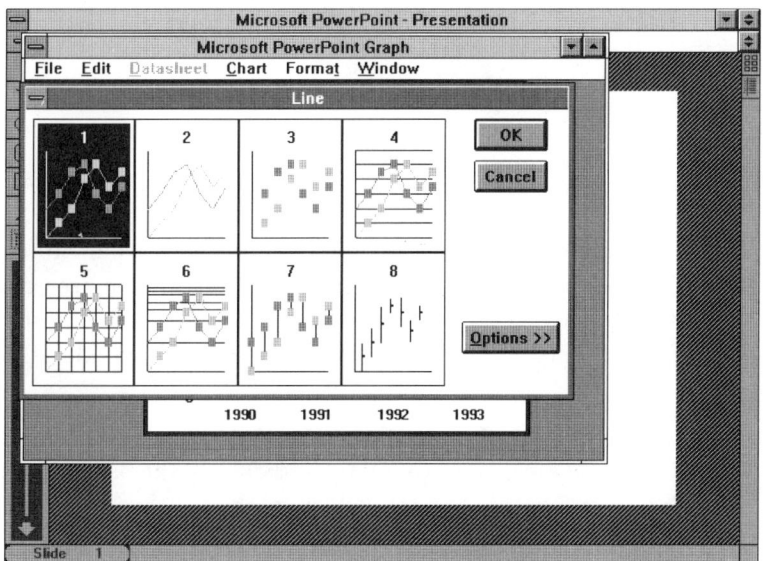

Figure 7-5. *You can choose one of PowerPoint's line-chart options to emphasize trends.*

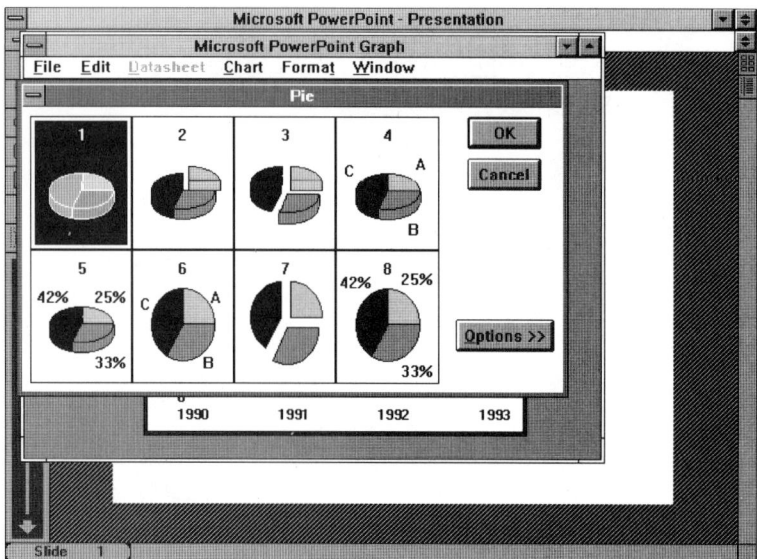

Figure 7-6. *A pie chart displays part/whole relationships.*

Scatter

Scatter charts display the distribution of data. (See Figure 7-7.) Notice that options 4 and 5 are logarithmic charts, which you can use when the rate of change is exponential.

Additional options

You can further customize your choices by clicking on the Options button, which is available for all chart types except scatter charts. Each chart type offers a unique set of options. For example, with bar charts, you can adjust the amount of three-dimensional offset or choose stacked bars. With area or line charts, you can add high–low lines, as shown in Figure 7-8. (In the figure, the Legend command on the Format menu was used to move the legend to the top of the chart.)

You can also change the way PowerPoint translates data into charts. While the Datasheet is selected, open the Datasheet menu and choose the Series In Rows command. Or if Series In Rows is already selected, choose the Series In Columns command. Notice how this dramatically changes the appearance of the various charts described above.

Chapter 7: Translating Numbers into Charts and Graphs

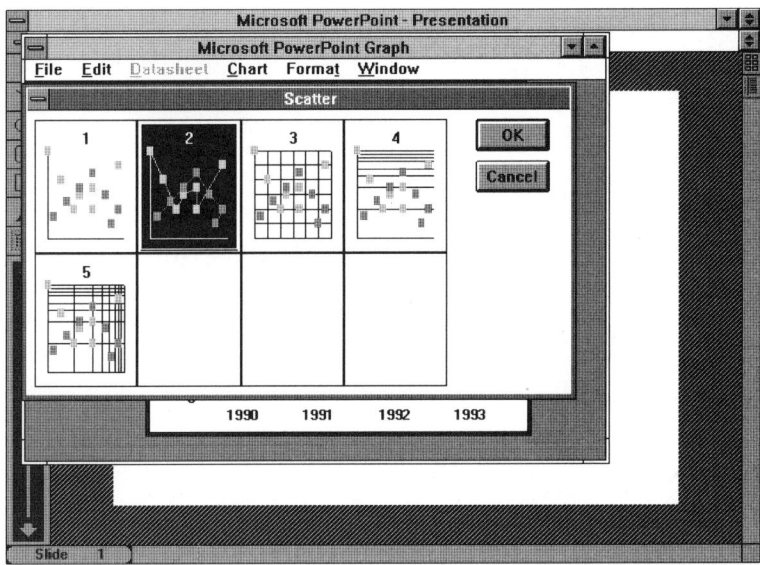

Figure 7-7. Scatter charts emphasize the distribution of data.

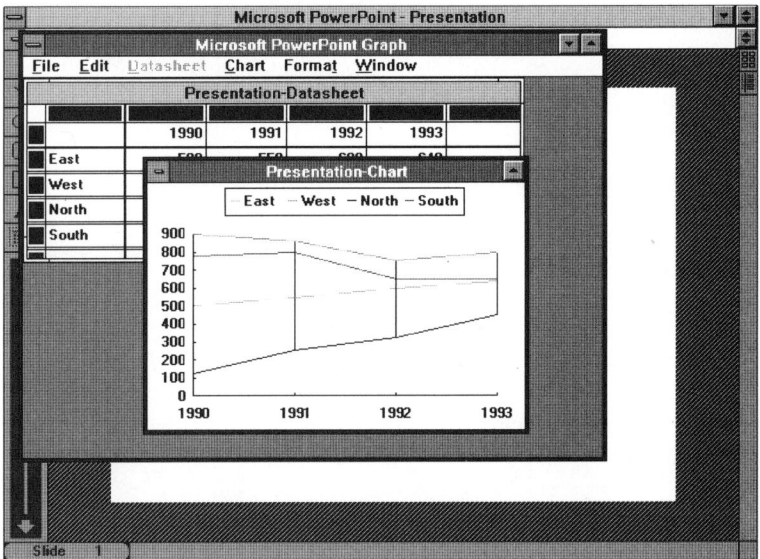

Figure 7-8. Add high–low lines when you want to emphasize data differences.

Working with Microsoft Excel

Microsoft Excel offers similar choices and operation. The following procedures are essentially the same for both Macintosh Excel and Windows Excel. After you've entered the sample data provided in the table on page 169 in an Excel worksheet, do the following.

1. Select the data you've just entered in the worksheet by holding down the mouse button and dragging the cursor through the data.
2. Release the mouse button.
3. Choose the New command from the File menu.
4. Choose Chart.
5. Click OK or press Return.

Excel's default chart will appear. When it appears, choose Gallery. To choose the appropriate type of chart, you follow a two-step process.

1. Choose a basic category of chart (for example, area, pie, or line).
2. Choose the particular version of each type of chart by double-clicking on its reduced-size image, clicking OK, or pressing Return. Notice that several versions of each chart include value labels that display the exact amounts represented by each segment of the chart.

Excel then immediately transforms your data into the type of chart you selected.

The Next and Previous commands

Excel's Next and Previous commands make it easier to view your chart options. (See Figure 7-9.) By choosing the Next command, you can easily advance from area-chart to bar-chart to column-chart options without needing to open the Gallery menu and choose the name of the chart type.

By clicking on Previous, you can review the chart options you just viewed.

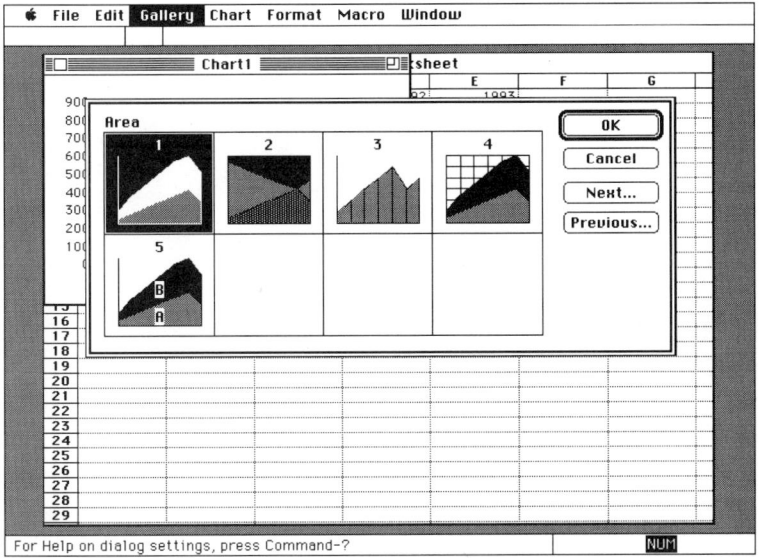

Figure 7-9. Microsoft Excel's Next and Previous commands let you compare chart options.

Combination charts

Microsoft Excel allows you to create combination charts, such as bar or column charts combined with area or line charts. These permit the simultaneous display of two types of data.

FORMAT THE CHART

Windows PowerPoint and both Macintosh and Windows versions of Microsoft Excel allow you to format the chart exactly as you want. Following is a discussion of some of the formatting options available.

Formatting Charts Created with Windows PowerPoint

Windows PowerPoint allows you to control all aspects of the appearance of your charts. Following are some of the ways you can format charts. (Note: Not all options are available with every chart type.)

Typeface, type size, type style, and color options

To format the text used to identify the horizontal or vertical axis information, do the following.

1. Click on the chart.
2. Click on the horizontal or vertical axis, legend, or data label.
3. Open the Format menu.
4. Choose Font. (See Figure 7-10.)

You can now choose a different typeface, type size, type style, and color for text used on the item you've selected.

Line width and color

To choose a desired line thickness and color for the horizontal or the vertical axis, the legend box, a data series, frame, or gridlines, do the following.

1. Click on the chart.
2. Click on the item you want to format.
3. Open the Format menu.
4. Choose the Line Style command. (See Figure 7-11.)
5. Choose a line thickness and color.
6. Click OK or press Enter.

Data labels

To display the names of, or the exact amounts represented by, each slice of a pie chart or by each segment of a bar or column chart, do the following.

1. Click on the chart.
2. Open the Format menu.
3. Choose the Data Labels command. (See Figure 7-12 on page 180.)
4. Click on Show Value or Show Label.

You can also modify the typeface, type size, type style, and color used to display value and label information by doing the following.

1. Choose one of the Data Labels.
2. Open the Format menu.
3. Choose Font.

Chapter 7: Translating Numbers into Charts and Graphs

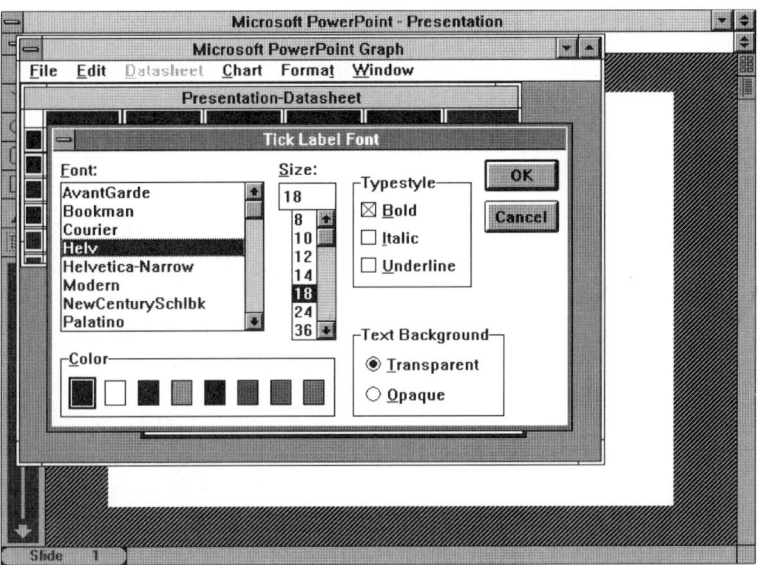

Figure 7-10. You can format the text for the axes, legend, and data labels of a chart.

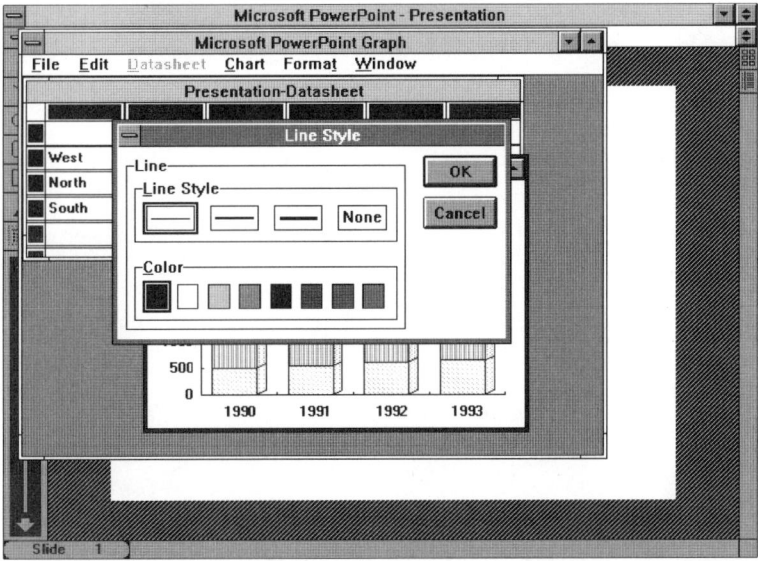

Figure 7-11. The Line Style command lets you choose a line width and color for axes, legend boxes, data series, frames, and gridlines.

4. Choose typeface, type size, type style, and color.

5. Choose Opaque if you want data label text to appear against a different-colored background.

6. Click OK.

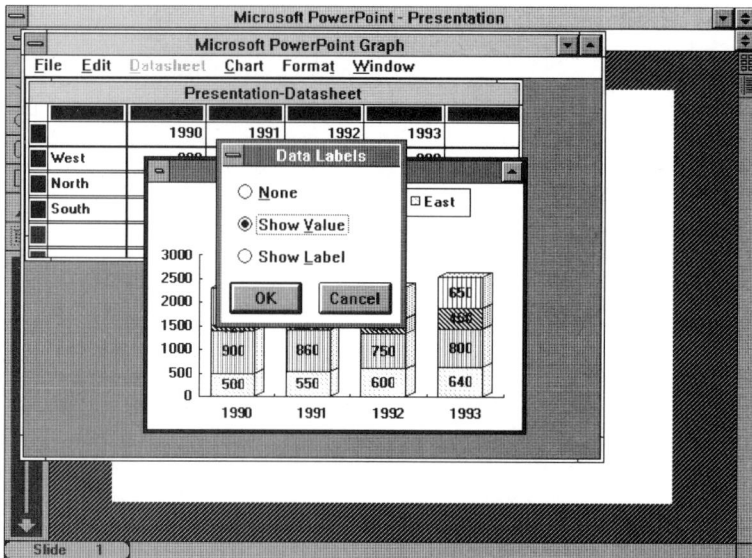

Figure 7-12. The Data Labels command lets you add value or label information to each data series.

Legend

To place the legend that identifies each pie chart slice or bar chart segment, do the following.

1. Click on the chart.

2. Open the Format menu.

3. Choose the Legend command. (See Figure 7-13.)

4. Click on an option.

(If you don't want to display a legend, choose None.)

As you try out the options, notice how the legend reformats itself.

Chapter 7: Translating Numbers into Charts and Graphs

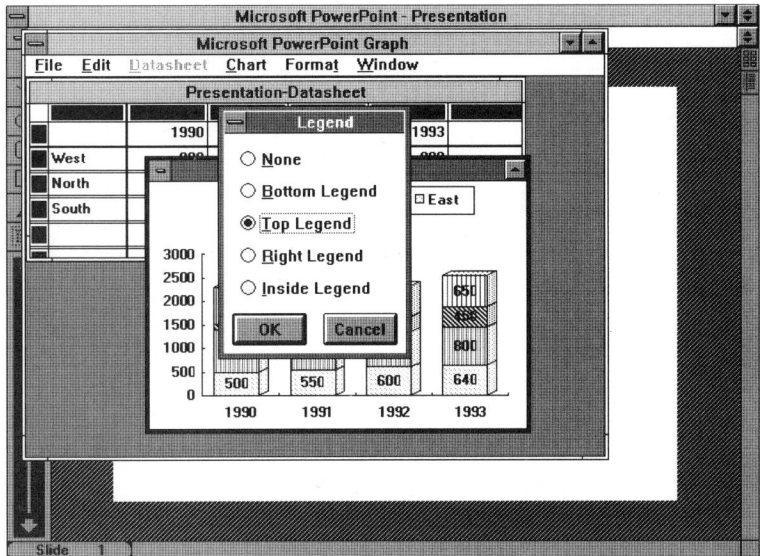

Figure 7-13. *The Legend command lets you place legends below, above, to the right of, or inside a chart.*

You can format the legend by choosing a typeface, type size, and type style as well as a background fill pattern and line style.

To format legend text, do the following.

1. Click on the chart.
2. Choose the Legend command.
3. Open the Format menu.
4. Choose the Font command.
5. Choose a typeface, type size, type style, and color. If you want to emphasize the legend by providing it with its own background, choose Opaque.
6. Click OK or press Enter when you've made your choices.

The Legend reformats itself to accommodate a larger or smaller type size.

181

SECTION II: BASIC SKILLS

To choose a different line thickness and color for the frame around the legend, do the following.

1. Click on the chart.
2. Choose the Legend command.
3. Open the Format menu.
4. Choose the Line Style command.

To add a distinct background to the legend, do the following.

1. Click on the chart.
2. Click on the legend.
3. Open the Format menu.
4. Choose the Fill command. (See Figure 7-14.)
5. Choose background patterns and colors.

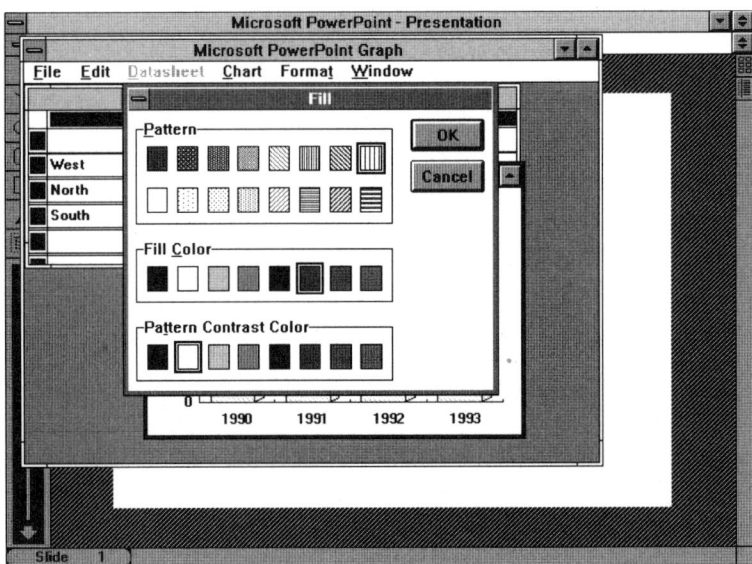

Figure 7-14. The Fill command lets you choose fill colors and background patterns.

Frame and gridlines

A frame unifies a chart and isolates it from the rest of the slide or overhead, resulting in a more formal appearance. Gridlines provide a visual frame of reference.

To add a frame to a chart, do the following.

1. Click on the chart.
2. Open the Format menu.
3. Choose the Gridlines command.
4. Click on Frame.

To add gridlines to a chart, do the following.

1. Click on the chart.
2. Open the Format menu.
3. Choose the Gridlines command. (See Figure 7-15.)
4. Choose an option for the horizontal and vertical axes. (You can add lines either at major or at minor intervals or at both.)

To choose a different line thickness and color for either the frame or the gridlines, do the following.

1. Click on the chart.
2. Click on either the frame or one of the major or minor horizontal or vertical gridlines. (Notice that Windows PowerPoint allows you to individually format major and minor gridlines.)

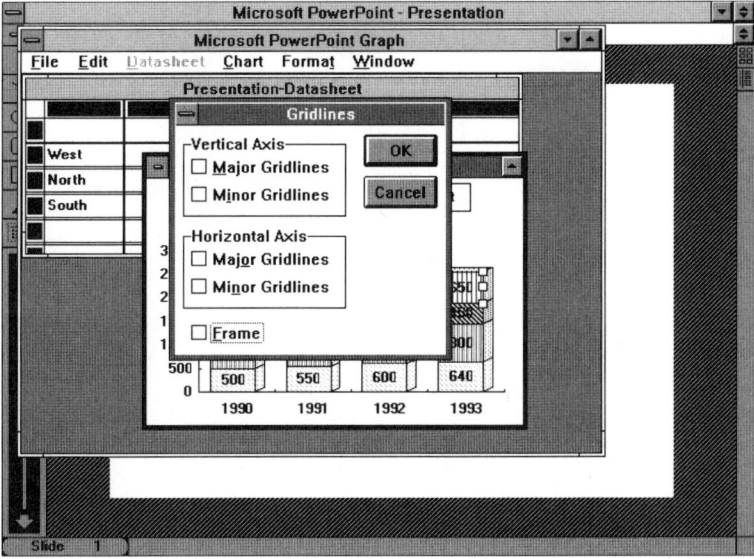

Figure 7-15. *The Gridlines command lets you choose horizontal or vertical gridlines that provide a visual frame of reference.*

3. Open the Format menu.
4. Choose the Line Style command.
5. Choose a line thickness and color.
6. Click OK or press Enter.

Tick marks

Tick marks provide an additional frame of reference. Tick marks indicate minor divisions of the horizontal or the vertical axes. You can often improve the appearance of a chart by using tick marks instead of gridlines. To add tick marks to your chart, do the following.

1. Click on the chart.
2. Open the Format menu.
3. Choose Horizontal Axis or Vertical Axis. (See Figure 7-16.)

You can choose whether to display the axis itself and whether to format the tick marks. You can add tick marks inside, outside, or crossing the horizontal or the vertical axis. You can also determine the tick mark interval.

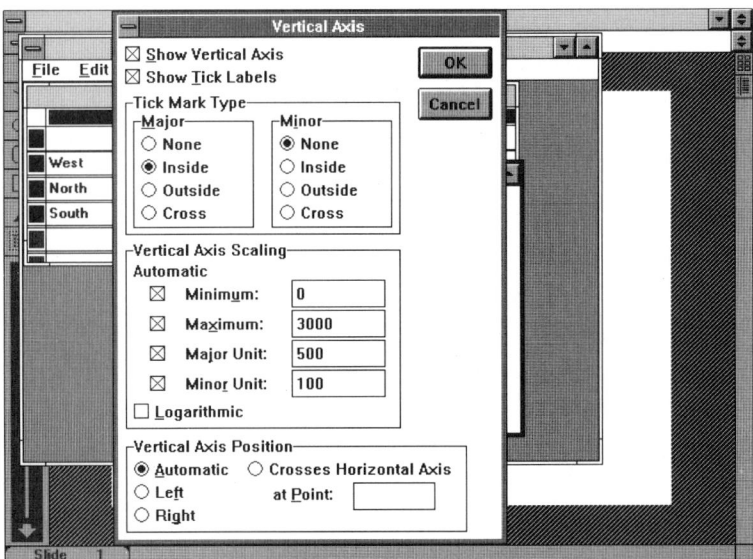

Figure 7-16. *The ability to format tick marks lets you control the smallest details of a chart.*

Colors, lines, and patterns

You can also format your chart by modifying the colors, lines, and patterns used for each slice of a pie chart or each segment of a bar or column graph. To recolor the information displayed in a chart, do the following.

1. Click on the chart.
2. Click on a single slice of a pie chart or on one segment of a bar or column chart.
3. Open the Format menu.
4. Choose the Fill command.

You can now choose Pattern, Fill Color, and Pattern Contrast Color. Pattern Contrast determines the color that is used to replace the white spaces in the selected pattern.

You can also choose a different line thickness and color for the lines outlining each pie chart slice or segment of a chart. To choose a different line style, do the following.

1. Click on the chart.
2. Click on the segment you want to reformat.
3. Open the Format menu.
4. Choose the Line Style command, and then choose a line thickness and color.
5. When you've finished, click OK or press Enter.

Image size

When you format charts with Windows PowerPoint, you can work more accurately by using the Maximize command to temporarily increase chart size. The Maximize command is located under the horizontal line at the upper left of the chart screen. You can also increase chart size by clicking on the up arrow located at the upper right of the chart screen.

To return to normal view, which shows both the chart and the source Datasheet, choose Restore from the left bar or click on the down arrow at the upper right of the screen.

Creating a default chart

You can reuse your formatting options by creating a default chart. Each time you choose Insert Chart, the default chart incorporates the formatting options you've chosen above.

To create a default chart, do the following.

1. Click on the chart.
2. Open the File menu.
3. Choose Set As Default Chart.

PowerPoint will verify that you want to replace the current default chart with your newly formatted option. Click OK or press Enter.

This default chart will last as long as your current presentation is open. To make your default chart permanent, see "Creating a Default Presentation" in Chapter 8.

Formatting Charts with Microsoft Excel

With Microsoft Excel, you can format charts with precision. The following are merely some of your options. These procedures are essentially the same in both the Windows and the Macintosh versions of Excel.

Frame, background color, and shadow

To enhance your chart with a frame, background color, and shadow, do the following.

1. Select the entire chart by opening the Chart menu and then choosing Select Chart.
2. Open the Format menu.
3. Choose Patterns. (Border options are listed in the left half of the Patterns dialog box, as shown in Figure 7-17.)
4. To add a border, click on Automatic followed by your choices of a solid or dashed border, border color, and line width. Choose Shadow if you want to add a three-dimensional effect to the frame.
5. To choose a background option, use the options available in the center of the dialog box, labeled Area.

Typeface, type size, type style, and color options

To simultaneously change the appearance of the text used for both the horizontal and the vertical axis, do the following.

1. Select the entire chart by opening the Chart menu and then choosing Select Chart.

2. Open the Format menu.

3. Choose Font.

4. When the Font dialog box appears, choose a typeface, type size, type style, and color.

5. When you've finished, click OK or press Return.

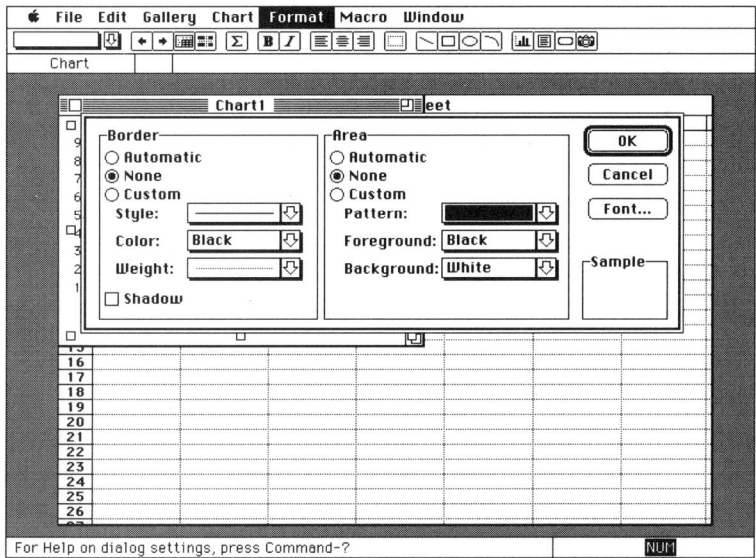

Figure 7-17. The Patterns command lets you choose the frame and background options for a chart with Microsoft Excel.

Formatting the horizontal and vertical axes

To choose a line width and a color for the horizontal and vertical axes, do the following.

1. Select the horizontal or the vertical axis by clicking on it.

2. Open the Format menu.

3. Choose Patterns. (See Figure 7-18 on the following page.)

4. Choose a line style, color, and line weight from the Axis section of the dialog box.

5. If you want to include Tick Marks or Tick Labels or both, choose from among the options in the center portion of the dialog box.

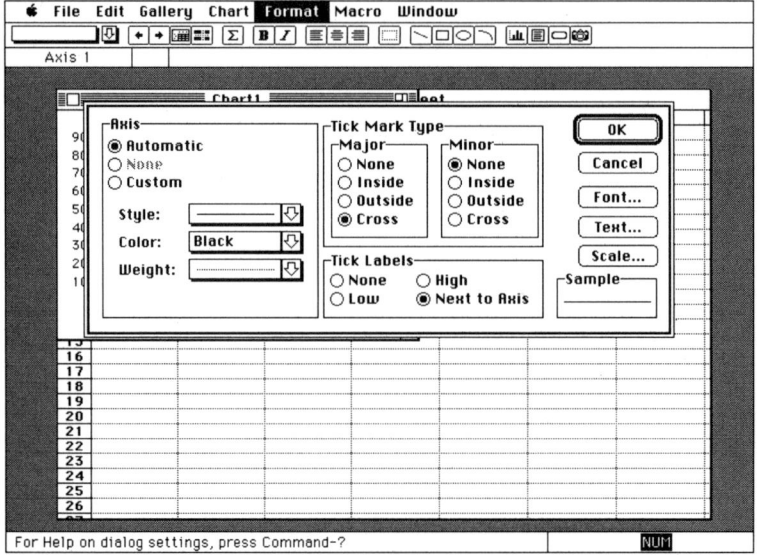

Figure 7-18. The Patterns command lets you choose from among line style and tick mark options.

Before returning to the chart, you can choose a different typeface, type size, type style, and color for either the horizontal or the vertical axis by clicking on the Font button at the right side of the dialog box.

When you've finished, click OK or press Return.

Legend

To add and format a legend identifying the individual segments of your chart, do the following.

1. Open the Chart menu.
2. Choose Add Legend. When the legend appears, select it by clicking on it.

When the legend is surrounded by eight small boxes, do the following.

3. Open the Format menu.
4. Choose Legend. (See Figure 7-19.)
5. Choose a legend placement: Bottom, Corner, Top, or Vertical.

Chapter 7: Translating Numbers into Charts and Graphs

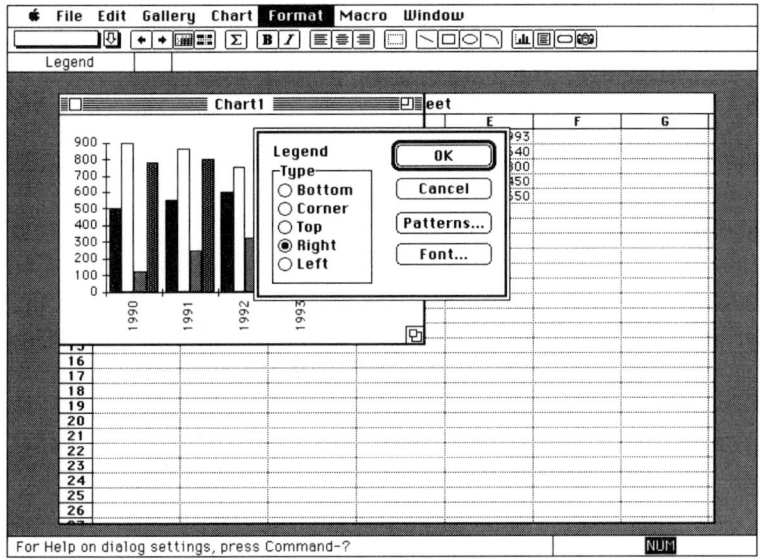

Figure 7-19. *The Legend command lets you place the legend.*

You can then format the type and appearance of the legend, using the commands on the Format menu.

1. Choose Font to choose the typeface, type size, type style, and color used for the legend text.

2. Choose Patterns to choose Border options for framing the legend with a line style, line thickness, and line color.

3. Choose Patterns to choose Area options to select a one-color or two-color background for the legend.

4. When you've finished, click OK or press Return.

Gridlines

To add gridlines to provide a visual frame or reference behind your chart, do the following.

1. Select the entire chart by opening the Chart menu and choosing Select Chart.

2. Open the Chart menu.

3. Choose Gridlines.

4. Choose major or minor gridlines options for the horizontal and vertical axes.

5. When you've finished, click OK or press Return.

Plot area

To emphasize the plot area of your chart (the area between the horizontal and vertical axes), do the following.

1. Open the Chart menu.

2. Click on Select Plot Area, or click on a portion of the chart inside the horizontal or the vertical axis.

3. Open the Format menu.

4. Choose Patterns to choose Border options for framing the plot area with a line style, line thickness, and line color.

5. Choose Area options to select a one-color or two-color background for the plot area.

Colors, lines, and patterns

To individually format any segment of any type of chart, do the following.

1. Select a chart segment by clicking on it.

2. Open the Format menu and choose Patterns.

3. Use the Border options to adjust the style, thickness, and color of the line bordering each segment.

4. Use the Area options to select a fill pattern and color.

Adding and formatting value labels

Although some Excel chart options include value labels, you can add an individual value label to an individual chart segment. To add a value label to an individual segment, do the following.

1. Open the Chart menu.

2. Choose Attach Text. (See Figure 7-20.)

3. When the Attach Text dialog box appears, click on Series And Data Point and enter the Series Number and Point Number you want to enhance with a value label.

4. When you've finished, click OK or press Return.

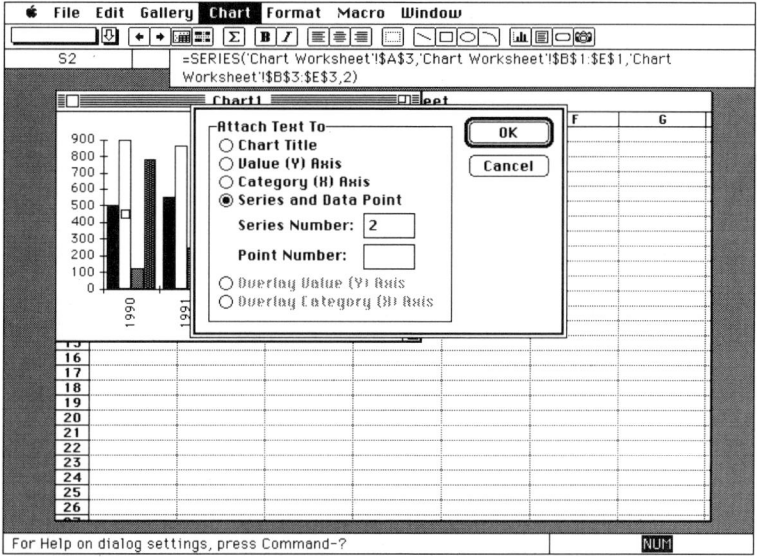

Figure 7-20. *You can add a value label to an individual chart segment to emphasize the segment while discussing it.*

When the value label appears, it is surrounded by eight small boxes. To format the text, do the following.

1. Open the Format menu.
2. Choose Font.
3. Choose a typeface, type size, type style, and type color, as well as whether you want the text to appear against a transparent or an opaque background.
4. When you've finished, click OK or press Return.

Creating a default chart

To use the chart you just created as the default chart for Microsoft Excel, do the following.

1. Click on the chart.
2. Open the Gallery menu.
3. Choose Set Preferred.

Future charts that you create will reflect these new default settings.

SECTION II: BASIC SKILLS

PLACE, RESIZE, AND ENHANCE THE CHART

A significant amount of work remains to be done after you've created a chart for a PowerPoint visual. Typically, you need to move, resize, and recolor the chart after placing it into your presentation. In addition, you can add a frame or a shadow to the graphical image of the chart to further enhance the chart.

Placing Charts into a PowerPoint Presentation

Windows PowerPoint offers an integrated approach to adding charts to presentation visuals. Macintosh PowerPoint offers you a choice of two methods.

Placing charts with Windows PowerPoint

After you've created a chart with PowerPoint Graph, do the following.

1. Open the File menu in PowerPoint Graph.
2. Choose Exit And Return.
3. Press Enter.

The chart will immediately appear on the currently selected slide of your presentation.

If you have used the Windows version of Microsoft Excel to create your PowerPoint chart, do the following.

1. With the chart window (named "1PowerPoint") active, open the File menu.
2. Choose Update.
3. Press Enter.

The chart will appear in the currently selected slide.

Placing charts with Macintosh PowerPoint

You can use either the Macintosh Clipboard or the Macintosh Scrapbook to import charts created with Microsoft Excel into a presentation that you're creating with Macintosh PowerPoint.

Using the Macintosh Clipboard

To use the Macintosh Clipboard, do the following.

1. Copy the chart to the Clipboard.
2. Close Excel.

3. Open Macintosh PowerPoint.
4. Open the Edit menu.
5. Choose Paste.

Using the Macintosh Scrapbook

The limitation of the Clipboard, of course, is that it's restricted to one image at a time. To speed your work, you can use the Scrapbook feature or the Smart Scrap desk accessory included with PowerPoint. Smart Scrap allows you to save multiple Scrapbook files.

While working in Excel, for example, you might schedule a major chart-building session and create several charts—perhaps all the charts needed for your presentation. These can be pasted one at a time into the Macintosh Scrapbook.

When you've finished, open PowerPoint and select the individual charts from the Scrapbook; then copy and paste the charts into your presentation as needed.

Moving Charts

To move a chart, click on it. This exposes its fuzzy border. Simply grab the border and hold down the mouse button as you drag the chart to the location you want. Release the button.

Moving a chart created with Windows PowerPoint is even easier. Simply click on the chart using the right mouse button. Hold down the right mouse button as you reposition the chart, and then release the button.

Resizing Charts

Typically, you have to resize a chart to fit its surroundings. To resize a chart, grab one of the corner handles and drag it in the direction you want.

- ◆ Moving the corner handle horizontally or vertically distorts the chart horizontally *or* vertically.
- ◆ Moving the corner handle diagonally distorts the chart horizontally *and* vertically.

You can often improve a chart's effectiveness by stretching a chart to fit the slide. Stretching a chart vertically adds emphasis to column charts, and stretching a chart horizontally adds emphasis to bar charts.

Horizontally distorting pie charts helps them fill the slide, eliminating "wasted" space to the left or the right. (See Figure 7-21.)

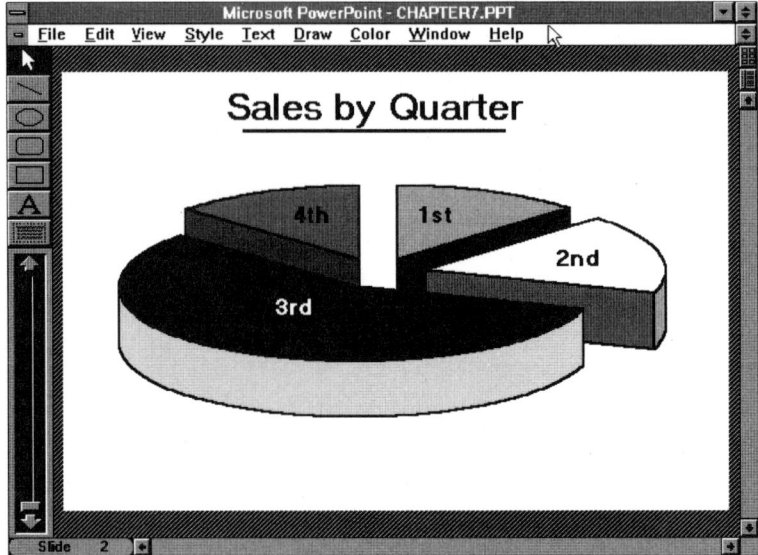

Figure 7-21. *You can stretch a pie chart horizontally to decrease empty space to its right and left.*

Maintaining a chart's original proportions

To preserve a chart's original aspect ratio, or height-to-width ratio, hold down the Shift key while dragging the corner handle diagonally.

Enhancing Charts

You can enhance a chart by employing the commands located in the Draw menu. Start by clicking on the chart to select it. Open the Draw menu. Then choose one or more of the following commands.

Opaque

Choose the Opaque command if you want the chart to share the Slide Master background colors but appear in front of existing text or graphical objects.

Framed

Choose Framed from the Draw menu if you want to add a frame around the entire chart—including or not including the legend. (See Figure 7-22.) This frame will help focus attention on the chart.

Chapter 7: Translating Numbers into Charts and Graphs

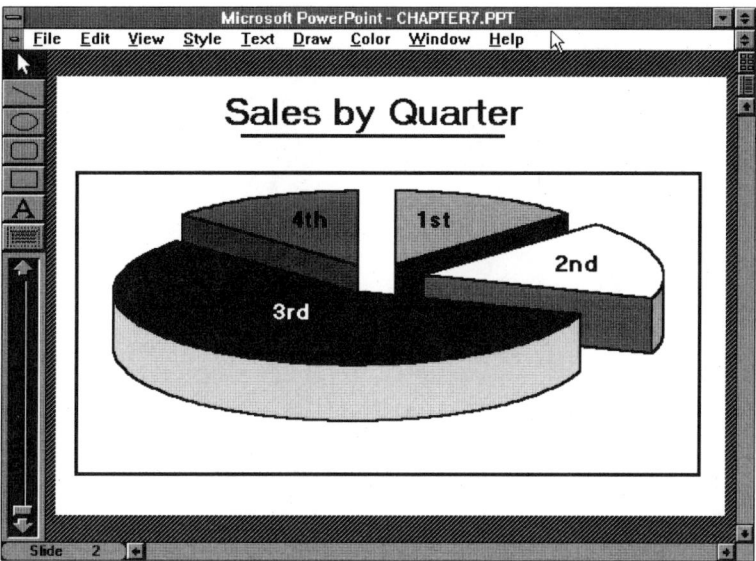

Figure 7-22. *You can use a frame to isolate a chart from other objects on the slide.*

You can adjust the thickness of the frame by choosing a line thickness. Open the Draw menu and choose Line Style if you want to modify the frame's line thickness.

Filled

Choose Filled from the Draw menu if you want to provide a contrasting background for the chart, one that will help the chart stand out from the slide background created by your presentation's Color Scheme. (See Figure 7-23 on the following page.)

Choose Pattern from the Draw menu if you want a background pattern different from the default that appears when you choose Filled. Open the Color menu and choose Fill to choose a different-colored background. Choose Pattern Contrast if you want a two-color background.

Shadowed

You can add emphasis to a chart by choosing the Shadowed command from the Draw menu. This supplies a contrasting shadow to the right of and below the chart.

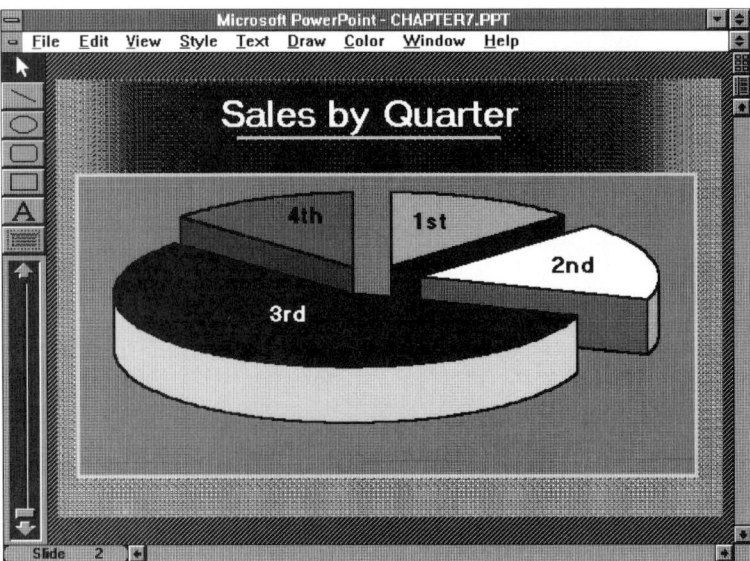

Figure 7-23. Use a solid or patterned background to emphasize a chart.

Recoloring Images

There are two reasons to recolor charts placed in PowerPoint slides. One is to restore color lost during the placement process. The other is to integrate the chart's colors with those of your existing presentation Color Scheme.

Adding color to a chart created with Microsoft Excel

When you import a chart created with Microsoft Excel into a Macintosh PowerPoint presentation through the Clipboard or the Scrapbook, the chart appears as a patterned, black-and-white image. The original colors are replaced by solids, gray shades, and patterns.

Restoring color to an Excel chart involves three steps.

1. Select the chart by clicking on it.

2. Choose Recolor Picture from the Color menu.

3. Choose Change Patterns when the Recolor dialog box appears. First, click on the ballot box next to each pattern in the From column that you want to replace with a color. (See Figure 7-24.) Next, click on the pop-up menu in the To column associated with each pattern and choose the color that best matches your presentation's Color Scheme.

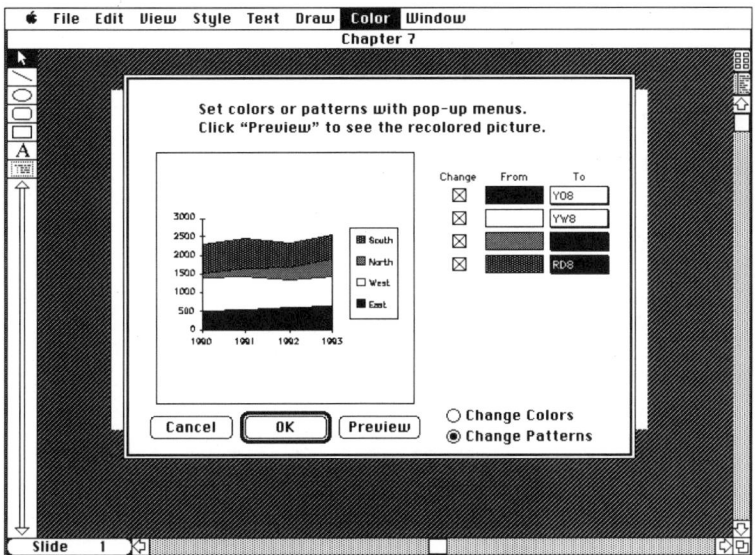

Figure 7-24. You can use the Recolor Picture command to add color to a chart created with Microsoft Excel.

Recoloring charts in Windows PowerPoint

One of the most important reasons to recolor a chart is to maintain consistency with the Color Scheme chosen for your presentation.

To recolor a chart created with Windows PowerPoint, do the following.

1. Select the chart by clicking on it.
2. Choose Recolor Picture from the Color menu.
3. Select the down arrow next to the color you want to modify. When you click on the arrow, you see the color options available in the Color Scheme selected for your presentation. (See Figure 7-25 on the following page.)

Adding callouts

You can also enhance charts by adding callouts. Callouts are short explanatory phrases attached to a chart by a line with an arrow. To add a callout to a chart, do the following.

1. Choose the Line tool.
2. Click on the part of the slide where you want the text to appear, and then drag the mouse to the chart segment to which you want to point.

SECTION II: BASIC SKILLS

3. Open the Draw menu.
4. Choose Line Style and pick an appropriate line thickness.
5. Again, open the Draw menu.
6. Select Arrowheads style.
7. Add text at one end of the line using the Labeler tool. (You might find it useful to open the Text menu and choose Right.)

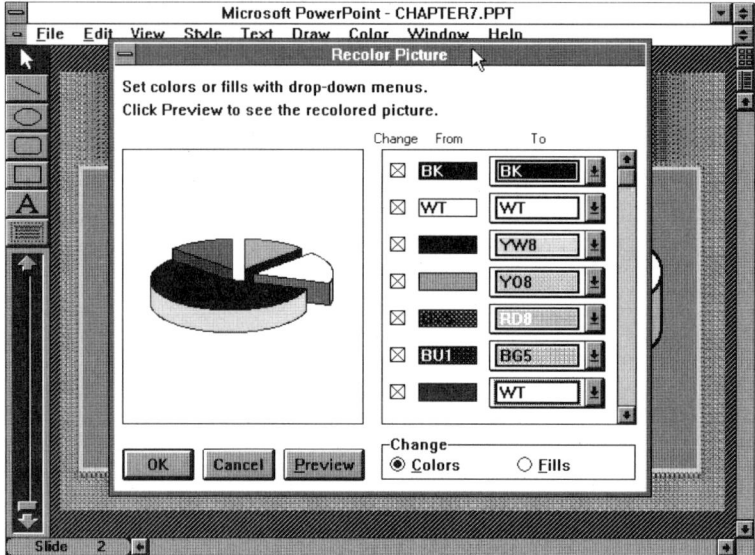

Figure 7-25. *You can use the Recolor Picture command to integrate a chart's colors with the colors used in your presentation's Color Scheme.*

Editing Previously Created Charts

The Windows and Macintosh versions of PowerPoint differ in the ease with which you can edit previously prepared charts.

Editing charts with Windows PowerPoint

You can edit a chart prepared with Windows PowerPoint in either of two ways.

◆ By double-clicking on the chart
◆ By opening the Edit menu and choosing Edit Graph

Both alternatives return you to the Datasheet and the Edit Chart window. By clicking on the chart, you can reformat the chart. By clicking on the Datasheet, you can enter new data.

To return to your presentation after you've finished, choose Exit And Return from the File menu and press Enter.

Editing charts prepared with Microsoft Excel

To edit information in a chart created with Microsoft Excel, you first need to delete the chart. You then return to Microsoft Excel to edit and reimport the chart.

If you saved your original charts, you can open them by clicking on their filename. If you linked the chart to the spreadsheet when you saved it, this will also open the spreadsheet the chart is based on.

After entering new data or reformatting the chart, you'll (again) have to save it to the Macintosh Clipboard or Scrapbook. After you return to PowerPoint, delete the old chart and paste the new one in its place.

EVALUATING YOUR PROGRESS

As you review your work, ask yourself the following questions.

- Did I use the type of chart that best displays the data and interpretation I want to communicate?
- Can readers, at a glance, understand the intent of my chart?
- Did I clearly identify all segments of my chart?
- Did I include gridlines and tick marks to assist my audience?
- Did I place the legend in the correct location?
- Did I recolor my chart to match my presentation's Color Scheme?

PowerPoint Tips and Techniques

You can combine PowerPoint commands to create a variety of special effects.

- *Builds.* Builds introduce information step by step, preventing your audience from reading ahead of you.
- *Embossing.* Embossing adds three-dimensional effects to color slides.
- *Graduated fills.* You can create graphical objects that contain smooth gradations from light to dark.
- *Shining graphics.* You can emphasize a graphic by making it appear as if light is shining out of it.
- *Organizational charts.* You can easily create organizational charts to show cause-and-effect relationships and to illustrate hierarchies of information or responsibility.
- *Tables.* Tables provide a framework to communicate information in a clear, concise format.
- *Callouts.* A callout is a short phrase "attached" to a graphic with a line that ends in an arrowhead pointing at a graphic or at part of a graphic. Callouts make it easy to draw the audience's attention to one or more elements on a slide.

- *Logos.* You can quickly create a logo for a special occasion. You can also use a scanned image of your firm's logo as a background for your slides and overheads.

- *Three-dimensional text* (aka *shadow lettering*). You can add a shadow behind a few large words—say, in a title—so that the words look three-dimensional.

In addition, PowerPoint helps you work more efficiently by allowing you to create standardized formats and to reuse your work.

- *Import outlines.* You can prepare an outline for your presentation by using word processing software (such as Microsoft Word) or dedicated outlining programs and then importing the text into a PowerPoint presentation.

- *Create default presentations.* New presentations open with the correct Slide Master, Color Scheme, Styles, Text, and Draw defaults.

- *Share slides between presentations.* You can create a library of slides that can be used over and over.

- *Share Slide Masters between presentations.* You can base a new presentation on a previously created Slide Master or update an existing presentation by adding a Slide Master from a previous one.

- *Share Color Schemes between presentations.* You can easily recolor a presentation to match a previously created one.

- *Transfer files between Windows PowerPoint and Macintosh PowerPoint.* You can use a presentation created with Macintosh PowerPoint as the basis for a Windows PowerPoint presentation, and vice versa.

SPECIAL EFFECTS

You can create a variety of special effects by using PowerPoint commands in conjunction with one another. As you work with PowerPoint, you'll undoubtedly develop your own ways to do this.

Builds

Whenever a new slide or overhead appears on the screen, the audience *reads* instead of *listens*. Audiences also often read ahead of the presenter. "Builds" eliminate these problems. Builds permit you to introduce new ideas step by step and to focus your audience's attention on the particular idea you're discussing. Builds can be used when introducing various visual material.

- Items in a list
- Slices of a pie chart
- Levels of an organizational chart
- Maps or geographic territories

Text builds

The first step in developing a text build is to create the finished, or last, slide that will be shown. (See Figure 8-1.)

Next, choose the Slide Sorter command from the View menu, or click on the Slide Sorter icon at the upper right of the screen.

Click on the finished slide. Choose the Copy command from the Edit menu.

Choose the Paste command. Paste as many copies of the slide as there are layers to the build.

Select the first slide in the series by double-clicking on it. This returns you to the Slide view. Choose the Word Processor tool, and highlight the text and graphics that will be introduced on the second, third, and fourth slides. Delete the text by opening the Edit menu and choosing Clear, or use the Delete key (in Macintosh PowerPoint) or the Backspace key (in Windows PowerPoint).

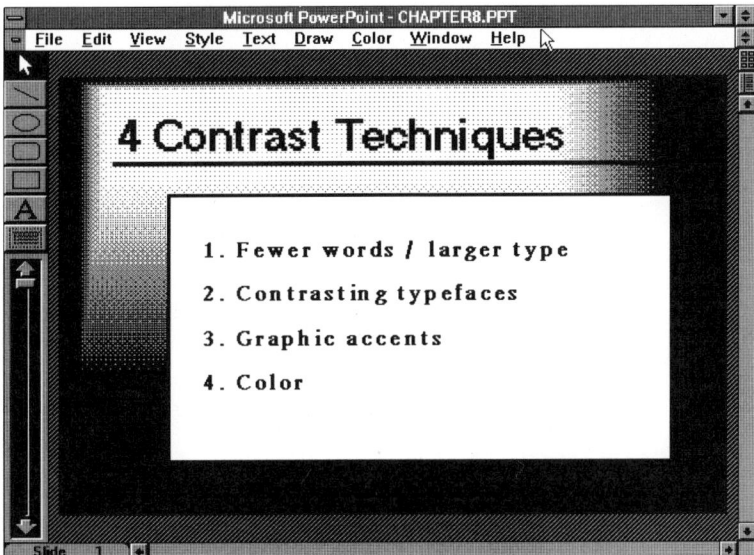

Figure 8-1. *The first step in creating a text build is to create the last slide containing all the text.*

When you've finished, only the information you want on the first slide in the series should remain. (See Figure 8-2.)

Click on the Downward arrow of the Slide Changer tool to advance to the next slide in the series. Carefully select and delete the information that will be introduced on the remaining builds—in this case, the third and fourth slides. (See Figure 8-3.)

On Slide 3, eliminate the fourth line of text. The fourth, or last, slide does not require any changes. (See Figure 8-4.)

To preview your build, use the Slide Show feature. Notice that you don't have to run the entire Slide Show to preview only the slides that you're working with. The Slide Show dialog box allows you to specify a range of slides.

Double-check your work to be sure you've selected and deleted the appropriate information each time. Now, when you deliver your presentation, you'll be able to focus the audience's attention on the points you're discussing as you discuss them.

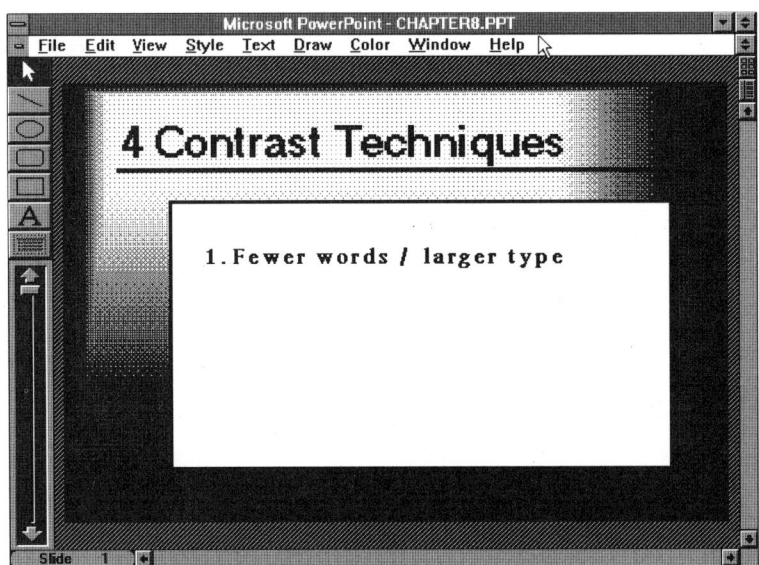

Figure 8-2. After you delete the text to be introduced on the second, third, and fourth slides, the first slide contains one important idea.

Chapter 8: PowerPoint Tips and Techniques

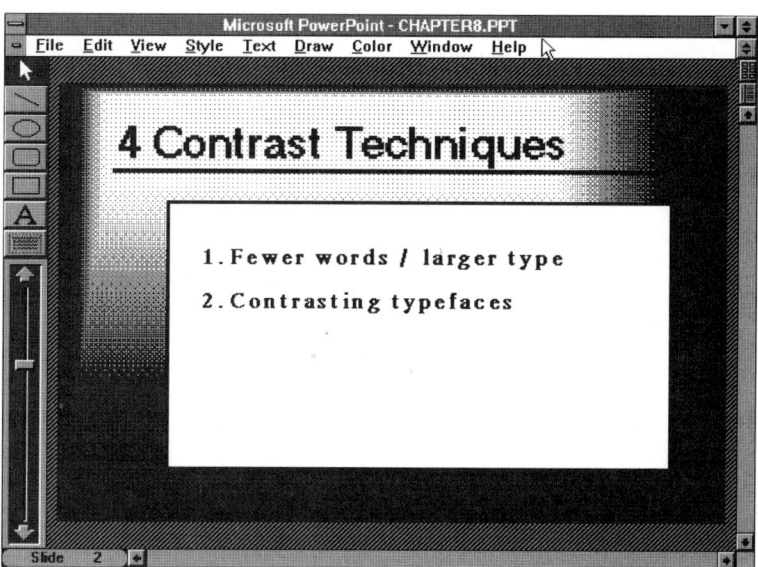

Figure 8-3. *After you delete the text to be introduced on the third and fourth slides, the second slide contains the first two ideas.*

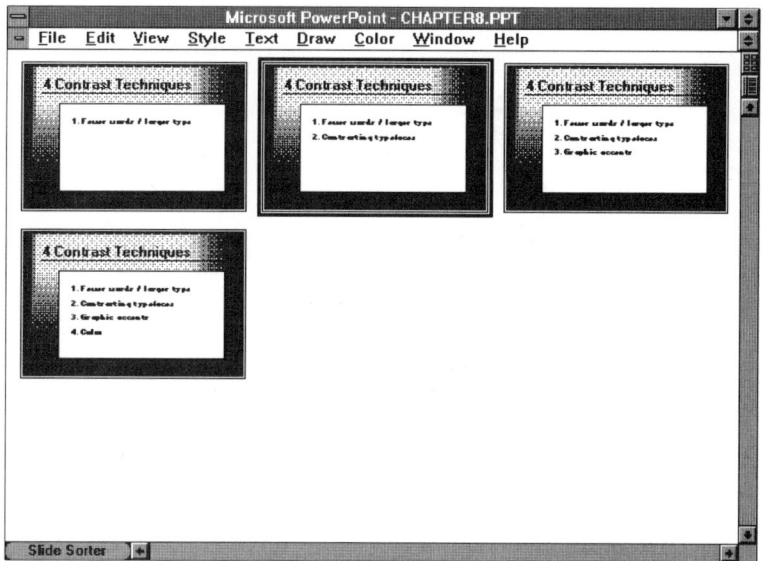

Figure 8-4. *The Slide Sorter view shows the completed text build.*

205

Creating text builds with color

Another way to create a build is to change the color of previously introduced text and to use a strong color to emphasize new text. (See Figure 8-5.) To create a color build, do the following.

1. Create the last slide in the series, the one containing the full list.
2. Highlight the text.
3. Open the Color menu, choose Text, and select a strong color for the text.
4. Change to Slide Sorter view. Double-click on the slide and copy it. Paste as many copies as there are steps in the build.
5. Double-click on the first slide. As you did above, delete the information that you'll introduce on the second and third slides.
6. Use the Downward arrow to advance to the second slide.
7. Highlight the text introduced in the first slide.
8. Open the Color menu and choose Text.
9. Repeat the process for the third and fourth slides (the remaining slides in the text build).

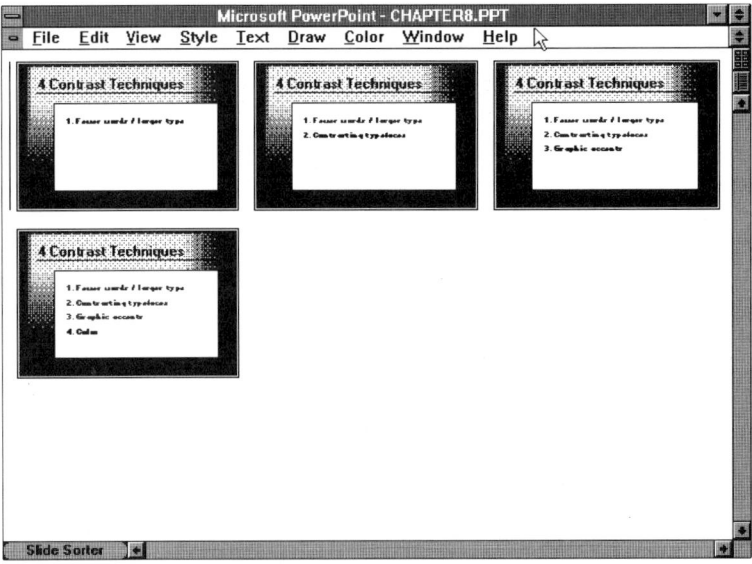

Figure 8-5. *The Slide Sorter view of a text build that uses color to set off the new point being made from the previously introduced ones. ("Colors" are represented here by shades of gray.)*

10. Choose a different, perhaps lighter, color. This will de-emphasize the text introduced on the first slide.

The resulting slide clearly focuses the audience's attention on the newest information, yet it allows the audience to refer to previously introduced information.

Creating chart and table builds

You can use the same basic build techniques for progressively introducing information in charts and tables. Always create the last slide first, make as many copies of it as needed, and delete information not being introduced.

You can use the Recolor Picture command to create impressive chart builds. To create a chart build, do the following.

1. Create the chart.
2. Make as many copies of the chart as necessary.
3. Double-click on the slide containing the first chart segment you want to introduce.
4. Click on the chart.
5. Open the Color menu and choose Recolor Picture.
6. Do not change the color used for the first chart segment.
7. Recolor the chart segments that will be introduced later. Choose a color that matches either the Slide Master background or the background Fill color used for the chart. (See Figure 8-6 on the following page.)

As each new chart segment is introduced, color it with a foreground color that contrasts with the color used for the Slide Master background or with the Fill color used for the chart.

Embossing

You can add three-dimensional effects to Slide Masters or individual objects. "Embossing" is based on the way the PowerPoint color palette contains subtly lighter and darker shades of the colors.

To create an embossed effect, do the following.

1. Create a framed object by using one of the line-drawing tools. (The frame, which will be removed shortly, helps you select the objects while working on them.)

SECTION II: BASIC SKILLS

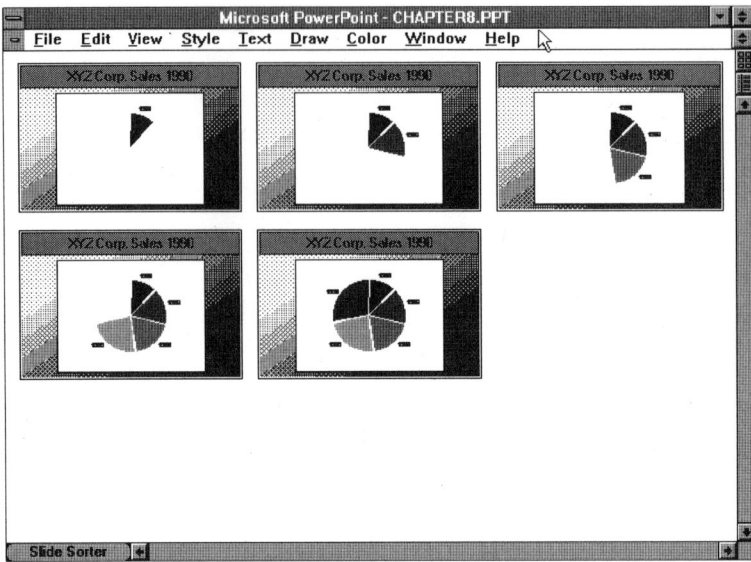

Figure 8-6. *The Slide Sorter view of a chart build that uses color. ("Colors" are represented here by shades of gray.)*

2. Make two additional copies of the object by using the Copy and Paste commands.

3. One at a time, select each of the objects and reposition them until they slightly offset each other. (See Figure 8-7.) The rear object should be slightly above and to the left of the original object. The front object should be slightly to the right and below the middle object. (The example shown in Figure 8-7 has been exaggerated for clarity.)

4. Select the rear object by clicking on it.

5. Choose Fill from the Color menu, and choose a lighter shade of the color used for the Slide Background.

6. Select the middle object.

7. Choose Fill, and then choose the same color used for the Slide background.

8. Select the frontmost object.

9. Choose Fill, and then choose a darker shade of the color used as the Slide background.

208

10. Select the middle layer by clicking on it.
11. Choose Bring To Front from the Edit menu, or use the appropriate keyboard shortcut: Command-= (in Macintosh PowerPoint) or Ctrl-= (in Windows PowerPoint).

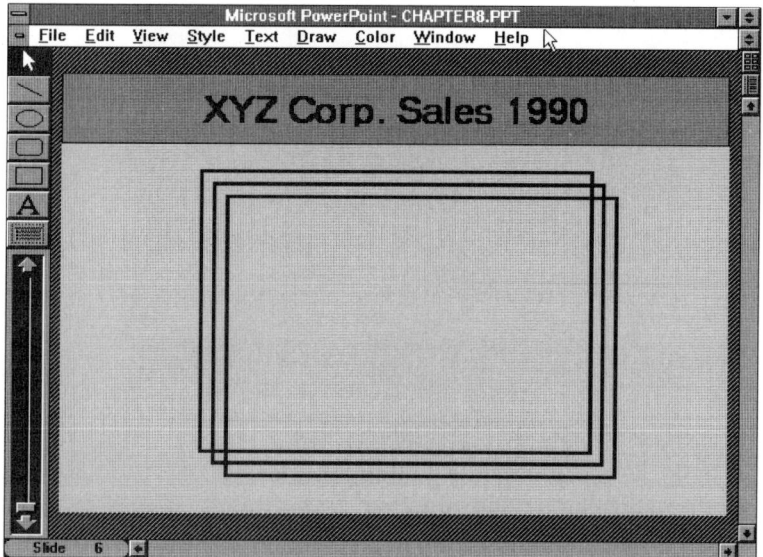

Figure 8-7. *You can use the Copy and Paste commands to create multiple objects—the first step in achieving an embossed effect.*

The final steps are to select each layer and deselect Framed from the Line menu. (The frames were originally included to help you locate each layer.) Figure 8-8 on the following page shows the resulting embossed effect.

By selecting and adjusting the offset, you can increase or decrease the amount of highlight or shadow.

When you're pleased with the effect you've created, you can select all three layers and use the Cut and the Paste As Picture commands. This allows you to easily move, resize, and make additional copies of the embossed object.

Embossing works especially well with Slide Masters containing shaded backgrounds. If you're shading backgrounds from the upper left, for example, with the slide background forming a smooth transition from light to dark, the highlight area will appear to be "lit" from the upper left. Or if you're shading backgrounds from the title, you can adjust the embossed object so that the title appears to "light" the object.

SECTION II: BASIC SKILLS

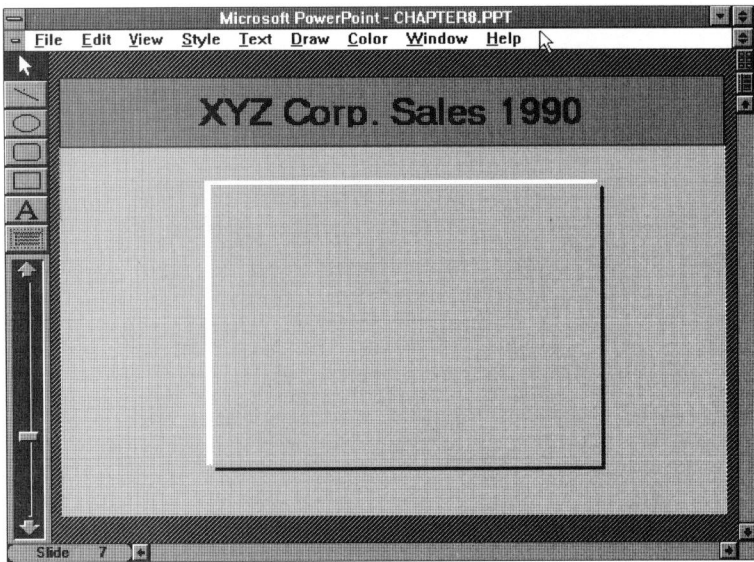

Figure 8-8. *This is the completed embossed object.*

Graduated Fills

You can add impact to your slides and overheads by creating graduated fills for rules and boxes. These can form dramatic borders or accents, or you can use them as backgrounds for artwork, charts, or text. You can also use this technique to create three-dimensional "pipes" to connect objects.

Let's assume that your current presentation contains a shaded horizontal background that is light at the top and dark at the bottom. Your goal is to create a shaded box that contains the same colors but that is dark at the top and light at the bottom. To create such a shaded box, do the following.

1. Open a new presentation. Choose the Use Format Of Active Presentation option. In Macintosh PowerPoint, the presentation is named "Untitled"; in Windows PowerPoint, it is named "Presentation."

2. Choose a shading direction (from among the Shade Background options) that is the opposite of the one already chosen.

3. After applying your background, open the Draw menu and choose Opaque. (This is crucial. Be sure that Opaque is the only option selected.)

4. Choose the Rectangle tool and, while holding down the mouse button, create a box that encompasses as much of the light-to-dark range of background as you want to use, as shown in Figure 8-9. (You can choose a more limited range of shading by including a smaller portion of the Slide background.)

5. With the box selected, choose Copy from the Edit menu.

6. Close the new presentation. (This returns you to your original presentation.) Or switch to your original presentation by choosing its name from the Window menu.

7. Choose Paste As Picture from the Edit menu. The box now appears, with the shading running exactly opposite to the shading in the original Slide background. (See Figure 8-10 on the following page.)

Because the box has been pasted as a picture, you can resize it as desired. If the box is given a large size, it can be used as a background for text or graphics. Or a thin version can frame the top or bottom of your slides. (See Figure 8-11 on the following page.)

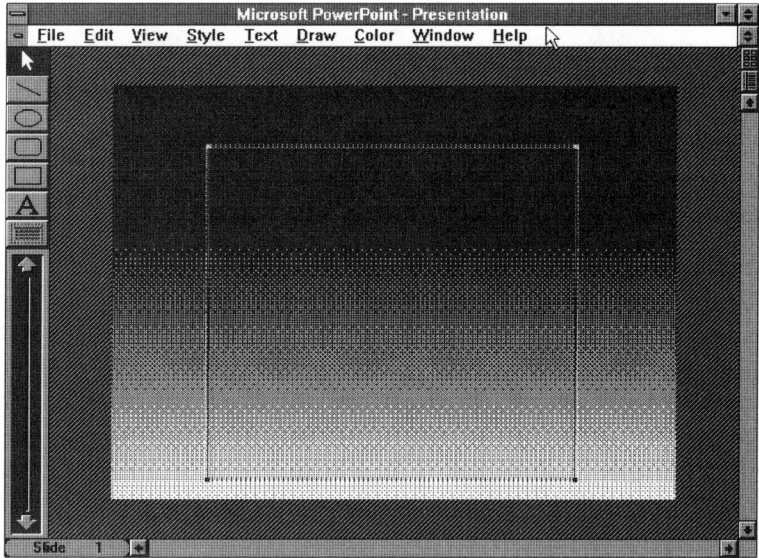

Figure 8-9. *You can define the graduated fill area that you import into an existing presentation.*

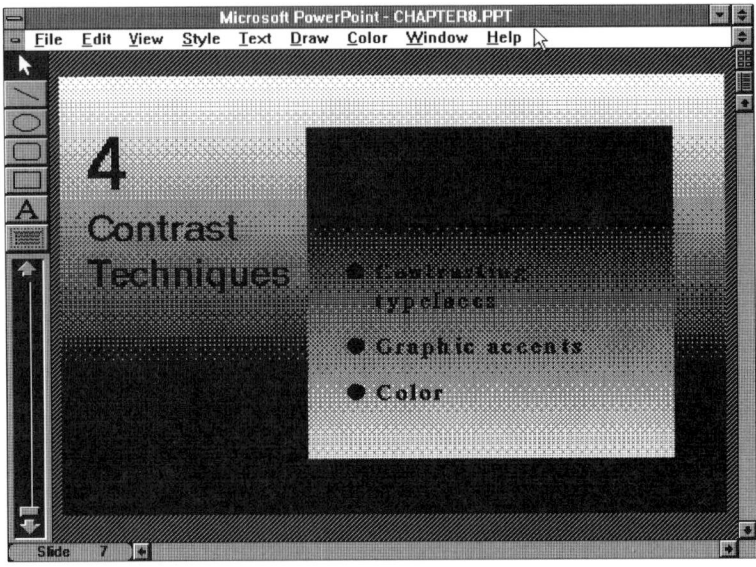

Figure 8-10. You can set text against a graduated background.

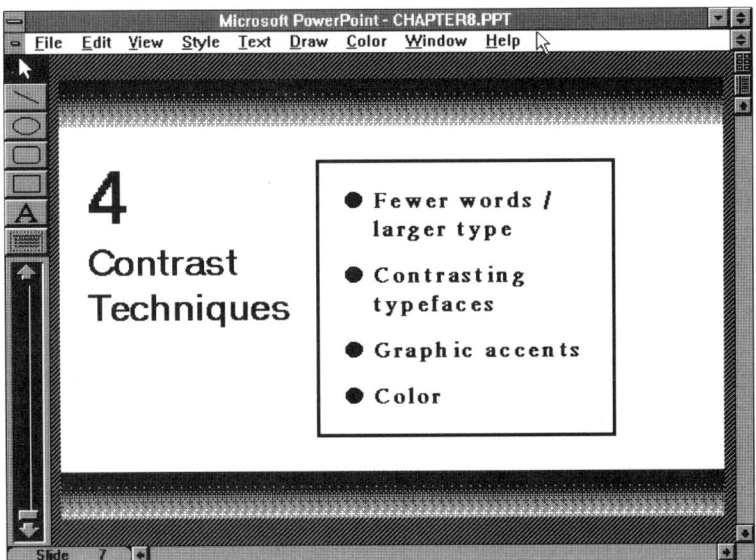

Figure 8-11. You can frame the top or bottom of visuals with graduated fills.

A wide version can be used to draw attention to information at either the left or the right side of the slide. (See Figure 8-12.)

To free computer memory, close the "Untitled" or "Presentation" slide after you've copied the box into your original presentation.

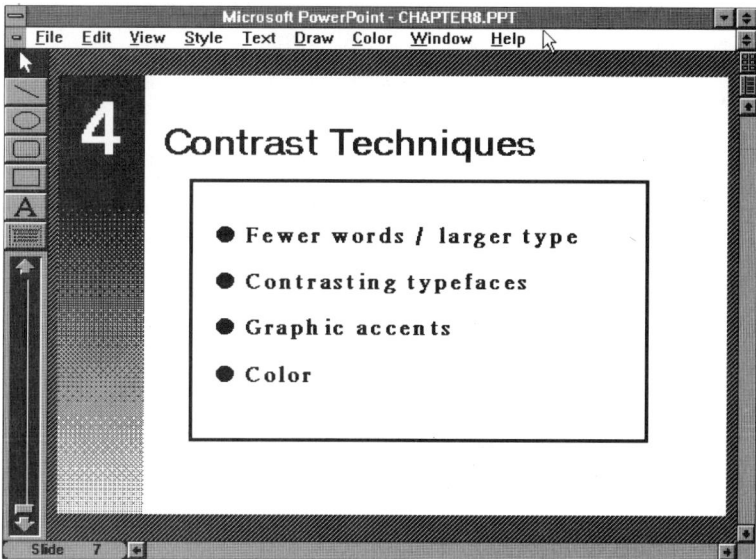

Figure 8-12. Using a graduated fill as a vertical accent to the left of the text area.

Creative options

As you become comfortable using graduated fills, you'll find they offer tremendous creative possibilities. For example, you can create horizontal or vertical "pipes" (as shown in Figure 8-13 on the following page).

To create a pipe, choose the Shade Horizontal or the Shade Vertical option, using one of the two shaded-from-center variations, and center the box you're copying over the shaded area.

In the example in Figure 8-14 on the following page, graduated fill pipes are used to connect items in an organizational chart.

If you want the graduated fill to appear on every slide, place it on your presentation's Slide Master.

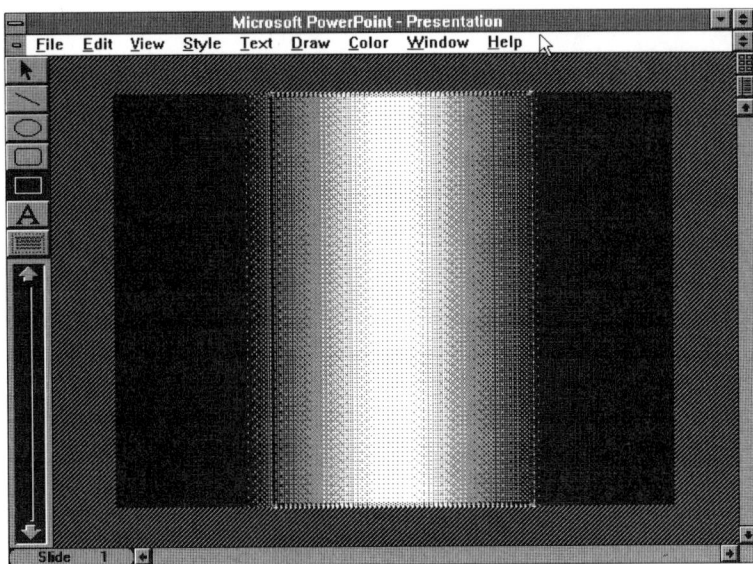

Figure 8-13. You can create a piping effect by using the Shade Horizontal or the Shade Vertical option and centering the box over the shaded area.

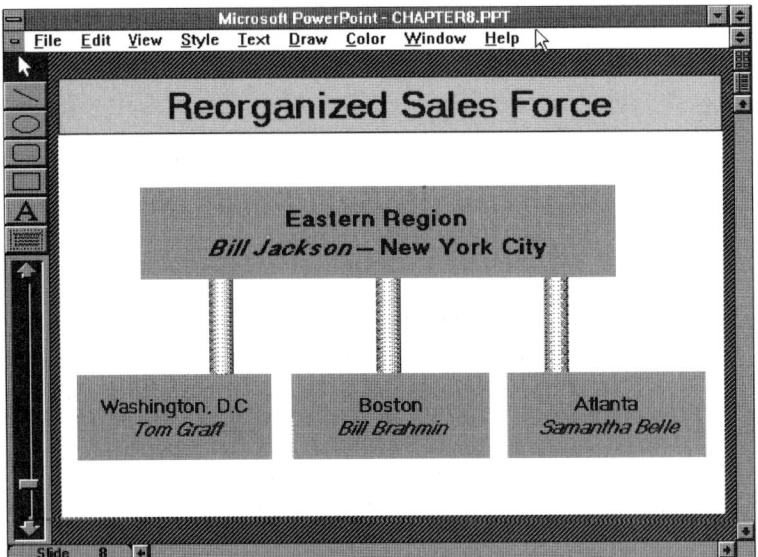

Figure 8-14. You can use three-dimensional pipes to connect items in an organizational chart.

Another effective use of this technique is to change the format of your new presentation by changing the order of the colors in the Color Scheme. Simply replace the Background color with the Foreground color or with one of the Accent colors, and choose Apply. This ensures that the graduated fill will match your presentation's Color Scheme.

Shining Graphics

You can create a highlight that appears to illuminate the rest of the slide. This is an especially useful technique if you have a symbol that you want to have appear as if it were shedding light on a problem.

"Shining graphics" is an especially effective technique to use in conjunction with the embossing technique or the Recolor A Picture tool. To create a shining graphic, do the following.

1. Click on the slide *Title*. Select the fuzzy border and move *Title* to the location from which you want the "light" to appear to originate.

2. While the title is selected, highlight the word *Title* and press the Spacebar.

3. Choose Color Scheme from the Color menu.

4. Choose Shade Background and then Choose From Title.

5. Select the option at the right by clicking on it. This indicates a light area that is surrounded by darker shades. To emphasize the shining-graphics effect, adjust the scroll box to the right. When you've finished, click on OK.

When you leave the Color Scheme box, be sure you choose the proper Apply To option to apply the effect only to the slide or slides you want to modify. Cover *Title* (which is now only a space) with the graphic that will represent the light source that "illuminates" the rest of the slide. (See Figure 8-15 on the following page.) Import and resize the desired graphic and place it over *Title* (that is, the space).

To maintain continuity with the rest of your presentation, you should add a second title using the Word Processor tool. The only disadvantage with this approach is that the new title will not appear in the Title Sorter view. If this bothers you, here's how to get around this problem.

SECTION II: BASIC SKILLS

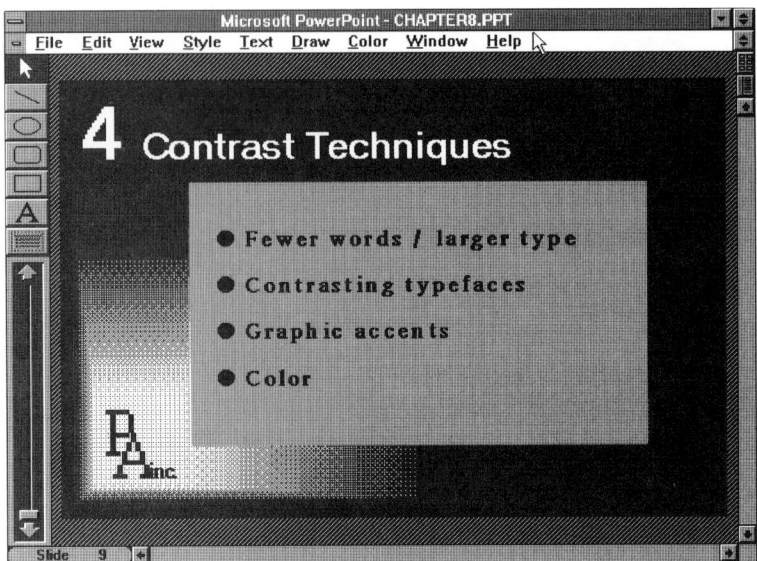

Figure 8-15. A slide background can be "lit" by an imported graphic (a "shining graphic").

1. Enter the title text in the normal way.
2. Copy the text and paste the copy into the slide location you want.
3. Select the original title by clicking on it.
4. Choose Color from the Color menu, and recolor the text the same color as used for Slide Background.

You can increase the size of the "light source" by pressing the Spacebar as many times as necessary. If you inadvertently create a light source that is too large, you can reduce it by pressing the Backspace key. By experimenting, you can adjust the light source so that the source of the light is exactly the same size as the graphic it's supposed to emanate from.

Organizational Charts

The Guides and Object Label tool allows you to create organizational charts. Organizational charts are useful for displaying dominant-subordinate relationships as well as for displaying sequences of events in flow-chart style.

Creating the boxes

To create the boxes for the organizational chart, do the following.

1. Choose Show Guides from the Draw menu (if Guides are not already displayed).

2. Deselect Sized To Text from the Draw menu.

3. Create a box for the top level of the organizational chart by using the Rounded Rectangle or Rectangle tool. Select the box and center it over the vertical guide.

4. While the box remains selected, use the Copy command to copy the box.

5. Drag the horizontal guide to the level you want for the top of the second level of the organizational chart. Use the Paste command to paste as many copies of the box as needed for the second level of your organizational chart. (See Figure 8-16.) Use the vertical guide as a measuring tool to ensure equal horizontal spacing.

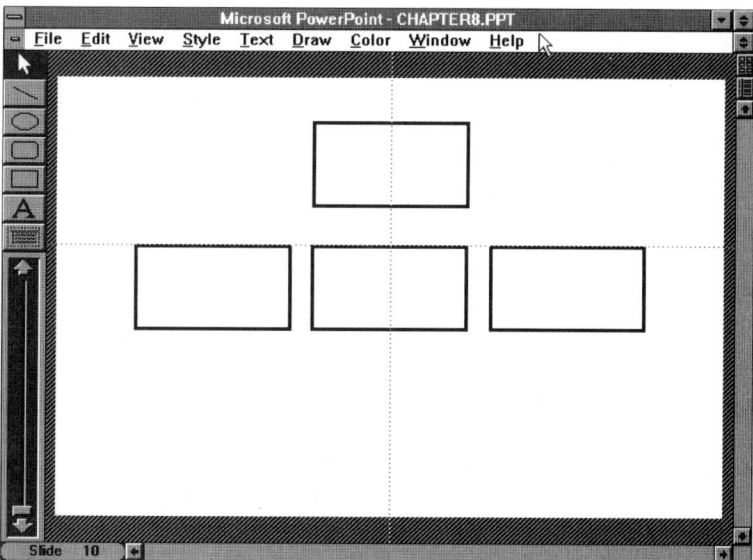

Figure 8-16. *You use the horizontal and vertical guides, the Copy and Paste commands, and the drawing tools to create the second level of an organizational chart.*

6. Drag the horizontal guide to the top of the third level of your organizational chart. Paste in as many copies of the box as needed. (See Figure 8-17.) Again, use the vertical guide as a measuring tool to ensure equal horizontal spacing. (Alternatively, you can use one of the box-drawing tools to create a filled placeholder to separate the boxes.)

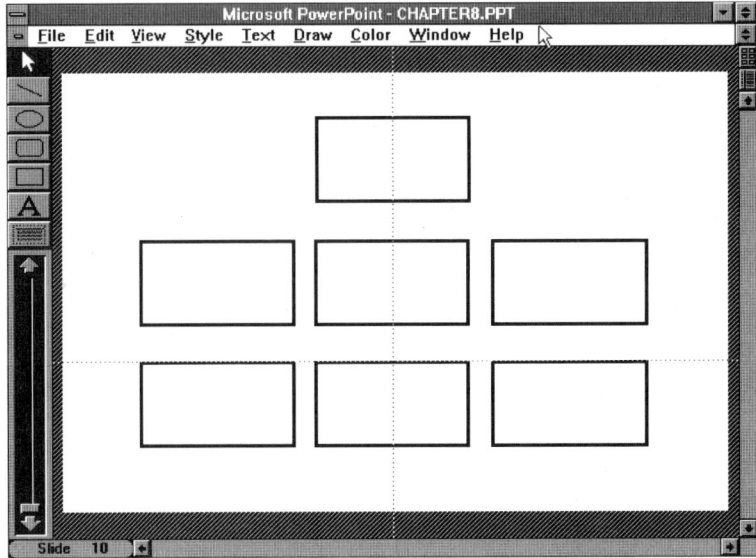

Figure 8-17. *You again use the guides, the Copy and Paste commands, and the drawing tools to create the third level of an organizational chart.*

Adding text

The Attached Label feature allows you to add text to each box. Simply select each box and begin typing. Text will automatically be centered. (See Figure 8-18.) Use a hard return if you want text placed on another line.

All levels of an organizational chart need not be contained in boxes. You can create the lowest level of an organizational chart as a list using the Word Processor tool. This permits you to adjust line spacing as well as alignment. You can also include bullets and hanging indents to emphasize each point.

After you size and format the first list, use the Copy and Paste commands to create as many identically formatted lists as needed. Use the horizontal guide to align the tops of each word processing box. Use the vertical guides to ensure equal spacing.

Chapter 8: PowerPoint Tips and Techniques

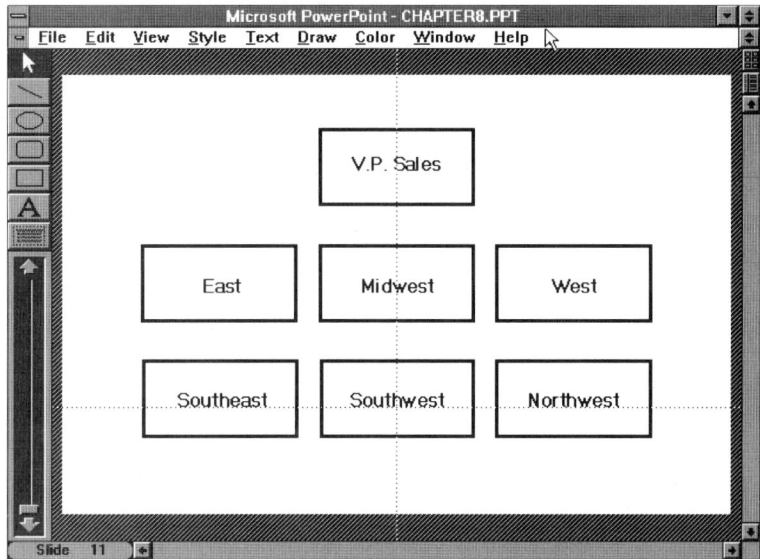

Figure 8-18. *You can add text to each box by using the Attached Label feature.*

Connecting the boxes

Now you can use the Line tool to connect the boxes. You can connect the boxes with lines of identical thickness, as shown in Figure 8-19 on the following page, or you can add character to your presentation by using heavier rules for either the horizontal or the vertical lines.

Accurate placement is made easy by the tendency of the lines to "bond" themselves to the box borders if you release the mouse button near the borders. Here are some line-drawing hints worth remembering.

- ◆ Hold down the Shift key as you use the Line tool. This ensures that the lines connecting the boxes will meet at right angles.

- ◆ When lines meet at a 90-degree angle, simply click and begin drawing the next line.

- ◆ To work with greater precision, choose the Full Size command from the View menu.

Organizational charts can have either a horizontal or a vertical orientation. The presentation of organizational charts can be enhanced by builds: Simply introduce one level at a time. Other possible enhancements include choosing Shadowed from the Draw menu and then choosing an appropriate Shadow Color from the Color menu.

SECTION II: BASIC SKILLS

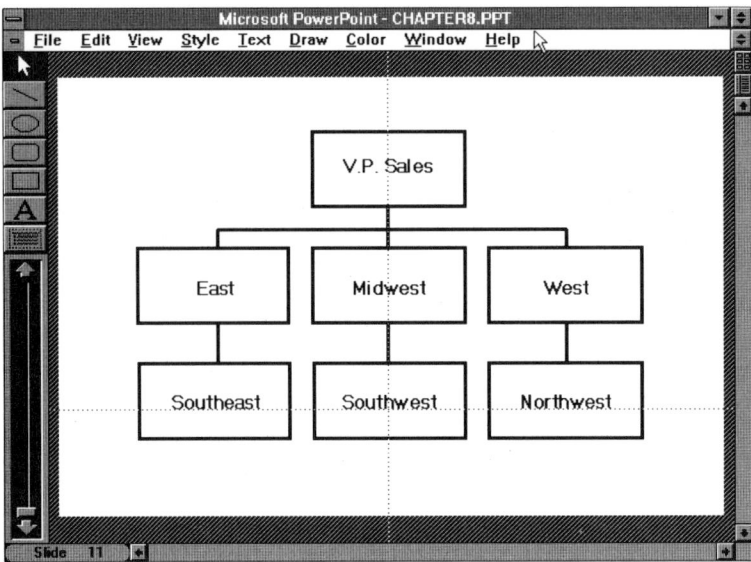

Figure 8-19. Organizational chart with lines connecting the boxes.

Tables

You can use a table to display names or numbers in a minimal amount of space. Tables can organize even the most complicated lists.

Creating a table

To create a table that contains 12 boxes (three rows by four columns), do the following.

1. Create a box by using the Rectangle tool.
2. Copy the box.
3. Choose Paste 11 times—once fewer than the total number of boxes needed. (The first box has already been created.)
4. Select the first box, and move it into approximate position.
5. Select another box and place it next to the first. Complete the first row by placing the last two boxes next to each other.
6. Select another box and place it under the first box. Complete the second row by placing the remaining three boxes next to each other. As you work, notice how the boxes are automatically attracted to each other. All you need to do is drag a box near its neighbor—and it automatically snaps into place.

7. Complete the third row in a manner similar to the completion of the first and second rows. (See Figure 8-20.)

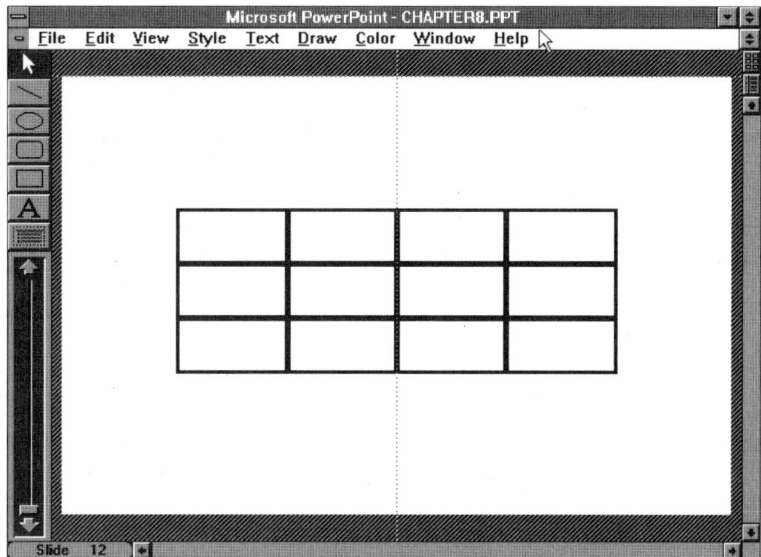

Figure 8-20. *You can create a table by copying and pasting boxes.*

Entering text in a table

You can use the Attached Label feature to enter text in each box.

1. Be sure that Sized To Text on the Draw menu is turned off.

2. Choose an appropriate typeface, type size, and type style from the Style menu. Choose Center from the Text menu unless it's already selected.

3. Click on each box. Enter the text you want. Text will be centered both horizontally and vertically. Text will not wrap, so press the Return key whenever you want to begin a new line of text.

After text has been entered, the table can be moved as a unit. You can select the table in two ways.

◆ Choose Select All from the Edit menu, and click on the slide title, while holding down the Shift key, to deselect it.

◆ You can use the selection tool and create a marquee box—or flashing box—surrounding the table.

SECTION II: BASIC SKILLS

Text can be edited, even after the box has been moved. You can enhance the table by using contrasting background patterns and by using various line thicknesses and colors. You can also introduce rows and columns as builds.

Callouts

You can use callouts to add selective emphasis to one or more elements on a slide. Callouts consist of a short phrase or an explanatory sentence attached to a graphic by using a rule that ends in an arrowhead. (See Figure 8-21.)

To add a callout to a slide or graphic, do the following.

1. Start with a slide containing a properly sized and placed graphic.
2. Choose Line Style from the Draw menu, and then choose a line of appropriate thickness.
3. Choose Arrowheads from the Draw menu, and then choose either the single or the double arrowhead option.
4. Choose the Line tool, and while holding down the mouse button, drag the pointer *in the direction you want the arrow to point.*
5. Choose the Labeler tool, and click on the slide location where you want to add the callout. Format the text as described in Chapter 5.

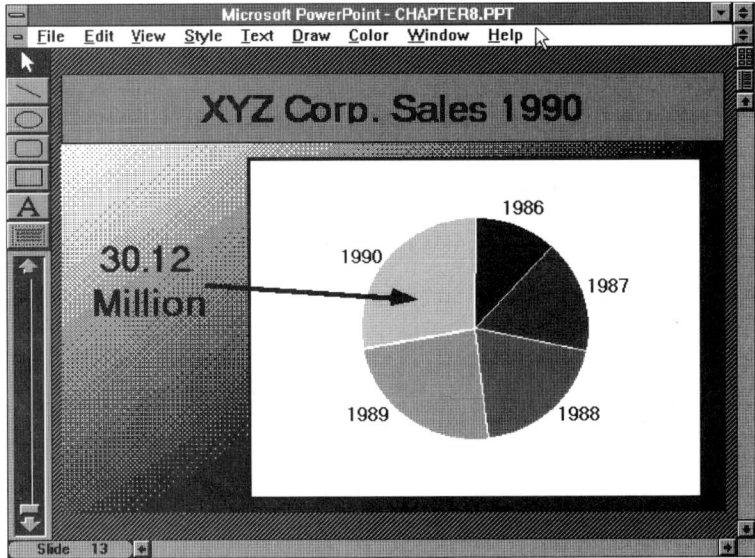

Figure 8-21. *A callout (phrase plus rule with pointing arrow) draws attention to an individual chart segment.*

Callouts are especially effective when you use them in conjunction with builds. You can use callouts to draw attention to new text or portions of a chart or graph as they are added. For example, you can use callouts to add emphasis as new slices of a pie chart appear on successive slides.

Logos

PowerPoint makes it easy to create a logo for special occasions. If you have access to an image scanner, you might also be able to use your firm's logo as a background element.

Creating a logo

The Cut and Paste As Picture commands can be used to create a logo out of individual letters. Let's assume that your firm's—or your client's—name is Presentation Associates, Inc., and that you need to create a logo fast. Here's what you do.

1. Choose the Labeler tool, and type an uppercase *P*. (The pointer is now an I-beam.) Highlight the letter you just created by dragging the I-beam through it.

2. Choose Font from the Style menu. If you're using Macintosh PowerPoint, hold down the mouse button, move the pointer to the right, and scroll down until Times is highlighted, and then release the mouse button. If you're using Windows PowerPoint, hold down the left mouse button, move the pointer to the right, and scroll down until Tms Rmn is highlighted, and then release the mouse button.

3. Choose Size from the Style menu. When the submenu appears, move the mouse to the right and select *48*.

4. Choose the Arrow tool, click on the letter you just created, and then choose Copy from the Edit menu.

5. Choose Paste from the Edit menu.

6. When a second *P* appears on the screen, select it by clicking on it.

7. Highlight the second *P* by dragging the I-beam through it. Type in an uppercase *A* followed by a lowercase *inc*.

8. Highlight *inc.* by dragging the I-beam through it. Choose Size from the Style menu. Scroll through the list of available type sizes. Release the button when *14* is highlighted. (See Figure 8-22 on the following page.)

SECTION II: BASIC SKILLS

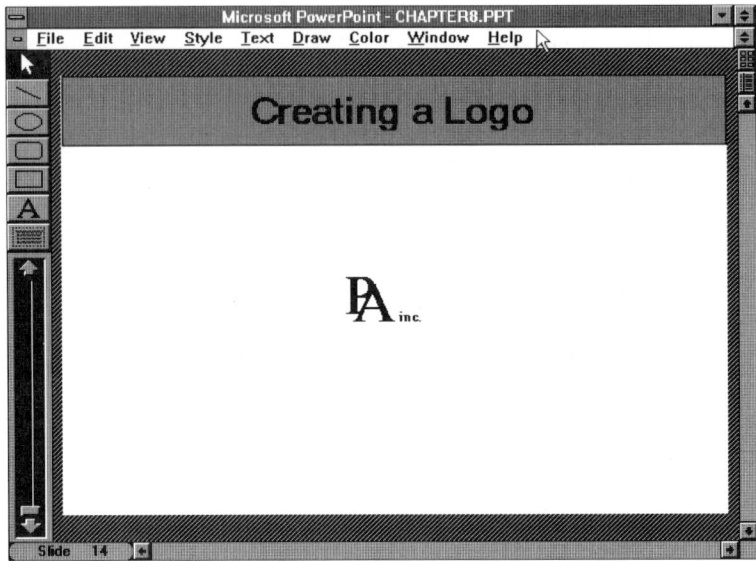

Figure 8-22. *Here are the elements of the Presentation Associates logo before repositioning.*

9. Select Full Size from the View menu.

10. Select the *Ainc.* text block. Click on one of the fuzzy borders surrounding the text block, and position it a bit lower and to the right of the *P*. (See Figure 8-23.)

11. When you're satisfied with the relative position of the *P* and the *Ainc.*, select them both by clicking on them while holding down the Shift key, or by dragging a marquee around them with the Arrow tool.

12. While both are selected, choose Cut from the Edit menu.

13. Choose Paste As Picture. When the Presentation Associates logo appears on the screen, it can be resized as needed. Simply hold down the Shift key as you increase or decrease the size of the logo by dragging one of the corner handles. (See Figure 8-24.)

If you're working with Macintosh PowerPoint, you can now paste the Presentation Associates logo into the Macintosh scrapbook. If you're working with Windows PowerPoint, you might want to save the presentation containing your logo in a special file, perhaps in the Samples subdirectory. This will allow you to find it when you need it.

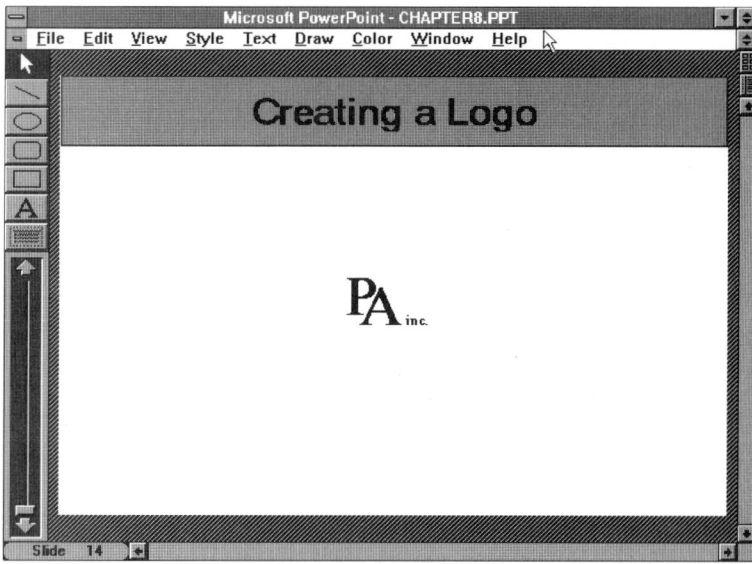

Figure 8-23. Here are the elements of the Presentation Associates logo after repositioning.

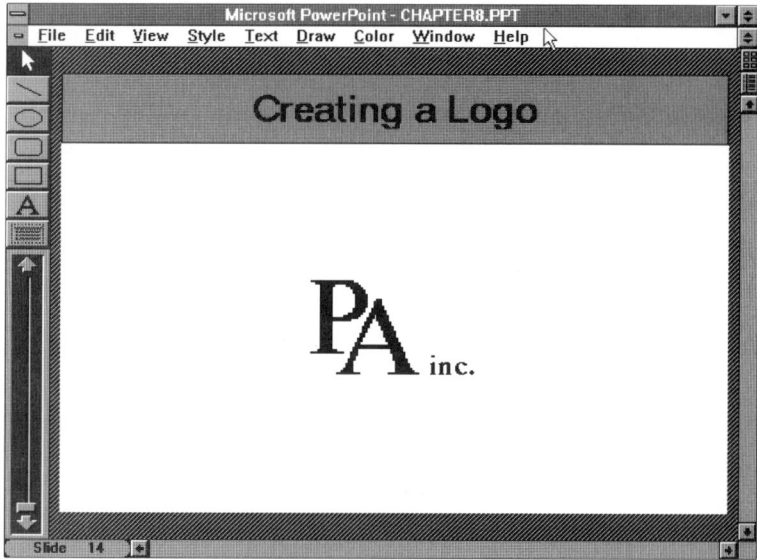

Figure 8-24. You can maintain the aspect ratio of the Presentation Associates logo by holding down the Shift key as you resize the logo.

Using an existing logo as a background element

If you have access to an image scanner and are sending your presentation to Genigraphics for production, you can use an enlargement of your firm's logo as a background element on your Slide Masters. Your logo treatment can be as literal or as abstract as you want. This technique works especially well if your logo consists of a few thick letters or a large, simple shape.

To use a logo as a background element, do the following.

1. Locate or print out a high-quality version of your firm's logo. If the logo was created with a drawing program such as Aldus Freehand or Adobe Illustrator, consider printing it about 6 inches square on a high-resolution Linotronic phototypesetter.

2. Scan your logo and save it as a PICT file. (As described in the previous chapter, PICT files can be reproduced by both laser printers and the high-resolution film recorders Genigraphics uses to produce slides and overheads.)

3. Open the File menu, and then choose Paste From to import the scanned image.

You can use your logo as a background element in your presentation in several ways.

- You can use it as a repeating element across the top or bottom of your slides and overheads.
- You can stack logos vertically along the right or the left edge.
- You can use a large, simple outline of your logo behind the text. (This works especially well on title and conclusion slides.)

You must be careful, of course, not to allow the logo to interfere with the legibility of your message. (See Figure 8-25.) This technique works best if you use the Recolor Picture command to select a shade from the Color Scheme slightly lighter or slightly darker than the Slide Background color and if you choose solid background colors. (Note: You should avoid the use of shaded backgrounds because some logos will appear lighter or darker than others, which can attract unnecessary attention.)

The large scanned image of your logo can be enhanced even further by the embossing effect described earlier in this chapter. This effect can be as dramatic or as subtle as you want.

Figure 8-25. *You can use a scanned image of a logo as a background for your title slide.*

By choosing colors that contrast with the Slide Background you've chosen, you can make the logo "pop" (stand out). Or by choosing lighter and darker shades of the Slide Background color, you can "quietly" enhance your presentation without danger of overkill.

Three-Dimensional Text (aka *Shadow Lettering*)

To create a dramatic, three-dimensional title for your presentation with the "shadow lettering" technique, begin by entering the words with the Word Processor tool (instead of the Labeler tool) so that you can adjust line spacing for maximum impact.

Highlight the words, and choose Font from the Style menu. Choose a typeface and type size. While the words are highlighted, you'll probably want to choose the Line Spacing command on the Text menu and reduce line spacing to 80% of the original. With a little experimenting, you'll soon be able to accurately estimate appropriate line spacing for a variety of type sizes. (If you're using uppercase text, you have even more opportunity to reduce line spacing, because uppercase type lacks descenders.)

While the text is still highlighted, choose the alignment you want—perhaps centered if you're creating a title slide.

Next, select the text box with the Arrow tool, and then choose Copy and then Paste. After you paste a copy of the text, it will be offset slightly below and to the right of the original text.

While the pasted text is still selected, choose Text from the Color menu.

Choose a color that will enhance the original text. Options include a lighter or darker shade of the original text or a shade of gray. If the appropriate color doesn't appear on your presentation's Color Scheme, choose Other.

While the image remains selected, you can adjust its degree of offset from the original lettering by selecting the shadow and moving it. For added precision, choose Full Size from the View menu and then Ignore Grid from the Draw menu if Snap To Grid is activated.

When you're satisfied with both color and offset, select both the original and the offset text. After you've selected both the original and the offset text, choose Cut from the Edit menu, and then choose Paste As Picture. You've just created shadow lettering! (See Figure 8-26.)

When the text reappears, the original and the offset text will be permanently locked. You can now move, resize, or recolor them as a single object. (You might want to experiment further with different colors, using the Recolor Picture command.)

Figure 8-26. *You can create shadow lettering for title slides by using the Text command on the Color menu.*

More important, you can now enhance the text with commands from the Draw menu.

1. Add a frame around the words by choosing Framed and an appropriate line thickness from the Line Style dialog box.

2. Place the text against a contrasting background by choosing Filled and an appropriate pattern from the Pattern dialog box.

3. Add a shadow around the text by choosing Shadowed.

You can choose the Fill, Line, Shadow, and Pattern Contrast commands from the Color menu to add further impact to the title. In addition, because the text is now a graphic, it can be distorted by horizontal or vertical stretching. (Always use discretion when distorting type, however.)

In addition to titles, shadow lettering can be used to create slides such as "The End" or "Any Questions?"

TIMESAVING TIPS

If most of your presentations are based on a common format, PowerPoint makes it easy to begin working on a new presentation. You can create a default presentation reflecting your firm's visual identity. You can also incorporate previously created slides, Slide Masters, and Color Schemes into both new and existing presentations.

Import Outlines

You can import previously prepared outlines into your open PowerPoint presentation.

In Macintosh PowerPoint, you can import outline files created with the outlining programs More and ThinkTank. In Windows PowerPoint, you can import ASCII text files created with any word processing application, or Microsoft Word files saved as RTF (Rich Text Format) files. This allows you to save time and avoid retyping. To import a previously prepared outline, do the following.

1. Select the Title Sorter view from the View menu.

2. Open the File menu and choose Paste From. Scroll through the various folders (in Macintosh PowerPoint) or subdirectories (in Windows PowerPoint) until you find the file you want to use.

3. Double-click on the filename.

PowerPoint will place the first level of each topic as the title of each visual, followed by subordinate information.

Create Default Presentations

If all your presentations are going to share the same basic look, you can save a lot of time by creating a default presentation that is loaded automatically when you start PowerPoint and every time you choose New from the File menu.

This default presentation defines the following.

- ◆ Format and output device
- ◆ Slide Master (including borders, Color Scheme, title treatment, and logo placement)
- ◆ Style, Text, Line, Draw, and Color defaults
- ◆ Word Processor box fills, frames, shadows, tabs, indents, and line spacing
- ◆ Notes and Handouts formats

In Windows PowerPoint, the default presentation can also include a formatted default chart created with the PowerPoint Graph program.

Note: If you're creating a default format based on an existing presentation, be sure you carefully go through each slide and remove all text and graphics specific to the presentation. Otherwise, these will become a part of your default presentation.

After you've defined your default presentation, choose Save As from the File menu.

If you're using Macintosh PowerPoint, choose the System folder or the PowerPoint folder, and name your presentation *Default format*. If you're using Windows PowerPoint, choose the PowerPoint subdirectory, and name your presentation *DEFAULT.PPT*.

Now, whenever you start PowerPoint, the default format appears. In addition, whenever you choose New from the File menu, you're given an opportunity to base your presentation on the default format or the format of the currently active presentation. (See Figure 8-27.)

Chapter 8: PowerPoint Tips and Techniques

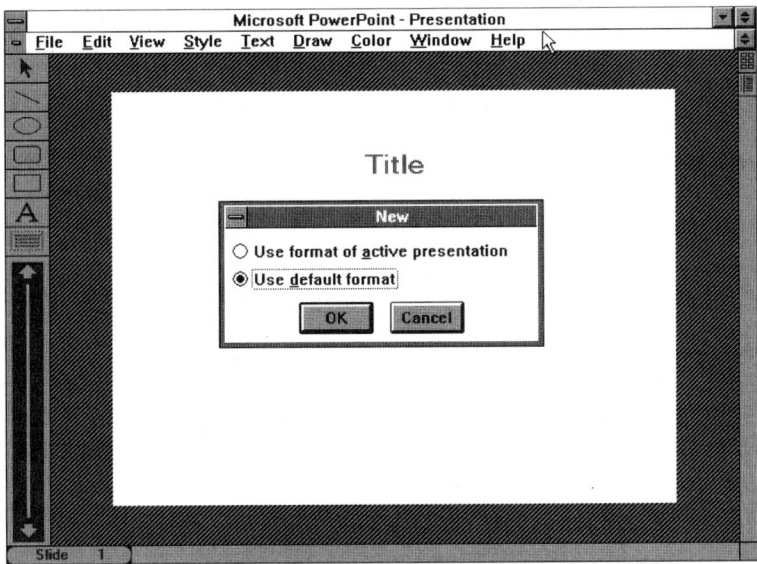

Figure 8-27. *You can save a presentation that can be used as the basis for future presentations.*

Share Slides Between Presentations

You might find yourself using the same slides or overheads in more than one presentation. For example:

- If you're an advertising agency, you might always include the same slides describing past successes or the backgrounds of key personnel.

- In a corporate setting, you might include the same economic assumptions and projections in more than one presentation.

- In governmental environments, you might reuse the same demographic projections in several presentations.

You might even go so far as to create a "resource" presentation that might never be presented to an audience but will serve simply as a "database" for creating other presentations.

Working in the Slide Sorter view

- To share slides between presentations, open the first, or "source," presentation. Choose Slide Sorter from the View menu. (See Figure 8-28 on the following page.) To fit more slides into the window, choose either 50% view or 33% view.

231

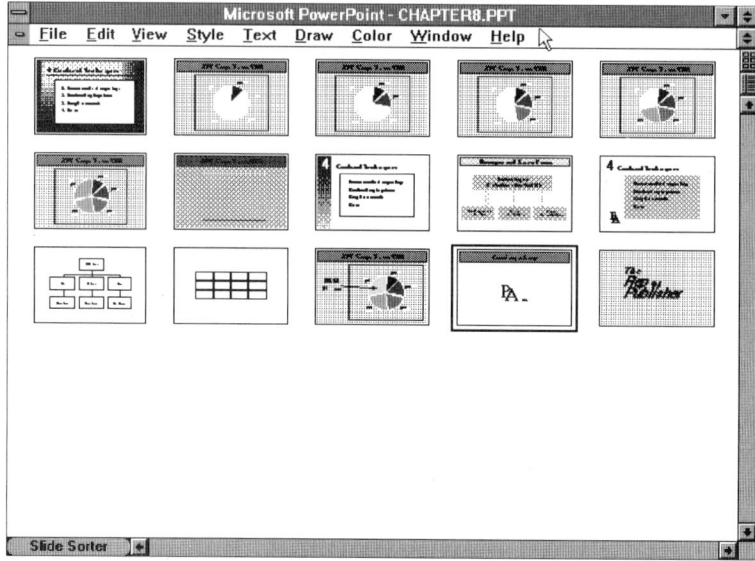

Figure 8-28. *You can use the Slide Sorter view when you want to copy slides from one presentation to another.*

- Next, create or open a new or existing "target" presentation. (See Figure 8-29.) Choose Slide Sorter, and then choose 50% view or 33% view to fit more slides into the screen.

- To copy a slide from the source presentation to the target presentation, select a slide by clicking on it and then choosing Copy from the Edit menu.

- Activate the target presentation. Click at the point where you want the new slide to be inserted. A vertical flashing cursor will appear at the insertion point. Choose Paste from the Edit menu. A copy of the source slide will appear in the target presentation. (See Figure 8-30.)

If you hold down the Shift key while selecting slides from the Source presentation, you can copy more than one slide at a time. When you paste them into the target presentation, however, they will be pasted together.

Working in the Title Sorter view

If you have provided each slide with a title that identifies its contents, you can copy slides between presentations using the Title Sorter view. Working in Title Sorter view saves time because your computer doesn't have to redraw the slides shown on the screen after each change.

Chapter 8: PowerPoint Tips and Techniques

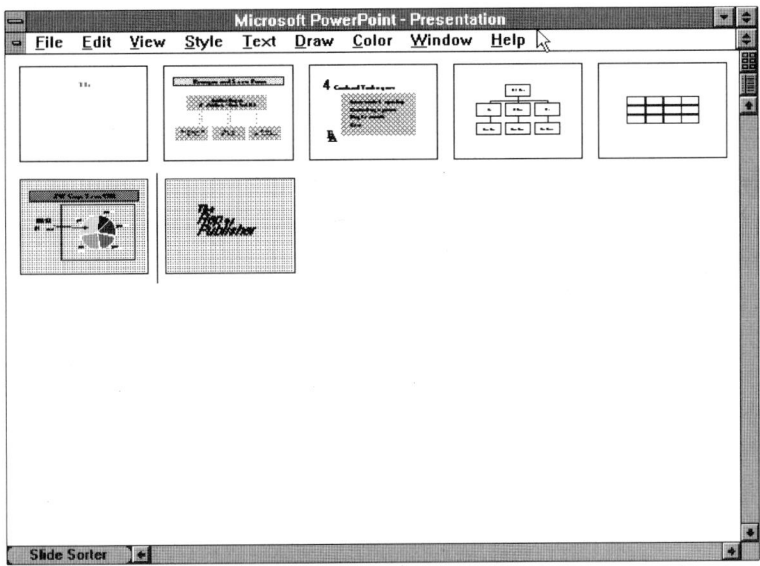

Figure 8-29. This Slide Sorter view shows a "target" presentation. The vertical line between the two slides in the second row shows the insertion point for the new slide.

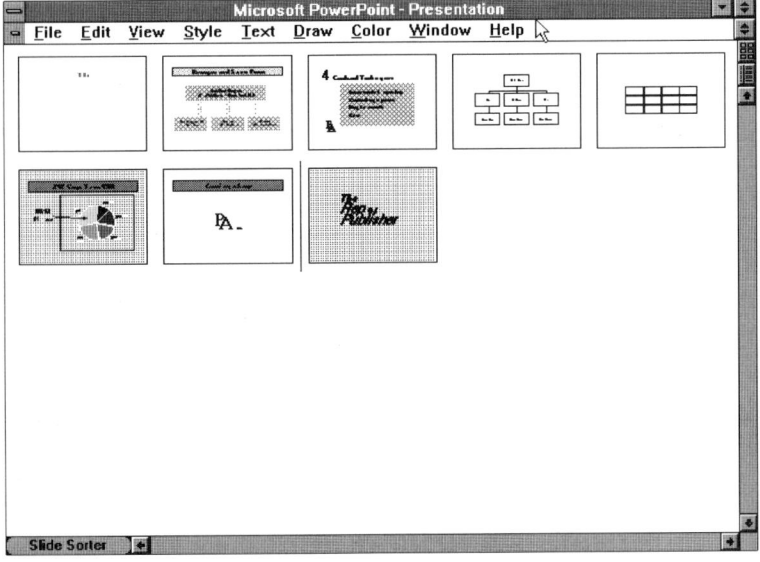

Figure 8-30. Target presentation with added slide.

233

Slides can be edited after they've been pasted in a target presentation. This permits you to create standard slide types—or templates—that will be modified after they've been copied to a different target presentation.

For example, you might create a series of organizational charts and tables that can be copied from your "resource" file as needed.

Share Slide Masters Between Presentations

With PowerPoint, you can base new presentations on previously created Slide Masters. In addition, you can update existing presentations with previously created Slide Masters.

New presentations

You can use a Slide Master that you created previously as the basis for a new presentation.

1. Open the original presentation by clicking on its title.
2. Choose New from the File menu.
3. A dialog box appears, as shown in Figure 8-31, and asks if you want to base your new presentation on the format of the active presentation.

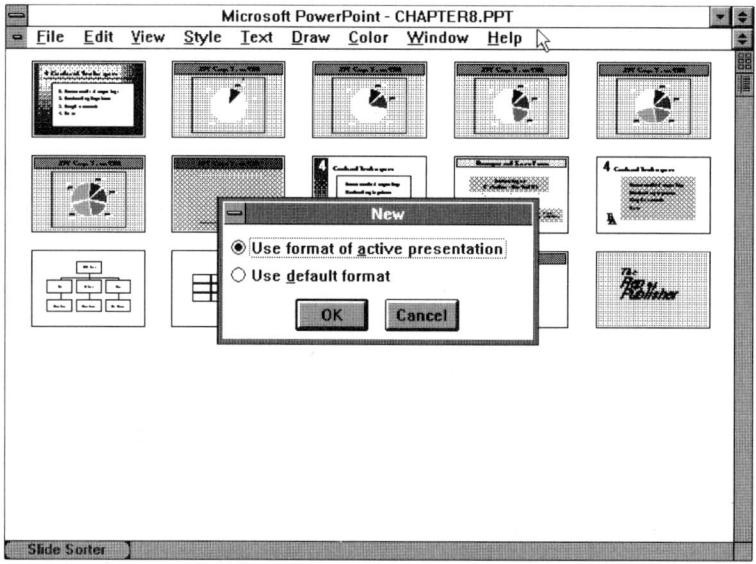

Figure 8-31. You can base a new presentation on the Slide Master of an open presentation.

Click OK, or press Enter. Your new presentation will now share the Slide Master—including Color Scheme—of the original presentation.

Share Color Schemes Between Presentations

You can apply a previously created Color Scheme to an existing presentation.

1. Open the presentation containing a slide with the Color Scheme you want to reuse.

2. Open the Color Scheme dialog box—but do not close it!

3. Choose Open from the File menu, and click on the name of an existing presentation you want to recolor.

4. When the new presentation appears, choose Color Scheme from the Window menu at the upper right of your screen. Notice that the dialog box still displays the Color Scheme of the source presentation. (See Figure 8-32.)

5. Choose Apply To All Slides, and click on Apply.

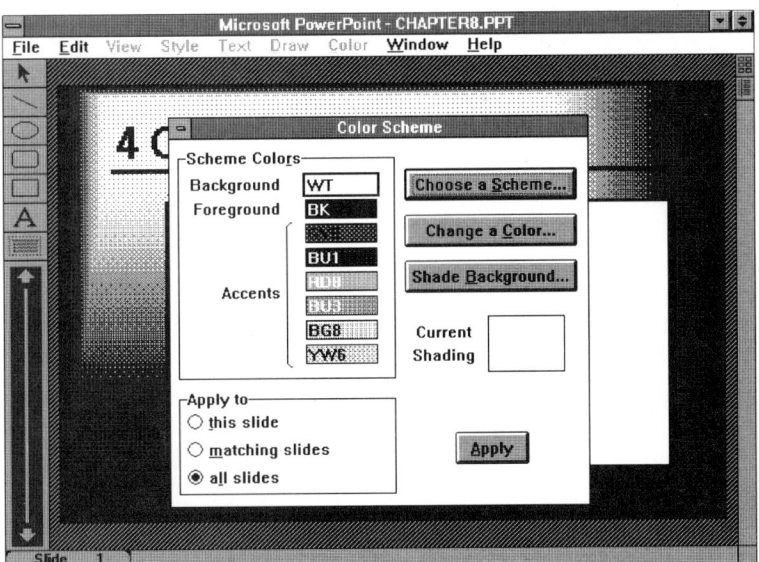

Figure 8-32. Original presentation's Color Scheme superimposed over presentation to be recolored.

All the slides in your target presentation will be recolored using the Color Scheme of the original presentation.

6. Choose Apply To This Slide if you want to apply the new Color Scheme only to the active slide.

7. Choose Apply To Matching Slides if you want to apply the new Color Scheme only to slides that share the Color Scheme of the active slide.

Transfer Files Between Windows PowerPoint and Macintosh PowerPoint

The PowerPoint file translator utility, available from Microsoft, allows you to share files between Windows PowerPoint and Macintosh PowerPoint.

EVALUATING YOUR PROGRESS

As you review your work, ask yourself the following questions.

- ◆ Did I use builds to introduce information step by step?
- ◆ Did I add impact to my presentation by using special effects such as embossing and shining graphics?
- ◆ Have I created organizational charts and tables to display information as effectively as possible?
- ◆ Did I use the vertical guides to ensure that the boxes and the lines connecting them are centered?
- ◆ Did I create a default presentation that incorporates the design attributes of my most frequently used presentation format?
- ◆ Am I working as efficiently as possible by sharing slides and Color Schemes among presentations?

III

HANDS-ON POWERPOINT

Preparing Handouts, Notes, and Visuals

Presentations become tangible when you create 35mm slides or overhead transparencies or when you display your presentation on a computer screen or projection device. You can add value to your presentation by preparing notes and by supplying handouts to the audience. Notes help you rehearse and deliver your presentation by reminding you of important points. Handouts help your audience review your presentation at a later date and share it with those unable to attend.

In contrast to desktop publishing, where a single output device is often used for both proofing and preparing final artwork, presentations frequently involve a close partnership between two or more output devices, each used to produce part of the presentation. You might use one output alternative (say, a color printer or an outside service bureau such as Genigraphics) to produce color slides or overhead transparencies or both, and you might use a second output device (such as a black-and-white laser printer) to proof your visuals and to produce notes and handouts—or Notes pages and Handout pages (as they appear on the PowerPoint screen).

Successful presentations are typically based on a three-step process.

- *Proof your work.* You can perform on-screen proofing with Power-Point's Slide Show feature, which allows you to view your presentation from the audience's perspective. In addition, you can use black-and-white laser printers or color ink-jet or thermal printers to proof your work. Hard-copy proofs help you identify errors that aren't obvious on your computer screen.

◆ *Prepare notes and handouts.* With PowerPoint, you can create a Notes page to accompany every visual. The best time to prepare your Notes is while the ideas are fresh, while you're working on each slide or overhead. You can also prepare Handout pages to give to your audience.

◆ *Produce slides or overheads.* The final step is to print your overheads or to send your slide or overhead transparency files to Genigraphics via floppy disk or by using a modem.

PROOF YOUR WORK

Successful presentations are based on careful attention to detail. Audiences are very critical, and their evaluation of your presentation will be affected by the presence or absence of errors. Therefore, you want to ensure that your presentation is as professional—and error free—as possible.

Even if you've used PowerPoint's spelling checker earlier in your preparations, you should go through a two-stage proofing process before printing final copies of your slides and overheads and before sending your files to Genigraphics for imaging.

1. Preview your work using the Slide Show feature.
2. Prepare hard-copy proofs of your visuals.

Using the Slide Show Feature

PowerPoint's Slide Show feature allows you to become an audience at your own presentation. Slide Show fills the screen of your computer with your presentation visuals, one after the other. Slide Show displays only your presentation visuals; tools and menus are omitted.

To activate the Slide Show feature, choose Slide Show from the File menu, and then choose Manually or Automatically as the preferred way to advance through the slides. (See Figure 9-1.)

If you choose Manually, a new slide is displayed each time you click on the mouse button (for Macintosh PowerPoint) or click on the left mouse button (for Windows PowerPoint). You can also advance to the next slide by pressing the Spacebar, the letter N, or either the Up or the Right direction key.

Chapter 9: Preparing Handouts, Notes, and Visuals

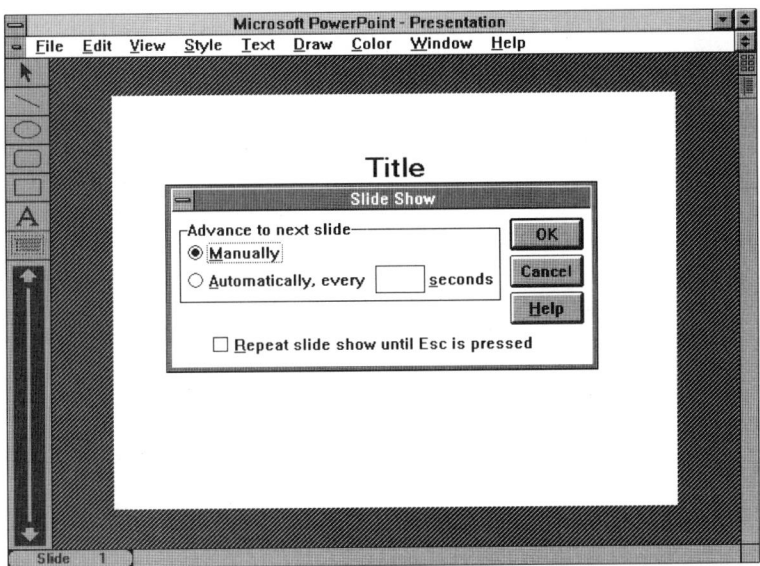

Figure 9-1. *The Slide Show feature lets you preview your presentation from the audience's perspective.*

To review a previous slide using Macintosh PowerPoint, hold down the Command key as you click on the mouse button. Using Windows PowerPoint, you can review the previous slide by clicking on the right mouse button. You can also repeat slides in both Macintosh and Windows PowerPoint by pressing either the Backspace (or Delete) key, the letter P, or either the Left or the Down direction key.

To go directly to a specific slide, enter that slide's number and press Return.

If you choose Automatically, you can define how long each slide will remain on the screen. You can stop the automatic Slide Show at any point by pressing Shift-S or the plus sign (+) key. Pressing Shift-S or the + key again will resume the Slide Show.

On-screen computer-based presentations

You also use PowerPoint's Slide Show feature when you present computer-based on-screen demonstrations using your computer monitor, projection pads placed on top of overhead projectors, or big-screen monitors. When you use the Slide Show feature as your final presentation medium, you'll appreciate the following Slide Show keyboard shortcuts.

- *B or . (period)*—Blacks the screen, or returns the slide if you have already blackened the screen. This feature is useful if you want to interrupt your presentation to address an audience comment or question.

- *W or , (comma)*—Whites the screen, or returns the slide image if the screen has already been made white.

- *A or = (equal sign)*—Adds an on-screen arrow that you can use to draw the audience's attention to a specific point in or segment of a chart. You control the arrow's position by using the mouse. Because the arrow is permanently pointed to the upper left, you'll generally place it below and to the right of the information you want to highlight.

- *I or \ (backslash)*—Inverts the screen. Changing light colors to dark, and vice versa, often makes proofing easier because colors that will reproduce well on overhead transparencies or slides might not be sufficiently bright for accurate proofing on a computer screen.

- *Command-. (period) or – (minus)*—Returns you to the Slide Show dialog box when you're using Macintosh PowerPoint.

- *Esc, Ctrl-Break, or – (minus)*—Returns you to the Slide Show dialog box when you're using Windows PowerPoint.

As you proof your work on screen, watch for consistent placement of repeating elements such as borders, titles, and presentation information. Be especially alert to titles that appear to jump around from slide to slide. In addition, watch out for colors that show up unexpectedly.

Preparing Hard-Copy Proofs

No matter how carefully you proof your presentation on screen, it's virtually impossible to catch every error. That's why it's important to print hard-copy proofs of your presentation—hard copy is easier to read.

If both black-and-white and color printers are available, you might want to prepare two proofs: the first on a black-and-white printer for the content, and the second on a color printer to check for the proper use of color.

Proofing with black-and-white printers

If you have more than one printer connected to your Apple Macintosh, use the Chooser command to switch between the output device that you originally targeted for producing 35mm slides or overhead transparencies and the printer that you'll use to print your proofs. (See Figure 9-2.)

If you're using Macintosh PowerPoint, choose Gray Scale or Inverse Gray Scale from the Slide Colors options in the Print dialog box. These choices speed printing and increase the legibility of your slides. (Experiment with both options to decide which option looks best with the colors used in your presentation.)

In Windows PowerPoint, you use the Printer Setup command to select a printer for printing proofs. (See Figure 9-3 on the following page.)

If you're using Windows PowerPoint, the first step in preparing proofs with a black-and-white laser printer is to choose Draft from the Printer options in the Print dialog box. (See Figure 9-4 on the following page.) At the same time, choose Inverse Gray Scale to reverse light and dark areas, thus increasing the legibility of your slides. Choosing Inverse Gray Scale also speeds printing. If you click the Draft button (located above the Printer options), a dialog box appears with which you can specify a printer to be used only for draft printing.

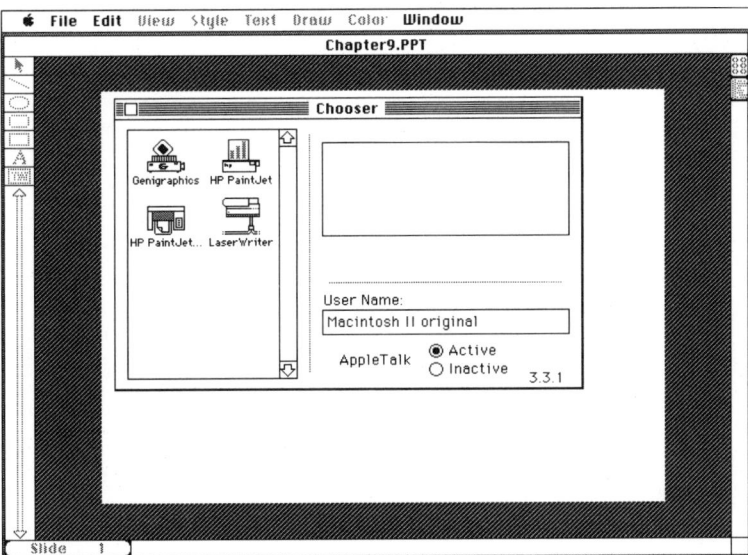

Figure 9-2. *You can switch between printers by using the Chooser command (in Macintosh PowerPoint).*

SECTION III: HANDS-ON POWERPOINT

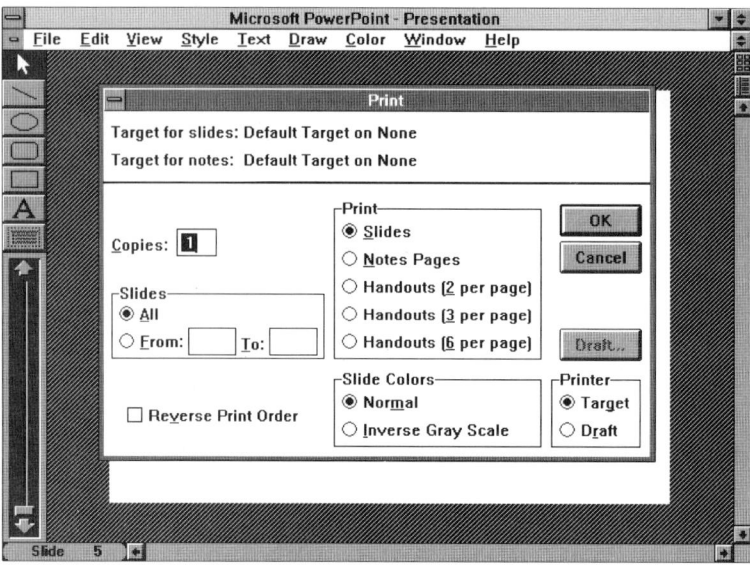

Figure 9-3. You can use the Printer Setup command to select a printer.

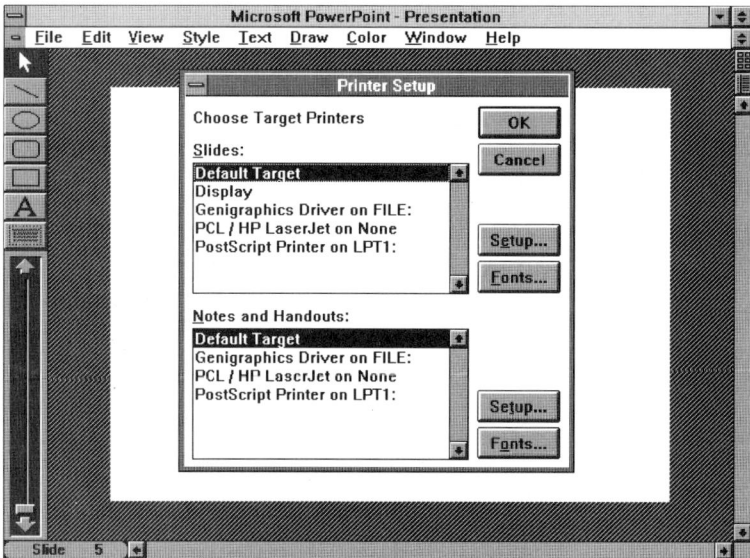

Figure 9-4. You can use the Print dialog box to prepare for proofing your visuals by choosing Inverse Gray Scale.

Proofing with color printers

Even if you're going to send your slides or overhead transparencies to Genigraphics for imaging, you should prepare color proofs if you have access to a color printer. Color proofs are far more revealing of mistakes. For example, you'll be surprised at how often tiny errors—such as inconsistent coloring of text bullets—become obvious at the color-proof stage.

If you're using Macintosh PowerPoint, choose a color printer from the Chooser dialog box. If you're using Windows PowerPoint, select a color printer in the Draft dialog box, available via the Print command.

When printing color proofs, you can save time by printing your proofs three to a page. This also saves on supply costs and might make it easier to file your proofs. To print proofs three at a time, select Handouts [3 per page] from the Print dialog box.

PREPARE NOTES AND HANDOUTS

PowerPoint's Notes pages (or Notes) are presentation aids that contain a reduced-size image of each of your slides and overheads plus a list of points you want to emphasize while displaying each individual visual. Notes pages are ideal for reviewing your slides and overheads the night before your presentation or while on the airplane traveling to it.

PowerPoint's Handout pages (or Handouts) contain reduced-size versions of your slides and overheads that your audience can review after your presentation. As you'll see later in this chapter, you can also prepare Handouts that will make it easier for your audience to take notes during your presentation.

Preparing a Notes Master

To create a Notes Master page, choose the Notes Master command from the View menu. (See Figure 9-5 on the following page.)

The Notes Master view allows you to

- ◆ Decide on the size and placement of the slide or overhead thumbnail (which is reproduced in Figure 9-5). You can resize the thumbnail by grabbing one of the corner buttons and moving it in the direction you want, holding down the Shift key to maintain the proper height-to-width ratio. To relocate the slide thumbnail using Macintosh PowerPoint, click on it to expose its fuzzy borders, and drag the thumbnail into the proper position. If you're using Windows PowerPoint, click on the slide thumbnail with the right mouse button and drag it into the proper position.

- Use one of PowerPoint's text tools to add repeating information—such as presentation title and date—to each Notes page.
- Add a page number, using the page-number symbol ##, to each Notes page by using one of the text tools.
- Use Line tool or one of the box-drawing tools to add graphics accents—such as borders—to each page. (You might, for example, add a box or a drop shadow around the slide thumbnail to help separate it from its background. This is especially important if your visuals appear against a white background or if you're preparing black-and-white overheads.)
- Add a box to define the text area you're going to create on each Notes page by using one of the Rectangle tools. (See Figure 9-6.) This helps ensure page-to-page consistency among your Notes. (After you've created your Notes, you can remove this box from the Notes Master if you want.)
- Add needed graphical objects, such as logos or drawings that you want to appear on each Notes page.

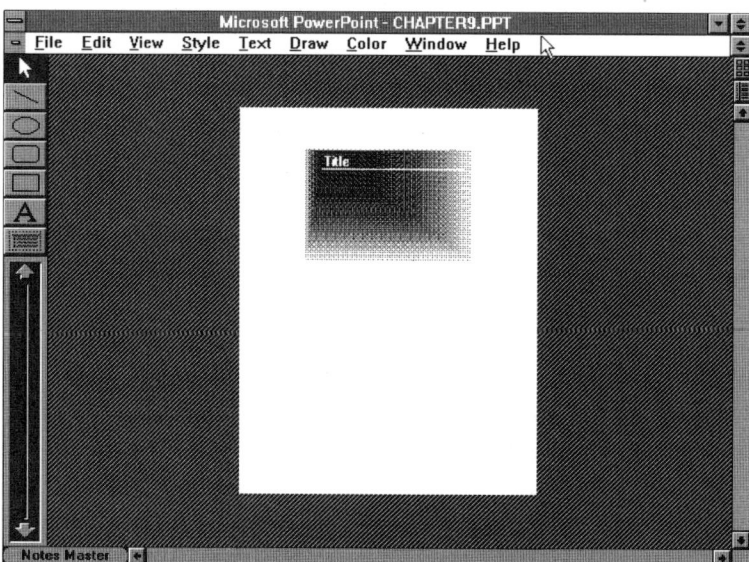

Figure 9-5. *This is an unformatted Notes Master page shown with its thumbnail image of a formatted slide.*

Chapter 9: Preparing Handouts, Notes, and Visuals

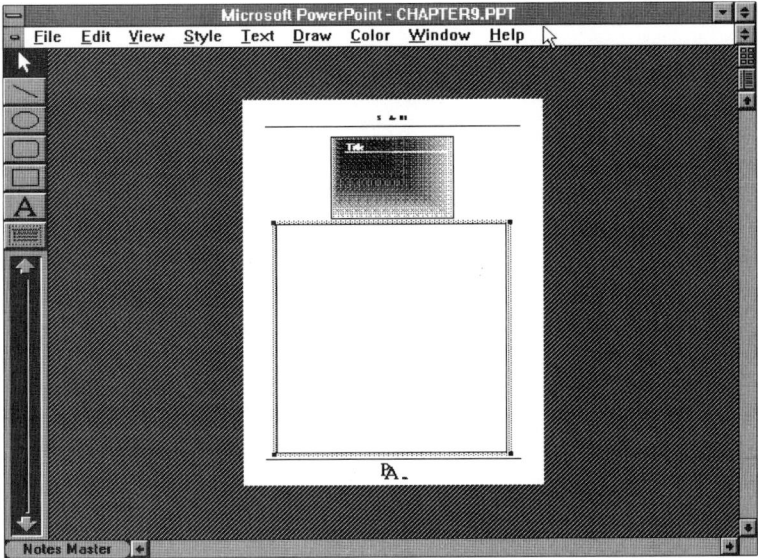

Figure 9-6. *This is a Notes Master page after formatting. The large box to be used to define the text area will be deleted later.*

Preparing Notes

Each slide or visual will have its own Notes page. As you work on each of the slides in your presentation, prepare an accompanying Notes page. You'll find it easier to prepare a Notes page while the ideas you want to include with it are still fresh in your mind. To prepare a Notes page while working in Slide view, do the following.

1. Choose Notes from the View menu, or use a keyboard shortcut: Command-E (in Macintosh PowerPoint) or Ctrl-E (in Windows PowerPoint).

2. Use the Word Processor tool to create a word processing box for your text.

3. While the box is selected, choose an appropriate Font and Size from the Style menu. Alternatively, choose a previously defined Style from the Style menu.

   Use as large a type size as possible. You don't want to be squinting at your Notes as you read them. You'll probably read your Notes from a farther-than-normal reading distance. Experience has shown that 36-point type is ideal for Notes pages. Large type also forces you to be brief!

4. Enter the Notes text. Be sure to use PowerPoint's spelling checker before printing your Notes so that you won't be distracted by a typographical error while delivering your presentation.

When you've finished entering the Notes for your current slide, return to the Slide by using a keyboard shortcut: Command-D (in Macintosh PowerPoint) or Ctrl-D (in Windows PowerPoint). Or use the mouse to select Slide [#] from the View menu. (See Figure 9-7.)

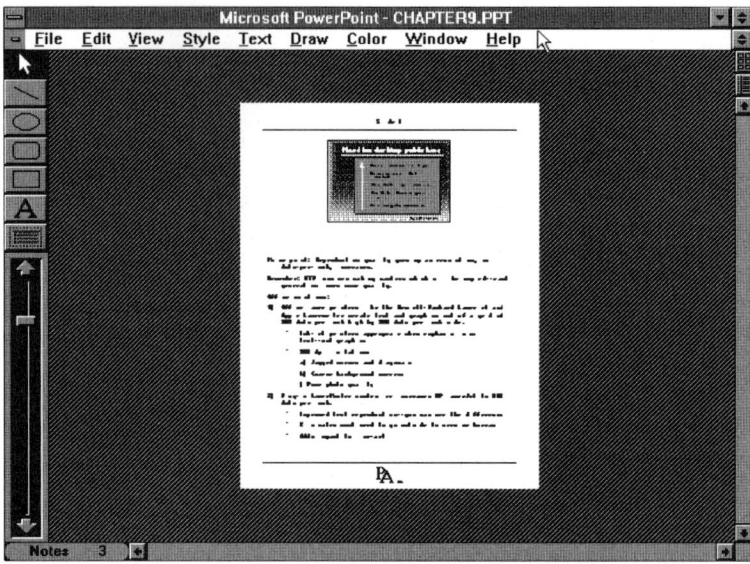

Figure 9-7. This is an example of a completed Notes page.

Printing Notes

To print your Notes, choose Notes Pages from the Print dialog box. (See Figure 9-8.) Choose All or specify the range of Notes pages you want to print. For Slide Colors options, choose Normal if you're using a color printer. Choose Gray Scale (in Macintosh Powerpoint) or Inverse Gray Scale (in Windows PowerPoint) if you're using a black-and-white printer.

Chapter 9: Preparing Handouts, Notes, and Visuals

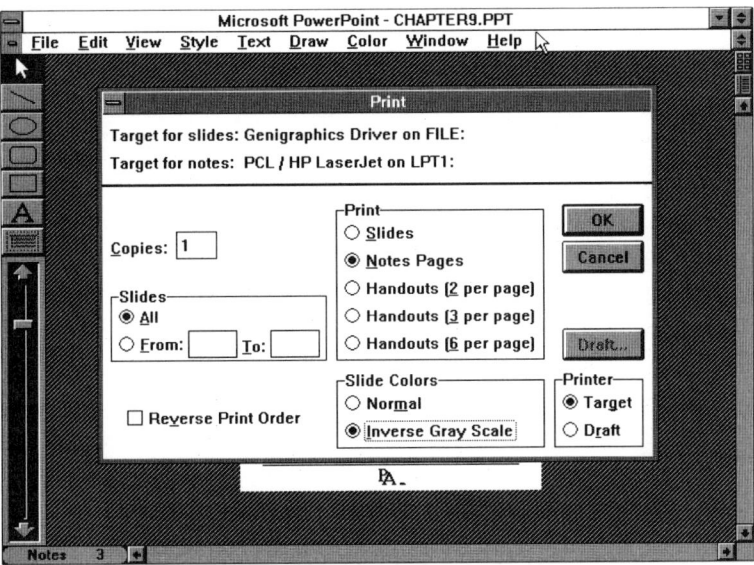

Figure 9-8. *You use the Print command to set up the printer for printing Notes pages.*

Formatting Audience Handout Pages

PowerPoint allows you to print audience handouts—called Handout pages, or Handouts—that contain two, three, or six slide or overhead thumbnails. The positions of these thumbnail options are indicated by the various dotted outlines that appear on the Handout Page, as shown in Figure 9-9 on the following page.

To prepare audience Handouts, you must first format the Handout Page.

1. Choose Handout Page from the View menu.

2. Use one of PowerPoint's text tools to add repeating information (such as presentation title, copyright information, and presentation date).

3. Add a page number symbol [##] to each page.

4. Add borders or other graphical accents by using the Line tool or one of the rectangle-drawing tools. If your slides do not have strong borders, for example, you might want to outline them with a box or a drop shadow. (See Figure 9-10 on the following page.)

249

SECTION III: HANDS-ON POWERPOINT

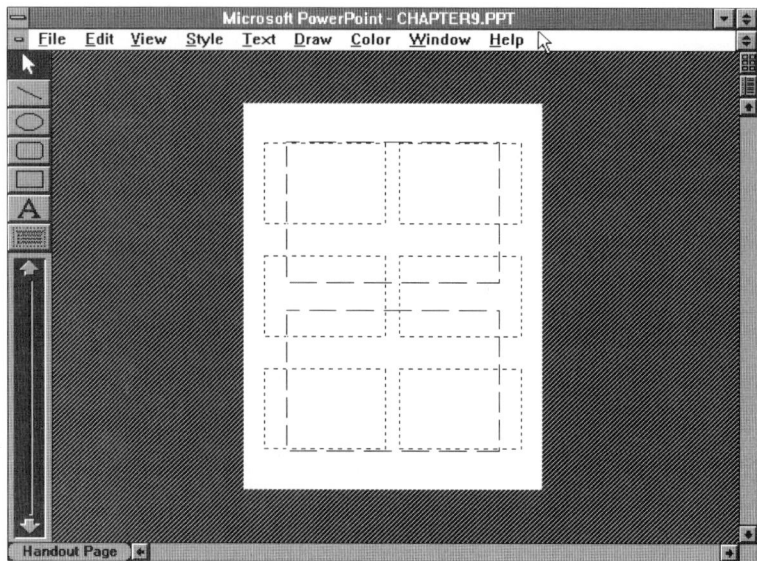

Figure 9-9. This is an unformatted Handout Page.

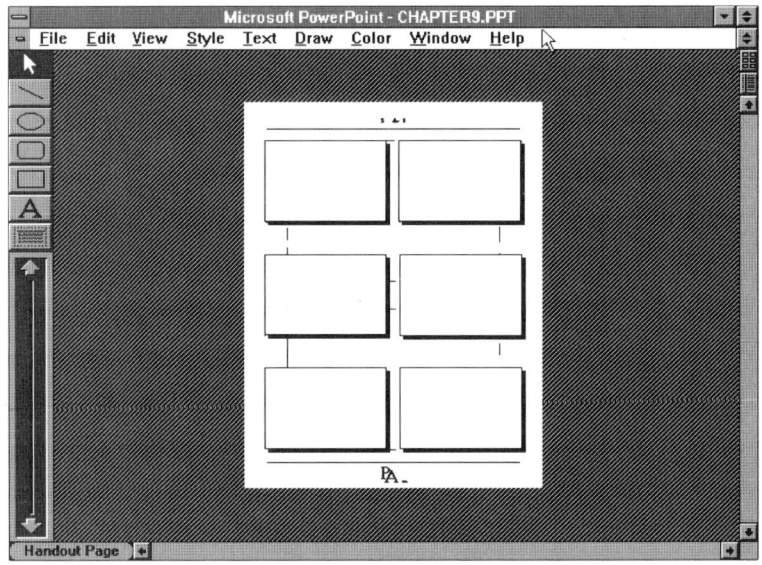

Figure 9-10. This is a Handout Page after formatting.

Handouts with space for audience notes

You can make it easier for your audience to take notes during your presentation by preparing a Handout Master page that contains a series of parallel lines (as in blank, lined paper) next to each thumbnail. Your audience will be able to follow along, entering notes adjacent to each slide or visual.

To prepare these "interactive notes pages," format your Handouts as described earlier, and then use the Line tool to draw a series of horizontal rules in the three vertical thumbnail locations indicated by dotted lines in the right "column" of the Handout Page.

Choose Full Size from the View menu to create consistent line spacing. (You'll find it easier to work in Full Size mode.)

You don't need to individually draw the lines for each of the three right-hand thumbnails. After you've drawn the lines for the top box, use the Arrow tool to draw a marquee box around the lines you've drawn. Then choose Copy from the Edit menu. Choose Paste, and move the lines into the second thumbnail location. Choose Paste again, and move the lines into the third thumbnail location. Your finished Handout Page should look like the one shown in Figure 9-11.

If you choose this option, be sure to choose the Handout [3 per page] option from the Print dialog box when you print your Handouts.

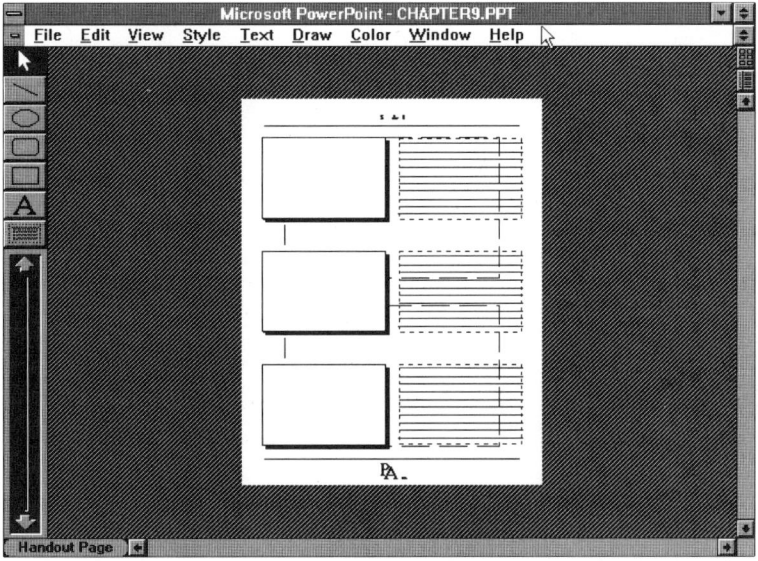

Figure 9-11. This is a Handout Page formatted with lines for taking notes.

Printing Handouts

To print Handouts, choose Print from the File menu. Choose the number of thumbnails you want to appear on each page. (If you're using Macintosh PowerPoint, be sure to deselect Slides or Notes if they were selected previously.) If you're using Windows PowerPoint, choose the appropriate Target or Draft printer, depending on the level of quality you want.

If you have access to a color copier, you might consider printing your Handouts in color and providing your audience with color copies. (The cost of low-volume, in-office color copying is coming down, and many copy centers offer this service at low cost.)

If you're using a black-and-white laser printer for Handouts, choose Gray Scale or Inverse Gray Scale as appropriate.

PRODUCE SLIDES OR OVERHEADS

PowerPoint includes specialized software needed to save and transmit files to Genigraphics for conversion to high-quality 35mm color slides and color overhead transparencies.

You can provide Genigraphics with your presentation saved on floppy disk. Better yet, you can transmit the files to Genigraphics using a modem. Depending on the delivery option you've chosen, you'll receive your completed 35mm slides or color overheads as quickly as the next morning (if you're using a modem) or within a few days.

You can also produce overheads by using your printer and overhead transparency sheets. Blank transparency sheets are available at most office-supply stores and allow you to quickly and inexpensively create overheads with your own laser printer. The steps involved in doing this are identical to those discussed earlier in this chapter for printing proofs.

Preparing and Transmitting Genigraphics Files

To transmit files to Genigraphics for imaging, you must target the Genigraphics Driver before you begin working on your presentation.

Files for Windows PowerPoint

If you're using Windows PowerPoint, choose Printer Setup from the File menu and then select Genigraphics Driver as the target printer. (See Figure 9-12.) Next, choose Slide Setup from the File menu to verify that you'll be using the full screen area (Full Printer Page) for the image. (See Figure 9-13.)

Chapter 9: Preparing Handouts, Notes, and Visuals

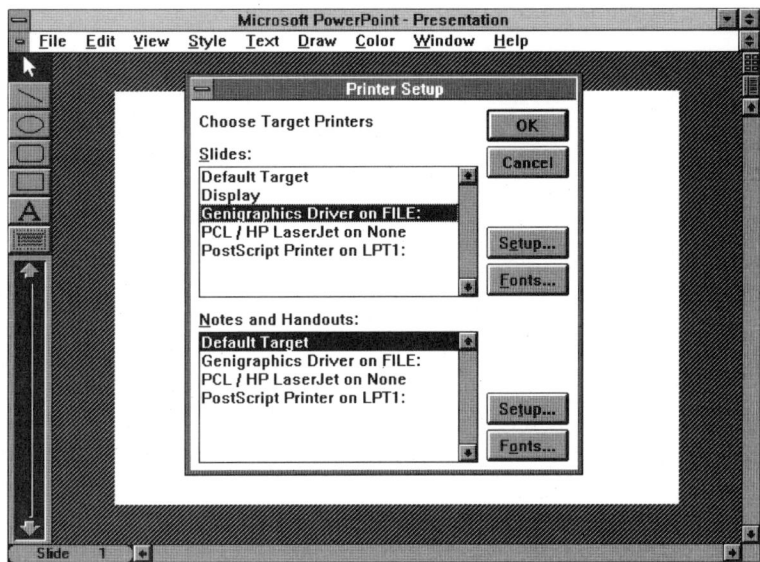

Figure 9-12. *You select the Genigraphics Driver as the target printer if you're using Windows PowerPoint to transmit files to Genigraphics.*

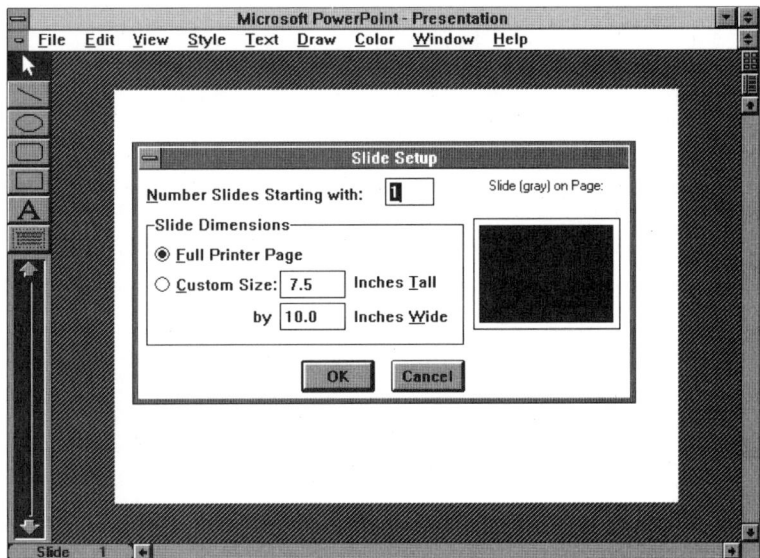

Figure 9-13. *The Slide Setup dialog box lets you determine how much of the screen will be used by the imager.*

Files for Macintosh PowerPoint

If you're using Macintosh PowerPoint, use the Chooser to select the Genigraphics Driver. (See Figure 9-14.)

Next, choose Page Setup from the File menu. The regular Macintosh Page Setup dialog box appears, overlapping the dialog box shown in Figure 9-15. After making your choices in Page Setup, click OK. You can now make your choices in the Slide Setup dialog box. (See Figure 9-15.) If you want to return to the Page Setup dialog box, click on the Page Setup button at the bottom of the Slide Setup dialog box.

Choose Genigraphics Presentation Format for standard 35mm color slides or overhead transparencies. If you need to prepare the highest-quality overheads, choose Overhead Shape for the printer. (This option offers sharper, more color-saturated overheads, but it also costs more.) You can enter a custom size as well.

While preparing your presentation, save your work as you normally do.

After you've finished preparing your presentation, save it in Genigraphics file format. To do this, choose Print, which brings up the Genigraphics Job Instructions dialog box. (See Figure 9-16.)

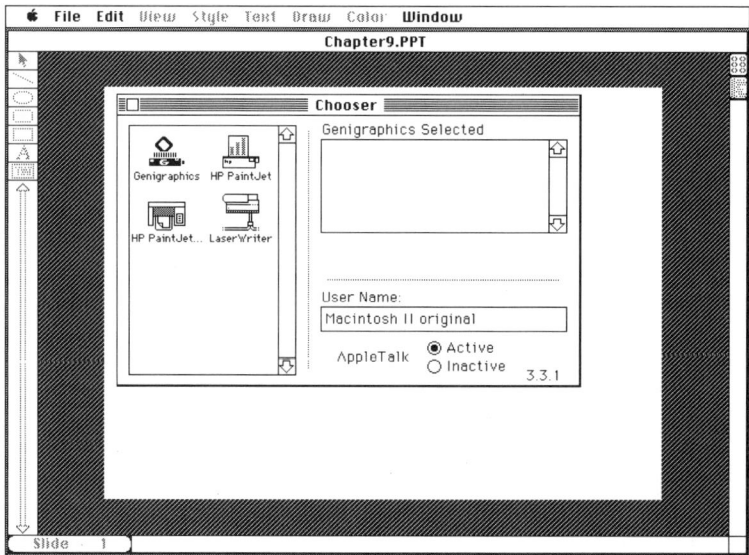

Figure 9-14. You use the Chooser command (in Macintosh PowerPoint) to select the appropriate output device.

Chapter 9: Preparing Handouts, Notes, and Visuals

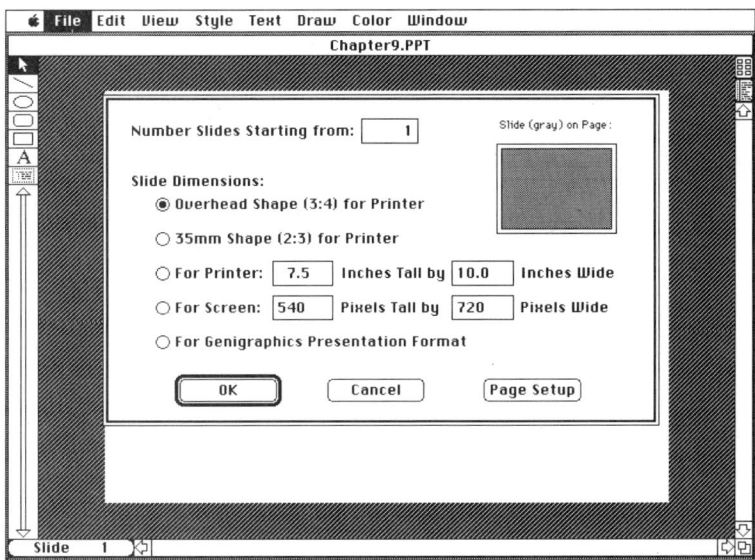

Figure 9-15. These are Slide Setup options in Macintosh PowerPoint, which you access by choosing Page Setup from the File menu.

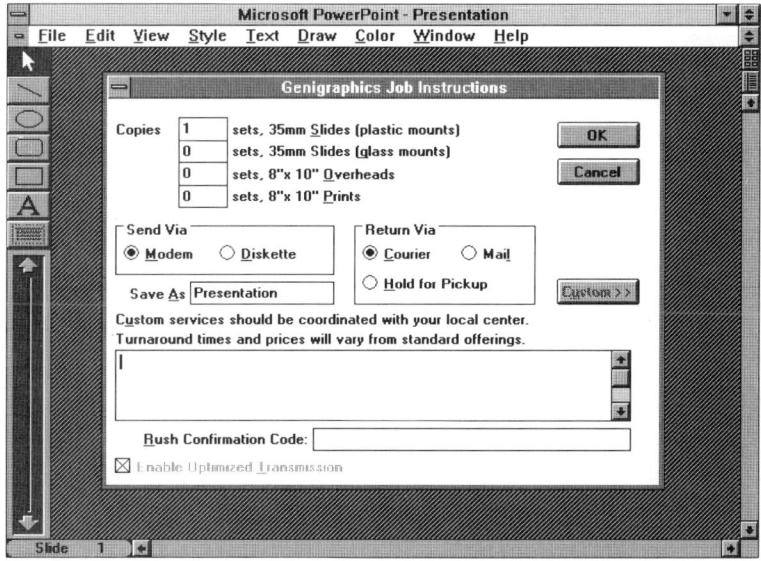

Figure 9-16. This is a Genigraphics Job Instructions dialog box.

The same basic Genigraphics dialog box then appears in both the Macintosh and the Windows versions of PowerPoint. The screen will prompt you to indicate the desired number of copies of 35mm plastic-mount slides, 35mm glass-mount slides, or 8-inch-by-10-inch overheads or prints.

The Job Instructions dialog box also prompts you to indicate whether you'll be transmitting your files to Genigraphics via modem or floppy disk and how you want your completed presentation returned: by overnight courier, by first-class mail, or held for pickup.

Choose the Custom option if you want Genigraphics to speed your order or offer customized service—and only if you've already checked with the local Genigraphics office.

Choose OK when you've properly entered all information. Your file will now be saved in Genigraphics format. As the file is being saved, you'll be kept informed of progress.

Error Codes

PowerPoint and Genigraphics have included a sophisticated method of informing you in advance of any potential imaging problems you might encounter. This helps you identify errors *before* your slides or overheads have been imaged.

As your files are saved in Genigraphics format, error codes might appear on the screen in the Genigraphics Warnings dialog box. (See Figure 9-17.) The most likely problem areas include the following.

- Graphical objects that extend beyond the edge of the slide (or the imaging area)
- Type that extends beyond the edge of the slide
- Use of typefaces and type sizes not supported by Genigraphics
- Inclusion of graphics files that Genigraphics does not support

Both the error and the number of the individual slide containing the error are indicated, so you can quickly locate and correct the error. By clicking on the appropriate box, you can copy the error-code list to the Clipboard and print it for easy reference.

If you encounter problems, choose Cancel. This returns you to the Slide view. Correct the errors and again save your file in Genigraphics format by choosing Print from the File menu.

Chapter 9: Preparing Handouts, Notes, and Visuals

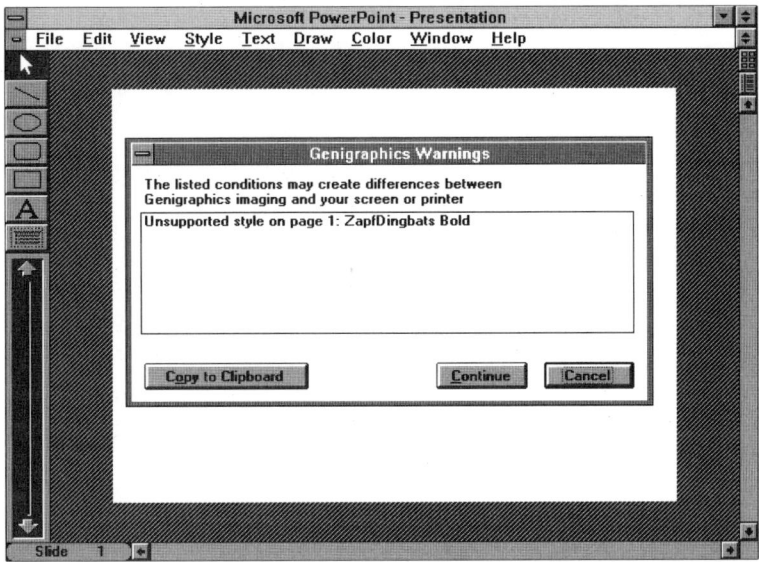

Figure 9-17. The Genigraphics Warnings dialog box informs you of errors that you need to correct.

If no errors are found—or if you choose to ignore the error warnings—you advance to the Genigraphics Billing Information dialog box. (See Figure 9-18.) Here you can specify shipping and billing addresses, telephone numbers, and payment options.

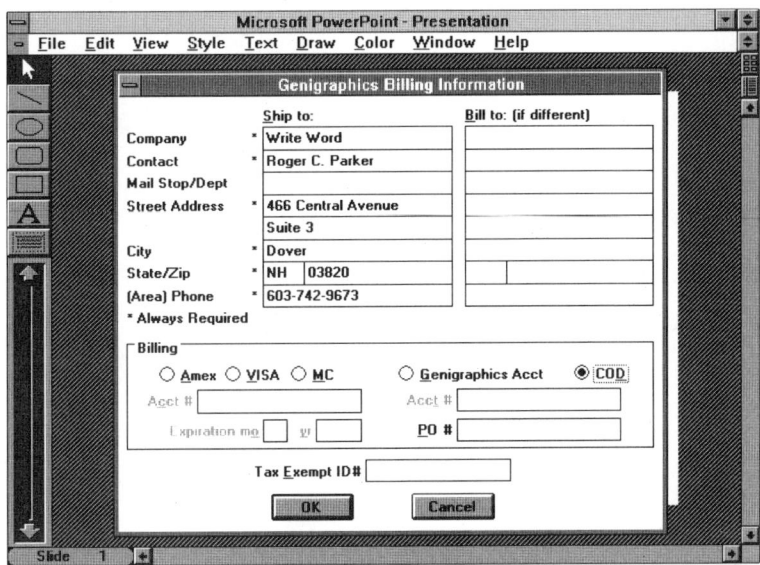

Figure 9-18. The Genigraphics Billing Information dialog box.

257

After you've filled in all information, click on OK. PowerPoint will confirm that your presentation has been saved in Genigraphics format. Once again, an on-screen error message will inform you if any problems are encountered while your presentation is being saved.

After you've saved your presentation in Genigraphics format, you can close PowerPoint.

Transmitting Files via Modem

If you've chosen the Diskette option, remove the floppy disk and send your files to Genigraphics via courier or mail. If you've chosen Modem, however, close PowerPoint and start the Genigraphics GraphicsLink program—a special communications program that transmits your files to Genigraphics.

Using Windows PowerPoint, click on the GraphicsLink icon. After GraphicsLink loads, you'll see a list of all available presentations saved in the Genigraphics format. (See Figure 9-19.)

Notice that the Genigraphics GraphicsLink dialog box informs you of the estimated time it will take to transmit each file.

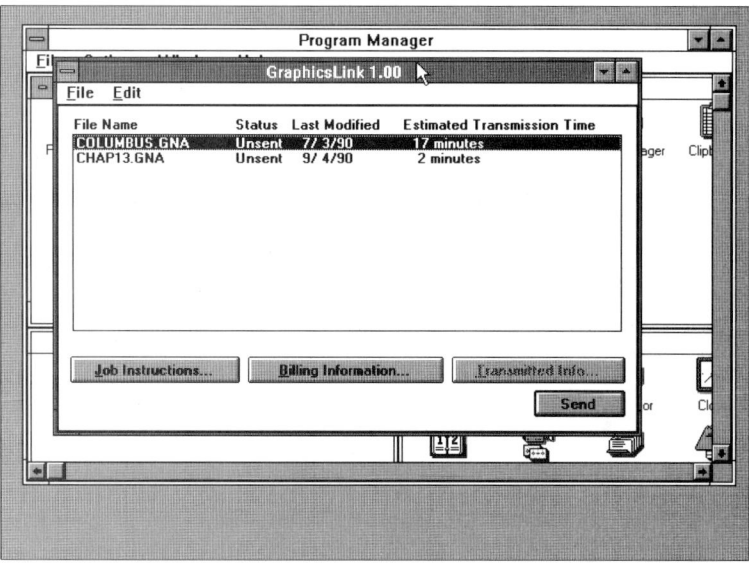

Figure 9-19. The Genigraphics GraphicsLink dialog box displays a list of the presentations you've saved.

Using Communications Setup

The first step in using GraphicsLink is to configure it by using the Communications Setup dialog box so that GraphicsLink works with your computer and modem. (See Figure 9-20.)

In the appropriate boxes, you can choose the speed of modem, the type of telephone you have, and the port where your modem is connected. You can also select from the Destination list the particular Genigraphics location to which you want your files sent.

You can also add the telephone number of your local Genigraphics office.

To send a Genigraphics file, click on the location where you want your files to be imaged, and click on Send.

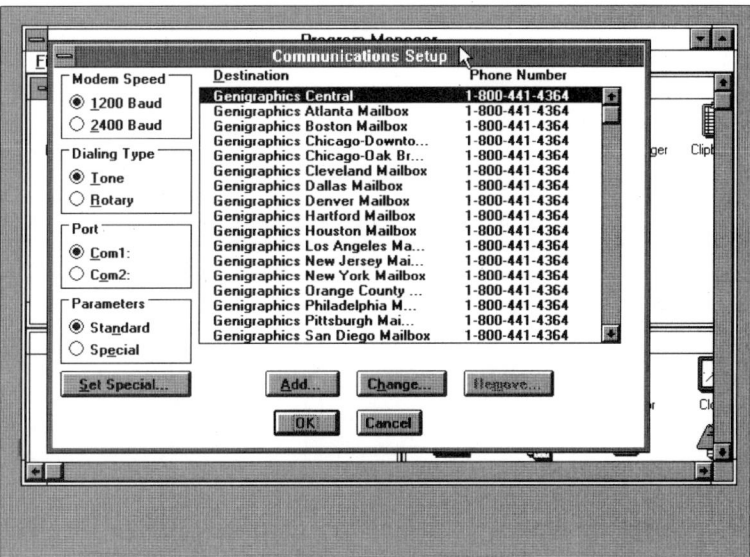

Figure 9-20. *You use the Genigraphics GraphicsLink Communications Setup dialog box to connect to your computer and modem.*

Changing Presentation Format

Each output device differs in its printing area. This is why you need to review your presentation every time you target a different printer after you've begun working on your presentation. If you don't, there's a pretty good chance that text or graphical elements will extend beyond the imaging area of the printer or screen used to display your visuals.

Targeting a different output device by using the Printer Setup dialog box, as shown in Figure 9-21, also influences the appearance of Notes pages because the new output device might create a larger or smaller thumbnail on the Notes page.

When changing presentation formats, you must review both the Slide Master and each individual slide or overhead to ensure that all borders and repeating information are within the imaging area of the new output device. You also need to double-check that the new imaging device can reproduce the typefaces, type sizes, and graphics file formats used in your presentation.

Although a PowerPoint alert (as shown in Figure 9-22) will remind you that the new format will likely create visuals with a different size and shape, it is up to you to change the size and placement of text and graphics.

Figure 9-23 is the opening slide of PowerPoint's "Columbus" sample presentation, with a PostScript laser printer targeted. Figure 9-24 on page 262 shows what happens when you open the same sample presentation, which was designed for on-screen display, and target the Genigraphics Driver.

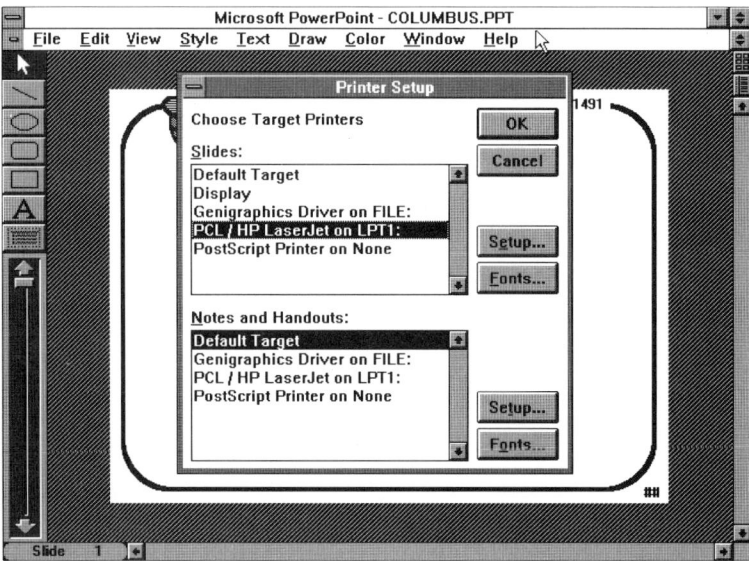

Figure 9-21. *You can target a different output device by using the Printer Setup dialog box. This might require you to resize and replace existing text and graphics.*

Chapter 9: Preparing Handouts, Notes, and Visuals

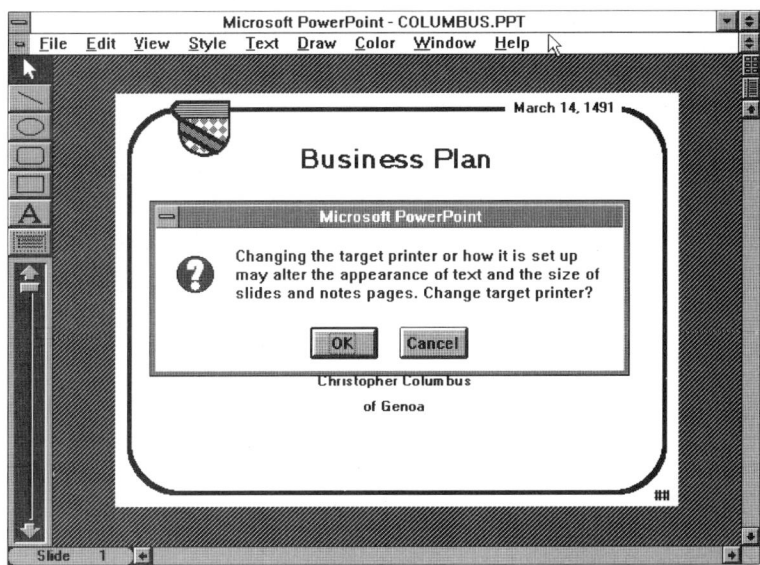

Figure 9-22. *PowerPoint will remind you that targeting a different output device can change the size and shape of your visuals. However, it is left to you to edit the Slide Master and adjust the contents.*

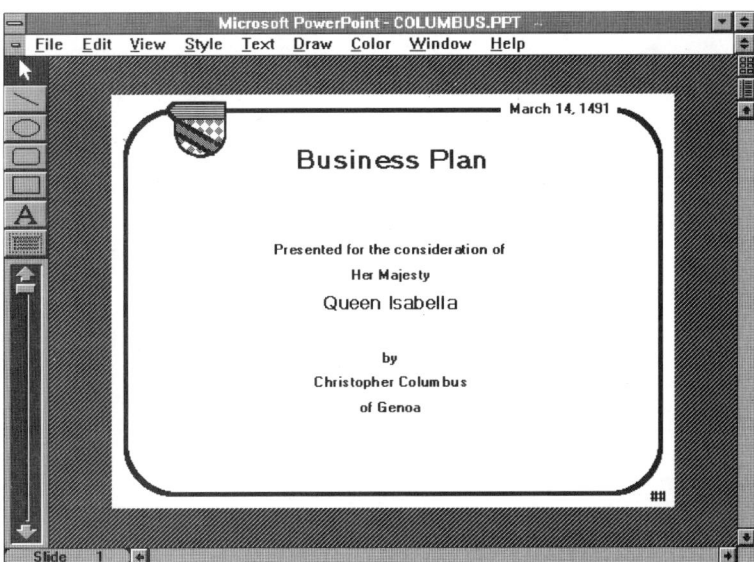

Figure 9-23. *This is how the screen display looks when the default target printer (an appropriate output device) is used—in this case, a PostScript laser printer.*

SECTION III: HANDS-ON POWERPOINT

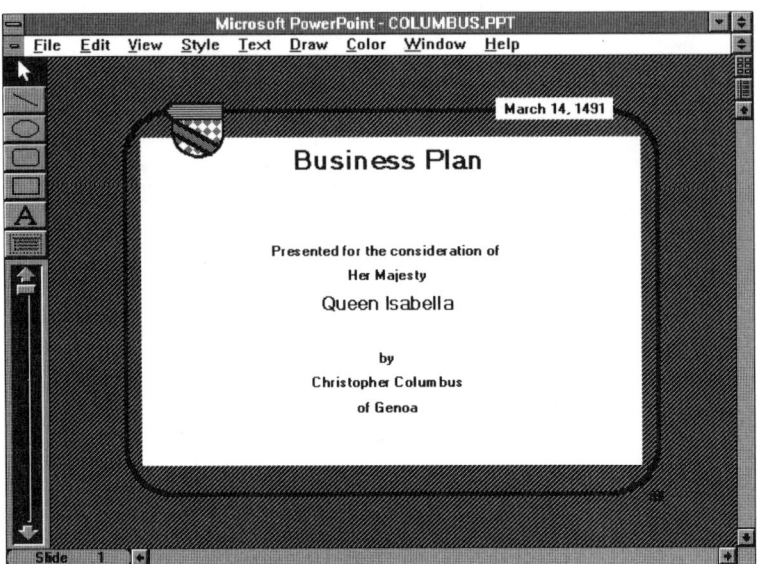

Figure 9-24. Here is an example of what can happen to your presentation when you target a different (inappropriate) output device.

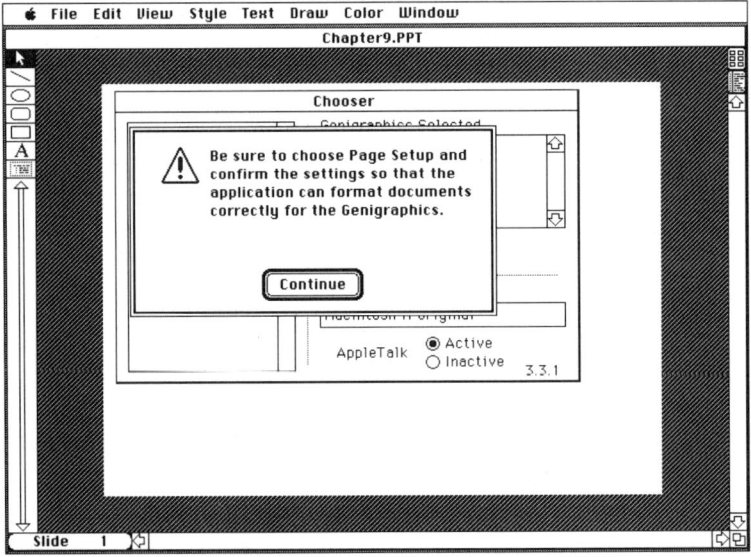

Figure 9-25. Macintosh PowerPoint requires that you choose Page Setup after targeting a new output device.

Whenever you change presentation format in Windows PowerPoint, you must choose Slide Master from the View menu and adjust the border and repeating information, and then you must go through the slides, one by one, repositioning and resizing the text and graphics.

In Macintosh PowerPoint, you can't print in the new format unless you go back to Page Setup. (See Figure 9-25.)

EVALUATING YOUR PROGRESS

- ◆ Given that PowerPoint presentations are output-device dependent, did I remember to target the appropriate output device when I began planning and working on my presentation?

- ◆ Did I proof my presentation on screen (using PowerPoint's Slide Show feature) and on hard copies that I printed?

- ◆ Are my typeface and type size choices and imported graphics file formats compatible with the output device that I'll use to prepare my presentation?

- ◆ When I saved my presentation in Genigraphics format, did I go back and correct the problems displayed in error messages?

- ◆ Did I fill in all necessary information in the Genigraphics Billing Information dialog box?

- ◆ If I changed presentation format after beginning work on my presentation, did I carefully review each slide and Notes page to ensure that no elements extend beyond the edge of the printing or the imaging area?

Working with the "Steps to Success" Template

In the "Steps to Success" template that we create in this chapter, and in the templates we create in the chapters that follow, you'll see how easy it is to put PowerPoint to work organizing and producing an effective presentation. If you use these templates for your first presentations, you can use them to review the basics of presentation design as well as the most frequently used PowerPoint commands. The templates reinforce the concept that effective presentations are based on simplicity, unity, and rigorous editing. In addition, the templates enable you to produce high-quality presentations at the last minute.

Remember that the templates described are only the starting point. You can easily customize them to reflect your unique presentation needs.

The "Steps to Success" template uses numbers as an organizing tool. Numbers help break complicated subjects into manageable and memorable bite-size pieces. In addition, numbers help audiences and presenters to measure progress through a presentation, maintaining the presenter's morale and at the same time eliminating audience boredom.

Numbers also keep you focused, and they are a hedge against your becoming too abstract. The "Steps to Success" template, for example, evolved from a presentation originally titled "How to Revitalize Your Business." This title did not provide a useful structure for developing the ideas to be presented. When renamed "Eighteen Steps to Greater Profits," however, the presentation became both easier to create and more interesting for audiences to watch.

The "Steps to Success" template demonstrates the impact that can be achieved by using a single typeface throughout your presentation, varying only size, style, and color for contrast and emphasis.

Two steps are needed to create the "Steps to Success" presentation template.

- ◆ *Create the Slide Master.* The Slide Master provides unity throughout the presentation, so each slide or overhead will have a consistent "look."

- ◆ *Create the subtemplates.* The three subtemplates—Organizers, Developers, and Contrasters—are used to display different categories of information. Organizers provide structure, Developers provide clarification or added detail, and Contrasters allow you to compare two points of view.

To use the "Steps to Success" presentation, you need to do the following.

- ◆ *Create empty subtemplates.* To do this, open an untitled copy of the presentation and make as many copies of each subtemplate as necessary. Then use the Slide Sorter view to organize them in the desired sequence.

- ◆ *Place text and graphics.* To do this, click on each slide or overhead and replace the titles, numbers, and placeholder copy with the specific contents needed for each slide or overhead.

- ◆ *Edit and review your work.* To do this, use the Slide Show and Spelling commands to refine your work.

CREATE THE SLIDE MASTER

The starting point for creating the "Steps to Success" template is to choose New from the File menu. Next, target your appropriate output device. If you're using Windows PowerPoint, choose the Printer Setup command. If you're going to send your files to Genigraphics for production of slides or overheads, select Genigraphics Driver on FILE as your target printer; then click on the Setup option and choose the Presentation format. If you're using Macintosh PowerPoint, use the Chooser to select Genigraphics Driver; then choose Genigraphics Presentation Format from the Page Setup menu.

Note: The dimensions that follow are appropriate for the presentations created for the Genigraphics Presentation Format. Slight adjustments will be required if you're using another output device to produce your presentations.

Creating the Slide Master Template

The Slide Master determines the overall look of your presentation. It provides the background for the individual Developer, Organizer, and Contraster subtemplates.

Choose Slide Master from the View menu to create the Slide Master.

Placing and formatting the title

The Slide Master for our "Steps to Success" presentation contains a title that extends to the left of the information area contained on each of the subtemplates. This asymmetrical title placement adds character to the presentation, avoiding the all-too-common "centered" look shared by many presentations. The title is enhanced by a heavy horizontal rule that not only draws attention to it but separates it from the information area of each slide or overhead. (See Figure 10-1 on the following page.)

Activate the Horizontal and Vertical guides (if they're not already visible on your screen) by choosing Show Guides from the Draw menu or by using a keyboard shortcut: Command-G (in Macintosh PowerPoint) or Ctrl-G (in Windows PowerPoint).

Click on the Vertical guide and move it 3 inches to the left of center. As you drag the guide, you'll see the exact position displayed. Move the guide to the left until it reads *3.00*. This will determine the left-side placement of the title and the horizontal rule.

Select the title by clicking on it. (Its fuzzy border becomes visible.) Grab one of its borders and move it so that its left edge is aligned with the vertical guide.

While the title is still selected, do the following.

1. Choose Left from the Text menu. (The default title alignment is usually Center.)

2. Choose Font from the Style menu. Scroll through the list of available typefaces, and choose Helvetica (in Macintosh PowerPoint) or Helv (in Windows PowerPoint) or the most similar sans serif typeface your output device supports.

3. Choose Size from the Style menu, and then choose 48 Point.

4. Choose Bold from the Style menu, or use the keyboard shortcut: Command-B (in Macintosh PowerPoint) or Ctrl-B (in Windows PowerPoint).

5. Click on the horizontal guide and move it up until it reads 2.75. Grab the title and raise it until the top of its border is aligned with the horizontal guide.

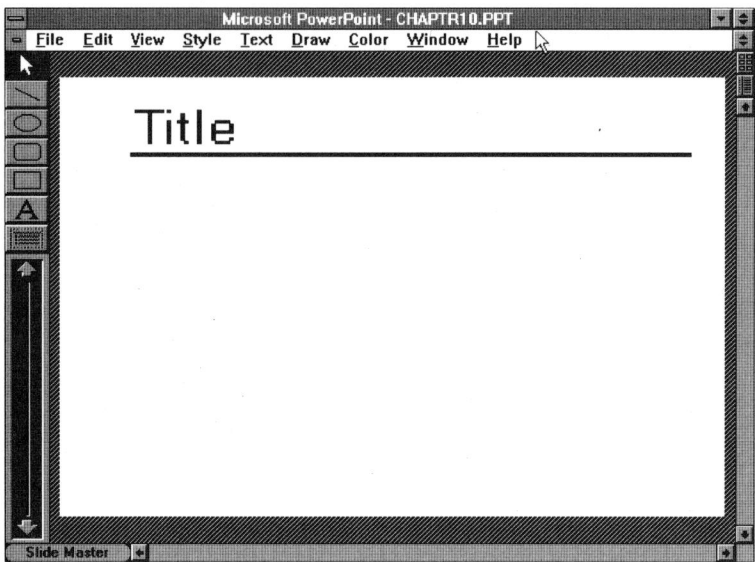

Figure 10-1. You can add emphasis to a title by positioning it asymmetrically and adding a rule.

Emphasizing the title

Choose Line Style from the Draw menu and release the mouse button when the third line down is highlighted. Choose the Line tool from the left side of the screen. Position the pointer below the title, aligned with the vertical guide. While holding down the Shift key, drag the pointer toward the right side of the screen until it almost reaches the right edge of the screen.

Temporarily relocate the vertical guide 4 inches to the right of center. Click on the line and, while holding down the Shift key, extend or shorten the line until it touches the vertical guide. Then reposition the vertical guide back to 3 inches left of center.

Choosing a color scheme

Next, specify an appropriate color scheme by choosing Color Scheme from the Master menu. Choose background, foreground, and highlight colors (as described in Chapter 4).

- If you're creating color overhead transparencies, choose a light-colored background.

- If you're creating 35mm color slides, choose a color scheme with a dark background color that will be shaded to provide visual contrast.

- If you're unsure of your color choices, copy one of the sample color schemes that Genigraphics provides. (See "Sharing a Color Scheme Between Presentations" in Chapter 9.)

Next, choose Shade Background from the Color Scheme dialog box. Choose Shade From Title. Choose the option on the right side, with the darkest area in the center of the sample. We'll assemble the "Steps to Success" presentation template on a Slide Master that is darkest behind the title and that gradually becomes lighter farther from the title. This will emphasize the title by placing it against the darkest part of the slide. The size of the darkest area of each slide background will depend on the number of words in the title—providing a subtle visual contrast between slides.

In the next section, we'll create rectangles and circles of consistent size to use as containers for text and graphics. We'll fill each container with a contrasting color so the information area of each slide or overhead will stand out against the Slide Master background.

To return to Slide View, choose Slide (#) from the View menu, or use a keyboard shortcut: Command-D (in Macintosh PowerPoint) or Ctrl-D (in Windows PowerPoint).

CREATE THE SUBTEMPLATES

Now it's time for us to create the three types of subtemplates: Organizers, Developers, and Contrasters.

Organizer Subtemplate

The Organizer subtemplates form the core of the presentation. Each one consists of the title in large type followed by three points (set in smaller type) that you want to make.

The decision to include three points was deliberate. First, most people have trouble remembering more than three points at a time. Second, by limiting each Organizer to three points, each line can be set in a large, easy-to-read type size. Individuals sitting at the back of the room will appreciate this!

In addition, the use of three points eliminates the unwanted parallelism, balance, or "opposition" that occurs when only two points are made. If each Organizer contained only two points, readers would often unconsciously try to compare and contrast them. If Organizers contained more than three points, say four points, you would need to use a smaller text size—which would limit legibility, and the reader would be tempted to read ahead of the presenter.

To prepare for creating all three subtemplates, select and grab the vertical guide and place it 2.50 inches to the left of center. This will indent the rectangles relative to the title. Relocate the horizontal guide 1.50 inches above the midpoint. Then choose Line Style from the Draw menu and release the mouse button on the second width option. Finally, choose Framed, Filled, and Shadowed from the Draw menu.

By making these choices *before* you choose the Rectangle tool, these choices become defaults, so they are automatically chosen when you create all three subtemplates.

Creating a text box

Next, choose the Rectangle tool to create the text box. Create a rectangle that extends from the vertical guide on the left to the approximate length of the line under the title.

Then relocate the horizontal guide 0.50 inch above the midpoint. Select the rectangle and drag on one of the bottom corners until it touches the guide.

Finally, select the vertical guide and relocate it 3.75 inches to the right. Drag one of the rectangle's right-hand corners until it touches the vertical guide.

Coloring the text box

Next, choose appropriate Fill (for the background color) and Line (for the frame color) from the Color menu. A multitude of choices are available. Sometimes the strongest effects are achieved by filling the text box with a solid version of the shaded background color.

Experiment with various combinations of Fill and Line colors—until you discover one you especially like.

Formatting Organizer text

1. Click on the text-box rectangle.
2. Choose Left from the Text menu.
3. Choose Font from the Style menu, and then choose Helvetica or Helv.
4. Choose 56 Point from the Size menu. Enter the number *1*, and press the Spacebar twice.
5. Choose 36 Point from the Size menu, and type in a few words, perhaps *Text Placeholder*.

Now go back to the beginning of the line, select the number, and change its color. The type size and text-color contrast between the oversized numbers and the words of each point being made provides visual interest. Accordingly, select an accent color that forms a strong contrast with the adjacent text. At this point, your Organizer should look similar to the one in Figure 10-2.

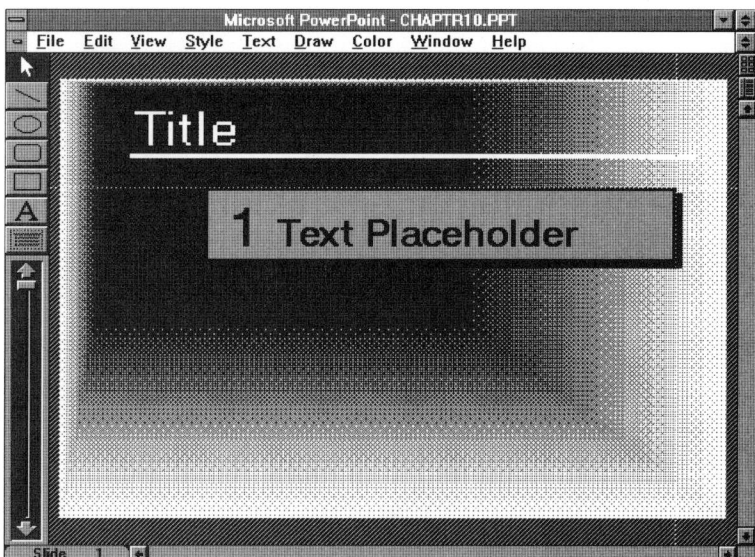

Figure 10-2. *You can create a text box that is indented under the title.*

Creating additional text boxes

Click on the text-box rectangle, and choose Copy from the Edit menu. Choose Paste twice. In turn, select each rectangle and drag it into position, aligning the right edge of each rectangle with the vertical guide. Then, using the horizontal guide as a measuring tool, provide 0.25 inch of vertical separation between the rectangles.

Click on the second rectangle. Select the number by holding down the mouse button to the left of the number and dragging the I-beam through it. Replace the *1* with a *2*.

Click on the third rectangle. Select the number and replace it with a *3*. Your Organizer subtemplate should now look like the one shown in Figure 10-3.

Notice that the total area occupied by the three text-box rectangles can be defined by the following dimensions.

- ◆ Top border of top rectangle: 1.50 inches above center
- ◆ Left border of each rectangle: 2.50 inches left of center
- ◆ Right border of each rectangle: 3.75 inches right of center
- ◆ Bottom border of bottom rectangle: 2.00 inches below center

You'll be using these same dimensions when you create the Developer and Contraster subtemplates later in this chapter.

Now is the time to add information—such as presentation title, copyright information, and your firm or association's name—to the Slide Master. To do

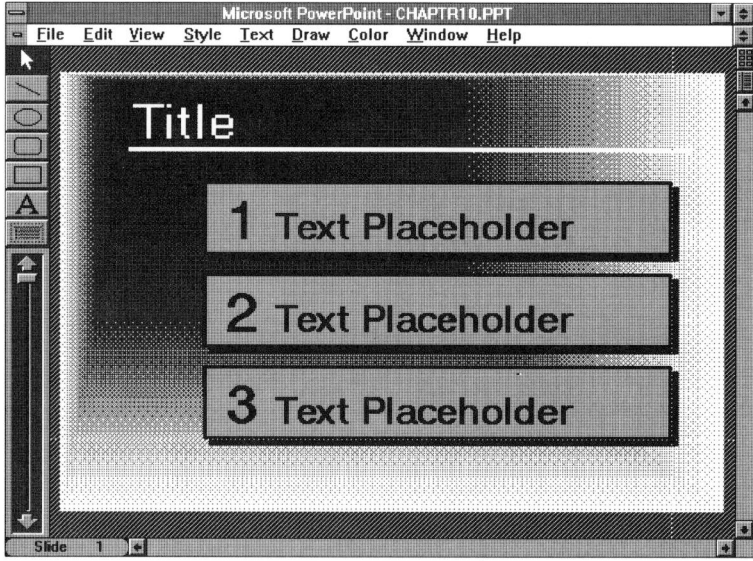

Figure 10-3. *Here is an Organizer subtemplate with three correctly numbered text boxes.*

this, return to Slide Master view and position the horizontal guide 2.00 inches below midpoint. Be sure that any information you add is located well below the horizontal guide.

If you haven't done so already, now is a good time to save your work. You might name the file STEPSTMP (steps template). You might also want to create a special template folder or subdirectory for your presentation templates to keep them separate from specific projects.

Creating additional Organizers

To create additional Organizers, choose Slide Sorter from the View menu, or click on the Slide Sorter icon at the upper right of your screen. When the Organizer subtemplate appears, select it by clicking on it. When it is selected, choose Copy from the Edit menu. Then choose Paste four times to make three additional copies. (See Figure 10-4.)

Double-click on the second slide. When the slide appears, highlight the 1, 2, and 3 and change the numbers to 4, 5, and 6. Select the third slide and change the numbers to 7, 8, and 9. Change the numbers on the last slide to 10, 11, and 12. (The result is shown in Figure 10-5 on the following page.)

If additional Organizers are needed, they can easily be added later.

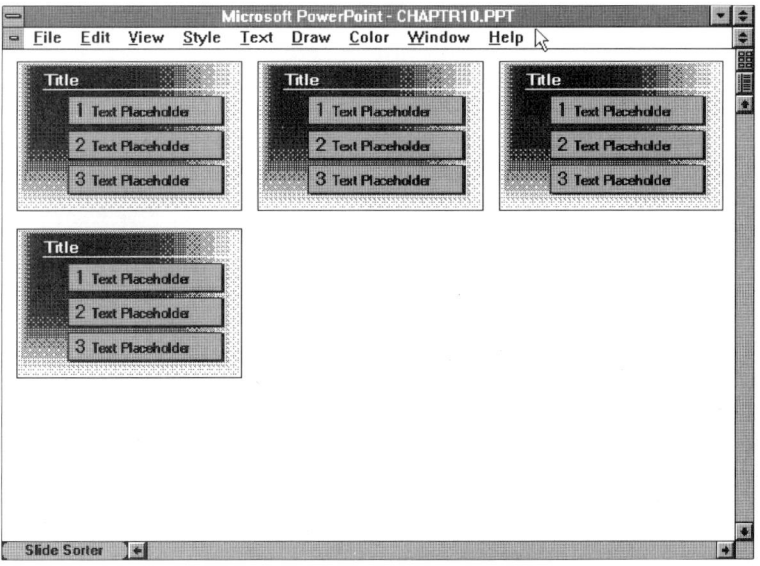

Figure 10-4. You can create additional Organizer subtemplates in the Slide Sorter view by using the Edit menu's Copy and Paste commands.

SECTION III: HANDS-ON POWERPOINT

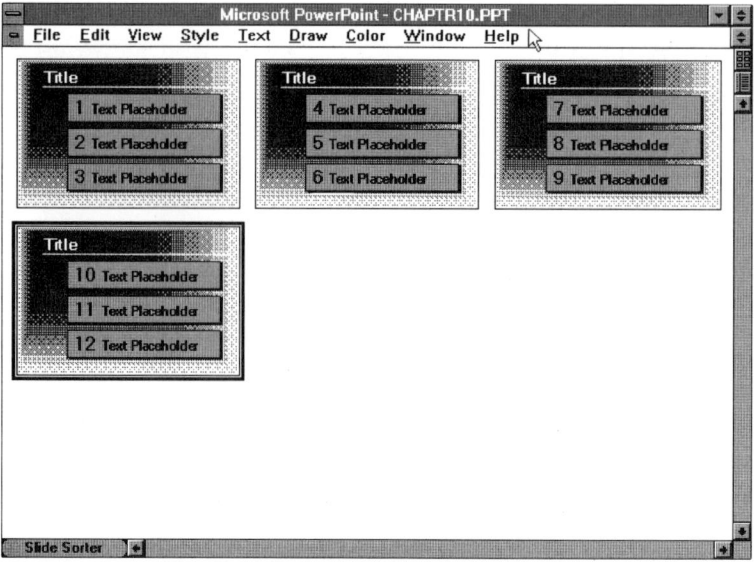

Figure 10-5. *Here is the Slide Sorter view of the Organizer subtemplates after the text boxes have been consecutively numbered.*

Developer Subtemplates

The Developer subtemplates provide a large rectangle that can be used to elaborate on one or more of the points introduced on a preceding Organizer. Here is a list of five types of Developers you might use.

- *Title slide.* You might introduce your presentation with a title slide that states, in large type, the presentation's goal or point of view.

- *Indented outline introduced by bullets.* Use full-sentence outlines to describe a sequence of steps and the reasons for them. Or use full-sentence outlines when discussing the source of points introduced on Organizer subtemplates.

- *Two-column list of short phrases preceded by bullets.* These provide added details to support one or more points on a preceding Organizer.

- *Quotation slide.* Often you can strengthen your recommendations or conclusions by a "call to authority" consisting of a quotation set off by oversized quotation marks.

- *Empty box.* The empty box provides a container for graphs, organizational charts, or illustrations.

274

Because you placed the title and highlight rule on the Slide Master, they will be located in the same place on Developers as they are on Organizers. This helps maintain a strong family resemblance—or unity—throughout your presentation.

When creating Developers, be sure that the dimensions of the Developer text boxes remain identical to those of the three rectangles found on Organizer templates. If the top and bottom borders or left and right margins are different, the concentration of viewers will be disturbed by the constantly "jumping" margins. (To observe this for yourself, try modifying these dimensions and then running PowerPoint's Slide Show feature. You'll see how distracting it is when visuals jump around on the screen.)

Creating Developers

Choose New Slide from the Edit menu, or press Command-N (in Macintosh PowerPoint) or Ctrl-N (in Windows PowerPoint).

Using the same Line Style, Shadowed, Framed, and Filled choices you made before, create a single large rectangle. The rectangle's dimensions should be as follows.

- Top: 1.50 inches above center
- Left: 2.50 inches left of center
- Right: 3.75 inches right of center
- Bottom: 2.00 inches below center

Choose the same Shadowed, Framed, and Filled color choices that you used previously for the Organizers.

When you've finished, your Developer subtemplate should look like the one shown in Figure 10-6 on the following page.

As before, choose the Slide Sorter icon and make two copies of the slide.

Click on the first copy, and use the Word Processor tool to create a single wide column of text that extends almost the full width of the rectangle. Enter the following formatting options from the Style menu.

- Left
- Font—Helvetica
- Size—24 Point

Open the Text menu and choose Show Text Ruler to adjust the indents. Then choose Line Spacing to adjust the line spacing. Enter a bullet at the beginning

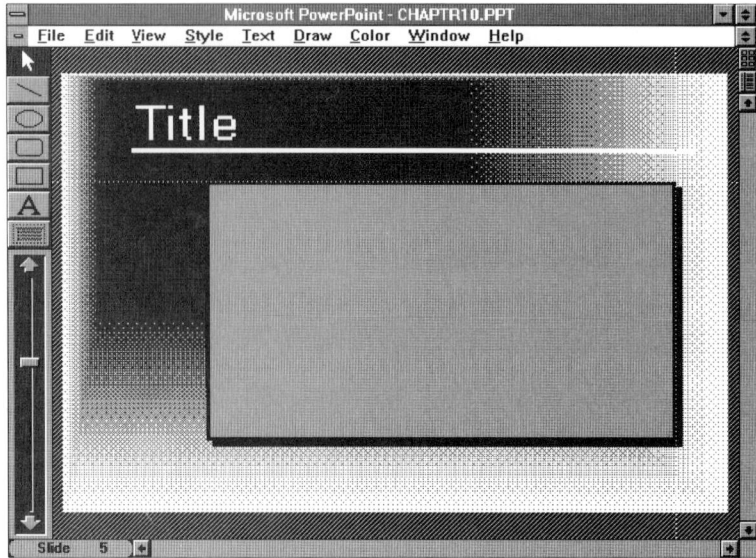

Figure 10-6. *This is the Developer subtemplate with the empty rectangle that you created.*

of each line, and then add a few words on each line. (Remember that to create a round bullet, press Option-8 in Macintosh PowerPoint; in Windows PowerPoint, type a lowercase "l," highlight it, and then change its font style to Zapf Dingbats.) This Developer will be used for indented lists. When you've finished, the Developer subtemplate should look like the one shown in Figure 10-7.

Return to the Slide Sorter view, and click on the second Developer.

Choose the Word Processor tool. Choose Text Ruler and select a smaller indent. Use the Word Processor tool to create a narrow column less than half the width of the rectangle. Select and copy this box. Choose Paste. Select the copy and place it to the right of the original box.

Use PowerPoint's horizontal guide to align the tops of these two Word Processor boxes. They'll be used for creating parallel lists. Select 24-point type, and then enter bullets and brief text placeholders on each line. The completed "phrase Developer" should look similar to the one shown in Figure 10-8.

As you prepare your presentation, make additional copies of these subtemplates in the Slide Sorter view by using the Copy and Paste commands.

Again, save your work.

Chapter 10: Working with the "Steps to Success" Template

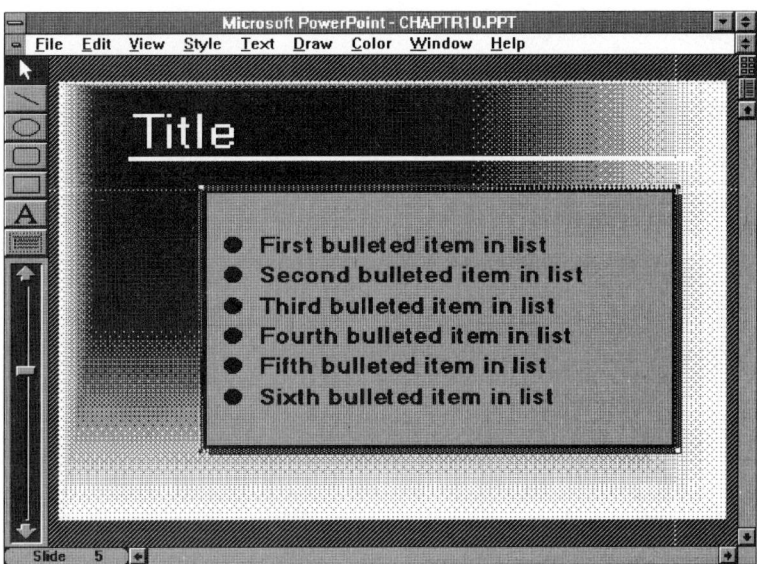

Figure 10-7. Here is a Developer subtemplate with a one-column list.

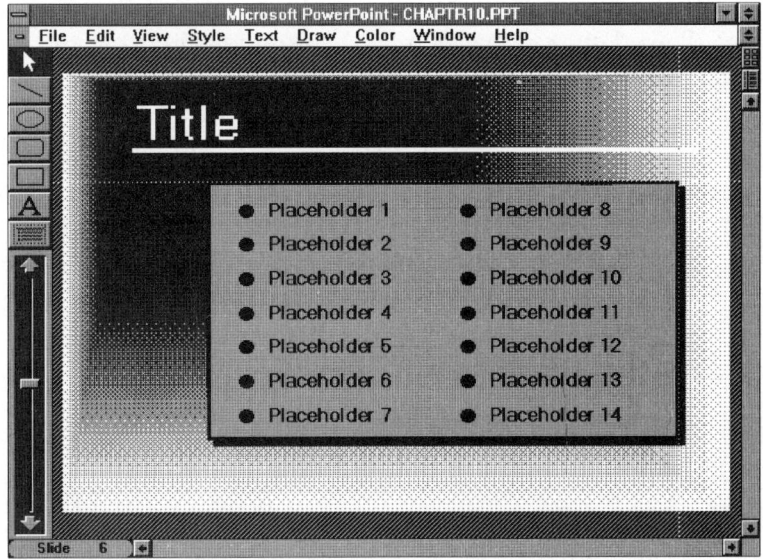

Figure 10-8. Here is a Developer subtemplate with a two-column list that you can create with the Word Processor tool.

Contraster Subtemplates

You use the Contraster subtemplate to contrast two major points—for example, the pros and cons of an argument. Contrasters use circles, instead of rectangles, as an organizing tool. This adds variety to your presentation. As before, however, the top, bottom, left, and right margins of the circles must be consistent with the margins of the Organizer and Developer subtemplates.

Creating Contrasters

1. Before you begin creating a Contraster, relocate the horizontal guide 0.25 inch below center. Relocate the vertical guide 0.75 inch to the left of center.
    - If it is selected, deselect Sized To Text from the Draw menu.
    - Choose the same Line Style, Framed, Filled, and Shadowed options from the Draw menu and color choices from the Color menu—as used previously.
2. Choose the Oval tool to draw a circle. Place the pointer at the intersection of the horizontal and vertical guides. While holding down Shift-Option (in Macintosh PowerPoint) or Shift-Ctrl (in Windows PowerPoint), draw a circle that extends almost to the horizontal line under the title. (Notice that the circle grows from the center.)
3. Relocate the vertical guide to 2.50 inches to the left of center and the horizontal guide to 1.50 inches above center.
4. Choose the Oval tool, and again, while holding down Shift-Option or Shift-Ctrl, resize the circle until its left and top borders touch the guides.

Formatting Contraster text

1. Choose Center from the Text menu.
2. Choose Helvetica, 36 Point, and Bold from the Style menu.
3. Type *PRO* and press Return.
4. Return to the Style menu; choose 18 Point from the Size options.
5. Enter three to five lines of type, ending each line with another hard return.

When you've finished, your Contraster should look like the one shown in Figure 10-9.

Chapter 10: Working with the "Steps to Success" Template

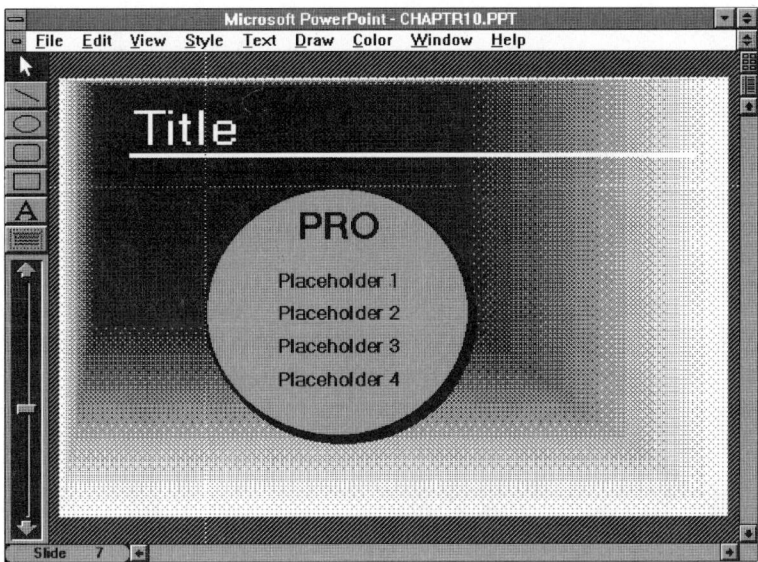

Figure 10-9. *Partially completed Contraster subtemplate with centered text.*

Alternatively, choose Left from the Style menu. Enter three or four single-word bulleted points, each followed by a hard return. When you've finished, your Contraster should resemble the one shown in Figure 10-10.

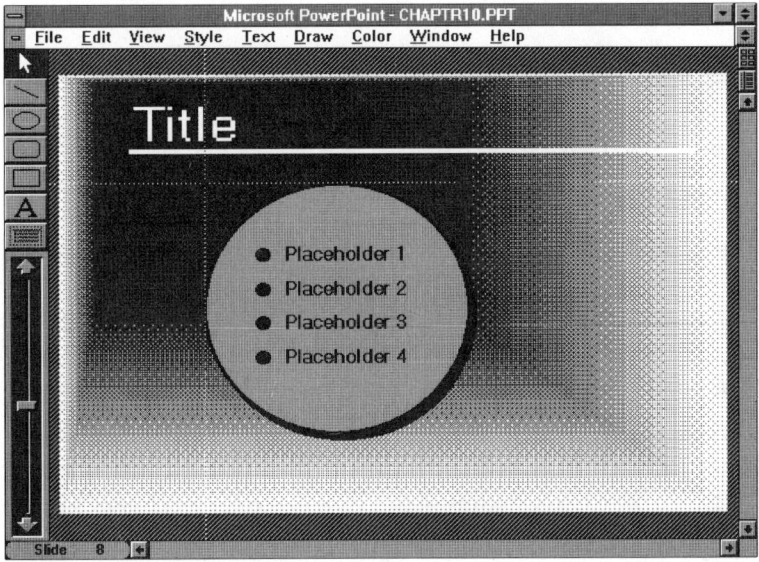

Figure 10-10. *Partially completed Contraster subtemplate using a bulleted list with flush-left text.*

Creating a "Con"

Begin by relocating the vertical guide 3.75 inches to the right. Select both the circle and the text block by clicking on each while holding down the Shift key. Choose Copy from the Edit menu, and then choose Paste. Select the new circle and text block and position them so the top and right edges of the circle touch the horizontal and vertical guides.

Highlight *PRO* and replace it with *CON*. When you've finished, your Contraster should resemble the one shown in Figure 10-11.

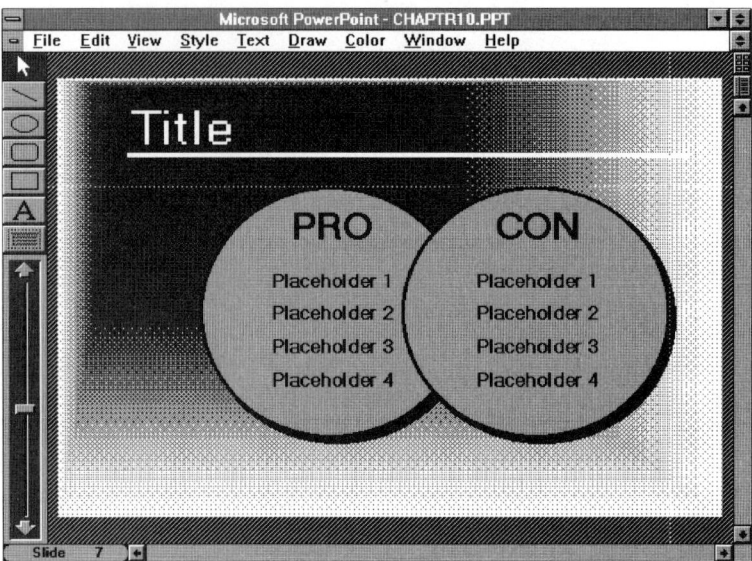

Figure 10-11. *Completed Contraster subtemplate.*

Checking Your Work

The last step in preparing your presentation template is to run the Slide Show and observe the transitions between the various subtemplates that make up the "Steps to Success" presentation. Be sure that you've maintained an overall unity. Also, be sure that the slides don't jump around on the screen—a result of slight differences in object size or placement.

Finally, print out a reference set of the "Steps to Success" presentation template. This will help you plan your specific presentations. You might want to store copies of your presentation templates in a three-ring binder.

Now take a well deserved break! In the next section, you'll see how easy it is to put the template to work.

THE "STEPS TO SUCCESS" TEMPLATE

In this section, we'll use the "Steps to Success" template to prepare an actual presentation. Then we'll take a look at ways to customize the template to give it your personal touch.

Preparing a Presentation

The first step in using the "Steps to Success" template is to print Storyboard forms (as described in Chapter 2). These Storyboards help you plan the content and sequence of your presentation. Storyboards also help you determine how many copies you need of each "Steps to Success" subtemplate.

As you plan and sketch the contents of each slide or overhead, make a rough drawing of each type of subtemplate on each Storyboard. This lets you see at a glance how many copies of each subtemplate you're going to need.

Creating empty subtemplates

To begin work on your actual presentation, open an untitled copy of the "Steps to Success" template. Immediately after you open an untitled template, you must save it with the title of your current presentation—for example, *JAN 90 BOARD MEETING* in the Apple Macintosh environment or *JANBRD90* if you're working with Windows PowerPoint.

Then choose Slide Sorter from the View menu. Make as many copies of each subtemplate as necessary by clicking on each "submaster" and choosing Copy and Paste as many times as necessary.

While still in Slide Sorter view, grab the individual subtemplates and drag them to the new locations. This usually involves inserting Developers and Contrasters between Organizers.

Replacing placeholder text with actual text

While still in Slide Sorter view, double-click on the first slide. When it appears on your screen, do the following.

1. Click on *Title*. Drag the cursor through the word *Title* to select it, and while it is highlighted, replace it with the title of your first visual.

2. Click on the first rectangle. Again, select the placeholder words, and then replace them with the actual words you want in your presentation.

3. Repeat this for the second and third boxes.

4. Click on the Downward arrow at the left of your screen. This advances you to the next slide. Repeat the same steps—that is, enter a new title and replacement text for points 4, 5, and 6.

5. Repeat the above steps until you have modified all of the Organizers.

Adding, deleting, and moving subtemplates

If you need additional Organizers—perhaps your presentation is based on "Eighteen Steps to Greater Profits"—click on the Title Sorter icon at the upper right of your screen (or choose Title Sorter from the View menu). Again, click on one of the Organizer slides. Choose Copy from the Edit menu. Place your cursor after the slide where you want an Organizer inserted. Choose Paste. A blank Organizer appears. Return to Slide View, highlight the numbers and text, and enter replacement numbers and text.

If, on the other hand, your presentation was based on "Six Steps to Greater Profits," simply click on the slides containing Steps 7–9 and Steps 10–12 and remove them by using the Cut or Clear command or by using the Backspace key.

Likewise, you can use the Slide Sorter view to add and relocate Organizers and Contrasters as needed. Select the Slide Sorter icon, click on the template you want, and move it to the location where it's needed.

Working with Developers and Contrasters

You use the same basic procedure when working with Developers and Contrasters.

1. Select the appropriate subtemplate.

2. Select the placeholder text, and replace it with the actual words that will support your recommendations or conclusions.

Use empty Developers as a container for creating tables or for placing imported charts, maps, or other graphics.

Editing and Reviewing Your Work

While replacing placeholder text with actual text, you're likely to encounter instances when the phrase you want to enter is too long to fit on one line.

Whenever this occurs, you might be tempted to reduce the type size to accommodate the extra words or run the copy on two lines or both.

Neither alternative is desirable. If you reduce type size in only one Organizer, you'll call unwanted attention to it. You might also be creating text that is difficult to read.

When you find that your Organizer headings are too long to fit on single lines, remember that the function of Organizers is simply to provide a sequence for your presentation, a guide for your narrative. *The story should be contained in the words you speak.* Thus, short phrases are acceptable—even preferable.

Ruthless editing is called for when you find that there are too many words to fit on a single line. You have two basic choices. Consider the following when you need to shorten a line.

- *Find replacement words.* Look for long words that can be replaced with short words. You'll probably find many occasions when you've used long words such as "exemplary" when you could have used short words such as "fine." Keep a thesaurus at your side as you work.

- *Eliminate unnecessary words.* Look for phrases containing unneeded modifiers—especially adjectives. In addition, eliminate verbs whenever possible. Because the point of the Organizers is to provide a sequence for the introduction of new ideas, verbs are not always needed.

You should consider reducing type size only when you're running into problems on all—or on a significant majority—of your slides and overheads *and* you're convinced that a smaller type size will not compromise legibility. If you do consider reducing type size, of course, remember to reduce type size on *all* the slides and overheads throughout your presentation. Otherwise, your presentation's unity will be seriously compromised.

As Chapter 5 cautioned, you should always run PowerPoint's spelling-checker program one last time before printing your slides and overheads or sending them to an outside service bureau. (Typographical errors inevitably creep into titles or phrases added at the last minute.)

In addition, you'll probably want to use PowerPoint's Find and Find Next commands, which can be used to search for overused or repeated words.

CUSTOMIZING THE "STEPS TO SUCCESS" TEMPLATE

Consider the "Steps to Success" template a starting point for developing your own custom presentation template. Here are some of the ways you can customize the presentation to fit your specific needs.

Modifying the Slide Master

You can add information to the Slide Master. For example, you might add the presenter's name, the date of the presentation, the name of the meeting, or the name of the client or prospect.

If you're using the "Steps to Success" template as the basis for color slides, you might customize the Slide Master background by using the embossing technique described in Chapter 9 instead of using Shadowed boxes. Embossing adds great impact to the areas of the Organizers, Developers, and Contrasters that contain text and graphics.

Modifying Organizers

Another way to make a dramatic change in the appearance of your presentation is to replace the numbers with symbols such as empty or filled ballot boxes, bullets, or check marks. (Note: This makes sense only when numbers are not necessary.)

Use the Macintosh Keycaps Desk Accessory or the Keyboard Help menu in Windows PowerPoint to quickly find the location of the Zapf Dingbats you want to use.

Adding Builds

As described in Chapter 8, builds allow you to introduce information step by step. If you plan to spend a lot of time discussing each of the three points contained in each Organizer, you might consider introducing each point one at a time.

You could add builds to your Organizers by making three copies of each Organizer and deleting the second and third rectangles the first time each Organizer appears and the third rectangle the second time each Organizer appears.

Preparing Notes and Handouts

Attractive, effective slides and overheads are only part of the presentation story. A great deal of the success of your presentation depends on the quality of the Notes you prepare for your own use and the Handouts you distribute to the audience.

Accordingly, the last step in preparing your "Steps to Success" presentation template is to create formats for Notes and Handouts. Masters should contain page numbers as well as specific audience and date information.

The more you work with the "Steps to Success" template, the more variations you're likely to come up with.

EVALUATING YOUR PROGRESS

- Did I place titles and text in the same position on each slide?
- Did I choose appropriate background fill patterns and colors?
- Have I avoided the temptation to reduce type size to squeeze in more words?
- Do the numbers provide a pleasing contrast with the slide titles and text that they introduce?
- Have I created various categories of Developer subtemplates (such as large quotations, single-column lists, and two-column lists)?
- Have I used Contraster subtemplates to develop opposing points of view?
- Did I preview the presentation's continuity and progression of ideas by using the Slide Show feature?

Using a Chart to Add Interest to Text Presentations

By creating four-slice, six-slice, and eight-slice pie-chart templates in advance, you can quickly prepare a presentation by simply choosing the template that contains a pie chart with the number of slices needed to represent the number of points you're going to cover in your presentation.

THE "ADVANCING PIE CHART" TEMPLATE

The "Advancing Pie Chart" template provides a structure for adding memorable text to a presentation—even if prepared under last-minute conditions. The template is based on a pie chart that paces your presentation. Each time you introduce a new topic, you fill in another slice of the pie chart. If you're using Macintosh PowerPoint, you create the pie chart with Microsoft Excel. If you're using Windows PowerPoint, you create the pie chart using either Microsoft Excel for Windows or PowerPoint's built-in charting tools. The Recolor A Picture command plays an important role in both environments.

Prepare the Slide Master

1. Target the output device that you're going to use to prepare your slides and images. As in the previous chapter, we've chosen the

Genigraphics Driver and Genigraphics Presentation Format. If you've chosen a different output device, you'll need to modify the prescribed dimensions to preserve the look of the following example.

2. Choose an appropriate Color Scheme. Do not shade the background, however.

3. Activate the alignment guides (if they're not already visible) by choosing Show Guides from the Draw menu. Reposition the horizontal guide 1.50 inches above center. Reposition the vertical guide 2.75 inches to the left of center.

4. Be sure that the Slide Master view is active, and then click on the title. While the title is selected, choose these formatting options.

    ◇ Choose Left from the Text menu.

    ◇ Choose Font from the Style menu, and then choose Helvetica or Helv.

    ◇ Choose Bold from the Style menu.

    ◇ Choose Size from the Style menu, and then choose 56 Point.

    ◇ Choose Text from the Color menu, and then select an appropriate color.

5. While it's still selected, grab the title and position it 2.75 inches to the left of center.

6. Open the Draw menu. If a check mark appears next to Sized To Text, deselect it by clicking on it. Choose Filled and—if you want—Shadowed from the Draw menu.

7. Choose Fill and Shadow Colors from the Color menu.

8. Deselect the title by clicking on a blank area, and then choose Line Style from the Draw menu, and select the third option down. Choose a line color from the Color menu.

9. Use the Line tool to create a line extending from the vertical guide to the right about the same distance up from the bottom of the slide as the title rectangle is down from the top of the slide.

    Temporarily reposition the vertical guide 4.00 inches to the right of center. Click on the title rectangle, and then click on and drag one of the black corner handles on the right until it touches the vertical guide. Adjust the length of the line at the bottom as well. Return the vertical guide to 2.75 inches to the left of center.

Your Slide Master should look like the one shown in Figure 11-1.

Return to Slide View by choosing Slide (#) from the View menu or by using the keyboard shortcut: Command-D (in Macintosh PowerPoint) or Ctrl-D (in Windows PowerPoint).

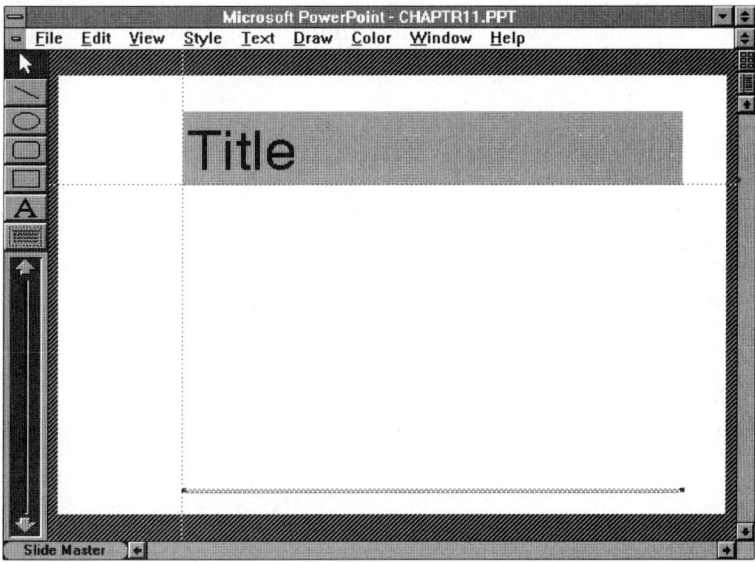

Figure 11-1. *This is the Slide Master that you just created.*

Creating the Pie Chart

Begin by deciding how many pie-chart slices you'll need to pace your presentation. A new slice should be filled in every time you introduce a major point.

Let's assume you're going to need eight slices. Use the Calculator of the Macintosh or Windows to divide 100 by 8, which yields 12.5—that is, each slice occupies 12.5 percent of the pie.

Importing a pie chart created with Microsoft Excel

The technique described here can be used with either the Macintosh or Windows version of Microsoft Excel.

Exit PowerPoint, and start Microsoft Excel.

Enter 12.5 in the first cell. Choose Copy from the Edit menu. Highlight the next seven cells, and choose Paste.

Highlight all eight cells and choose New from the File menu; then choose Chart. When the default chart appears, choose Pie Chart from the Gallery menu, and then choose chart type number 4, an exploded pie chart.

When the eight-slice pie chart appears, click on it and choose Copy. It is now in the Clipboard. Because you might frequently reuse the pie chart, however, use the Paste command to paste the chart into the Macintosh Scrapbook or into a Windows PowerPoint file that you use to store frequently used "clip art" images.

Before you quit Microsoft Excel, you might want to repeat the process, creating exploded four-, five-, six-, seven-, eight-, nine-, and ten-slice pie charts and saving them, so they can be accessed later.

Exit Microsoft Excel and start PowerPoint. Open the Macintosh Scrapbook or Windows clip-art file. Select the eight-slice pie chart. Choose Copy. Paste the eight-slice pie chart into your PowerPoint presentation.

Working with pie charts in Macintosh PowerPoint

Click on the chart and, while holding down the Command key, select one of the corner buttons. Crop the image rectangle until it is just slightly larger than the pie chart itself. Raise the horizontal guide to 2.00 inches above center. Position the pie chart so that it is centered on the horizontal guide and its right border is flush with the title block.

When you've finished, your screen should look like the Macintosh PowerPoint screen shown in Figure 11-2.

Working with pie charts in Windows PowerPoint

If you're using Windows PowerPoint, choose Insert Graph from the File menu. Click on the PowerPoint Datasheet, and choose Select All from the Edit menu. Choose Clear from the Edit menu. Choose Clear Data, and click OK (or press Return).

Enter 12.5 in the first data cell of the Datasheet. (The first visible row and column of cells in a Datasheet are for text labels. Enter the first number in the first *data cell*, which is in the second row and second column of visible cells.) Select the cell, and choose Copy from the Edit menu. Highlight the next seven cells to the right, and then choose Paste.

Chapter 11: Using a Chart to Add Interest to Text Presentations

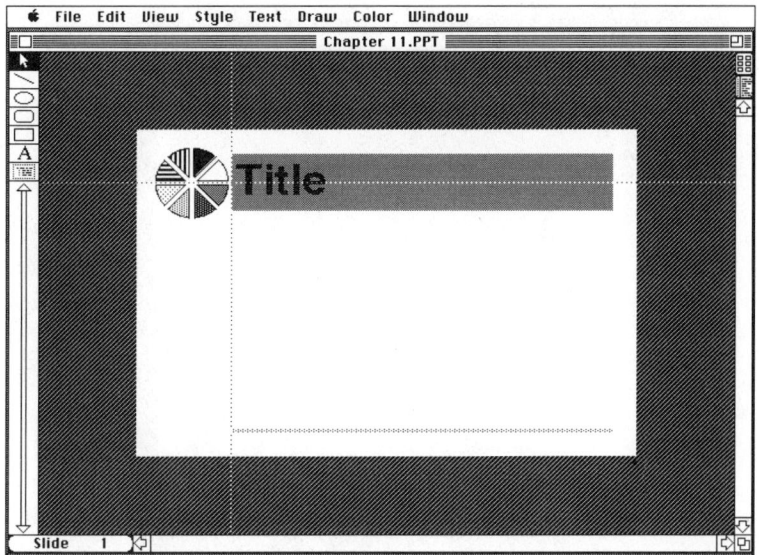

Figure 11-2. *You can place a pie chart (created in Microsoft Excel and imported into Macintosh PowerPoint) next to the slide title.*

Click on the chart and choose Pie from the Chart menu, and then choose chart type number 7 (an exploded, flat pie chart), then click OK. Choose Legend from the Format menu, choose None, and then click OK.

Choose the Exit And Return command from the File menu to insert the pie chart into your presentation. While holding down the Shift key, click on one corner of the chart and resize it to approximate size. (We'll soon fine-tune its position.) Using the right mouse button, click on the chart and move it into approximate position at the upper left of your screen.

Choose the Crop Picture command on the Edit menu, and then use the cropping tool to resize the pie chart until it is a bit smaller than the rectangle surrounding the title.

Raise the horizontal guide to 2.00 inches above center. Move the pie chart until it is centered on the horizontal guide and its right border is flush with the vertical guide.

Your slide should look like the one shown in Figure 11-3 on the following page.

If you have not yet saved your work, save it now—perhaps as PIE8TMP (pie template with eight slices).

SECTION III: HANDS-ON POWERPOINT

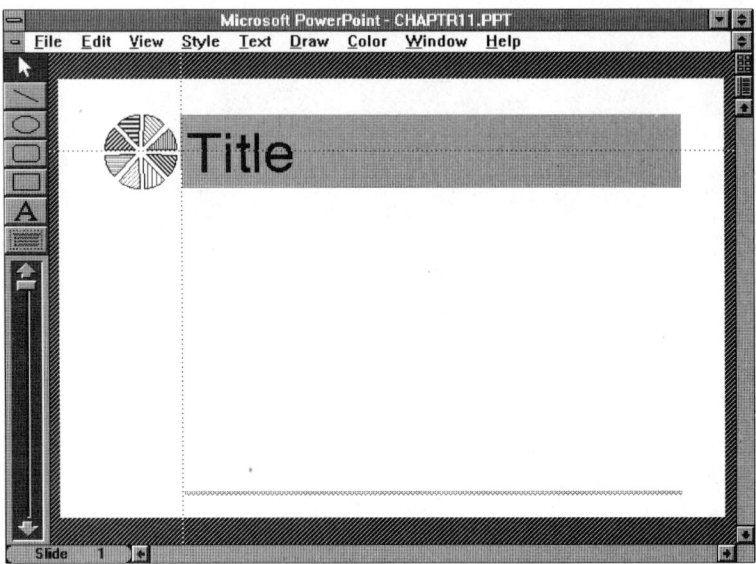

Figure 11-3. *You can place a pie chart (using Windows PowerPoint) next to the title of your presentation.*

Copying Slides

Whether you're using Macintosh PowerPoint or Windows PowerPoint, choose Slide Sorter from the View menu, or click on the Slide Sorter icon at the upper right of the screen.

You can use the Copy and Paste commands to make as many slide copies as there are slices in the pie chart. When the Slide Sorter appears, click on the slide to select it. Choose Copy, and then choose Paste seven times to paste seven copies into the Slide Sorter. (See Figure 11-4.)

Your presentation template is almost ready to be put to work. All that remains is to recolor the slices of each pie chart.

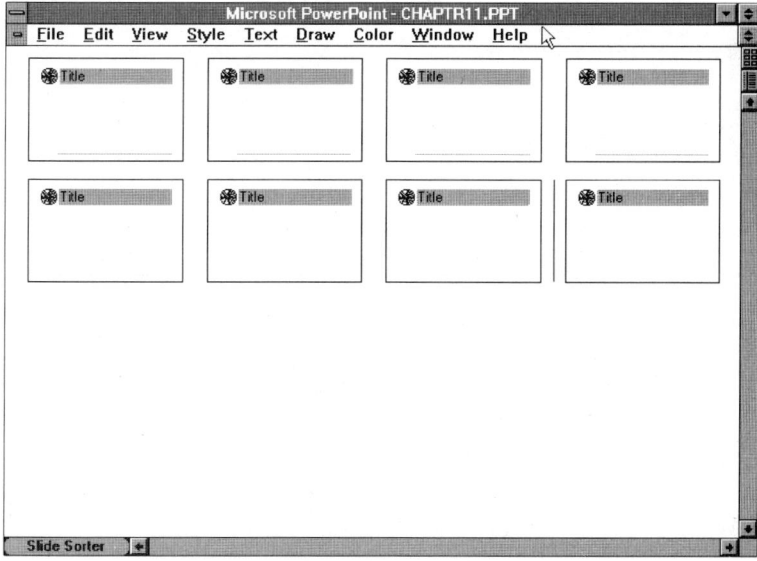

Figure 11-4. *You can use the Slide Sorter to copy slides with unformatted charts.*

Recoloring Pie-Chart Slices

Switch to Slide view, click on the pie chart, and choose Recolor Picture from the Color menu. If you're using Macintosh PowerPoint, choose Change Patterns. If you're using Windows PowerPoint, choose Fills.

The first row of the Recolor Picture dialog box refers to the first pie-chart slice—the one immediately to the right of "twelve-o'clock." Click on the To color box, and select your Color Scheme's foreground color, which is Black in our example.

The color box for the second slice is on the next row. Change its color to that of your Color Scheme's background color, which is White in our example.

Proceed through the remaining options, changing the color of each pie slice to match your Color Scheme's background color.

If you're using Windows PowerPoint, click OK or press Return, and then reopen Recolor Picture. This time, choose Colors. Replace Black—the default color for the rule outlining each pie-chart slice—with your presentation Color Scheme's foreground color.

Choose Preview. The pattern of the first pie-chart slice is now changed to a solid color that matches your Color Scheme's foreground color, as shown in

293

Figure 11-5. This foreground color also outlines—but does not fill—the remaining seven pie-chart segments.

Click OK (or press Return). Save your work now—before you recolor the remaining slices of your pie.

Click the Downward arrow along the left side of the screen to advance to the next slice.

Select the pie chart by clicking on it. Choose Recolor Picture from the Color menu. Choose Change Patterns (in Macintosh PowerPoint) or Fills (in Windows PowerPoint).

This time, however, choose the foreground color for *both the first and second* pie-chart slices. Choose your Color Scheme's background color for the remaining six slices.

If you're using Windows PowerPoint, reopen Recolor Picture, choose Colors, and replace Black with the foreground color of your presentation.

This time, your chart should look like the one shown in Figure 11-6.

Repeat the process with the remaining six slices.

When you've finished, your presentation should resemble the Slide Sorter view shown in Figure 11-7.

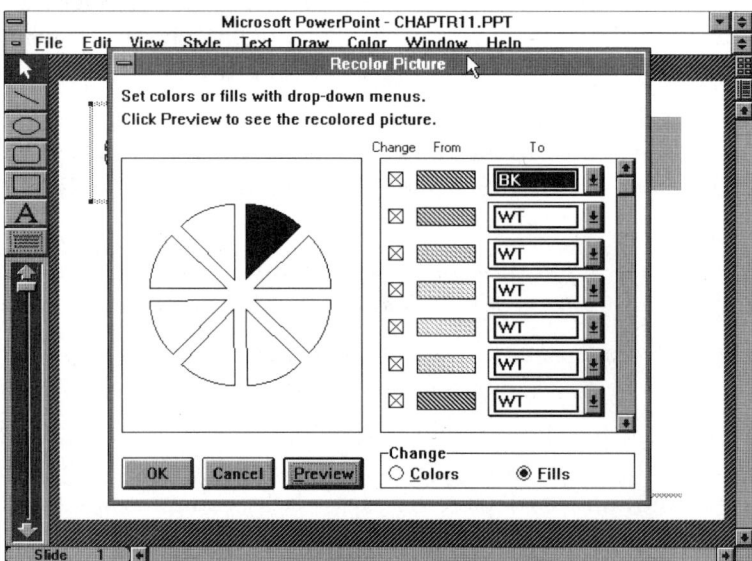

Figure 11-5. You can recolor pie-chart slices.

Chapter 11: Using a Chart to Add Interest to Text Presentations

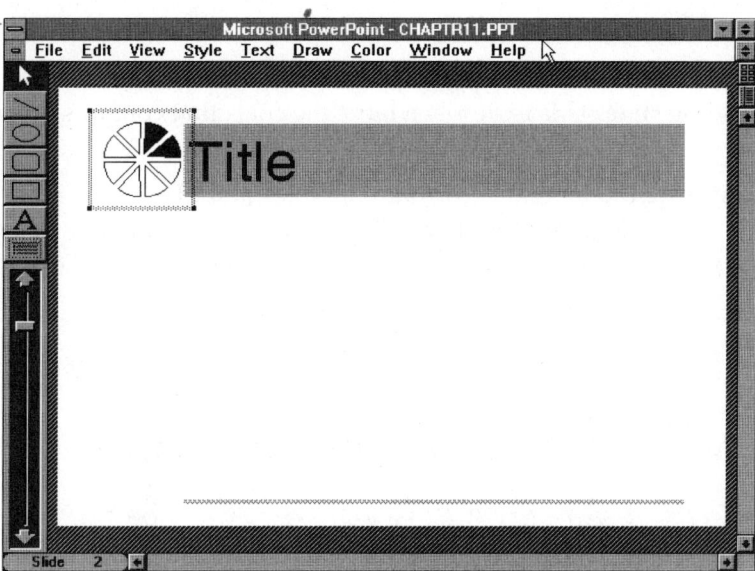

Figure 11-6. The second slide in the series contains two highlighted pie-chart slices.

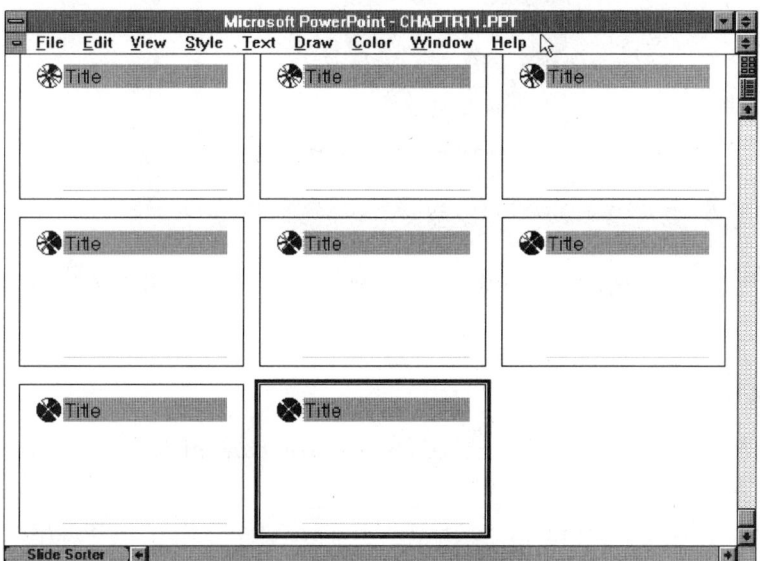

Figure 11-7. The Slide Sorter view now shows the entire series of slides, with each successive slide containing an additional filled-in pie-chart slice.

SECTION III: HANDS-ON POWERPOINT

Creating the Concluding Slide

The starting point is to create the pie chart that will form the dominant visual on the concluding slide. This is simply a large pie chart that contains the steps leading to your conclusion. (See Figure 11-8.)

After you complete the template, format the Notes and Handout pages, and save your work. As suggested earlier in the chapter, you can create several templates at once, based on pie charts using different numbers of slices.

The next section presents only a few of the options you can use to adapt the pie chart to your particular presentation needs.

Figure 11-8. The concluding slide of your presentation contains all the steps.

OPTIONS

The pie chart is only the beginning, of course. You can enhance the effectiveness of this procedure in many ways.

For example, you could add a box around the pie chart equal in height to the title box. Then you could choose an appropriate Fill color—perhaps White, or a lighter or darker version of the slide background color. This would help isolate the pie chart from the background and also visually "lock" the pie chart to the title.

Placing the pie chart against a filled box also allows you to use a shaded slide background for this template because the filled box behind the pie chart remains a constant color.

Although the template has been described so far in terms of "one slice/one title," you can use more than one slide to illustrate each slice of the pie chart if you're preparing a long presentation.

You could introduce each subtopic with a new slice of the pie chart and use as many slides as needed to elaborate on the topic. The pie-chart slice would remain the same regardless of the number of slides needed to discuss each topic.

Using this variation, you could identify each topic with a small title adjacent to the pie chart.

Now that you're comfortable with the idea of pacing your presentation using a pie chart, you might want to experiment with other visual devices. For example, you could create a grid of small vertical rectangles and pace your presentation by—once again—replacing outlined rectangles with filled-in rectangles, as shown in Figure 11-9.

You can also experiment with recoloring the newest slice of a pie chart to match the color of Title. This will visually connect the new pie-chart slice to the title of the presentation.

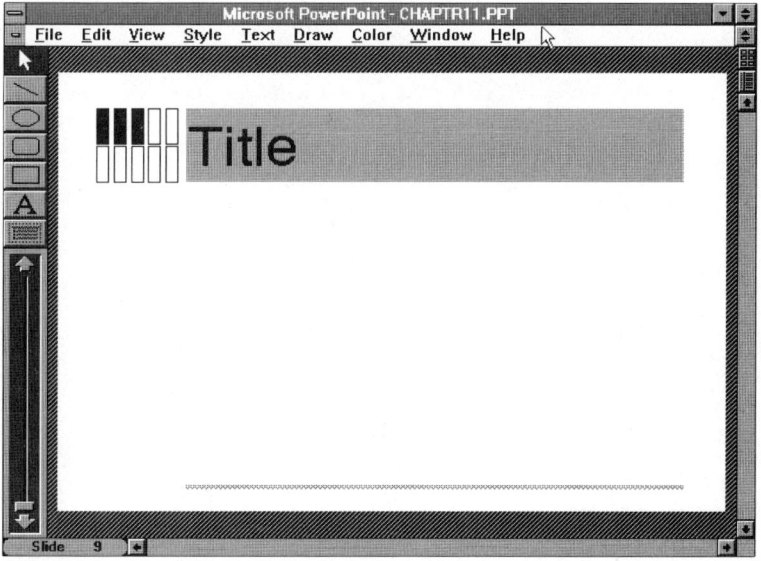

Figure 11-9. *You can use rectangles to pace your presentation.*

A final option, if you're explaining a "total" composed of parts of varying importance, is to use different-size slices for the pie chart. You can make the size of each slice proportionate to its importance to the completed chart by entering different values for each slice in the Excel worksheet or in the Windows PowerPoint Datasheet.

EVALUATING YOUR PROGRESS

- ◆ Does the pie chart appear in the same position on each visual?
- ◆ Did I use the Recolor Picture command to color all segments of the pie chart correctly?
- ◆ Did I preview the progression of the pie chart by using the Slide Sorter view and the Slide Show feature?
- ◆ Does the text area appear in the same position on each visual?
- ◆ Did I use horizontal rules to frame the text area of each visual?
- ◆ Have I added presentation information (such as the name of the audience and the presenter or the date of the presentation) to the Slide Master?
- ◆ Have I experimented with creative options (such as keying the color of the latest pie-chart slice introduced to the text color of the presentation title)?

Using Genigraphics Backgrounds with Black-and-White Overheads

All too often, black-and-white overhead transparencies exhibit excessive contrast. The presenter—say, an educator—appears in front of an intensely white screen containing black text. Typically no grays are used—no transitions in tonal values between the brilliant white screen and the black text. This all-or-nothing black-and-white effect is akin to shouting and can quickly tire an audience.

This doesn't need to happen. Even though the capability of laser printers to smoothly reproduce shades of gray is limited, this limitation can be mitigated if the grays are used for graphical highlights that soften the harshness of black against white and to accent (or draw attention to) text.

THE "PROMOTING SPECIALIST" TEMPLATE

The "Promoting Specialist" template described in this chapter provides a means of adding visual interest to black-and-white overheads. The careful use of various shades of gray can enhance the effectiveness of black-and-white transparencies and can help avoid the frequently encountered harshness of black type against a white background unrelieved by any middle tones. (Such usage is ideally suited to preparing low-budget transparencies for educational or training purposes.) This chapter also explains how the artwork included in the Genigraphics samples can be reused for other purposes.

The "Promoting Specialist" template also shows how visual interest can be added to black-and-white overheads by creating a banner at the top of each overhead that contains distinctive typography. This banner not only visually defines the top of each transparency and adds continuity to your presentation but also reinforces your presentation's title.

Three steps are involved in creating high-impact presentations that use artwork from the Genigraphics samples included with the Genigraphics software package.

- *Locate and isolate the artwork.* Identify the Genigraphics format containing the artwork that you want to incorporate into your presentation.

- *Select and copy the artwork.* Choose the background effect you want, and add it to a new Slide Master by using the Clipboard.

- *Place, resize, and recolor the artwork.* Use the Paste As Picture and Recolor A Picture commands to translate colored artwork into shades of gray.

To create a banner over each overhead, follow these steps.

- *Create a filled box on the Slide Master.* This should be filled with solid black.

- *Add reversed text.* This emphasizes the titles and unifies your presentation.

Locate and Isolate the Artwork

1. Open a new PowerPoint file. Target an appropriate output device by using the Chooser (in Macintosh PowerPoint) or Printer Setup (in Windows PowerPoint). Because you'll be preparing black-and-white overheads, choose the particular brand of laser printer you're going to use as an output device, typically either an Apple LaserWriter or one of the Hewlett-Packard LaserJet (or equivalent) printers.

Chapter 12: Using Genigraphics Backgrounds with Black-and-White Overheads

2. Choose the Slide Master view. Choose Color Scheme, click on Select A Scheme, and then select White as the background, Black as the foreground, and the third option from the left on the top row—the one filled with various shades of gray—for accent colors.

3. Choose Open from the File menu. Open the Color Special Effects folder (in Macintosh PowerPoint) or the \template\35mm subdirectory (in Windows PowerPoint). Scroll through the list of Genigraphics files until you find one containing a graphical image you want to include in your project.

4. The horizon perspective that we'll use as the basis for this template is found in the Horizon Grid Template file (in Macintosh PowerPoint) or the horizon.ppt file (in Windows PowerPoint). Open the file by double-clicking on it. An image similar to the one shown in Figure 12-1 should appear on your screen.

Note: The name and/or appearance of some Genigraphics templates can differ, depending on the version and release date of your PowerPoint package.

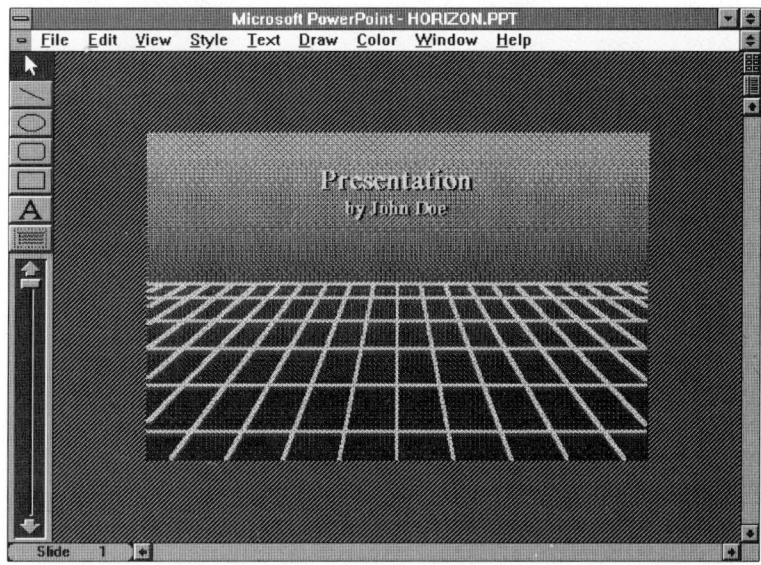

Figure 12-1. *You can access this sample presentation by double-clicking on the Horizon Grid Template file (in Macintosh PowerPoint) or the horizon.ppt file (in Windows PowerPoint).*

Select and Copy the Artwork

1. Choose the Slide Master view. Choose Select All from the Edit menu. Deselect the title by clicking on it while holding down the Shift key. (This is necessary because you cannot select the title for copying or cutting.)

2. From the Edit menu, choose Copy, and then choose Close from the File menu. Choose No if PowerPoint asks whether you want to save the template file.

3. Use the Paste As Picture command on the Edit menu to place the horizon grid into the Slide Master of your presentation.

   When you've finished, the Slide Master should look similar to the one shown in Figure 12-2.

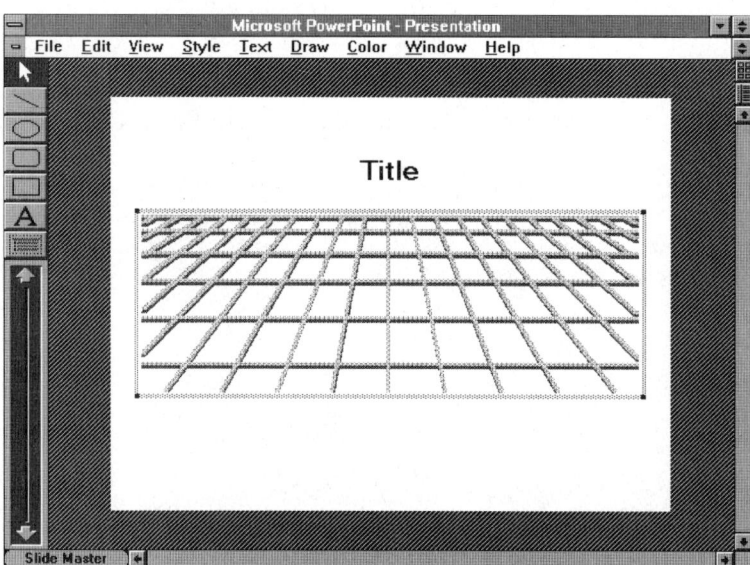

Figure 12-2. *You can place the Horizon Grid Template into the Slide Master by using the Paste As Picture command.*

Place, Resize, and Recolor the Artwork

Although the original horizon grid was created with numerous lines, you can now resize and recolor it as a single object because you pasted it as a picture into your presentation.

1. Select the grid and align the bottom with the bottom of your slide. Grab one of the top buttons and compress the grid until it extends only about one-third of the way up the screen. (See Figure 12-3.)

2. While the grid is still selected, choose Recolor Picture from the Color menu.

3. Choose Change Patterns (in Macintosh PowerPoint) or Fills (in Windows PowerPoint). Replace the blues with shades of gray—GY4 and GY7, in our example. If it turns out that the grays are too light or too dark, you can always choose different grays later.

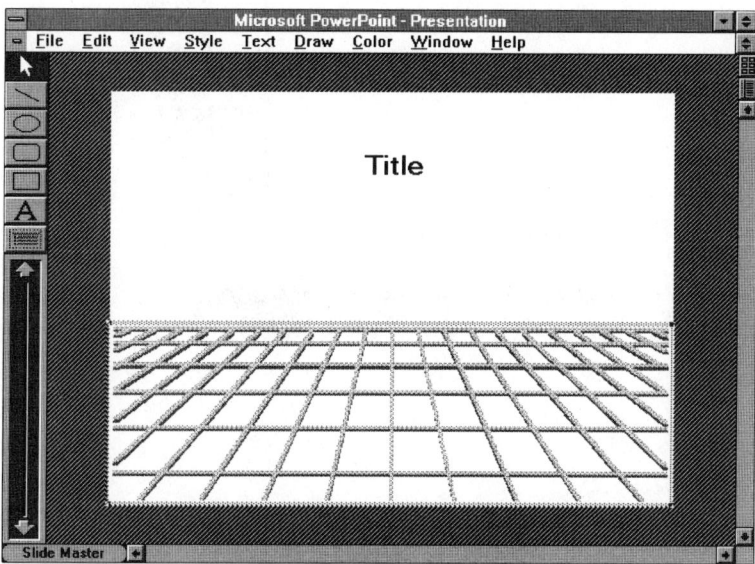

Figure 12-3. *You can move and resize the Horizon Grid Template on the Slide Master. Here the Horizon Grid has been compressed.*

Adding a "Contents Box"

The next step is to use the Rectangle tool to create a "contents box" for the text area of your presentation.

1. Be sure that the grid image and title are not selected, and then choose Opaque, Framed, and Shadowed from the Draw menu.

2. Choose Shadow from the Color menu, and then choose Black.

3. Choose the Rectangle tool and create a box that begins about one-fourth of the way down from the top of the screen and extends about five-sixths of the way down the screen.

SECTION III: HANDS-ON POWERPOINT

4. Select the title and reposition it within the contents box.

When you've finished, your Slide Master should look similar to the one shown in Figure 12-4.

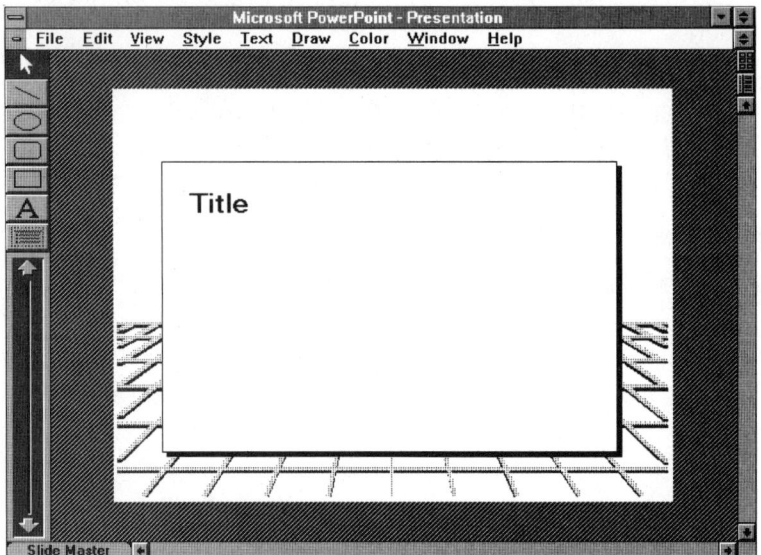

Figure 12-4. *You can create a contents box with a shadow added for emphasis.*

Adding a Title Banner

The final step is to add a title banner with reversed text across the top of your presentation. (Reversing the text, of course, is dependent on the capability of your laser printer to create reversed type.) The purpose of this banner is twofold. First, the blackness of the background provides a pleasing contrast to the whiteness of the remainder of the overhead. Second, repeating the title of your presentation as a banner on all of your overheads reinforces your presentation's identity.

To create the title banner, follow these steps while working in Slide Master view.

1. Be sure that nothing is selected, and then choose Filled from the Draw menu and deselect Shadowed.

2. Choose Fill from the Color menu, and then choose Black.

3. Use the Rectangle tool to create a black box across the top of the overhead.

4. Use the Labeler tool to add the title of your presentation. The example that follows is based on a short, two-word title supported by a longer subtitle that elaborates on the title and explains its focus.

To create a title similar to "Promoting Specialists," follow these steps.

1. Select the Labeler tool, click in the center of the black rectangle, and then choose these formatting options from the Style menu.

   ◇ Font: Helvetica

   ◇ Size: 36 Point

   ◇ Style: Bold

2. From the Color menu, choose Text, and then choose White.

3. From the Text menu, choose Center.

4. Type *Promoting Specialists* (or the title of your presentation), and then press Return.

5. While the Labeler tool is still selected, choose these formatting options from the Style menu.

   ◇ Font: Helvetica

   ◇ Size: 18 Point

   ◇ Style: Bold and Italic

6. Enter the subtitle of your presentation (if it has one).

Now your Slide Master should look similar to the one shown in Figure 12-5 on the following page.

Return to your Slide by choosing Slide (#) from the View menu or by using a keyboard shortcut: Command-D (in Macintosh PowerPoint) or Ctrl-D (in Windows PowerPoint).

The framework is ready to use. You can enter text by using the Word Processor tool. (See Figure 12-6 on the following page.)

You can prepare black-and-white overhead transparencies by using your laser printer. (Be sure that the brand of overhead transparencies you have is certified for use with your particular laser printer.) You can also run off standard black-and-white copies and use an office copier to prepare the transparencies.

SECTION III: HANDS-ON POWERPOINT

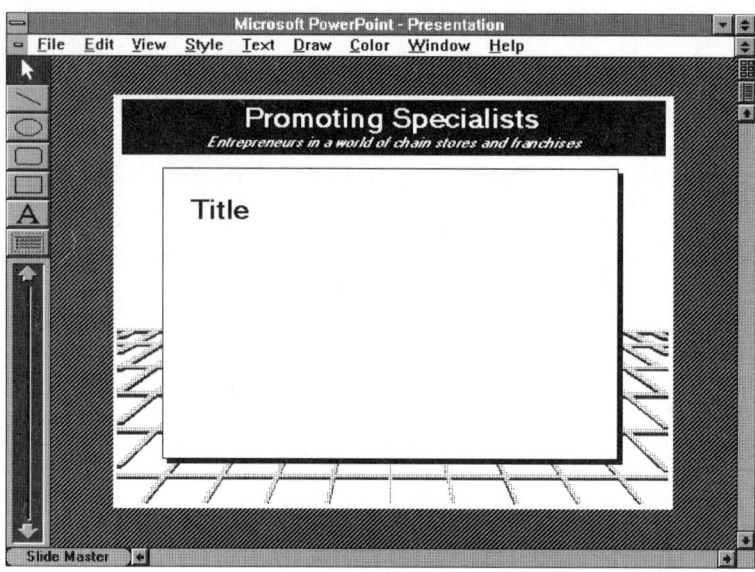

Figure 12-5. You can add a reversed title to your Slide Master.

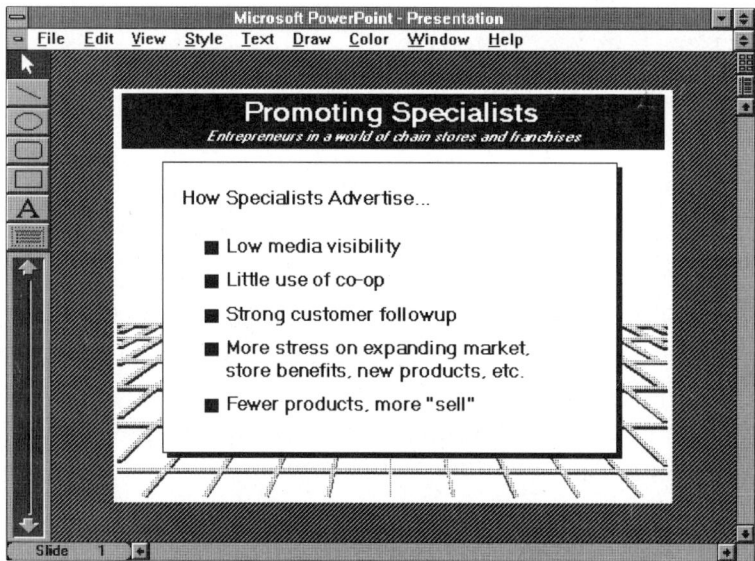

Figure 12-6. You can add text to a contents box by using the Word Processor tool.

Experimenting

You can use the same technique described above to create interesting backgrounds by selecting other Genigraphics color samples. In each case, the sequence is as follows.

1. Identify the Genigraphics color sample file that contains the artwork you want to incorporate into your Slide Master.

2. Open the file and choose Slide Master.

3. Select the artwork—often by using Select All and deselecting the title. Use the Copy and Paste As Picture commands to place the artwork into your existing Slide Master.

4. Resize the background image and use the Recolor Picture command to integrate the background into your existing presentation.

5. Use an Opaque box to provide a container for the contents of each slide.

EVALUATING YOUR PROGRESS

- Have I avoided using a background graphic so attention-getting that it detracts from the effectiveness of each visual's text and graphics?

- Did I use the Recolor Picture command to create a pleasing tonal contrast between foreground text and the subdued background?

- Did I include sufficient breathing room between the edges of the text box and the edges of the visual?

- Have I averted creating competition between the presentation's title banner and the title of each slide?

- Have I experimented with various shades of gray for recoloring the background?

PowerPoint at Work: A Color-Slide Portfolio

PowerPoint's capabilities provide you with an almost unlimited opportunity to communicate visually with an audience. You can create slides, overheads, computer-based presentations, notes, and audience handouts. You can incorporate text, photographs, symbols, illustrations, logos, charts, tables, graphs, and much more into any presentation you give.

The color slides are offered as inspiration. Many of the following examples make use of professionally created images included in the Genigraphics clip-art files provided with PowerPoint. The slides illustrate many effects that can be created by using PowerPoint's built-in graphing and drawing tools. The variety of concepts and designs in this portfolio are intended to encourage originality and excellence in your own slide-creation process.

POWERPOINT PRESENTATIONS BY DESIGN

The computer-grabbing-the-man illustration is part of the Genigraphics clip-art collection. Pastel shades in the bar graph and illustration soften the impact of potentially unpleasant news (down-time statistics). The graph has been stretched to fill a horizontal space.

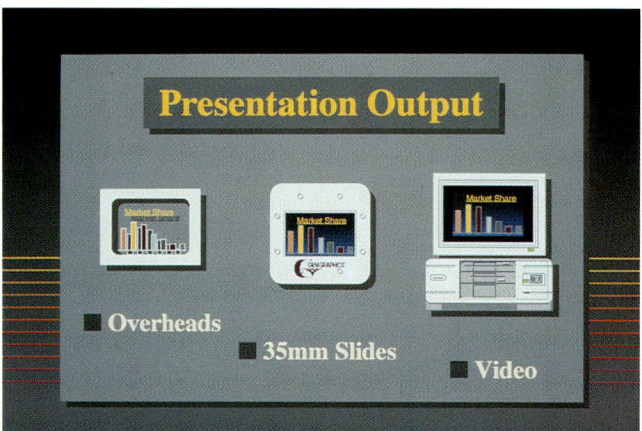

Visual unity is achieved by using drop shadows for the title box and for the three color graphics. In addition, the colors in the horizontal lines that flank the large rectangle blend nicely with colors used in the title and in the overhead, slide, and video versions of the bar graph.

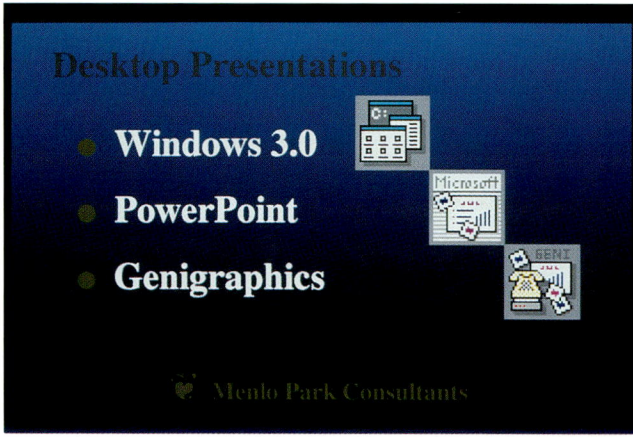

The three squares, connected at their corners, create a dynamic, step-down effect. Had the squares been stacked, too much space would have been required between text lines, thereby decreasing the cohesiveness of the design. Notice also that the toned-down color of the title allows the items in the bulleted list to "pop."

PowerPoint at Work

The design element across the top counterbalances the longish list, preventing the slide from becoming bottom-heavy. Pastels can be used to create a "strong" visual, even though they're usually considered to be "soft" colors.

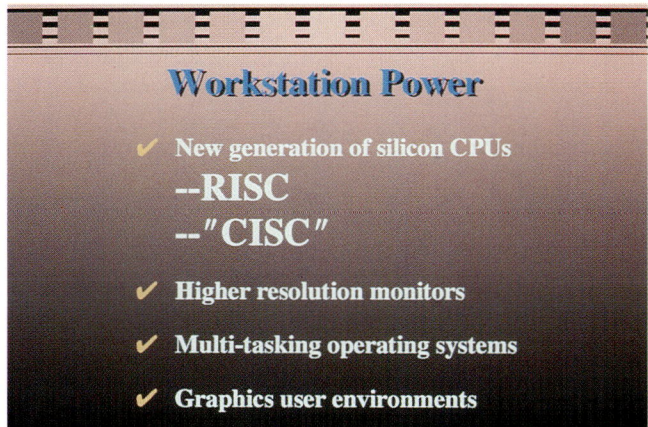

Compatibility—the main theme—is supported by the implied motion in three design elements— the radiating stripes in the background, the slanted sides of the title box, and the two-headed arrow.

The same color is used for the title, the bullets in the list, and the dots on the map—all of which relate to the location of sales offices. The gradation of "lighting" in the title box prevents it from being overwhelmed by the "lighting" of the globe. The horizontal lines of the background contain the globe so that it doesn't dominate the slide.

POWERPOINT PRESENTATIONS BY DESIGN

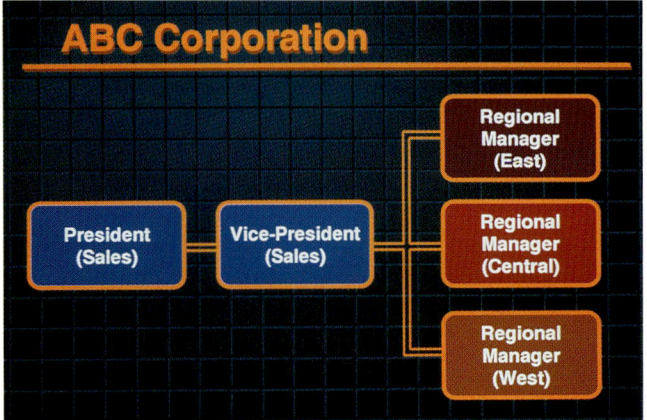

A horizontally oriented organizational chart emphasizes relationship and de-emphasizes hierarchy. Colors differentiate the job titles.

The entire design leads the viewer to "people." This is most obviously achieved by the lively colors of the clothing and less obviously achieved by having two backgrounds: the diagonal stripes and the solid but graduated color outside the "picture frame" and the solid but graduated color that forms the inner backdrop.

The use of a graphic (the magnifying glass) can underscore the subject matter (observations). White is used as a type color. A busy background can be acceptable when subdued colors are used.

PowerPoint at Work

By placing the words "Token Rings" inside the two orange rings and by using white letters against the darkest part of the background, the central mechanism becomes the center of attention.

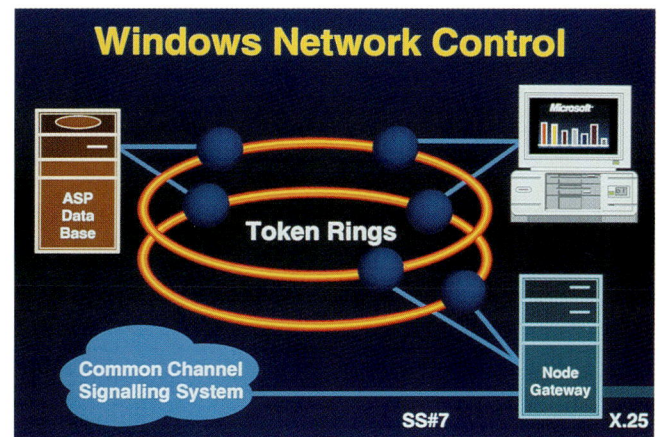

The venerable chart is refurbished by using distinct colors for each group of points/line/label and for the oversize and colorful arrow that dramatizes the overall trend. This "exploding" arrow is part of the Genigraphics clip-art collection.

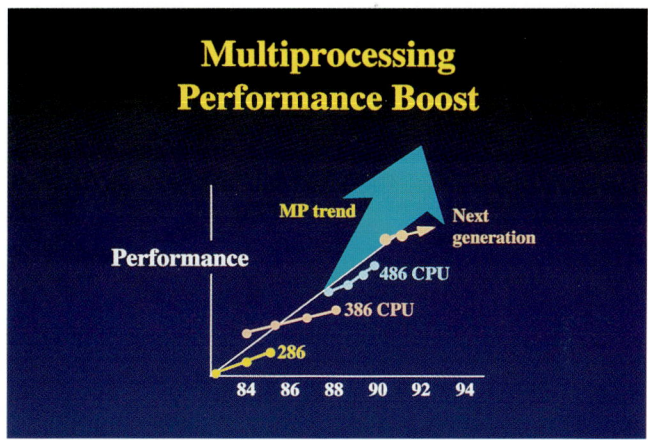

The slide-within-a-slide motif plus the use of overlapping frames, colors, and a pie chart suggest the sophistication of the available slide-creation tools. A graduated screen is used within a tall rectangle. The slide illustration is part of the Genigraphics clip-art collection.

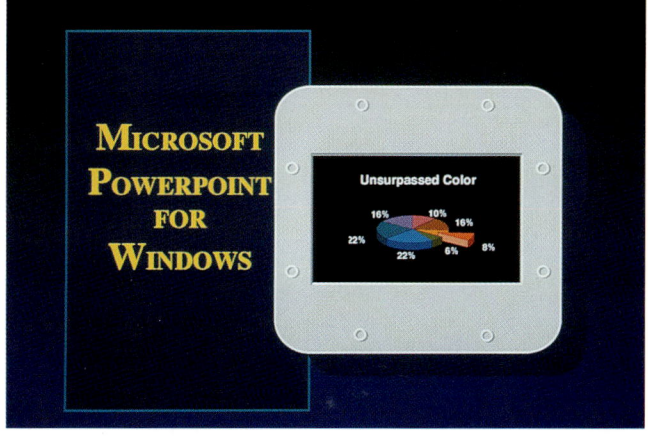

POWERPOINT PRESENTATIONS BY DESIGN

A sculpturelike design—in this case, two three-dimensional elements (initials forming a logo) with minimal but striking use of color—can be affecting. A graduated fill backlights the central design.

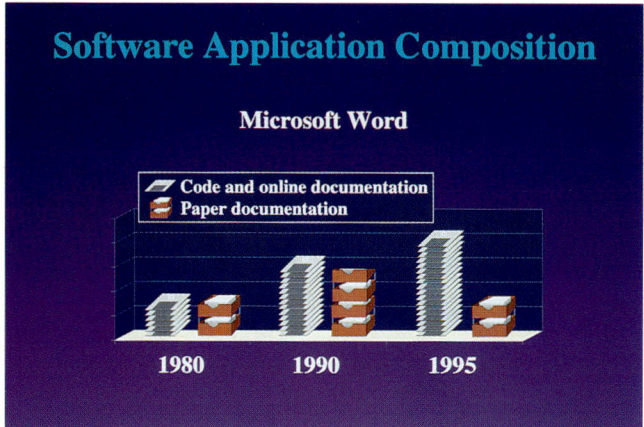

A bar chart takes on new life and can visually suggest content when the key graphics are the stuff of which each bar is made. The sheet of paper and the paper-holder box are part of the Genigraphics clip-art collection, here produced in multiple by using the Copy and Paste commands.

A complex background of short diagonal lines behind a rectangular frame of horizontal lines can be created easily with PowerPoint's tools. The title, "Customer Support," is in shadow lettering. The Genigraphics clip-art illustration is used twice—once with normal coloring and once with all colors changed to black (using the Recolor Picture command) to create the shadow.

PowerPoint at Work

An exquisite photograph has attention-grabbing power. The goal in this instance is to create a setting that enhances the "jewel" and that does not interfere with the viewer's focus. The same visual might have been boring if the object had been placed against a solid background.

If your output device can produce scanned images, a photograph can lend immediacy and drama to a slide by substantiating the slide's text. Part of the impact of this slide results from symmetry: The top and bottom borders of the photo align with the first and last lines of text, and the area devoted to the photo balances the area devoted to text.

The suggestiveness of a photograph can be intriguing. This could be an advertisement for a pen-based, grid-pad computer or for blue jeans. Or this could be part of a corporate-profile slide show, depicting a serious and competent employee performing his job with state-of-the-art equipment.

POWERPOINT PRESENTATIONS BY DESIGN

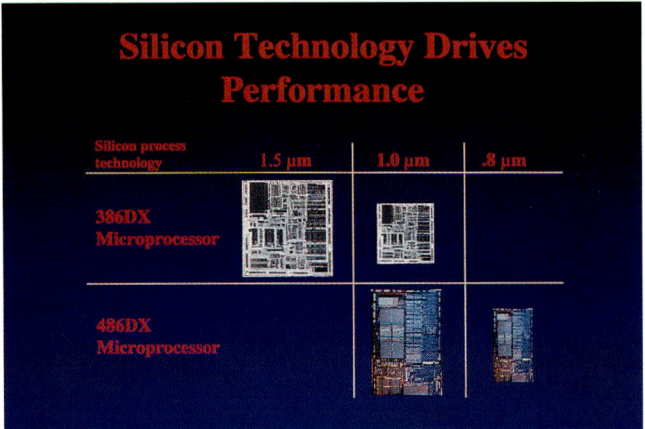

This table is unusual because it has a measurement as the column head (not as a column entry) and photographs as the data entered in the matrix. The introduction of color in the photographs of the newer chips emphasizes the generation of the more advanced chips.

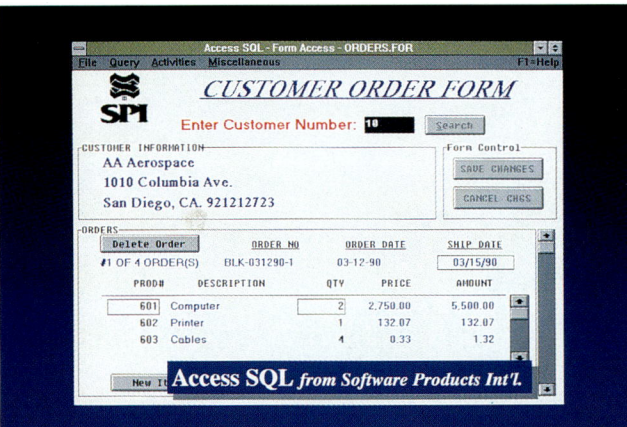

A real-world product can be shown to an audience that might not be receptive to an advertisement. By presenting a specific application, potential customers can see exactly what it is that they might be buying and using. In this case, a screen dump familiarizes viewers with the capabilities of a new software program.

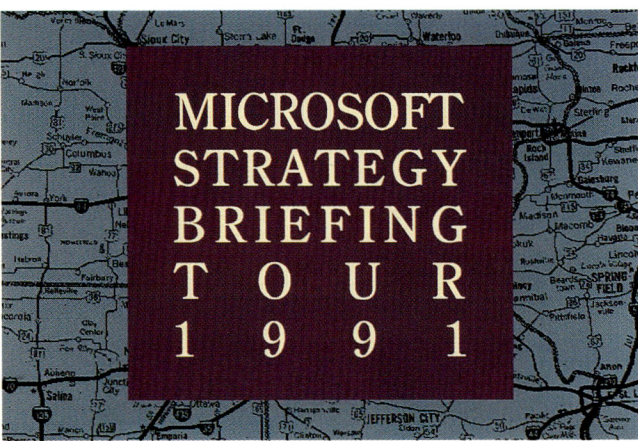

The temptations of color make it easy to overlook the effectiveness of black-and-white illustrations. A black-and-white graphic (in this case, a map) can provide a meaningful background for and serve as a counterpoint to a colorful and bold announcement (of a tour).

Working with the "Left-to-Right" Template

Most slides and overheads are based on a top-to-bottom arrangement. The title appears at the top, and lists or illustrations appear beneath it. This often can result in a boring, predictable presentation. Alternatives are available, however. The left-to-right format described in this template makes better use of space and is in accord with a person's natural tendency to read from left to right. Left-to-right formats can also be more visually interesting because they avoid the static look that is especially noticeable when both titles and text are centered.

The "Left-to-Right" template is ideal for text-heavy presentations. The template is based on an oversize slide number that provides a dominant visual focus for each slide and also paces the presentation. The template is particularly useful for presentations characterized by short titles and long lists.

Although this presentation is designed for maximum text density, the relatively large amount of space above and below the number, title, and subtitle on the left side, as well as the space surrounding the information frame, provides a pleasing space-to-text ratio.

Four tasks are involved in preparing this template.

- *Choose a color scheme, and shade the background from the title.* A light-to-dark transition works best, although you can experiment with dark-to-light transitions if you choose different colors for the slide number and the title.

- *Add your firm's or association's logo to the left side of the slide.* Logos provide important presentation reinforcement.

- *Format the slide number and title along the left side.* These help pace your presentation and identify the slide in the Title Sorter view.

- *Balance the slide number and title with a shaded container that has a solid background for text or graphics on the right.* The contrast between the solid background and the shaded background will help draw the audience's attention to the text.

GETTING STARTED

Begin by selecting an output device by using the Macintosh Chooser and PowerPoint's Page Setup command or by using the Windows PowerPoint Printer Setup command. The dimensions that follow are based on choosing the Genigraphics Driver and the Genigraphics Presentation Format.

Use the Color Scheme command to select a palette of background, foreground, and accent colors.

Most important, choose Shade Background and then choose From Title. If you're preparing color overheads with a light background, choose the option which indicates that the title will be the darkest part of the slide. If you're preparing 35mm slides with a dark background, choose the option indicating a light title background, and then do the following.

1. Choose Slide Master.

2. Choose Show Guides from the Draw menu, or use the keyboard shortcuts: Command-G (in Macintosh PowerPoint) or Ctrl-G (in Windows PowerPoint).

3. Grab the vertical guide, and reposition it 3.50 inches to the left of center.

4. Grab the horizontal guide, and reposition it 1.50 inches above center.

Add the Slide Number

To add the slide number, do the following.

1. Choose the Labeler tool, and add the slide number symbol—two pound signs (##)—to the Slide Master above and to the right of where the horizontal and vertical guides intersect.

2. Highlight the slide number symbol, and then choose Font from the Style menu. Choose a sans serif typeface such as Helvetica (in Macintosh PowerPoint) or Helv (in Windows PowerPoint). Then choose Size from the Style menu and select 72.

3. Choose and reposition the ##, if necessary, being sure that the left and bottom edges are aligned with the intersection of the horizontal and vertical guides.

4. While ## is still selected, choose Text from the Color menu, and then choose a color that will form the strongest contrast with the darkest or lightest (depending on the shading variant you chose) Slide Master background.

Add the Accent Rule

To add the accent rule, do the following.

1. Move the vertical guide 3.75 inches to the left of center.

2. Choose Line Style from the Draw menu, and select the third option down.

3. While holding down the Shift key, choose the Line tool and, beginning at the intersection of the horizontal and vertical guides, draw a line to the right.

4. Move the vertical guide 2.00 inches to the left of center. Click on the line, and extend it to the vertical guide. When you've finished, return the vertical guide to 3.75 inches to the left of center.

5. While the line is still selected, choose Line from the Color menu, and then choose an appropriate accent color.

Position and Format the Slide Title

To position and format the Slide title, do the following.

1. Select and highlight the title. While it is highlighted, add the formatting options.

SECTION III: HANDS-ON POWERPOINT

2. Choose Left from the Text menu.

3. Choose Font from the Style menu, and then choose a sans serif typeface such as Helvetica (in Macintosh Powerpoint) or Helv (in Windows PowerPoint).

4. Choose Size from the Style menu, and select 48.

5. While the title is selected, move it until the top and left edges of the title touch the lower right intersection of the horizontal and vertical guides.

6. While the title is still selected, choose Text from the Color menu, and then choose a color that will form the strongest contrast with the darkest or lightest (depending on the shading variant you chose) Slide Master background. (Choose the same color as you did for ##, or choose a contrasting color.)

Now you can add presentation information or your firm's logo to the lower left side of the Slide Master, perhaps lined up with the vertical guide.

Save your work.

At this point, your Slide Master should look like the one shown in Figure 13-1.

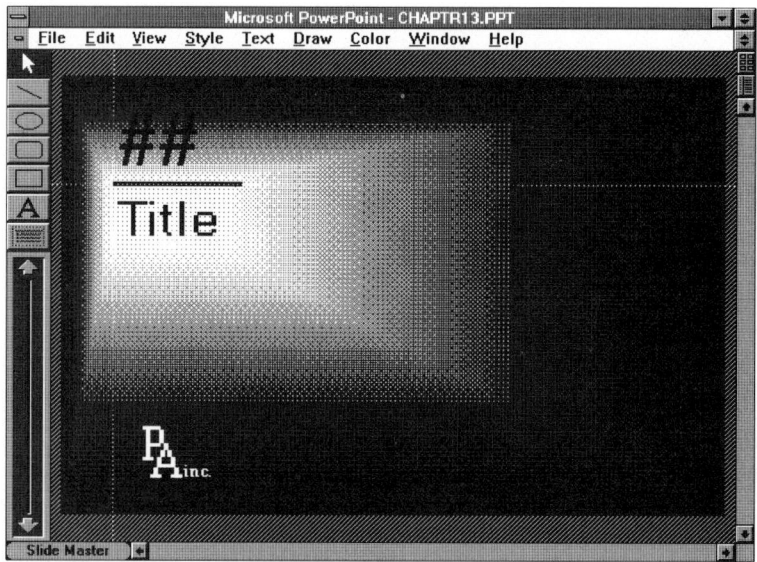

Figure 13-1. Slide number, title, and company logo appear at the left in the "Left-to-Right" template.

Create the Contents Box

To create the contents box, do the following.

1. Open the Draw menu, and choose Framed, Filled, and Shadowed.

2. Open the Line Style menu, and choose the second option.

3. Open the Color menu, and choose the Fill, Line, and Shadow colors you want. To integrate the slide number and title with the text they introduce, you might choose the same Line color that you selected for the rule separating the slide number and title.

   The fill color can be the same color as the Slide Background, or the next lighter or darker option. The contrast between the solid filled area of the contents box and the shaded Slide Master background will be quite pleasing.

4. Move the vertical guide 1.50 inches to the left of center.

5. Choose the Rectangle tool and, matching the height and vertical location of ##, draw a large box to the right.

6. When you've finished drawing the box, drag the box until it has the following dimensions.

   ◇ Left side: 1.50 inches left of center

   ◇ Right side: 4.0 inches right of center

   ◇ Top: 2.50 inches above center

   ◇ Bottom: 2.50 inches below center

7. Fine-tune your Slide Master by being sure that your firm's logo is lined up with the bottom of the contents box. Use the horizontal guide to ensure accurate alignment.

8. Before returning to Slide View, relocate the vertical guide to 1.25 inches left of center, and relocate the horizontal guide to 2.25 inches above center.

The completed Slide Master should look like the one shown in Figure 13-2 on the following page. When you're ready, return to Slide View by choosing Slide (#) from the View menu or by using a keyboard shortcut: Command-D (in Macintosh PowerPoint) or Ctrl-D (in Windows PowerPoint).

SECTION III: HANDS-ON POWERPOINT

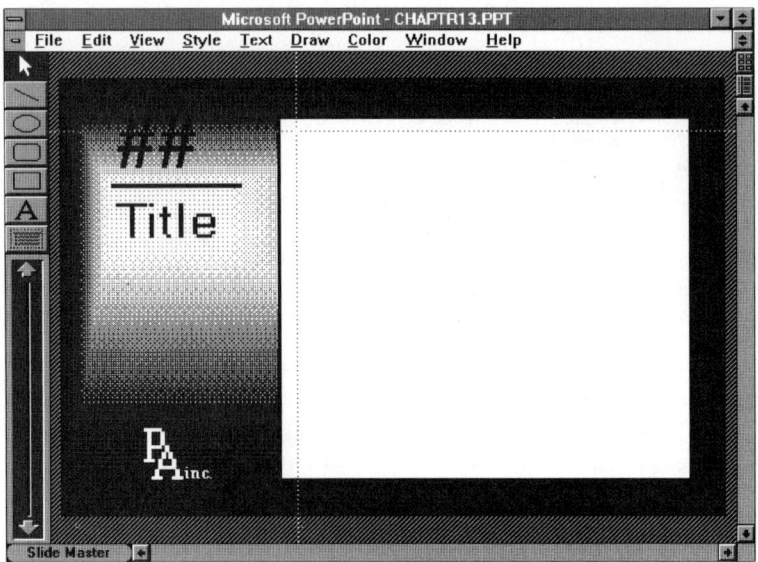

Figure 13-2. *A Slide Master with a shaded box easily accommodates text and imported visuals.*

ADDING TEXT TO INDIVIDUAL SLIDES

To add text to individual slides, do the following.

1. Use the Word Processor tool to create a text box that is a little smaller than the contents box. Position the pointer at the intersection of the horizontal and vertical guides and drag to the lower right of the box.

2. Choose a typeface, type size, type style, and color.

3. Choose Show Text Ruler from the Text menu to adjust the tabs to create hanging indents.

4. Choose Line Spacing from the Text menu to adjust line spacing as needed.

5. Add an appropriate title to the slide.

When you've finished, use the Macintosh Keycaps accessory, or, if you're using Windows PowerPoint, the Zapf Dingbats Help file, to locate the bullet symbols that will best introduce each text point.

Now your slide should look similar to the one shown in Figure 13-3.

Chapter 13: Working with the "Left-to-Right" Template

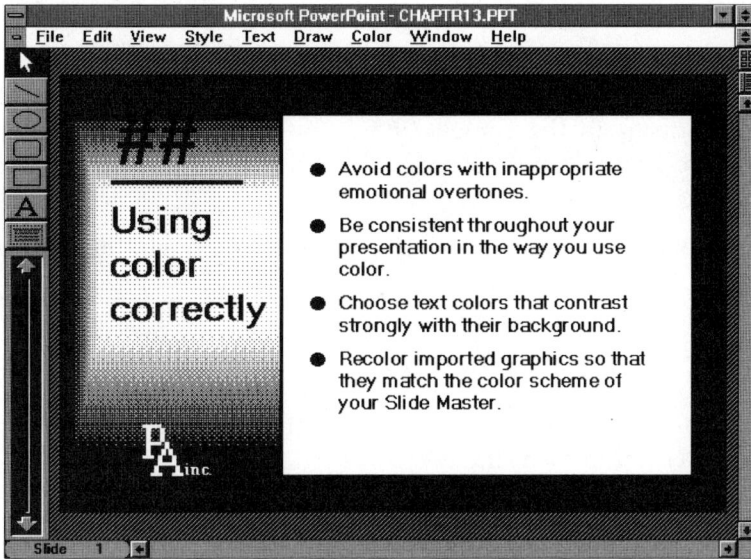

Figure 13-3. *This is the completed slide with text that you created.*

Fine-Tuning

Save your work, and then print out a sample slide. Be sure that the top of the slide number aligns with the top of the contents box. You might want to vertically center the text in the contents box, depending on the number of items it contains.

ADDING VISUALS

When adding artwork or charts to your presentation, always align them with the intersection of the horizontal and vertical guides in the upper left corner of the contents box. This will provide important slide-to-slide consistency.

OPTIONS

You can customize the "Left-to-Right" template in several ways. For example, you could shade the Slide Master background from left to right, or—by using the Graduated Fill technique described in Chapter 8—you could copy and paste a background shaded from right to left. Or you could use a solid Slide Background to offset a contents box shaded from top to bottom.

If you want to break the title at a specific point, be sure to use a hard return.

To create the necessary number of slides for your presentation, use the Copy and Paste commands in the Title Sorter view or the Slide Sorter view.

You can use flush-right alignment for the slide title, which "locks" the title to the text it introduces in the contents box. You can also experiment with various line thicknesses for the border and with eliminating the shadow around the contents box.

Finally, remember that—during printing—PowerPoint will number each slide.

EVALUATING YOUR PROGRESS

- ◆ Does the slide number of each visual clearly emerge as a dominant text element in each slide?
- ◆ Is the color contrast sufficient between the slide number and the slide title, and between these and the shaded Slide Master background?
- ◆ Have I correctly aligned the firm's logo and the presentation's title with the slide number and slide title?
- ◆ Did I use the Recolor Picture command to integrate the color of the firm's logo with the presentation's Color Scheme?
- ◆ Did I use the Slide Show feature to double-check that the text and visual areas appear in the same location in each slide and that the same type size is used in each slide?

Emphasizing Sequence with the "Index Cards" Template

The "Index Cards" template is useful for training applications, when you want to emphasize a sequence of steps. The presentation begins by showing the headings of six "index cards" needed to complete a given operation. As each step is completed, a new index card is revealed. The titles of the index cards that follow are always visible: At a glance, your audience can see what steps remain. This reinforces the sequence.

Although the template is ideally suited for presentations with six or fewer steps, you can adapt it for longer presentations by breaking it into two or more topics—each including six or fewer steps.

This template differs from previous templates in that most work is done on the slides themselves instead of on the Slide Master.

GETTING STARTED

Begin by selecting an output device by using the Macintosh Chooser and PowerPoint's Page Setup command or by using the Windows PowerPoint Printer Setup command. The dimensions that follow are those for the Genigraphics presentation format.

SECTION III: HANDS-ON POWERPOINT

1. Because accurate alignment is crucial to the success of this template, and because text will be used to align the elements, choose Show Edges from the Draw menu.
2. Choose Ignore Grid from the Draw menu. This will allow precise placement of the index cards.
3. Select the title and move it to the upper left of the screen.
4. Choose Show Guides from the Draw menu.

Note: Because of the complexity of the next few steps, we'll depart from our normal sequence and not choose the presentation's Color Scheme until the basic slide layout has been established. You'll find that this allows your screen to redraw much faster, and you'll be able to align the index cards much more quickly working in black and white. Later, you can choose an appropriate Color Scheme.

Creating the First Slide

To create the first slide (shown in Figure 14-1), do the following.

1. Working on Slide 1, draw a diagonal line extending from the upper right corner of your screen to the lower left corner. This line is used to ensure correct alignment of all of your index cards.

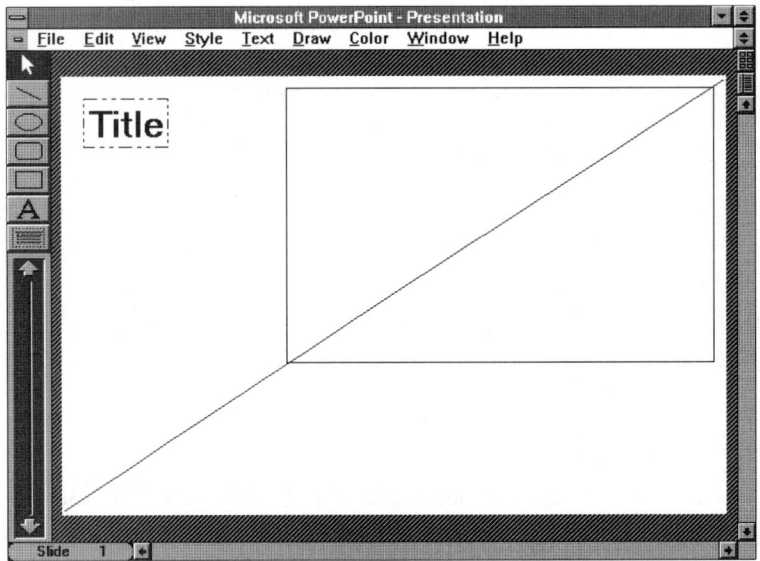

Figure 14-1. *This is the first "index card."*

2. Position the vertical guide 1.50 inches to the left of center. Position the horizontal guide 1.00 inch below center.

3. Choose the Rectangle tool, click at the intersection of the vertical and horizontal guides, and drag toward the upper right corner of the slide. Drag so that the upper right corner of the rectangle intersects the diagonal line.

Adding a Heading

To add a heading, do the following.

1. Choose the Word Processor tool, and click-and-drag a box approximately 0.5 inch high by 3 inches long.

2. Choose Font from the Style menu, and then choose Helvetica (or Helv).

3. Choose Size from the Style menu, and then select 18 point.

4. Type *Step X: Heading*. Position this text so that the left and top of its edges touch the left and top of the rectangle's edges.

Your "Index Cards" template should resemble the one shown in Figure 14-2.

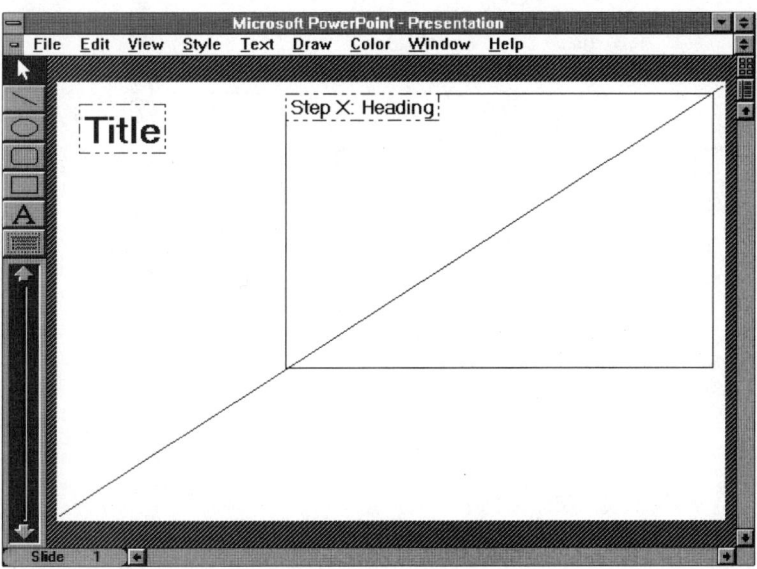

Figure 14-2. You add the heading to the first index card.

Copying and Placing Additional Index Cards

1. Hold down the Shift key, and select both the rectangle and the *Step X: Heading* text block.

2. Choose Copy.

3. Choose Paste.

4. When the second rectangle with text appears, align the upper right corner of the rectangle with the diagonal line. Align the top edge of the rectangle with the bottom edge of the first *Step X: Heading* text block. Position the new *Step X: Heading* text block to match the original "index card." When you've finished, your slide should look like the one shown in Figure 14-3.

To make it easier to align the top of each rectangle with the bottom of the text, you might want to choose Full Size from the View menu.

Note: You might have to reposition the horizontal guide if the last rectangle tries to center itself on the guide.

After you repeat this process five times, your slide should look like the one shown in Figure 14-4.

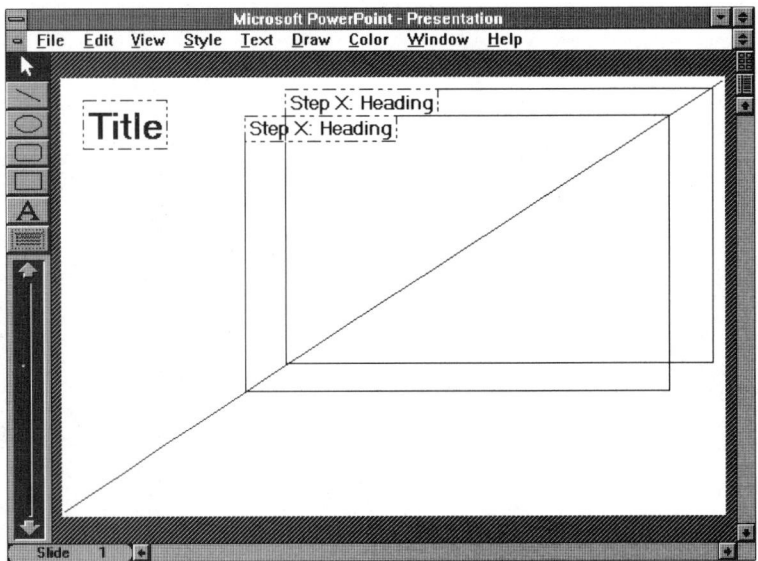

Figure 14-3. *You use the Copy and Paste commands to create the second index card.*

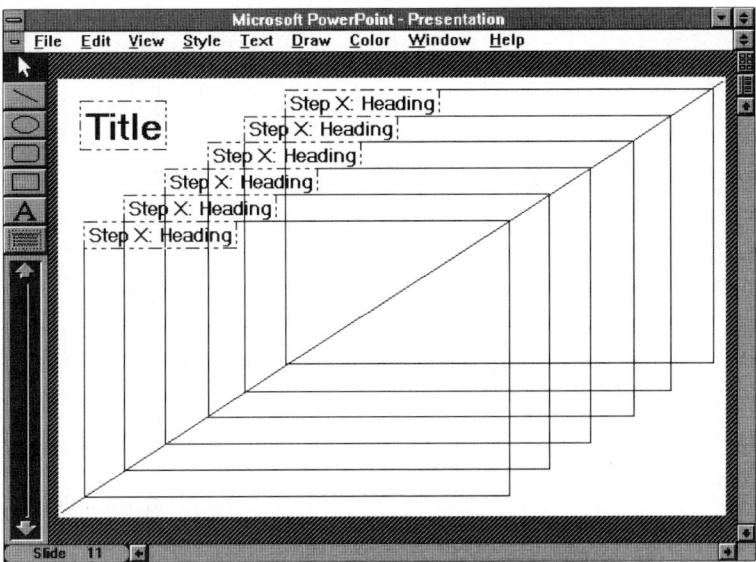

Figure 14-4. *Six index cards on the original slide.*

Finishing Touches

1. Click on each slide and—while each is selected—choose Opaque from the Draw menu.

2. Select the diagonal line and delete it, by using the Delete key (in Macintosh PowerPoint) or the Backspace key (in Windows PowerPoint) or choosing Clear from the Edit menu.

3. Choose Hide Edges from the Draw menu.

As the example in Figure 14-5 on the following page shows, your presentation is beginning to really take shape!

Choosing a color scheme

1. Select an appropriate Color Scheme to go with the 35mm slides or overhead transparencies that you create.

2. Choose Shade Background from the Color Scheme dialog box, and select From Corner. Choose the upper right option, which produces the darkest color along the left and bottom edges of the slide. (See Figure 14-6 on the following page.) This accent will help direct the audience's interest to the index cards, which advance toward the upper right.

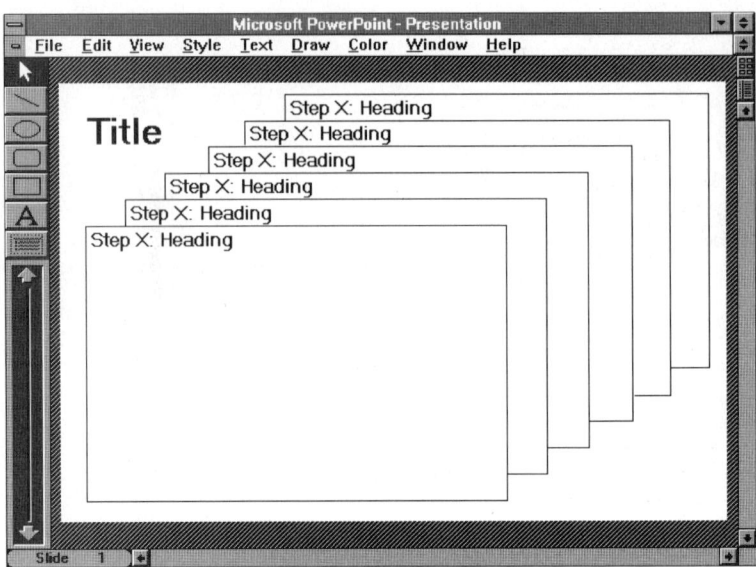

Figure 14-5. After you've chosen Opaque and Hide Edges and removed the diagonal alignment line, your slide should look like this.

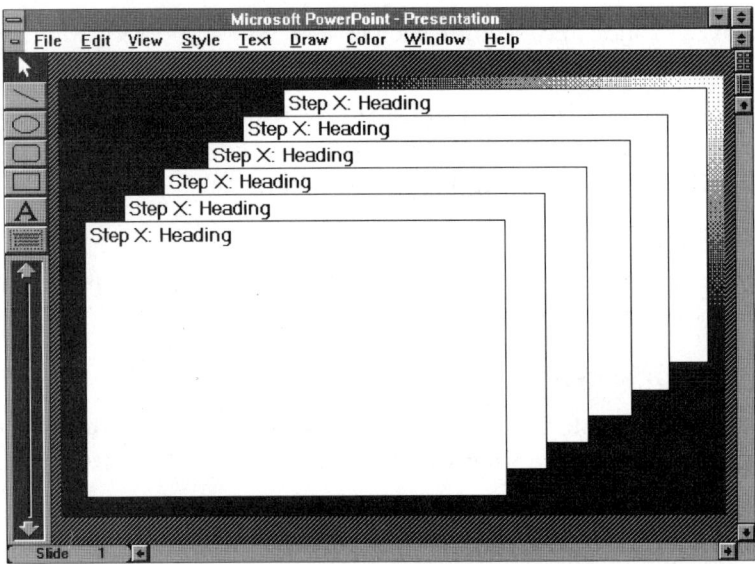

Figure 14-6. You can add emphasis to the index cards by adding a shaded background.

3. Be sure to choose All Slides before you select Apply to implement the Color Scheme that you've chosen.

Copying slides

Choose Slide Sorter from the View menu. Then select the completed slide and choose Copy. Make five copies of the slide by choosing Paste five times.

Creating individual index cards

1. Double-click on the second slide. Or return to the Slide view by choosing Slide [#] from the View menu.

2. When you're sure you are in the second slide, as indicated by *Slide 2* at the lower left, delete the lowest rectangle and *Step X: Heading*. (See Figure 14-7.)

3. Click on the down arrow. This takes you to Slide 3. Delete the two lowest rectangles and the two *Step X: Heading* index-card titles.

4. Continue this process for Slides 4 through 6, until only one rectangle and *Step X: Heading* remain.

When you've finished, the Slide Sorter view (as shown in Figure 14-8 on the following page) will reveal the progression of index cards that defines your presentation—or a portion of your presentation.

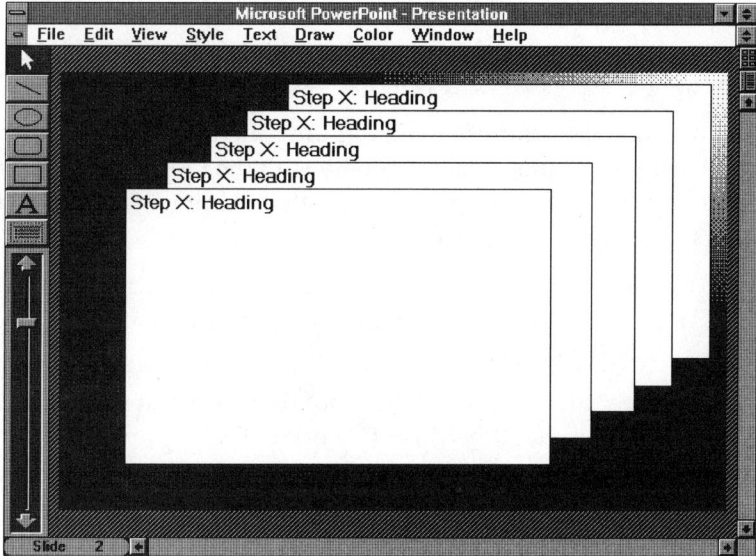

Figure 14-7. *After you delete the first index card, the second index card appears in front.*

SECTION III: HANDS-ON POWERPOINT

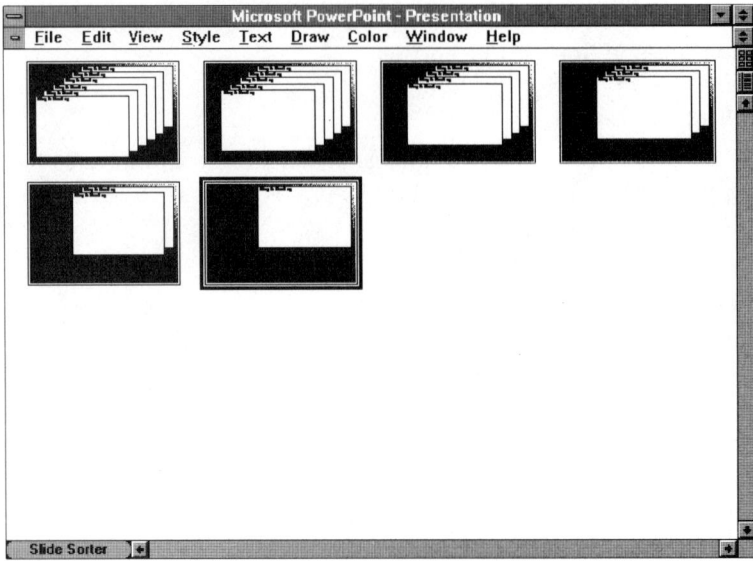

Figure 14-8. *The Slide Sorter view shows the completed slide sequence of the six index cards.*

Title considerations

The final step is to either hide the title that is to the left of the index cards or to change its color to white so that it stands out from the background. To hide the title, select it, highlight the text, and delete the title by choosing Clear from the Edit menu or by using a keyboard shortcut: the Del key (in Macintosh PowerPoint) or the Backspace key (in Windows PowerPoint).

You can also press the Spacebar after highlighting the title; doing this effectively hides the title so that it does not compete with the index-card headings. The disadvantage of this technique, of course, is that the title of each slide will not show up in PowerPoint's Title Sorter view.

If you color the title white, be sure that you choose a title that applies to all of the index cards in the sequence. This title might be an explanation of the purpose of the sequence being described.

Note: You cannot select the heading of the front index card in each slide and apply the Set As Title command because PowerPoint always places titles on the lowest level of each slide; otherwise, they would be hidden by the Opaque Fills of each rectangle.

WORKING WITH THE TEMPLATE

When you use the template, your first step will be to replace *Step #: Heading*, on each slide, with a new number and an appropriate index-card heading. Your second step will be to use the Word Processor tool to enter the text on each index card. (You can also, of course, place visuals—such as charts—on each card.)

You'll achieve optimal results if you use 24-point text for each step. Appropriate Zapf Dingbats will add to the effectiveness of the presentation.

Options

The "Index Cards" template offers great flexibility for coloring. As you refine the slides, use the Fill command to fill the frontmost index card with a bright background color. Use a darker version of the same color for the remaining index cards.

As your presentation proceeds, you'll find that the colors draw attention to your current index card as well as provide a visual connection to the remaining slides. You can also experiment with the Shadow command to emphasize the currently highlighted index card.

Preparing Longer Presentations

The index-card format can be easily adapted for longer presentations. Simply divide your presentation into four, six, or eight major steps and use index cards to discuss the component parts of each of the major steps.

Use an oversize number to subdivide the presentation into component parts. (See Figure 14-9 on the following page.) The large number will also provide a dominant visual on each page. If necessary, you can reduce the size of the index cards slightly to allow room for a title or subtitle to reinforce the topic that the number introduces.

Index-Card Size

When you work with this template, avoid the temptation to vary the size of the index cards if you don't need all six in a given slide. Instead, when you need only a few cards, omit the unneeded ones from the front of the deck.

As you work with the "Index Cards" template, you'll undoubtedly develop other, equally interesting, variations.

SECTION III: HANDS-ON POWERPOINT

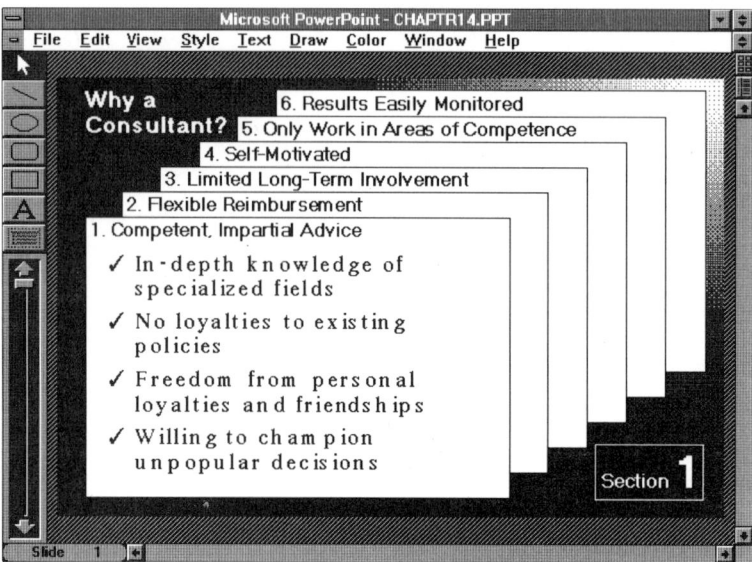

Figure 14-9. *You can add a category (section) number to divide long presentations into shorter segments.*

EVALUATING YOUR PROGRESS

- Did I correctly size the index cards that are in the "Index Cards" template?

- Did I align the index cards from the lower left to the upper right?

- Did I preview the progression of the index cards by using the Slide Sorter view and the Slide Show feature?

- Have I provided a sufficient border area at the top and right side of the slides to properly frame the index cards?

- Did I divide long presentations into shorter sequences, organized by *Section* or *Step*?

- Did I recolor the Slide Master title so that it doesn't compete with the individual index-card headings?

IV
MAKEOVERS

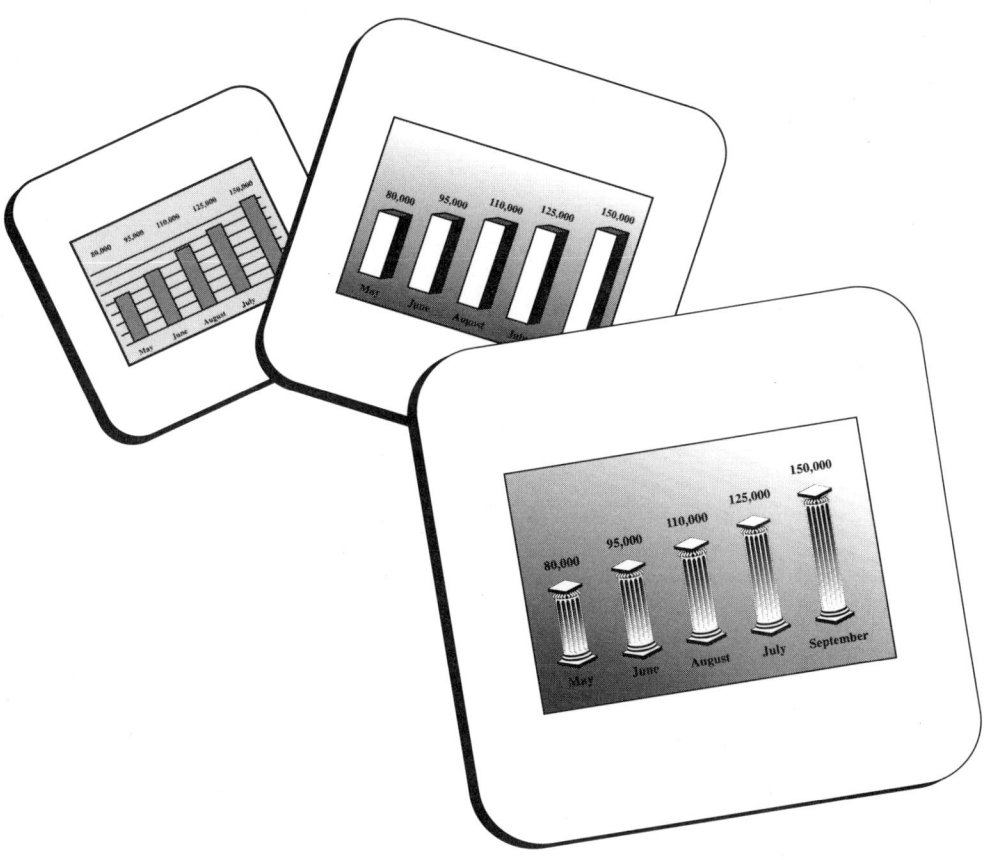

25 Ways to Improve Ordinary Slides and Overheads

If you've ever been forced to sit through a difficult-to-follow, boring presentation, chances are some of the reasons for your discomfort are illustrated in the examples in this chapter. Here are 25 frequently encountered problems and suggested solutions.

As you become more comfortable with your hardware and software, you'll find it easier to focus on design issues—thereby avoiding the common pitfalls that can undermine your ability to communicate with your audience.

As described in Chapter 9, proofing is best done by using PowerPoint's Slide Show feature and by printing hard copies of your slides and overheads. As you watch the Slide Show, use the hard-copy printout to note problem areas needing improvement. Analyze your slides and overheads in terms of the following four areas.

- ◆ *Review content and continuity.* Content problems occur when too much information is included in each slide or overhead. Continuity problems result from a lack of slide-to-slide consistency.
- ◆ *Evaluate text legibility.* Inappropriate typeface, type size, and line-spacing decisions as well as a lack of contrast between text elements are the causes of many problems.

- *Examine charts and imported graphics.* Often you can improve the appearance of your slides and overheads by adjusting the number, size, and placement of imported visuals.

- *Double-check use of color.* Inappropriate use of color can obscure, instead of enhance, your message.

REVIEW CONTENT AND CONTINUITY

The solution to most problems involving content is to rethink the goals of your presentation and to simplify the content of each slide or overhead as much as possible.

1. Too Much Information

The number one cause of boring, difficult-to-read slides and overheads is the inclusion of too many points in each slide or overhead. This is often a result of forgetting the principle that visuals should support your presentation, not replace your presence. Your slides and overheads should serve as road maps and references, not as word-for-word reiteration of every point you make.

Audience retention decreases when you include too many points in each slide because your audience spends too much time reading each slide—rather than listening to your discussion of each point. In addition, boredom increases because you're forced to leave the same slide or overhead on the screen too long while discussing each point.

Legibility also suffers because including too many points in each line necessitates the use of small type and results in too many words on each line. Figure 15-1 illustrates what frequently happens. In this example, three topics are introduced and too much information about each topic is included. As a result, the slide has a "gray" and cluttered appearance.

The example shown in Figure 15-2 is more inviting because the topic has been split into smaller, more visually digestible bites. In addition, the lowest level of supporting detail has been omitted; these details will be verbally delivered.

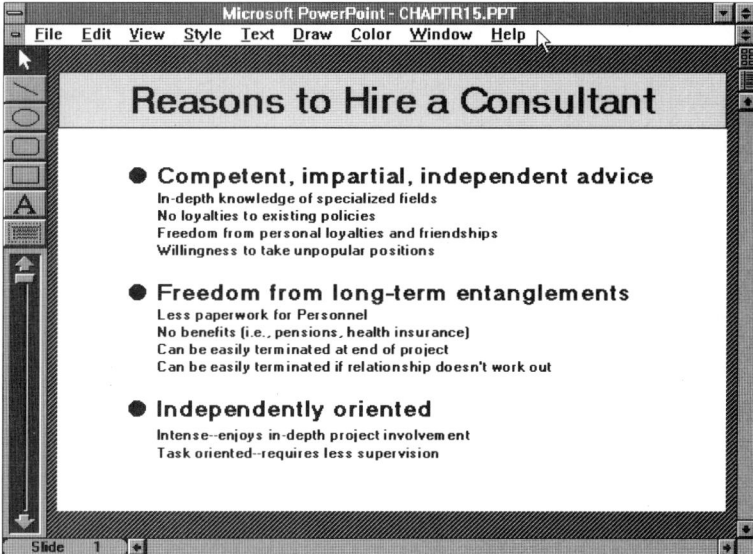

Figure 15-1. *Visuals that cover too many points and that use small type reduce legibility.*

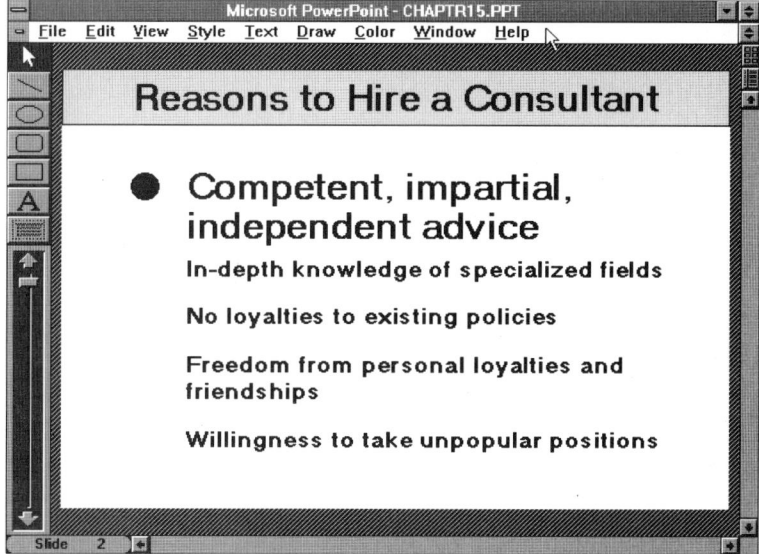

Figure 15-2. *When you focus each visual on a single idea, you can use a larger, easier-to-read type size that focuses the reader's attention on one point at a time.*

2. Lack of a Dominant Visual

Every slide or overhead should have one, and only one, dominant visual. A dominant visual organizes the slide and provides a starting point for the audience's eyes.

In Figure 15-3, the absence of a strong title gives an overall "gray" look to the slide—as does the lack of sufficient type size differentiation between the title and the supporting material.

Notice how much more comfortable you are when looking at the visual in Figure 15-4. Your eye goes immediately to the title, which reinforces retention. Your eye then moves naturally to the supporting material.

3. Inappropriate Tools

Strong presentations are based on the use of appropriate communications tools. Often words are used when a visual representation would better convey a given relationship. Numbers are often better described in graphs than in text. The list in Figure 15-5 on page 334, for example, does not do a very good job of describing the set of relationships.

The relationships are far easier to understand when an organizational chart is used, as shown in Figure 15-6 on page 334.

As mentioned earlier, one of the best ways to improve visuals is to have them focus on smaller chunks of information.

4. Cluttered Borders and Frames

Slide borders should frame, not overwhelm, your slide or overhead. In the example shown in Figure 15-7 on page 335, the border is so thick that it draws your audience's eyes to itself—instead of to the message.

Consider using a thinner border, perhaps with a solid fill pattern. Or consider replacing a border that surrounds a slide or overhead on all four sides with a top border that sets off the title and a bottom border that ends the slide, as shown in Figure 15-8 on page 335.

Frames around text or graphical objects should be used only when absolutely necessary. As the example in Figure 15-9 on page 336 shows, borders combined with the overuse of frames can create a very confusing "box within a box" effect.

One way to avoid the need for a border around the title is to use a larger type size, as shown in Figure 15-10 on page 336.

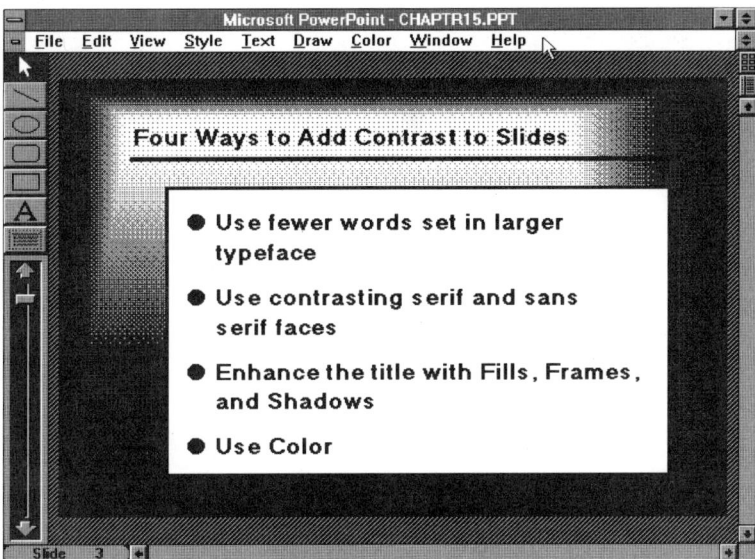

Figure 15-3. *The similarity in typeface and type size between title and supporting text results in uninteresting visuals.*

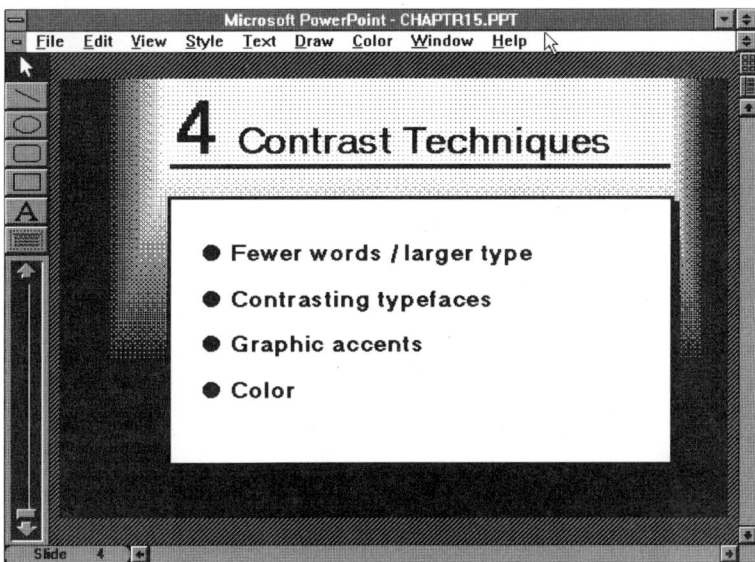

Figure 15-4. *An oversize number introducing a title of fewer words set in larger type results in a more interesting visual.*

SECTION IV: MAKEOVERS

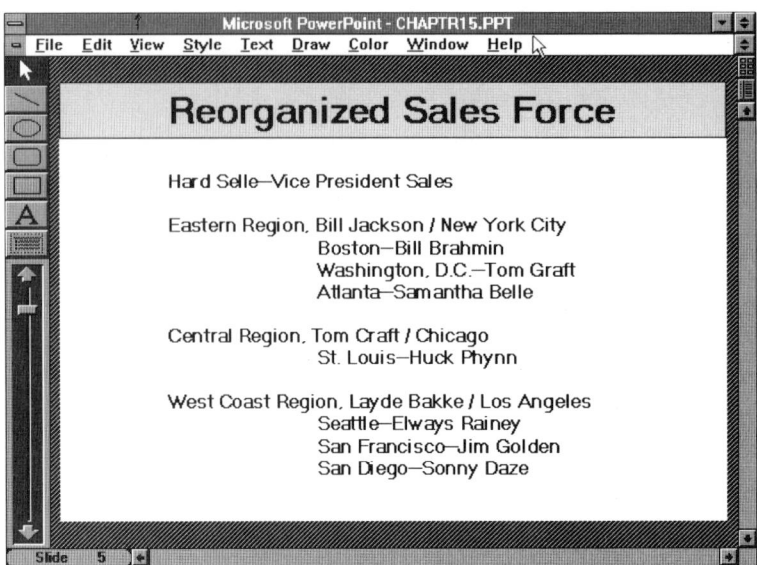

Figure 15-5. Indented lists are an inappropriate choice for displaying vertical relationships within an organization.

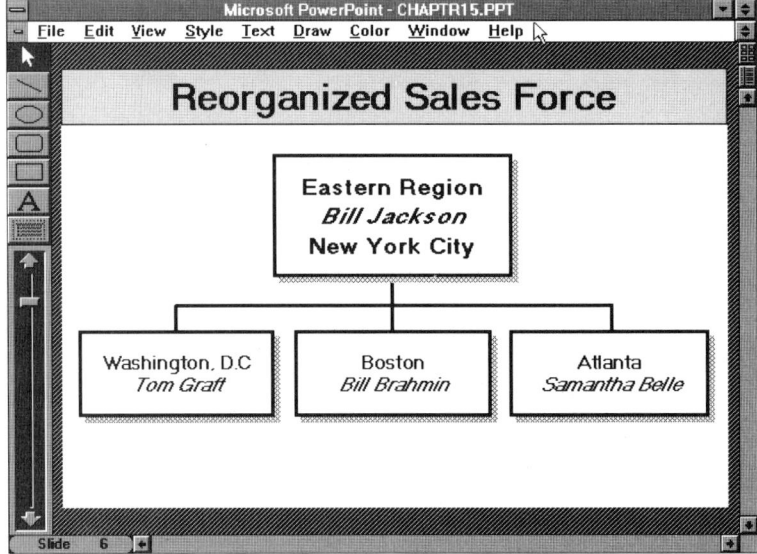

Figure 15-6. An organizational chart makes it easy to visualize vertical relationships. Visuals can communicate better when they are focused on single ideas or on parts of a whole.

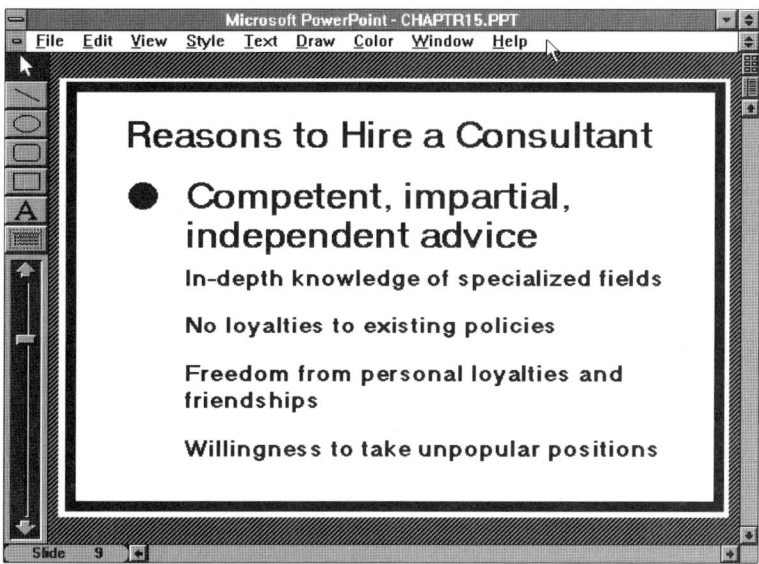

Figure 15-7. A thick border competes with the message for the audience's attention.

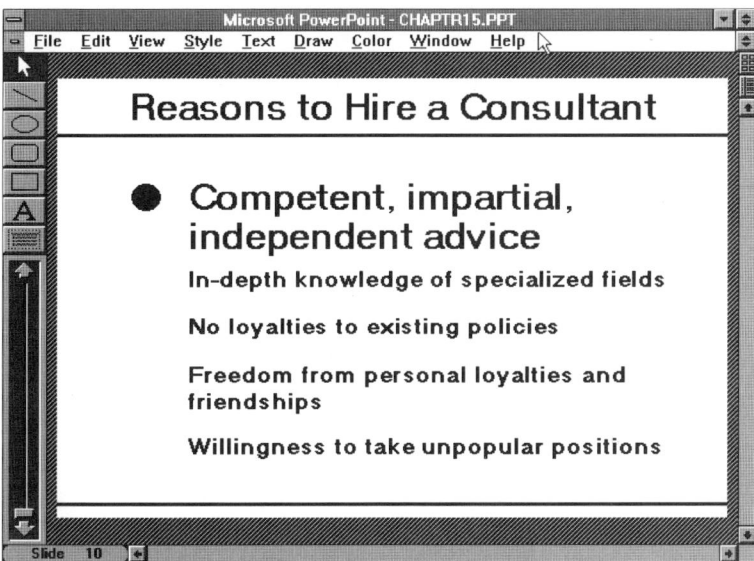

Figure 15-8. These borders let an audience focus its attention more easily on your message.

SECTION IV: MAKEOVERS

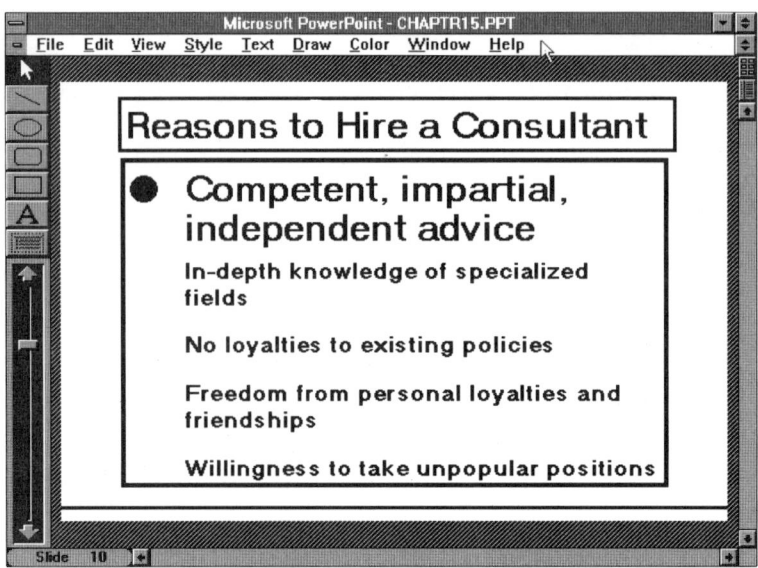

Figure 15-9. *If you place both title and text within a frame, you isolate each element (instead of allowing the title to lead into the text), and you create a potentially confusing effect.*

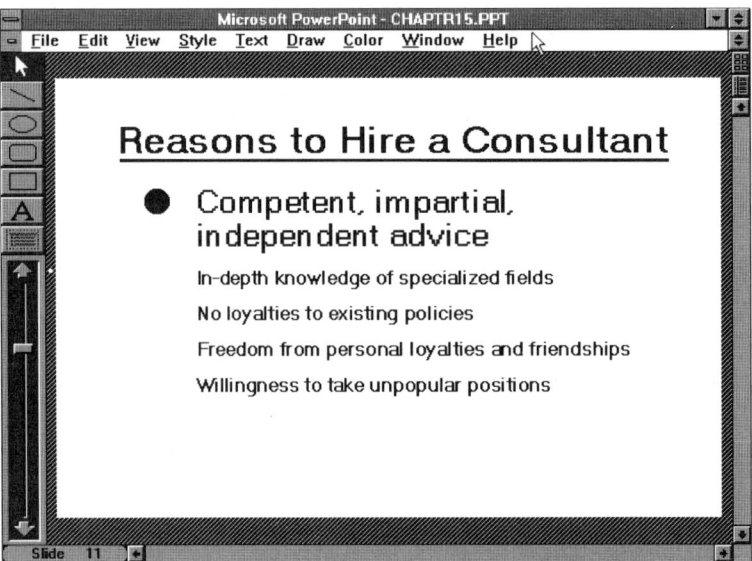

Figure 15-10. *A larger type size provides the emphasis that catches an audience's attention and then leads the audience into the text. Reducing the size and weight of the text makes it easier to read.*

5. Drifting Standards

A presentation's overall unity can easily be undermined by subtle slide-to-slide changes in border, title, or text placement. You must take great care to ensure that dimensions, colors, and type styles are consistent throughout your presentation.

In addition to using the Slide Show view, you can use the Slide Sorter view at a large magnification to check for continuity. If you study the slides in Figure 15-11, you'll notice differences in border placement and line thickness as well as gross inconsistencies in title and logo placement and alignment.

Such discrepancies can become very noticeable (and very annoying) to your audience—especially if you progress rapidly from slide to slide. One characteristic of a strong presentation is slide-to-slide continuity, as exhibited in Figure 15-12 on the following page. Be consistent—which requires that you be attentive to design details.

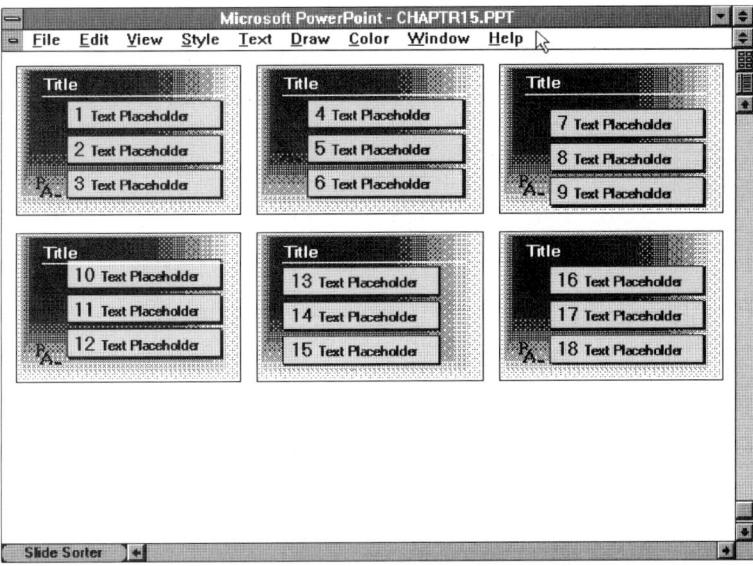

Figure 15-11. *Differences in the size and placement of text and graphical elements become apparent in the Slide Sorter view.*

SECTION IV: MAKEOVERS

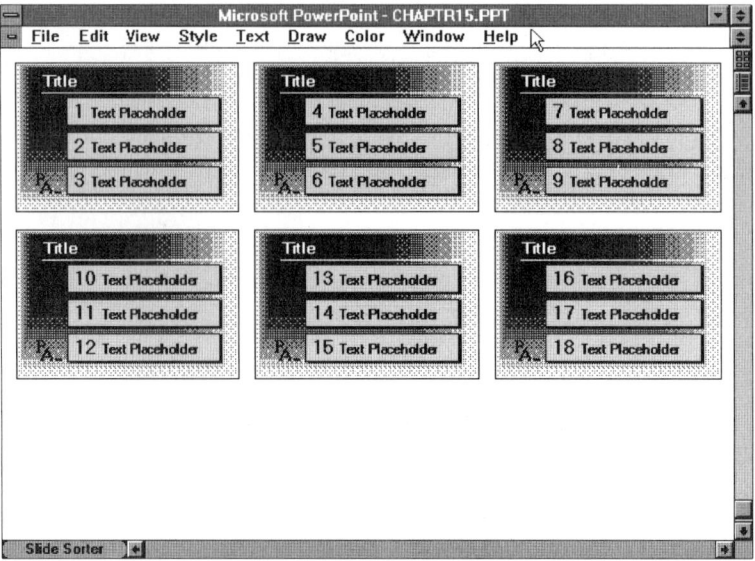

Figure 15-12. Attention to precise placement of text and graphics results in a quality presentation that presells your audience on your credibility and on the importance of your ideas.

EVALUATE TEXT LEGIBILITY

For your presentation to succeed, your audience must be able to read the text quickly and easily.

6. Insufficient Text Contrast

Effective presentations are based on slides and overheads that contain strong contrast among the various elements of text architecture. You can orchestrate the contrast by choosing the appropriate typeface, type size, and type style for each category of information.

The example shown in Figure 15-13 presents a boring appearance because the title and the presentation information are set in the same typeface and in type sizes that are too similar. The same information becomes far more interesting when the title is set significantly larger than the supporting information, as shown in Figure 15-14. Now your eye has a definite starting point, and it's clear which information is important and which is supportive.

Text contrast can be enhanced by changing both the typeface and the type size. In Figure 15-14, for example, the title is set in a large sans serif typeface and supporting information in a smaller serif typeface.

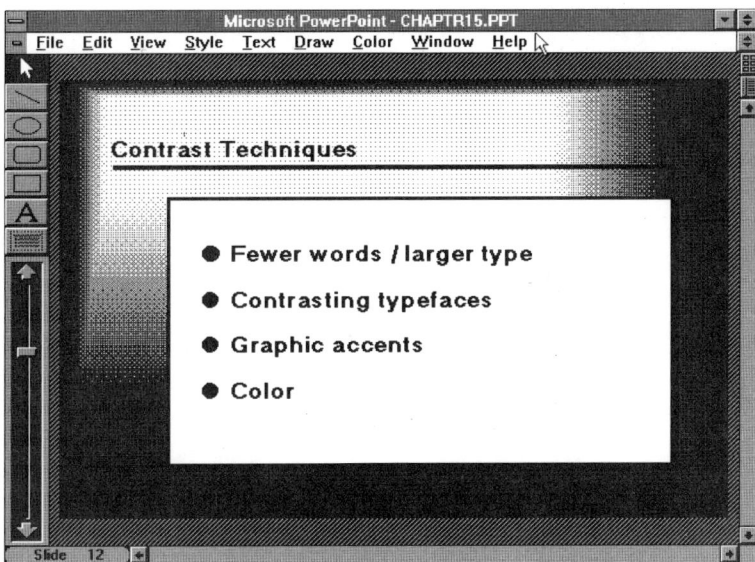

Figure 15-13. This slide is visually boring because the title and the text are set in similar sizes of the same typeface.

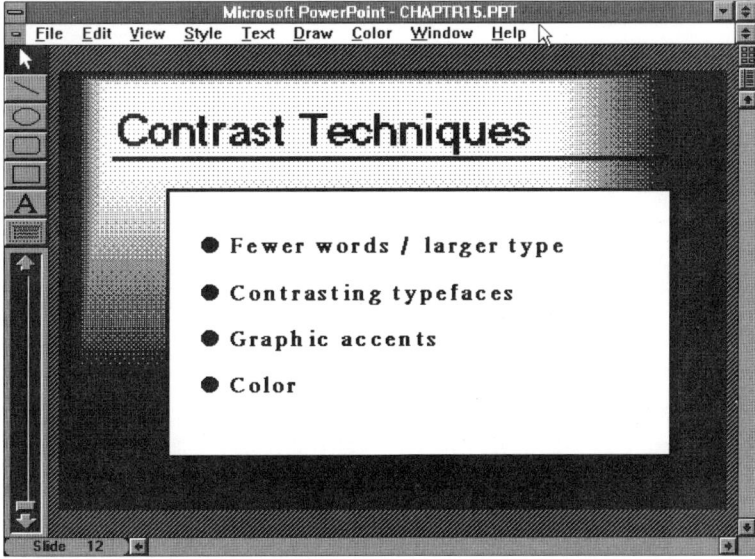

Figure 15-14. Increasing the size of the title and using a contrasting typeface for the text can provide the contrast necessary for interest.

7. Text in Small Type

Small, difficult-to-read type is common in slides that contain too much information; type size is often reduced to allow more words to fit on each line. (See Figure 15-15.)

Planning and editing can eliminate the need to fill your slides and overheads with too much text. By spending more time with PowerPoint's Storyboard feature to plan your slides and overheads, you'll often find ways to split topics among individual slides.

If you eliminate unnecessary words and replace long words with short words, you'll also eliminate the need to include so much text on your slides and overheads. (See Figure 15-16.)

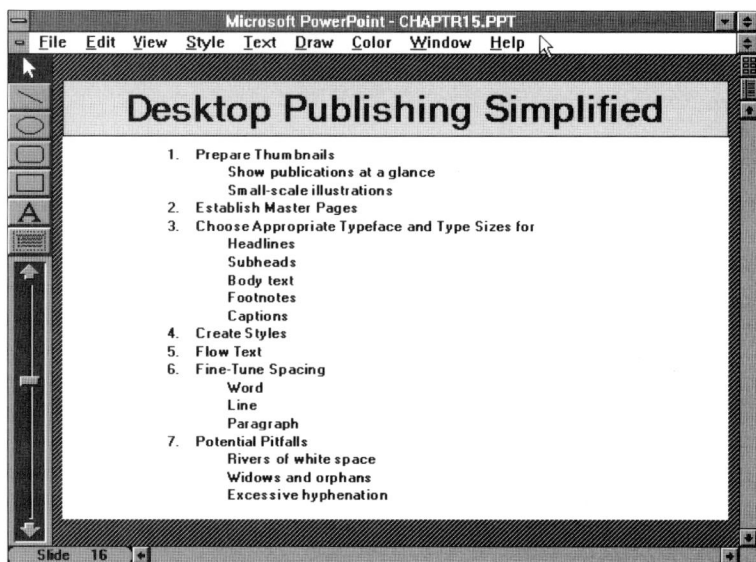

Figure 15-15. Visuals containing too much detail are often characterized by small, difficult-to-read type.

8. Too Many Typefaces and Type Sizes

Amateurish, difficult-to-follow presentations are characterized by the use of too many typefaces and type sizes. (See Figure 15-17.) Avoid such usage.

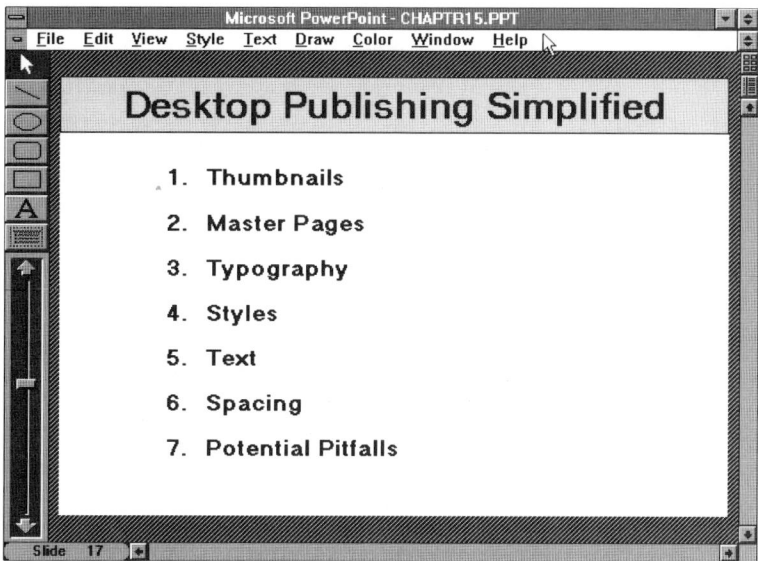

Figure 15-16. *Eliminating unnecessary words opens up the space needed for larger, easier-to-read text.*

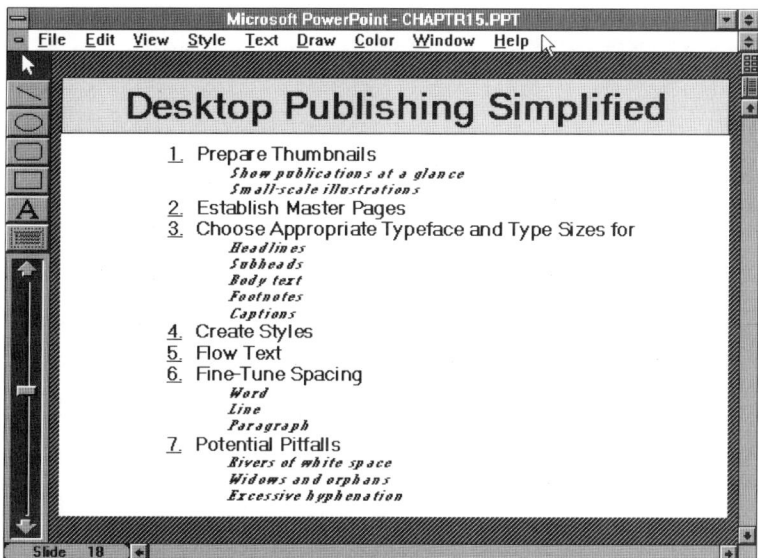

Figure 15-17. *Confusion results when too many typefaces and type sizes are used in a visual.*

As a rule of thumb, limit each slide or overhead to three combinations of typeface and type size. Use one typeface and type size for the title and a second typeface of a smaller size for the supporting copy. If you're including an indented list, use a smaller size of the second typeface for subordinate material rather than introducing a third typeface.

9. Overly Emphasized Text

Use discretion when using an italic or an outline typeface. Your audience will have great difficulty reading long blocks of text set in italic or outline type—especially if you use a small type size. (See Figure 15-18.)

Long blocks of text are easier to read when set in roman type. (See Figure 15-19.) Reserve the use of italics for quotations set in large size. Outline type works best for presentation titles or for a few words set in a very large type size.

Another style problem involves overuse of words set entirely in capital letters. Words set in uppercase type are more difficult to read than words set in lowercase type because there are no ascenders or descenders to provide visual clues—only uniform rectangles. (See Figure 15-20.) Readers depend on the shapes of words for recognition clues.

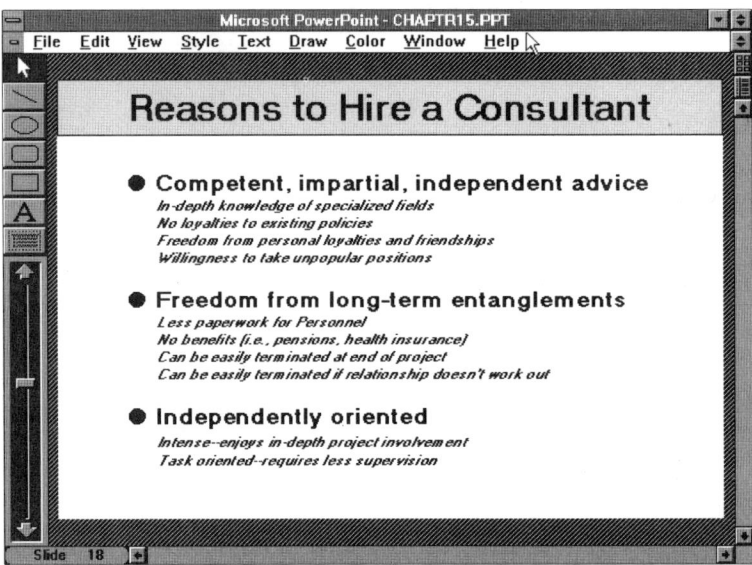

Figure 15-18. *Your audience will quickly tire of reading a lot of italicized text.*

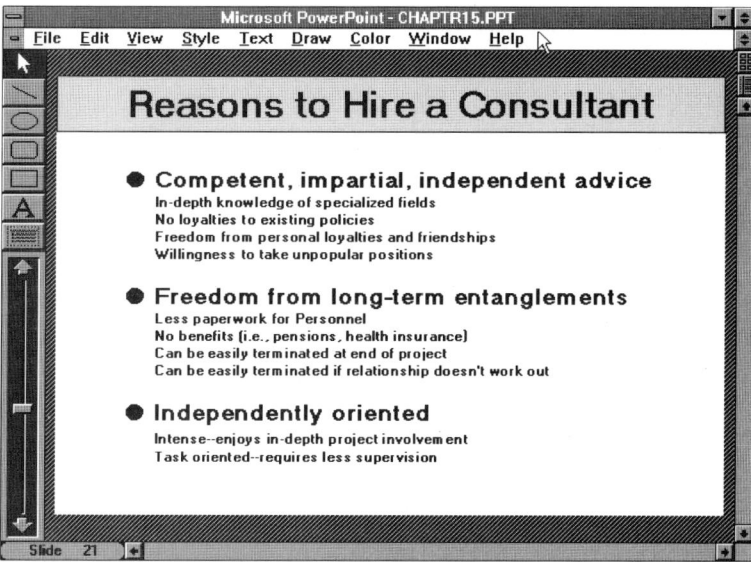

Figure 15-19. Roman, or upright, text is easier to read than italic text.

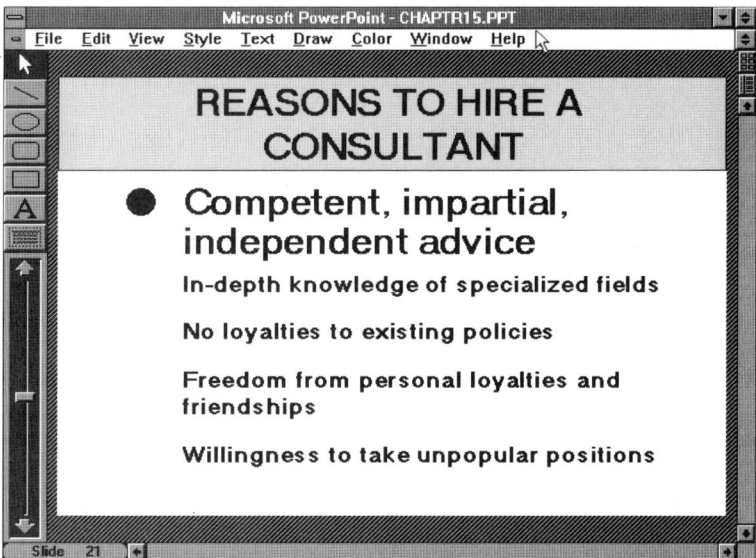

Figure 15-20. Avoid setting titles in uppercase letters because such titles are difficult to read.

Resetting titles and headings in uppercase and lowercase type can enhance legibility. (See Figure 15-21.) Titles set in uppercase and lowercase type also occupy less space, often reducing two-line titles to a single line.

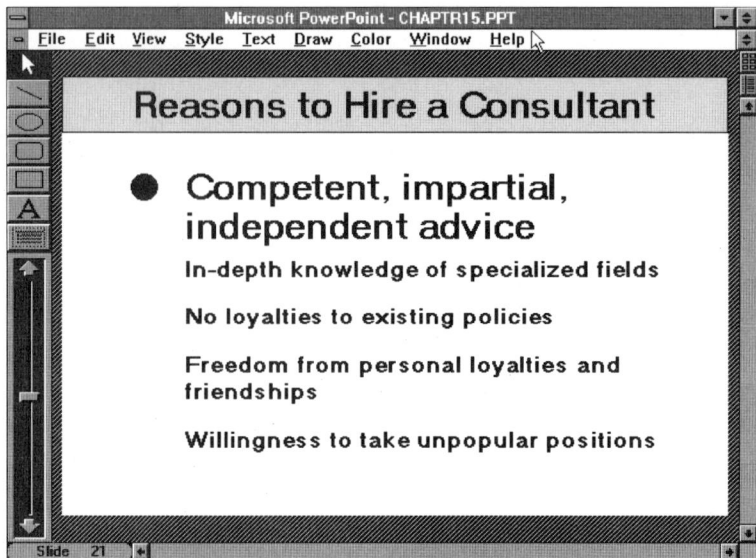

Figure 15-21. Titles set in uppercase and lowercase type are easier to read because each word has distinctive shapes.

10. Typefaces Not Supported by Output Device

When you include a typeface not supported by the output device used to produce your slides and overheads, one of two things typically occurs.

- ◆ The output device replaces the specified typeface with a default typeface—typically Courier.

- ◆ The output device substitutes a bit-mapped version of the typeface for the smooth font desired. Instead of containing smooth letters, your slides and overheads will contain rough, jagged letters.

In both of these instances, the appearance of your slide or overhead is seriously compromised.

Always verify the availability of your typeface selections by referring to the documentation that accompanies your output device or to the information provided by your service bureau.

11. Irregular Line Endings

When preparing slides and overheads for production by an outside service bureau such as Genigraphics, be sure you use only those type sizes listed in the Size dialog box. This ensures compatibility between line breaks shown on the screen of your computer and line breaks on your finished slides and overheads.

If you choose "other" and specify an in-between size, the line of type might be too short or the type might intrude into an adjacent graphic or—worse—extend beyond the edges of your slides and overheads.

Changing the type size to one of the sizes listed in the Size dialog box prevents this from happening.

12. Widows

A widow is a single or partial word isolated on its own line. Widows look worse in slide presentations than in word processed hard copy. Hyphens can be distracting in slide presentations and should be avoided.

Widows are especially noticeable when they occur in wide lines set in small type. (See Figure 15-22.)

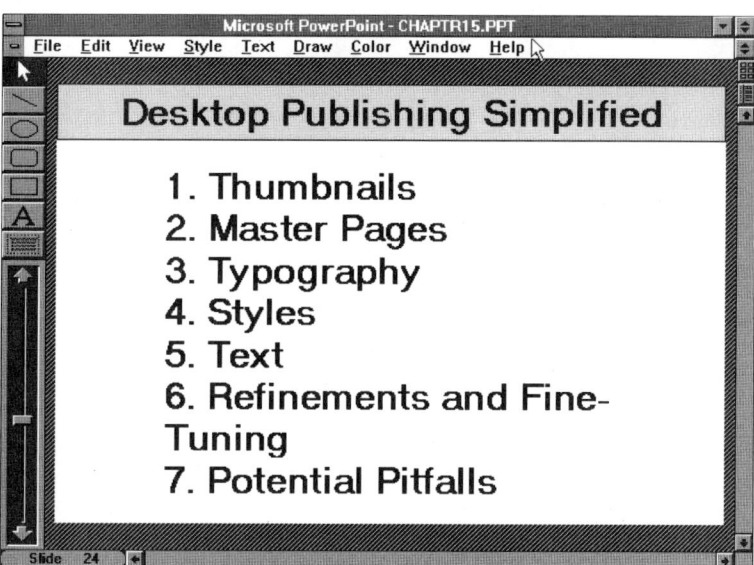

Figure 15-22. *A widow—a single or partial word on a line by itself—can be visually distracting, especially in an indented list.*

Editing the previous line is the best way to eliminate widows. Search for long words that can be replaced by short words or a phrase that can be replaced by one word, or eliminate unnecessary modifiers. (See Figure 15-23.) In addition, if the widow occurs after two or three lines of text, you can often eliminate it by transposing a few words in the preceding lines or deleting an unnecessary word, thereby "filling up" those lines.

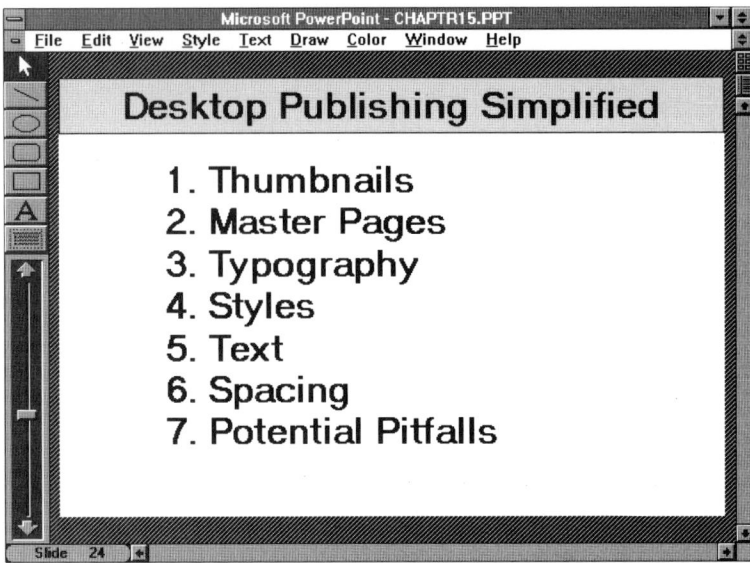

Figure 15-23. *You can often eliminate widows by transposing words, deleting words, or replacing long words with short words. In this case, replacing the three words of item number 6 in Figure 15-22 with one word eliminates the widow.*

EXAMINE CHARTS AND IMPORTED GRAPHICS

As you review your presentation, watch out for problem areas involving charts and imported graphics.

13. Visual Clutter

Visual clutter can occur when several pieces of clip art are included on each slide or overhead. Clip-art clutter diminishes your audience's ability to concentrate on the message you're trying to communicate. A comic-book effect often results. The clutter is made worse by the fact that the visuals must be made small. You can often avoid clip-art clutter by choosing only one piece of clip art and reproducing it in a significantly larger form—so that it becomes the dominant visual on the page. This opens up the slide and allows more space for the words. Instead of looking like an afterthought, the visual becomes an intrinsic part of the slide.

14. File Format Not Supported by Output Device

Although PowerPoint can import files created in other applications, not all output devices can reproduce them. For example, only PostScript printers can reproduce illustrations saved as Encapsulated PostScript files.

If you send slides and overheads containing Encapsulated PostScript Files to a service bureau or reproduce them on film recorders or on a Hewlett-Packard PaintJet or PaintJet XL, you'll receive a bit-mapped representation of the screen image instead of the crisp, sharp image you see on the screen of your computer.

Always read printer documentation and service-bureau information before printing your slides and overheads—and be alert for error messages.

15. Inappropriate Charts

Choosing the appropriate type of chart or graph will make it easier for your audience to understand the information you're presenting. Pie charts, for example, are adept at displaying part-whole relationships (as shown in Figure 15-24), but they're not as adept at displaying part-to-part comparisons.

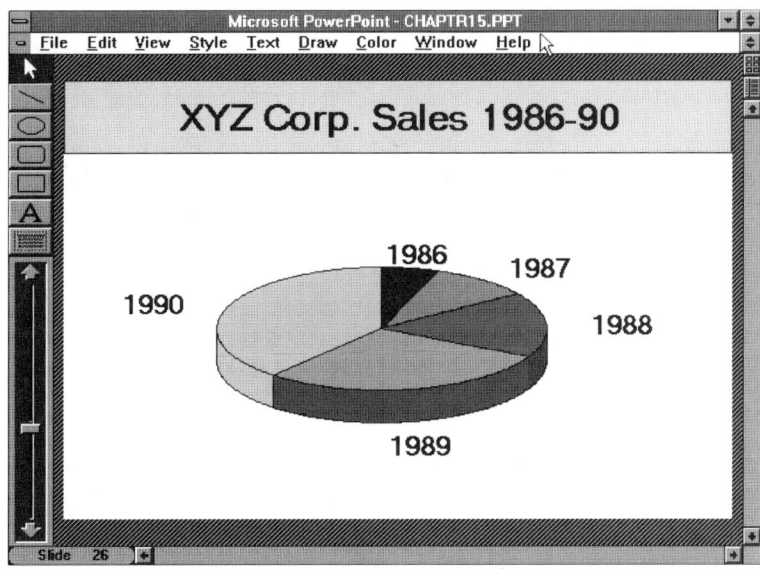

Figure 15-24. *Use a pie chart to display part-whole relationships.*

Column charts depict trends powerfully and are especially useful for month-to-month and year-to-year comparisons, as shown in Figure 15-25.

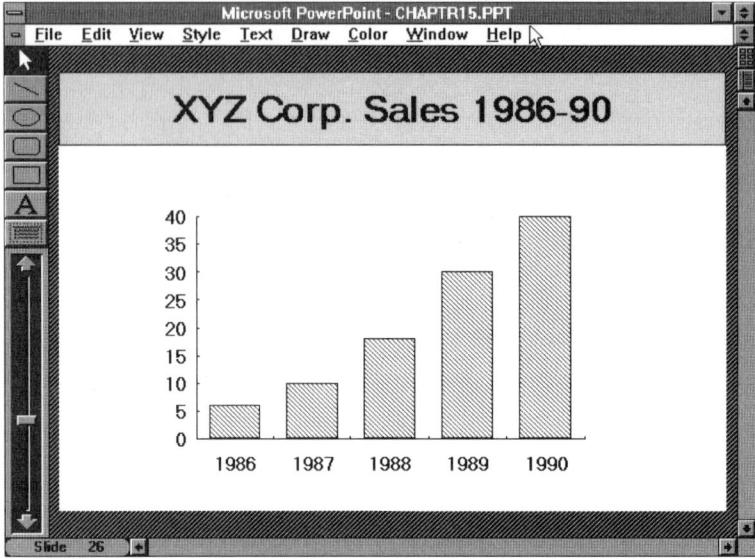

Figure 15-25. *Use a column chart to emphasize trends, such as increasing sales.*

16. Overly Complicated Charts and Graphs

Avoid including too much detail in your charts or graphs. This is especially a problem in black-and-white presentations that use different patterns and shades for the various segments of the chart or graph. (See Figure 15-26.)

Whenever possible, combine small segments into categories. For example, use a second graph—or a callout to a list—to identify the information in the "Other" segment. (See Figure 15-27.)

17. Undersized Graphics

When two or more charts and graphs are combined on a single slide or overhead, they often have to be so greatly reduced in size that the audience will have difficulty understanding and comparing them. Even two visuals of roughly equal size can be problematic because they tend to neutralize each other. (See Figure 15-28 on page 350.)

Chapter 15: 25 Ways to Improve Ordinary Slides and Overheads

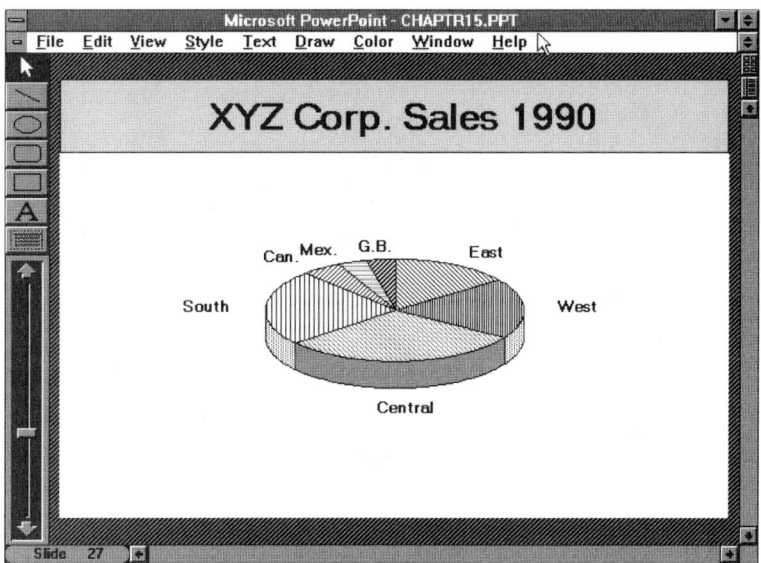

Figure 15-26. Charts containing too many segments are confusing, particularly black-and-white charts employing patterns and shades of gray to differentiate segments.

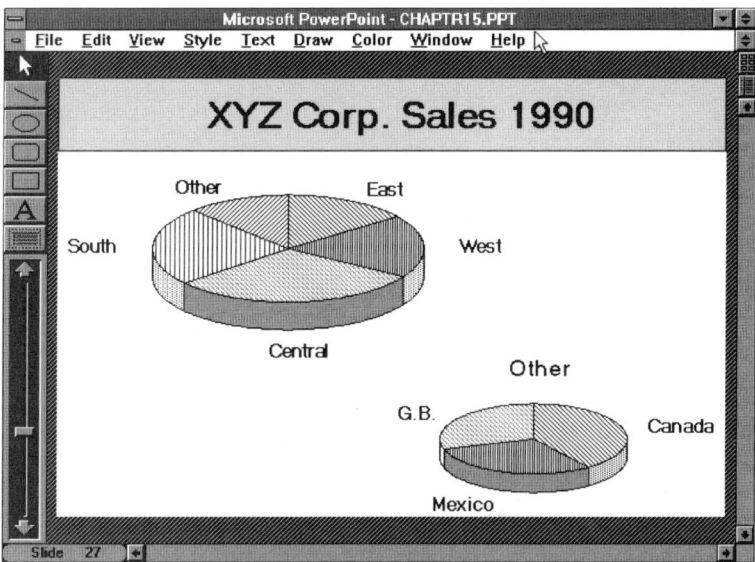

Figure 15-27. Use a second chart to represent the smaller, or "Other," segment.

SECTION IV: MAKEOVERS

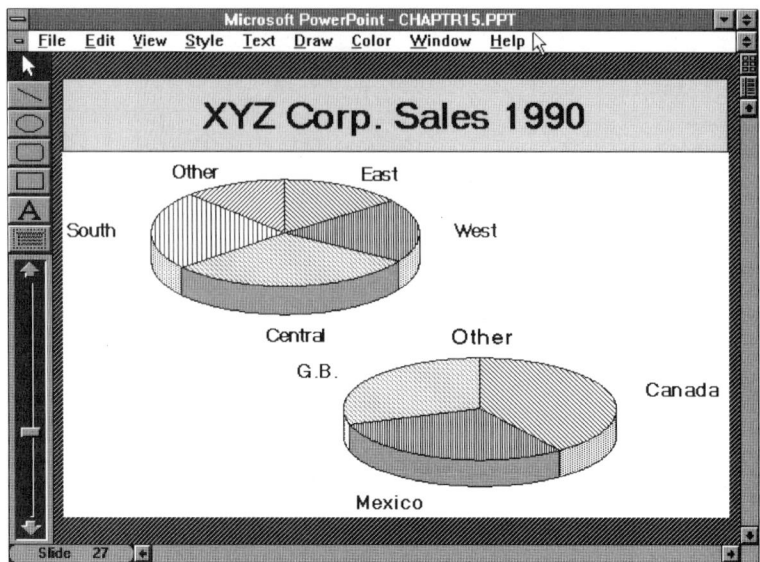

Figure 15-28. Two charts of roughly equal size compete with each other for the audience's attention. (See Figures 15-29a and 15-29b.)

One solution is to select the more important chart or graph and make it significantly larger. Another solution is to compare separate segments of data on two or more successive slides or overheads, as shown in Figures 15-29a and 15-29b.

Another very effective technique is to enlarge only a portion of an illustration instead of including the whole graphic. For example, if you're discussing West Coast sales, replace a map of the entire United States with a cropped and greatly enlarged portion of the same map showing the western states only.

18. Difficult-to-Read Supporting Information

Undersized legends, axis information, and totals can make it difficult for your audience to interpret the meaning of your chart or graph. In the graph shown in Figure 15-30 on page 352, the x-axis and y-axis information is so crowded that it is virtually unreadable.

Use "shorthand" to abbreviate information so that you can use a larger type size. You can note that figures represent larger units, instead of writing out long figures, as has been done in Figure 15-31 on page 352.

Chapter 15: 25 Ways to Improve Ordinary Slides and Overheads

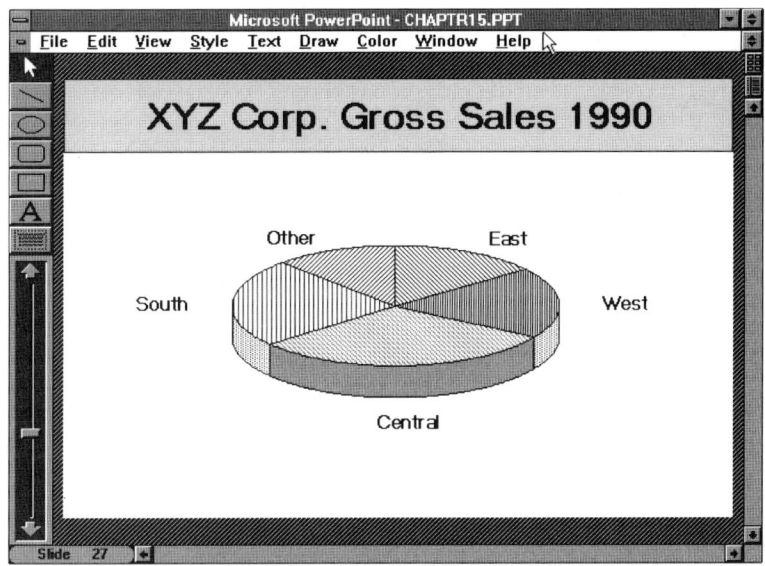

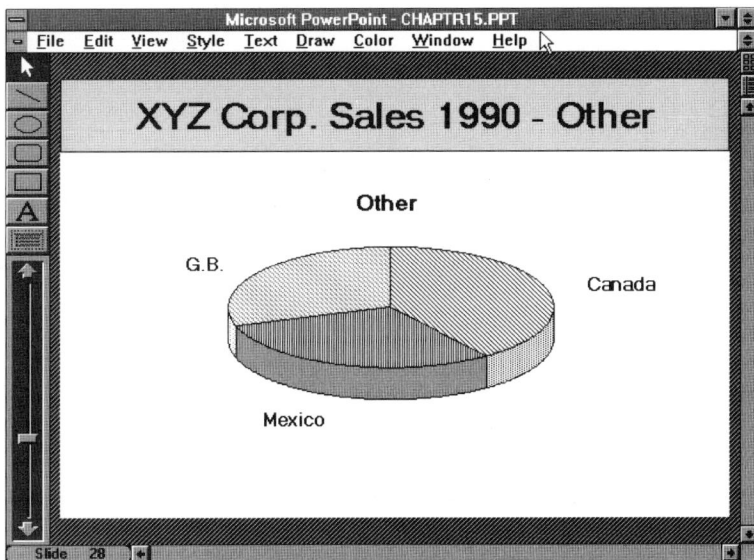

Figures 15-29a and 15-29b. *Focusing each visual on a single chart makes it easy to discuss that chart in detail. (See Figure 15-28.)*

SECTION IV: MAKEOVERS

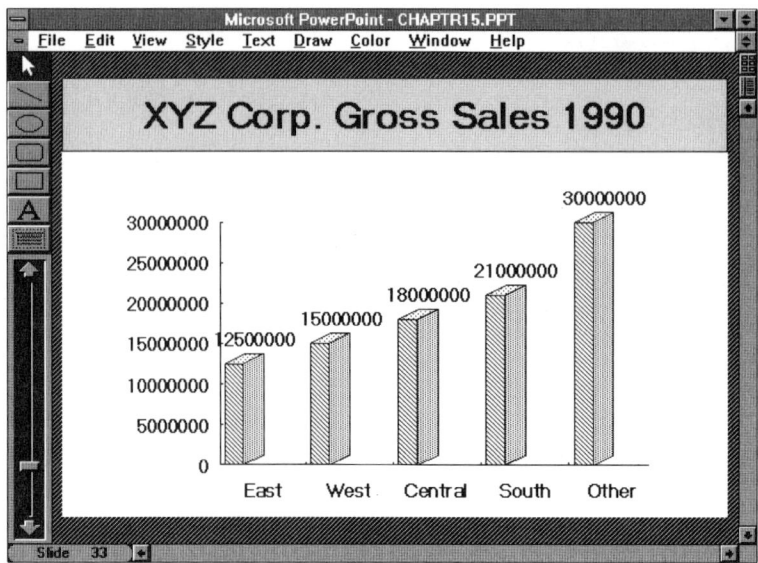

Figure 15-30. The label information for the x-axis, y-axis, and value labels is difficult to read because it had to be squeezed together to make it fit.

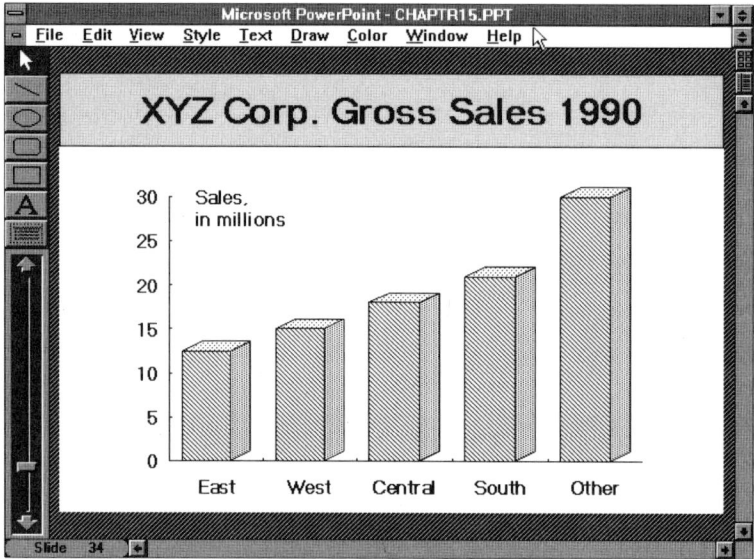

Figure 15-31. Reducing the scale of the information permits the chart's message to emerge with enhanced clarity.

19. Lack of a Background Grid

Use a background grid when you want to depict bar-graph quantities with greater accuracy.

When the background grid is omitted, as is the case in Figure 15-32 on the following page, it's difficult to make accurate column-to-column comparisons.

In addition to facilitating accurate comparisons, as shown in Figure 15-33 on the following page, a background grid also helps to visually separate the columns of information in your chart or graph.

DOUBLE-CHECK USE OF COLOR

Although PowerPoint's Color Scheme simplifies the effective use of color, color still introduces a new set of presentation design problems. These problems are based not only on how the colors affect the audience but on how the colors interact with the medium used to reproduce your presentation.

20. Inappropriate Color Choices

Colors—like words—can cause strong emotional reactions. A great deal of your success in communicating with your audience is based on choosing the correct colors. Appropriate color choice depends on both emotional and technical factors.

Colors that look good on the screen of your computer, for example, can arouse feelings of rejection in your audience. Red, for example, is a "high stress" color that can arouse subconscious feelings of panic or aggression. Grays and blues, on the other hand, are often experienced as relaxing colors.

You also have to take technical limitations into account. Certain colors and shades—light yellow, for example—tend to become easily washed out, especially when overhead transparencies are projected at large size.

Pay special attention to the atmosphere you're trying to create in your presentation. Avoid choosing colors with strong emotional overtones. Avoid the use of red, for example, when making a presentation to bankers and venture capitalists!

Choose cooler colors (blues and grays) for more formal presentations.

SECTION IV: MAKEOVERS

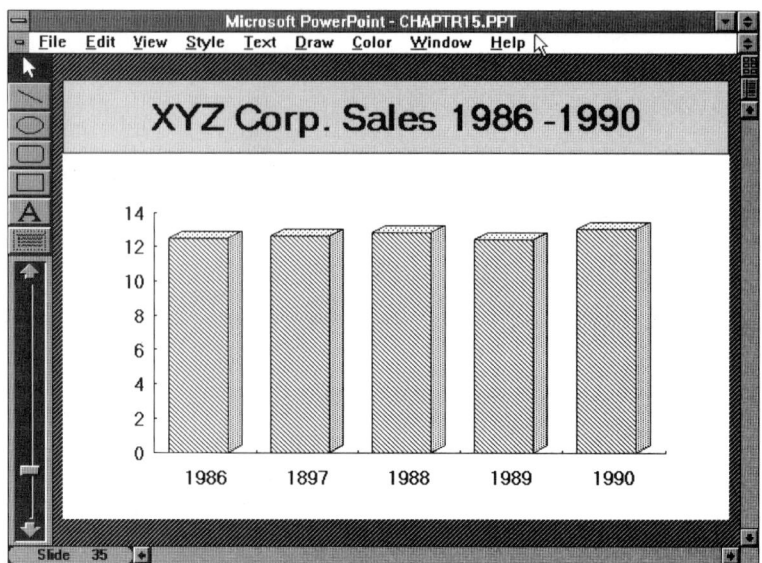

Figure 15-32. The lack of a background grid makes it difficult to appreciate subtle value differences.

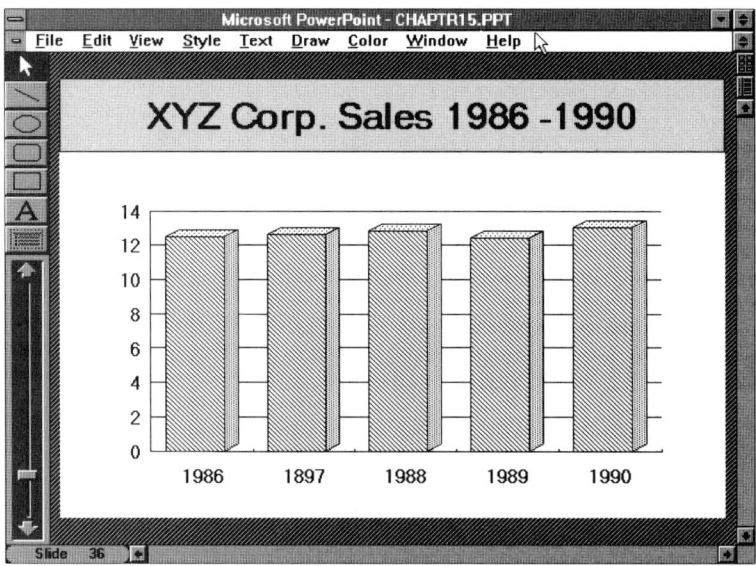

Figure 15-33. A background grid can function as a measuring tool, allowing an audience to quickly and accurately assess the value that a column represents.

21. Banding

Banding—that is, the phenomenon of the grouping of similar colors into a band instead of a smooth gradation of color—results when too many colors are included in a color slide or overhead. Regardless of whether you're working in the Apple Macintosh or the Windows environment, and regardless of how your color slides and overheads are being produced, there is a 256-color limit to the number of colors that can be included on a single slide. Banding occurs when more than 256 colors are included.

Although 256 sounds like a lot of colors, it isn't if you're including a shaded background fill as well as complex colored graphics—especially imported scanned photographic images. When using shaded backgrounds, remember that each step in the transition requires one of the available 256 colors.

Banding can also occur if you include both a shaded slide background and shaded text boxes or graphical accents.

If banding occurs, one solution is to substitute a solid background fill for the shaded background. Or if you want to continue using the shaded background, reduce the range of light-to-dark transition by adjusting the "light to dark" elevator box in the Shaded Background dialog box, which you can access by choosing Color Scheme and then choosing Shaded Background from the Color menu.

22. Lack of Color Contrast Between Text and Background

A great deal of the impact of your slides and overheads depends on a strong contrast between text and background colors. When there is insufficient contrast between text and backgrounds, the words become extremely difficult to read as they blend into the background.

In the example shown in Figure 15-34 (reproduced in grays on the following page), the title and text are difficult to read because they blend into the slide background.

Text is more legible when text color contrasts sharply with the background color. (See Figure 15-35 on the following page.)

SECTION IV: MAKEOVERS

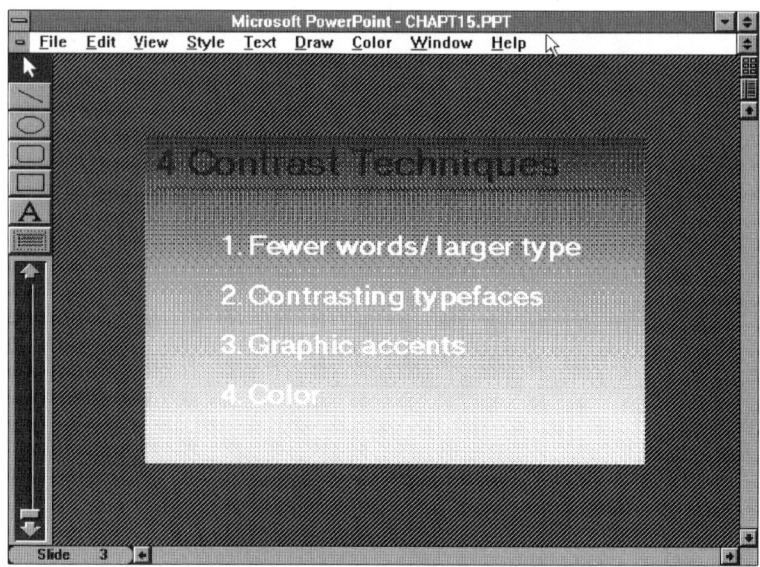

Figure 15-34. A lack of contrast between text and background colors interferes with legibility.

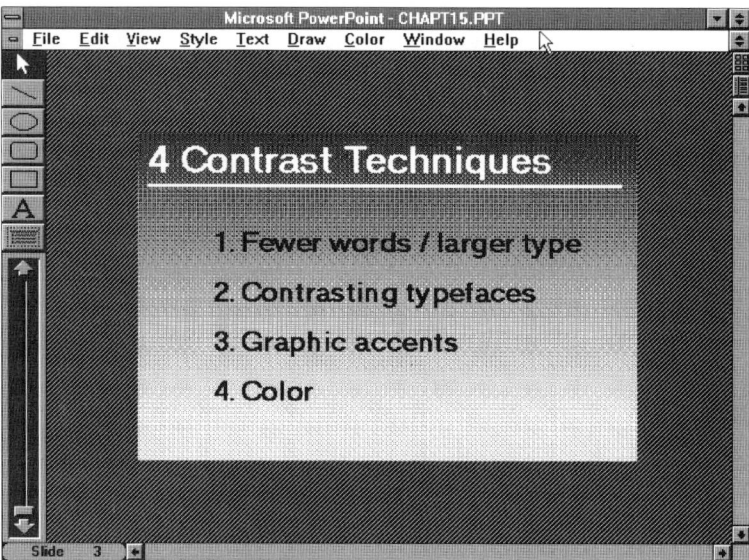

Figure 15-35. Text legibility is enhanced if the text color contrasts with the background color.

23. Graphics Clash with or Blend into Slide Background

When placing charts, graphs, and illustrations created with other programs, be sure that the colors do not compete with or blend into the Color Scheme of your presentation.

Use the Recolor Picture command to ensure compatibility between imported graphics and the Color Scheme of your presentation.

24. Too Much Color

A "circus" effect results when color is overused.

The use of a different background color for each element of the slide (titles, text, and graphics) creates a very confusing impression, especially if the colors are not chosen from a single Genigraphics Color Scheme.

One way to avoid this problem is to choose a typeface color that contrasts sharply with the slide background without the need for its own filled background.

25. Overly Bright Accent Colors

Some colors—like red and yellow—are "hot" colors. They "move forward" and attract more attention than other colors. When properly used, this directs your audience's attention to text and graphical elements that support your message. When inappropriately used, these hot colors can make it difficult for your audience to concentrate on your message.

CONCLUSION

The key to designing and preparing effective presentations is to carefully utilize PowerPoint's many text, drawing, file-importing, and color tools.

As the preceding examples show, most problems originate in a lack of *appropriateness*—from the overuse or underuse of basic design elements such as color, size, and typography, as well as from a lack of common sense, planning, and attention to detail.

By being aware of these 25 common problems, and by continually analyzing your work in terms of them, you'll be amazed at how quickly your presentation design skills improve.

EVALUATING YOUR PROGRESS

Use the following questions as a framework for reviewing your PowerPoint presentations. You might want to photocopy the following questions. Or you might want to use your word processing or page layout program to create a formal last-minute checklist that you and your co-workers can refer to each time you complete a presentation.

Content and Continuity

- Have I avoided including too much information in each slide or overhead?
- Does each slide or overhead contain a single dominant visual?
- Have I replaced text with charts and graphs whenever appropriate?
- Have I eliminated unnecessary borders and frames?
- Have I been consistent in placing text and graphics and in using colors and graphical accents?

Text Legibility

- Did I use contrasting typefaces to differentiate titles from presentation information?
- Have I avoided using type too small to be read easily?
- Have I avoided using too many typefaces and type sizes?
- Have I exercised restraint in the use of italicized and uppercase type?
- Are my typeface and type size choices supported by the service bureau or printer that will be preparing my slides or overhead transparencies?
- Have I eliminated single words isolated on lines?

Charts and Graphics

- Have I eliminated visual clutter by using a few large clip-art elements instead of numerous small ones?

- Does my printer or service bureau support the file format of imported graphics?
- Does the type of chart or graph that I used best illustrate the point I want to make?
- Have I broken complicated charts and graphs into smaller, more focused visuals?
- Have I avoided small difficult-to-understand visuals or visuals of equal size that compete with each other?
- Did I add a background grid whenever necessary to facilitate comparisons?

Color

- Have I avoided the use of colors with inappropriate emotional overtones?
- When using shaded backgrounds or imported graphics, have I included no more than 256 colors in a single slide or overhead?
- Is the contrast between text and background sufficient?
- Did I use the Recolor Picture command to integrate the color of imported graphics with those of the presentation's Color Scheme?
- Have I avoided using color for color's sake?

Index

A

accent rules 311
"Added Words" dictionary 144
Adobe
  Illustrator, importing images from 148
  Type Manager 110, 146
"Advancing Pie Chart" template
  concluding slide 296
  copying slides 292, 293
  creating the chart 289–91
  modifying 296–97
  recoloring pie slices 293–95
  slide master 287–89
Aldus Freehand, importing images from 148
aligning
  text 125–27, 143
  text and graphics 48–51
Analyzing Your Message Worksheet 13
Apple Chooser. *See* Chooser
Apple menu 27, 28
Apply To commands 95
area charts 171
Arrange All command 32
Arrow tool 33, 34
artwork. *See* graphics
ASCII files, importing 229–30
aspect ratio 158
Attached Label feature 105–6
audience
  consideration of 8, 9, 67
  handouts for 249–52
axes 178, 179, 187–88

B

background grid 353, 354
backgrounds
  adding to titles 83, 84
  color for 91, 355, 356
  filling 134, 135
  shaded 93–95
banding 355
bar charts 171, 172

Bitstream typefaces and utilities 110, 146
black-and-white
  printers (*see* printers)
  screens, preparing color presentations on 100–101
  transparencies 15, 16, 148, 299–307
boldface type, appropriate use of 124
borders
  adding to slide masters 80–82
  cluttered 322, 335, 336
  design considerations 72, 73
boxes
  empty 274
  in organizational charts 217–20
  tools for drawing 36–37, 82
brightness, excessive 357
builds 14, 202–7, 284
bullets 138

C

callouts 197–98, 222–23
cards, index. *See* "Index Cards" template
centering text and graphics 50, 125
characters. *See* text; typefaces
chart builds 207
charts and graphs
  area charts 171
  bar charts 171, 172
  callouts for 197–98
  default 185–86, 191
  editing 198–99
  entering data for 168–70
  formatting (*see* formatting, charts and graphs)
  graphic enhancements for 194–96
  inappropriate 347–48, 349
  labels 190–91
  moving 193
  overview 167–68
  placing in presentations 192–93
  PowerPoint features for 17
  problems with 346–53
  resizing 193–94
  types of 170–77, 216–20

361

Chooser 54–55, 254
clip art, cluttered 346–47
Clipboard 192–93
cluttered slides and transparencies 332,
 336, 346–47
color. *See also* color schemes
 adjusting to suit presentation rooms 88
 banding 355
 black-and-white screens and 100–101
 changing in graphics 160–61, 302–3
 changing in pie charts 293–95
 in charts and graphs 178, 186–87, 190,
  196–98
 contrast in 355, 356
 excessive brightness 357
 excessive intensity 357
 inappropriate choice of 353
 in numbers and bullets 138
 PowerPoint features for 17–18
 in slides (*see* slides)
 styles and 139–42
 in text 137–39
 in text boxes 270
 in text builds 206–7
 in transparencies (*see* transparencies)
Color menu 32, 137
colors, codes for 100–101
color schemes
 applying 95
 black-and-white screens and 100–101
 custom 90–93
 editing 96–97, 98–100
 Genigraphics Suggested 88–90
 hardware and 101
 overview 87–88
 PowerPoint system for 17–18
 presentation environments 88
 shaded backgrounds 93–95
 sharing among presentations 235–36
 in slide masters 269, 321–23
Color Special Effects folder 301
column charts 172, 173
combination charts 177
commands, keyboard shortcuts for 27,
 108, 241–42
Communications Setup dialog box 259
contents boxes 303–4, 306, 313–14

contrast
 in colors 355, 356
 in graphics 357
 in text 338, 339
Contraster subtemplates 278–80, 282
copying
 slides 44, 292, 293
 text and graphics 47–48, 302
Crop Picture command 29, 158–59
cropping images. *See* Crop Picture
 command

D

data labels 178–80
Datasheets 168–69
decimals, aligning 126
defaults, text 142–43
Define Styles command 139–40
deleting
 slides 44
 subtemplates 282
 text and graphics 47–48
Developer subtemplates 274–77, 282
dictionaries 143–44
drawing tools 34–39
Draw menu 31–32, 132–36

E

Edit Graph command 29
editing text 130–32
Edit menu 29
effects, special. *See* special effects
embossing 207–10
Encapsulated PostScript (EPS) files,
 importing 148
error codes, in transmitting files to
 Genigraphics 256–58
Excel
 coloring charts via 196, 197
 editing charts created with 199
 importing pie chart from 289–90
 PowerPoint graphs and 170, 176–77,
  186–91
exploded pie charts 172
exporting files to Genigraphics 252–59

Index

F

fever charts 172
File menu 28–29
files
  ASCII 229–30
  EPS 148
  exporting to Genigraphics 252–59
  importing (*see* importing files)
  support of format by output devices 347
Filled command 134–35, 163–65, 195–196
film recorders 52, 54. *See also* output devices
Find commands 31, 144-45
Fit To Page Size command 32
flush-right text 125
font metrics 114–15
fonts. *See* typefaces; type size; type style
formatting
  charts and graphs
    axes 187–88
    color 178, 185, 186–87, 196–97
    data labels 178–80
    Excel and 186–91
    frames and gridlines 182–84, 186, 189–90
    image size 185
    legends 180–82, 188–89
    lines 178, 179, 190
    pie chart slices 185
    plot area 190
    text 178, 186–87
    tick marks 184
  text
    appropriate time for 129
    charts and graphs 178–82
    individual words, phrases, or sentences 130
    Labeler tool and 37, 38
    line spacing and 128, 129
    output device limitations 109–10
    typeface 110–20
    type size 120–23
    type style 123–25, 342
Framed command 134, 163–65, 194–95
frames
  in charts and graphs 182–84, 186
  cluttered 322, 335, 336
Full Size command 40

G

Genigraphics library. *See* importing files
Genigraphics service bureaus. *See also* output devices
  black-and-white overheads and 299–307
  Color Scheme system and 17–18
  importing images from 150–54
  pros and cons 54
  Suggested Color Schemes 88–90
  transmitting files to 252–59
  typeface limitations 110
graduated fills 210–15
graphics. *See also* slides; transparencies
  aligning 48–51
  centering 50
  charts and graphs (*see* charts and graphs)
  cluttered 346–47
  contrast in 357
  cropping 29, 158–59
  deleting, moving, and copying 47–48
  design considerations 70–77
  drawing tools 34–39
  importance in presentations 4, 6
  importing (*see* importing files)
  logos 223–27
  PowerPoint features for 17
  resizing 47
  "shining" 215–16
  special effects (*see* special effects)
  types 68
  undersized 348, 350
  using in templates 300–304
graphs. *See* charts and graphs
gridlines 178, 179, 182–84, 189–90
grids 87, 353, 354

H

handouts 11, 21–22, 30, 249–52
hanging indents 127
hard-copy proofs 242–45
headings 319. *See also* titles
Help feature 27, 33
Hide Grid command 87
hiding text 132, 133, 324
Horizon Grid Template file 301
horizon.ppt file 301

horizontal axis 178, 179, 187–88
horizontal guide 48–50

I

image area, size of 40, 41
importing files
  adding frames, backgrounds, and shadows 162–66
  compatible file formats 148–49
  cropping images 158–59
  data for charts and graphs 169
  from Genigraphics library 150–54
  moving images 156
  outlines 229–30
  Paste commands and 149–50
  problems with graphics 346–53
  recoloring 160–61
  resizing images 156–58
  text and graphics 45–47
indents 127, 143
"Index Cards" template
  additional cards 320, 21
  card size 326
  color scheme 321–23
  first slide for 318–19
  headings 319
  individual cards 323, 324
  modifying 325, 326
  titles 324
ink-jet printers. *See* printers
italic type, appropriate use of 124, 342

J

justified text 126

K

keyboard shortcuts. *See* shortcuts
Keycaps desk accessory 116

L

Labeler tool 37, 38, 104–7
labels
  adding and modifying 104–7
  in charts and graphs 178–80, 190–91
laser printers. *See* printers

layouts, graphics 70–77
leading 128, 129, 143
left-aligned type 125
"Left-to-Right" template
  accent rule 311
  modifying 315
  positioning and formatting the slide title 311–12
  slide numbers 311
  text in individual slides 314–15
  visuals 315
legends, 178, 179, 180–82, 188–89
line charts 172, 173
line endings, irregular 345
lines
  accent rule 311
  adding and changing 34, 35
  in charts and graphs 178–79, 185, 190–91
  thickness of 81
line spacing 128, 129, 143
Line tool 31, 34, 35, 81
logos 223–27

M

Macintosh PowerPoint
  entering data for graphs 170
  importing files via Scrapbook 154–56
  keyboard shortcut for Word Processor tool 108
  output devices and 54–55
  pie charts and 290
  placing charts in presentations 192–93
  sharing files with Windows PowerPoint 236
  start-up 25
  transmitting files to Genigraphics 254–56
Macintosh Scrapbook. *See* Scrapbook
MacPaint II, importing images from 148
Maximize command 185
measuring distances 51
media, choosing for presentations 14–16
meeting rooms 8, 9–10
menus 27–33
Microsoft
  Excel (*see* Excel)
  Project for Windows 147
  Word, importing files from 229–30

modems, transmitting files via 258–59
monitors
  presentations on (*see* on-screen presentations)
  quality of color on 101
  type legibility and 146
More, importing files from 229–30
moving
  charts and graphs 193
  subtemplates 282
  text and graphics 47–48
MultiFinder, use in importing data 170

N

New Slide command 29
notes
  audience 251
  presenter 11, 21–22, 30, 245–49
numbering slides 86
numbers
  aligning over decimals 126
  color and 138

O

Omit Master command 87
on-screen presentations
  appropriateness of 15, 16, 53
  color presentations on black-and-white screens 100–101
  file formats for importing 149
  proofing 241–42
  type quality 146
Opaque command 132, 133, 162, 194
organizational charts 216–20
Organizer subtemplates 269–74, 284
outlines 70, 229–30, 274
outline type 124, 342
output devices. *See also* Genigraphics service bureaus
  changing presentations to suit 259–63
  choosing between 52–56
  pros and cons of 53–54
  setting up 54–56
  support of file formats 347
  support of typefaces 344
  targeting 52–56
  text-formatting limitations 109–10

Oval tool 36
overheads. *See* transparencies

P

paint programs, importing images from 148
Paste commands 45–47, 149–50
phrases, formatting individual 130
PICT files 149
pie charts
  color, lines, and patterns in 185, 293–95
  importing from Excel 289–90
  modifying 296–97
  overview 172, 174
  template for (*see* "Advancing Pie Chart" template)
pipes 213–14
planning presentations 7–10
plot area, formatting 190
point size 120. *See also* type size
PostScript 110, 48
PowerPoint
  Macintosh version (*see* Macintosh PowerPoint)
  overview of features 17–22
  Windows version (*see* Windows PowerPoint)
Presentation Planning Worksheet 8
presentations
  analyzing message of 12–14
  audience considerations in 8, 9
  changing to suit output device 259–63
  characteristics of 5–7
  choosing medium 14–16
  content and sequence 62–70
  default 230, 231
  designing (*see* storyboards)
  idea sources for 65
  notes for (*see* notes)
  organization of 13, 18
  planning and scheduling 7–14
  proofing 240–45
  purpose 13
  saving 230, 231
  special effects (*see* special effects)
  templates (*see* templates)
  use 3–5

Presentation Scheduling Worksheet 11
printers. *See also* output devices
   proofing presentations with 243–45
   targeting 52–56
printing
   handouts 252
   notes 248–49
   storyboard forms 60–62, 63
   use in proofing presentations 242–45
projector pads 52, 53. *See also* output devices
"Promoting Specialist" template
   contents boxes 303–4
   graphics in 300–303
   modifying 307
   title banner 304–5
proofing presentations 240–45

Q

quotations
   Developer subtemplate for 274
   as idea sources 65

R

Recolor Picture command 160–61, 196–97, 293–95
Rectangle tools 31, 36–37, 82
replace, search and 31, 144–45
reversed text 304
Rich Text Format (RTF) files 229–30
Rounded Rectangle tool 36, 37, 82
RTF files 229–30
rules. *See* lines

S

sans serif vs. serif type 111–13
scatter charts 174, 175
scheduling presentations 10–11
Scrapbook 154–56, 193
screen, description of PowerPoint 26–27
screens. *See* monitors
search and replace 31, 144–45
selection tools 33, 34, 40–41
sentences, formatting individual 130
serif vs. sans serif type 111–13

service bureaus. *See* Genigraphics service bureaus; output devices
Shade Background features 93–95
Shadow command 165, 166, 186
Shadowed command 135, 136, 195
shadowed type, appropriate use of 124
shadow lettering 227–29
"shining" graphics 215–16
shortcuts
   menus 27
   proofing 241–42
   views 42–44
   Word Processor tool 108
Show Guides command 48–51
Sized To Text command 106, 107, 135, 136
Slide Changer tool 40
Slide Master command 29
Slide Masters
   color schemes for (*see* color schemes)
   creating 80–87, 266–69
   omitting 87
   sharing among presentations 234–35
   in templates 267–69, 284, 287–89, 310–12
Slide Master view 80–81
Slide Number box 40
slide numbers, adding to template 311
slides. *See also* transparencies
   adding, copying, and deleting 44
   charts and imported graphics 346–53, 358–59
   choice as presentation medium 14–15
   color in 353–57, 359
   content and continuity 330–38, 358
   copying for template 292, 293
   file formats for importing 148–49
   moving between 39–40
   numbering 86
   PowerPoint features for 22
   producing via Genigraphics 252–63
   sharing among presentations 231–34
   text
      contrast via 117–19, 122–23
      excessive 330, 331
      legibility 338–46, 358
   titles for 311–12
Slide Show feature 28, 240–42
Slide Sorter view 20, 29, 42–44, 231–33

Index

special effects
  builds 14, 202–7, 284
  callouts 222–23
  embossing 207–10
  graduated fills 210–15
  logos 223–27
  "shining" graphics 215–16
  three-dimensional text 227–29
Spelling command 31, 143–44
stacked bar charts 171, 172
start-up 25–26
"Steps to Success" template
  customizing 284–85
  preparing presentation from 281–83
  slide master for 266–69
  subtemplates (*see* subtemplates)
storyboards
  content and sequence 62–70
  editing 68, 69
  graphics in (*see* graphics)
  idea sources for 65
  organizing ideas on 64
  outlines and 70
  overview 59–60
  printing forms for 60–62, 63
  refining 70
  simplicity in 65, 66, 67
stress of typeface 113–14
Style menu 30, 139–42, 143
subtemplates
  adding, deleting, and moving 282
  Contraster 278–80
  Developer 274–77
  empty 281
  Organizer 269–74, 284
symbols, in typefaces 115–17

T

table builds 207
tables 126, 220–22
tabs and indents 127, 143
Tag Image File Format (TIFF) 148
targeting output devices 52–56
telecommunication of files 258–59
\template\35mm subdirectory 301
templates. *See also* subtemplates
  "Advancing Pie Chart" (*see* "Advancing Pie Chart" template)

templates, *continued*
  "Index Cards" (*see* "Index Cards" template)
  "Left-to-Right" (*see* "Left-to-Right" template)
  "Promoting Specialist" (*see* "Promoting Specialist" template)
  "Steps to Success" (*see* "Steps to Success" template)
text. *See also* titles; typefaces; type size; type style
  adding to individual slides 314–15
  adding to slide masters 85
  adjusting to fit type size 135, 136
  aligning 48–51, 125–27
  backgrounds for 134, 135
  in charts and graphs 218–19, 350, 352
  colored 137–39, 355, 356
  defaults for 142–43
  deleting, moving, and copying 47–48
  design considerations 76, 77
  editing 130–32
  formatting (*see* formatting, text)
  framing 134
  hiding 132, 33
  importing (*see* importing files)
  legibility 146, 338–46
  line spacing 128, 129
  overemphasizing 342–44
  reversed (white on black) 304
  shadowed 135, 136
  spelling checker 143–44
  styles for 139–42
  in tables 221–22
  tabs and indents and 127
  in templates 270–73, 278–79, 281–82, 304–7
  three-dimensional 227–29
  tools for entering 39, 104–9
text boxes 270, 271–73
text builds 139, 203–7
Text menu 31
text-only files 229–30
thermal printers. *See* printers
ThinkTank, importing files from 229–30
three-dimensional charts 174
three-dimensional text 227–29
tick marks 184, 187–88

367

TIFF (Tag Image File Format) 148
title banners 304–5
titles. *See also* headings
  design considerations 72, 74
  Developer subtemplate for 274
  hiding 324
  shading 94
  in slide masters 82–84, 267–68, 311–12
Title Sorter view 20, 29, 43–44, 232–34
transparencies. *See also* slides
  charts and imported graphics 346–53, 358–59
  choice as presentation medium 15–16
  content and continuity 330–38, 358
  excessive text 330, 331
  file formats for importing 148–49
  with Genigraphics backgrounds 299–307
  numbering 86
  problems with color 353–57, 359
  text legibility 338–46, 358
typefaces
  appropriateness of (*see* formatting, text)
  in charts and graphs 178, 186–87
  choosing 117–20
  design and legibility 110–17
  excessive number of 340–42
  serif vs. sans serif 111–13
  special 113
  Style feature and 139–42
  support by output device 344
  x-height of 113–14
  variety of 146
type size
  adjusting text to fit 135, 136
  appropriateness of 120–23, 340
  in charts and graphs 178, 186–87
  considerations in planning presentations 67
  excessive number of 340–42
  Style feature and 139–42
type style
  appropriateness of 123–25
  in charts and graphs 178, 186–87
  Style feature and 139–42
typography, PowerPoint features for 21

U
underscored type, appropriate use of 124
uppercase type, avoidance of 124

V
value labels. *See* labels
vertical axis 178, 179, 187–88
vertical guide 51
VGA cards 101
View menu 29–30
views
  changing 87
  shortcuts for 42–44
  Slide Master 80–81
  Slide Sorter 20, 29, 42–44, 231–33
  Title Sorter 20, 29, 43–44, 232–34
visuals. *See* graphics

W
widows 131, 345–46
windows, opening multiple 32, 33
Windows menu 27, 28, 32–33
Windows PowerPoint
  coloring charts via 197
  entering data for graphs 168–70
  pie charts and 290–92
  placing charts in presentations 192
  printers and 55–56
  sharing files with Macintosh PowerPoint 236
  start-up 25
  transmitting files to Genigraphics 252–53
Word, importing files from 229–30
Word Processor tool 39, 107–9
words, formatting individual 130
word wrap 39

X
x-height of typeface 113–14

Z
Zapf Dingbats 115–17

Roger C. Parker is an internationally known author, consultant, and seminar leader. He has written 10 computer and design books and over 125 articles and columns. He travels extensively and has conducted desktop-publishing seminars and workshops throughout the world. He is president of The Write Word, an advertising and consulting firm located in Dover, New Hampshire.

The manuscript for this book was prepared and submitted to Microsoft Press in electronic form. Text files were processed and formatted using Microsoft Word.

Principal word processors: Debbie Kem and Judith Bloch
Principal proofreaders: Shawn Peck, Patrick Forgette, and Kathleen Atkins
Principal typographer: Ruth Pettis
Interior text designer: Peggy Herman
Principal illustrator: Lisa Sandburg
Cover designer: Rebecca Johnson
Cover color separator: Wescan Color Corporation

Text composition by Microsoft Press in Palatino with display type in Optima Bold Italic, using the Magna composition system and the Linotronic 300 laser imagesetter.

Printed on recycled paper stock.

Great Resources for Your Desktop Publishing Library— from Microsoft Press!

DESKTOP PUBLISHING BY DESIGN
Ventura Publisher® Edition
Ronnie Shushan, Don Wright, and Ricardo Birmele

Fact-filled, design-oriented resource that is packed with how-to information, layout ideas, and inspiration for anyone new to design, publishing, or computers. The authors offer a primer on the use of basic design elements—typeface, page layout, and graphics. Includes a series of hands-on projects to help you produce exciting, professional-looking printed pieces. The projects use Xerox Ventura Publisher version 2 for the IBM PC and compatibles.
368 pages, softcover $24.95   Order Code DEPUDV

DESKTOP PUBLISHING BY DESIGN, 2nd ed.
Aldus® PageMaker® Edition
Ronnie Shushan and Don Wright

"One of the most useful and attractive books we've seen on desktop publishing and design....Full of ideas and inspiration."   **The New York Times**

Here's a thoroughly updated edition—now with 16 pages of full color—of the book rated "Best How-to-Book" of the year by the Computer Press Association. This resource is really three books in one: a primer on design, a sensational portfolio of printed pieces, and a collection of hands-on projects. Covers version 4.0 for both the Apple Macintosh and Windows 3.
440 pages, softcover $29.95   Order Code DEPUD2

WORD FOR WINDOWS™ COMPANION
Mark W. Crane

WORD FOR WINDOWS COMPANION will make Word for Windows easier to learn and use. Regardless of your level of expertise, you'll find a wealth of useful information in this comprehensive resource. It's both an exceptional tutorial for new Word users and a master reference guide for experienced users. You'll learn basic concepts of word processing, typography, and design so that you'll be able to create professional-looking documents with confidence and ease. In addition to detailed explanations, the book offers scores of illustrations, examples, and tips to enhance your productivity. An extensive index and side-margin headings make information readily accessible.
896 pages, softcover $26.95   Order Code WOWICO

WORKING WITH WORD FOR WINDOWS™
Russell Borland

WORKING WITH WORD FOR WINDOWS is the most comprehensive book available for intermediate users of Microsoft Word for Windows. In-depth information, advice, and hands-on examples show you how to customize the user interface, use a variety of fonts and type sizes, insert graphics into documents, use macros to automate routine editing, position text and graphics, link text and graphics within documents, and more.
656 pages, softcover $24.95   Order Code WOWOWI

To order call **1-800-MSPRESS** *or use the order form on the next page.*

GETTING STARTED WITH MICROSOFT® EXCEL 3 FOR WINDOWS™
Ralph Soucie

This straightforward, no-nonsense introduction offers a fast and easy way for beginning users to become immediately proficient with Microsoft Excel. The authors address the basics of creating spreadsheets, charts, and databases. Includes step-by-step instruction, practical examples, scores of illustrations, and timesaving tips.

368 pages, softcover $22.95   Order Code GESTEX

RUNNING MICROSOFT® EXCEL, 2nd ed.
*The Cobb Group: Douglas Cobb and Judy Mynhier
with Craig Stinson and Chris Kinata*

Once you've mastered the fundamentals of Microsoft Excel, you'll want to delve deeper into this versatile spreadsheet program. Look no further than RUNNING MICROSOFT EXCEL, 2nd ed., a perfect companion to *Getting Started with Microsoft Excel 3 for Windows*. This book is packed with step-by-step instruction, superb examples, and dozens of screen illustrations to help you understand and use *every* function and command of Microsoft Excel version 3. This comprehensive reference will be your primary source of information and advice.

848 pages, softcover $27.95   Order Code RUEX2

ORDER FORM

BPP

QTY.	ORDER CODE	TITLE	PRICE PER BOOK	TOTAL PRICE
_____	DEPUDV	Desktop Publishing by Design, *Ventura Publisher Edition*	$24.95	_____
_____	DEPUD2	Desktop Publishing by Design, 2nd ed., *Aldus PageMaker Edition*	$29.95	_____
_____	WOWICO	Word for Windows Companion	$26.95	_____
_____	WOWOWI	Working with Word for Windows	$24.95	_____
_____	GESTEX	Getting Started with Microsoft Excel 3 for Windows	$22.95	_____
_____	RUEX2	Running Microsoft Excel, 2nd ed.	$27.95	_____

                                        SUBTOTAL _____
                                        SALES TAX _____
                                        SHIPPING _____
                                        TOTAL _____

NAME _____
ADDRESS (No P.O. Boxes) _____
_____
CITY _____ STATE _____ ZIP _____
(____) _____
DAYTIME PHONE NUMBER

To get your books faster...
call our toll-free line today
and place your credit card order.
1-800-MSPRESS*
Refer to campaign BPP.

Or mail your prepaid order to:
Microsoft Press
P.O. Box 7005
La Vergne, TN 37086-7005

SALES TAX
Please add applicable sales tax for the following states: AZ, CA, CO, CT, DC, FL, GA, HI, ID, IL, IN, KY, ME, MD, MA, MI, MN, MO, NE, NV, NJ, NM, NY, NC, OH, PA, SC, TN, TX, VA, WA, WI, and WV.

SHIPPING
One book—$2.50 Two books—$3.25 Each additional book—$.75
All orders shipped via UPS or RPS. Please allow 2-4 weeks for delivery.

PAYMENT: ☐ Check or Money Order
☐ VISA ☐ MasterCard ☐ American Express

CREDIT CARD NO. _____ EXP. DATE _____
CARDHOLDER SIGNATURE _____

In Canada, contact Macmillan Canada, Attn: Microsoft Press Dept., 164 Commander Blvd., Agincourt, Ontario, Canada M1S 3C7. ☎ 416-293-8141
In the U.K., contact Microsoft Press, 27 Wrights Lane, London W8 5TZ.

Microsoft Press books are available wherever quality computer books are sold.